A Political Companion to Walker Percy

A Political Companion to
Walker Percy

Edited by
PETER AUGUSTINE LAWLER
and
BRIAN A. SMITH

UNIVERSITY PRESS OF KENTUCKY

Copyright © 2013 by The University Press of Kentucky
Paperback edition 2014

Scholarly publisher for the Commonwealth,
serving Bellarmine University, Berea College, Centre College of Kentucky,
Eastern Kentucky University, The Filson Historical Society, Georgetown
College, Kentucky Historical Society, Kentucky State University, Morehead State
University, Murray State University, Northern Kentucky University, Transylvania
University, University of Kentucky, University of Louisville, and Western
Kentucky University.
All rights reserved.

Editorial and Sales Offices: The University Press of Kentucky
663 South Limestone Street, Lexington, Kentucky 40508-4008
www.kentuckypress.com

The Library of Congress has cataloged the hardcover edition as follows:

A political companion to Walker Percy / edited by Peter Augustine Lawler and
Brian A. Smith.
    pages cm
Includes bibliographical references and index.
 ISBN 978-0-8131-4188-6 (hardcover : alk. paper) — ISBN 978-0-8131-4190-9 (epub)
 — ISBN 978-0-8131-4189-3 (pdf)
 1. Percy, Walker, 1916-1990—Political and social views. I. Lawler, Peter
Augustine, editor of compilation. II. Smith, Brian A, editor of compilation.
 PS3566.E6912Z795 2013
 813'.54—dc23   2013008896

ISBN 978-0-8131-4742-0 (pbk. : alk. paper)

This book is printed on acid-free paper meeting the requirements of the
American National Standard for Permanence in Paper for Printed Library
Materials.

Manufactured in the United States of America.

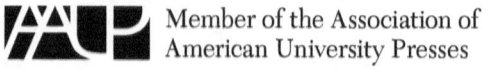   Member of the Association of
           American University Presses

Contents

Series Foreword   vii

Introduction: Walker Percy, American Political Life, and Indigenous American Thomism   1
Peter Augustine Lawler and Brian A. Smith

1. Walker Percy: A Brief Biography   11
Ralph C. Wood

2. *The Moviegoer*'s Cartesian Theater: Moviegoing as Walker Percy's Metaphor for the Cartesian Mind   29
Woods Nash

3. Walker Percy's Critique of the Pursuit of Happiness in *The Moviegoer, Lost in the Cosmos: The Last Self-Help Book*, and *The Thanatos Syndrome*   47
Elizabeth Amato

4. On Dealing with Man   69
James V. Schall, S.J.

5. Walker Percy's "Theory of Man" and the Elimination of Virtue   87
Nathan P. Carson

6. Confessing the Horrors of Radical Individualism in *Lancelot:* Percy, Dostoevsky, Poe   119
Farrell O'Gorman

7. Walker Percy's Alternative to Scientism in *The Thanatos Syndrome*   145
Micah Mattix

8. Love and Marriage among the Ruins   159
Richard M. Reinsch II

9. Walker Percy's Last Men: *Love in the Ruins* as a Fable of American Decline   179
Brian A. Smith

10. The Second Coming of Walker Percy: From Segregationist to Integrationist   207
Brendan P. Purdy and Janice Daurio

11. Walker Percy, Alexis de Tocqueville, and the Stoic and Christian Foundations of American Thomism   237
Peter Augustine Lawler

Selected Bibliography   267

List of Contributors   271

Index   273

Series Foreword

Those who undertake a study of American political thought must attend to the great theorists, philosophers, and essayists. Such a study is incomplete, however, if it neglects American literature, one of the greatest repositories of the nation's political thought and teachings.

America's literature is distinctive because it is, above all, intended for a democratic citizenry. In contrast to eras when an author would aim to inform or influence a select aristocratic audience, in democratic times, public influence and education must resonate with a more expansive, less leisured, and diverse audience to be effective. The great works of America's literary tradition are the natural locus of democratic political teaching. Invoking the interest and attention of citizens through the pleasures afforded by the literary form, many of America's great thinkers sought to forge a democratic public philosophy with subtle and often challenging teachings that unfolded in narrative, plot, and character development. Perhaps more than any other nation's literary tradition, American literature is ineluctably political—shaped by democracy as much as it has in turn shaped democracy.

The Political Companions to Great American Authors series highlights the teachings of the great authors in America's literary and belletristic tradition. An astute political interpretation of America's literary tradition requires careful, patient, and attentive readers who approach the text with a view to understanding its underlying messages about citizenship and democracy. Essayists in this series approach the classic texts not with a "hermeneutics of suspicion" but with the curiosity of fellow citizens who believe that the great authors have something of value to teach their readers. The series brings together essays from varied approaches and viewpoints for the common purpose of elucidating the political teachings of the nation's greatest authors for those seeking a better understanding of American democracy.

Patrick J. Deneen
Series Editor

INTRODUCTION

Walker Percy, American Political Life, and Indigenous American Thomism

Peter Augustine Lawler and Brian A. Smith

Why do two political scientists say that an American Catholic novelist can teach us what nobody else can about our nation's political life? In fact, we think it's important that Percy was an American, a Catholic, and a novelist, not to mention a physician and a philosophical essayist. Percy explains that the novel itself is a Christian medium. Who's read a really good Darwinian novel, or an atheistic novel, or a socialist novel? For all their wisdom, the classical Greeks never managed to write any novels. The characters in the dialogues and plays aren't quite—and aren't meant to be—fully fleshed-out human beings. The novel depends on the Christian discovery of irreducible inwardness or personal identity. In other words, the novel depends on the searching personal investigation found, maybe for the first time, in St. Augustine's *Confessions*.

Even the novels of the officially atheistic Sartre, which Percy admired, shared the Christian discovery that being human is all about being stuck in a predicament not of one's own making and about wondering and wandering in search of who you are and what you're supposed to do. For Percy, the existentialists—Sartre and especially Heidegger—offer personal or particular corrections to the impersonality of science ancient and modern. The existentialists observe that the human being is a leftover in the world described by modern science, and the Christians agree. Percy adds that the existentialists incorrectly slight or ignore the joyful discovery that the truth we can share in common is science. Percy painfully notes that the Christians have more than a bit of history of dropping the ball when it comes to science, but that's often been because they've made the mistake of believing that they must choose between science and what revelation teaches about the origin and destiny of each particular person.

The harmonization of what we know through science and what we know through revelation is the rather distinctively Catholic project called Thomism. There's a neglected American Catholic tradition composed of Orestes Brownson (author of *The American Republic,* 1865), John Courtney Murray (*We Hold These Truths,* 1960), and Percy that holds that a Thomistic interpretation of the greatness of our Founders' accomplishment is the gift American Catholics can offer their country. What Percy offers that Murray and Brownson do not is philosophical depth, psychological subtlety, and the novelist's gift for putting what he knows in action through the imaginative description of particular lives. Percy also offers, of course, the formidable literary and political resources of the Stoic/aristocratic and "Christ-haunted" American South. The Southern Agrarian criticism of the flourishing techno-republic of the industrialized North culminated in the indigenous Thomism of Walker Percy and Flannery O'Connor. What indigenous Thomism offers America, above all, is a better foundation for its liberalism than that our nation's most prominent political philosophers have provided us—one expressed, as G. K. Chesterton said, with "dogmatic lucidity" in our Declaration of Independence, but one rarely systematically explored.

Thomism is often called moral and metaphysical realism. There is, as Percy explains, a real world out there, and we the have natural capability to discover the real truth about it. We, the beings hardwired, so to speak, for language, are open to the truth about all things. We are like the other animals in some ways, but we are given excellences and responsibilities not given to them. As the existentialists say, we can live either authentically—not diverting ourselves from what we can't help but know—or inauthentically. We can't help knowing the bad news that we're born to trouble because of who we are as self-conscious, sinful beings, and there's no merely environmental or chemical remedy for what ails us. But we also know that compensations for our misery include the love of other particular persons and joyful shared discovery. It's not really true that each of us is absurdly locked up in him- or herself.

The founders of philosophy and science—the classical Greeks—taught that the human being is distinguished by the capability to wonder, and that the world, as Leo Strauss reminds us, is the home of the human mind. There is nothing more wonderful than the intelligible regularities of nature, and the philosopher dies to himself as a particular being in contemplating, for example, the stars. The Christians think of the human being as a wanderer or pilgrim or alien wherever he or she might live in this world. We are homeless because we can't help that our true home is somewhere else. The Christians correct the classical view, especially of Plato and Aristotle, that we are essentially natural or biological beings. We miss who we are as particular persons when we think of ourselves as essentially minds. Philosophy, so understood, is a kind of self-forgetfulness, which for the Christian places it as an only partially truthful diversion from insistently personal reality. Our longings, the Christians say, are personal, deep down. Personal longings point us beyond our apparent biological limitations; our deepest longing is to be transparent just as we are before a personal God.

The Christians discovered that the being with speech—with logos—is neither essentially mind, as Aristotle thought, nor essentially body, as materialists from Thales to Epicurus to today's "new atheists" and even less flamboyant neo-Darwinians and neuroscientists think, but a third kind of being that can't be reduced to mind or body or even some incoherent combination of the two. As Pope Benedict XVI often reminded us, logos, as we actually have experienced it, is animated by and present only in persons. Such reason appears only in the personal God and the persons made in his image. As Percy explains, any aliens that are intelligent enough to be discovered will be conscious, flawed persons too—not the benignly disembodied and apparently deathless alien minds described by the novelist Carl Sagan and not automatons of some sort. Like us, the aliens will be born to trouble and potentially a danger to us all.

Percy argued that beginning with Descartes, the characteristic modern philosophers agree that each of us is homeless—an alien—in the natural world. They quickly add that we can remedy this homelessness by transforming natural reality with the "I" in mind. The resulting scientific progress makes the "I" lonelier than ever. Such people know more and more about nature and less than ever about themselves, because science doesn't explain who they are. The failure of material science to make the "I" more at home in the world leads to existentialism, to the conclusion that we must simply embrace our destiny as absurd leftovers in the cosmos. The mistaken thought—one that's contradicted even by the joyful experiences of the real scientists and existentialist novelists who express it—that a conscious being could possibly be isolated and alone produces the misanthropic conclusion that the true goal of science ought to be to zap the malignity of self-consciousness out of existence altogether. As Percy puts it, these scientists seem to agree that it's better to be a contented chimp than a pointlessly dislocated human, and he directs our attention to the dystopian possibilities that flow from this desire to "fix" human life.

The Bible is right that it's not good to be alone, but it's just not true that to be human is to be truly isolated. If it were true, Percy explains, then there would be no real argument against suicide or devoting one's self to pointless diversions or to getting as drugged up as possible with mood-enhancing and consciousness-depressing drugs. We could erect no defense against the idea that our lives bear no meaning. Therefore, there would also be no argument against attempting to lose oneself in ideological wars about nothing, against the twentieth-century existentialism that culminated in Stalinism and Nazism. We now know that all those efforts to extinguish who we are are not only radically pernicious but also, thank God, destined to fail in their misanthropic objectives.

Percy's twentieth-century Thomism attempts, in our view with great success, to use what we really know these days through science—including evolutionary science and neuroscience—to show that the being who wonders is necessarily the being who wanders. The wondering being—the human self or soul, the human person—really can't integrate him- or herself into the world he or she can otherwise explain through science. The cosmos—in the sense of all that exists—isn't really a cosmos—in the sense of a homogeneous whole—as long as we're around. But that doesn't mean that the Cartesian/existentialist dualism between mechanistic (or stimulus-response) nature and mysteriously unnatural human freedom is correct.

Man breaking into the daylight of language introduced in nature a fundamental discontinuity—a discontinuity evolutionary theorists should address but usually don't, because it's such an obvious and seemingly invincible limitation to the explanatory power of their materialistic science. For physicists, such as the great Carl Sagan, nothing is more wonderful than the stars and the possibility of the unalienated pure mind that we can hope beings with extraterrestrial intelligence are. By contrast, for Percy, nothing is more strange and wonderful than the wandering aliens or pilgrims found right here on our planet. Percy observes that Sagan is so lonely that he hopes to make "contact" with beings elsewhere that he can't make with beings here. He has mistakenly raised himself to pure "mind" by reducing, in theory, the rest of us to pure body. But even the theoretical physicist is neither pure mind nor pure body, but a particular third kind of being that can't be integrated into theories that are all about minds and bodies. Because Sagan didn't really understand who he was, he didn't really understand how strange and lovable each of us is.

Percy's "theory of man" is, for him, a kind of Christian apologetics. It doesn't prove that the Christian account of who we are is true, but it does show that believing in its truth is compatible with what we can see with our own eyes as knowers. What we really know about evolution suggests, in fact, special creation of our species and particular persons and the deep, irreducible reality of personal love. It even suggests that our freedom is not for private, incommunicable experiences of conscience but for both shared scientific discovery and participation in the truthful, institutionalized community called the church, organized for thought and action. In other words, it suggests what our freedom—our wandering—is for. Percy's intention, of course, is not to politicize the church or to have public policy animated by the personal virtue of charity, but to show how our political life is limited and sustained by who we are as truthful, social, personal, joyful, and loving beings. We can be as home as we can be with our family, friends, and country and all the good things of this world when we understand the true cause—both through science and through faith—of our homelessness.

Percy reminds us that our Declaration of Independence isn't simply an expression of the Cartesian theory of Locke. That theory, in Percy eyes, is that man is nothing but a particularly clever organism transforming his environment in pursuit of this-worldly, self-won happiness. If that theory were simply true, people would be happier than ever in our free and affluent society, more at home than ever in the world we've made for ourselves. Scientists, as Percy would say, would know like angels. Ordinary people would flourish with expert help on how best to satisfy their needs. And morality would be on the way to perfection because people would understand better who they are and what they're supposed to do as "autonomous" selves. But all the evidence, Percy observes, suggests that the theory isn't true: people, Percy echoes Tocqueville, are more restless or miserably disoriented than ever in the midst of prosperity. And the pursuit of happiness has become the feverish, flaky, and increasingly futile pursuit of diversion from what we think we know—or don't know—about who we are.

The draft of the Declaration was the Lockean theory articulated by Jefferson and Locke. The draft was amended by the more Christian members of Congress. "Nature's God"—a past-tense God—became the judgmental and providential God—the living God—of the Bible. That compromise, Catholic Americans such as Brownson and Murray understand particularly well, really is providential. If our Declaration were simply Puritanical, it would theocratically criminalize every sin and be incompatible with the true freedom of persons and of the church. If our Declaration were purely Lockean, it would be too hostile to the whole Christian view of who we are. The compromise can even be called a kind of accidental Thomism—a reconciliation of reason and revelation not intended by either of the parties to the compromise.

But Percy suggests that absent a coherent theory of man that justifies it, this American compromise comes to nothing but confusion. The Christian understanding of who each of us is as a unique and irreplaceable being made in the image of God fades, and it's replaced by inexplicable experiences of homelessness that elude expert determination. So the providential accident of history that is our Declaration needs to be supported by a theory that understands better than our Founders did their political accomplishment and defends better than they did the liberty given by God and nature to each and every particular member of our singular species. That, we can say, can and should be Percy's contribution to American political science.

Peter Lawler named this theory, for the benefit of American political scientists and philosophers, "postmodernism rightly understood" (in his book of the same title) which, as far as we know, is the first effort to present Percy as an indispensable resource for our understanding of ourselves as a free, relational, and responsible people under God. Genuine postmodernism preserves what's true about modern science and the modern understanding of the self while incorporating those partial truths into a more comprehensive moral and metaphysical realism, a return to the idea that we're open by nature to the real truth about ourselves, others, and the cosmos in a way that gives us the guidance we need to know who we are and what we're supposed to do. The essays in this book are all meant to contribute to making the political thought of the philosopher-novelist-physician-Catholic available in an accessible and informed way.

Our collection opens with a biographical essay with particular focus upon Percy's political life by Ralph C. Wood. Tracing the author's family history and the particular problems of southern life that set him on his path to writing, Wood emphasizes how the Stoic legacy within which Walker grew to maturity shaped his thinking as well as the manner in which his predilection for scientific explanation opened up so many fruitful possibilities in his later work. This essay sets the stage for the more focused efforts that follow and provides the reader with a ready reference for the key events of Walker Percy's life.

In his essay, Woods Nash argues that Percy uses *The Moviegoer*'s character Binx Bolling's habitual moviegoing as a metaphor for the ways Descartes captured the modern mind. Along the way, Nash provides a vital introduction to the nature of the Cartesian mind by surveying the dominant view of this subject among philosophers, supplying the basis for demonstrating just how Percy uses the idea of the mind as a theater to explore the human condition. This analysis sets the stage for an exploration of Percy's *Moviegoer* as depicting the effects of extreme individualism on individuals and their communities.

Beginning with *The Moviegoer* and proceeding to later works, Elizabeth Amato inquires into the pursuit of happiness in Percy's America. She contends that Percy's contrarian efforts to understand our society led him to the conclusion that our *unhappiness* bears clues about the poor choices we make and, perhaps more important, that his novels' characters show Americans how their own self-destructive beliefs drive them to ever more impoverished conceptions of the good and happy life. Amato observes the ways Percy shows that our efforts to flee unhappiness through a kind of restless materialism in fact cause us to miss the clues that would lead us to consider a better sort of life.

Father James V. Schall's contribution turns our attention to Percy's distinctively Christian anthropology and the way he articulates this vision across his many essays and novels. Starting with Percy's observation that many bad novels are "about searching for one's self," Father Schall discusses the many ways Percy reminds us that any genuine search for the truth must lead us outside of ourselves to a recognition of our "transparency before God" and into an acquaintance with the essential nature of life as requiring participation in robust communities. In Father Schall's analysis, Percy ultimately emphasizes the vital importance of all our choices in how to live and why, and in the images of flawed creation, reminds us of our place as wayfarers.

Focusing on the internal problems at the heart of Percy's attempt to create a philosophical anthropology, Nathan P. Carson argues that Percy's vision of human nature contains a central flaw: Percy's deep and sustained critique of modernity does show our incoherence and provides us with significant resources for understanding our present state, but this demonstration comes at the expense of a significant loss in man's ability to develop a path out of this malaise. By diagnosing man's "unsignifiability"—his inability to fully describe or capture himself under the auspices of a symbol—Carson suggests that Percy may paradoxically describe a creature incapable of understanding or cultivating real virtue.

Farrell O'Gorman's contribution aims at demonstrating how Percy's 1977 novel *Lancelot* profoundly critiques a radical individualism that is both founded in and contributes to a displaced sense of the real. The essay also argues that this critique cannot be properly understood without due consideration of the novel's particular subgenre and historical context. Placing *Lancelot* in the context of the Southern Gothic novel, O'Gorman shows that in the intensely flawed narrator, Lance Lamar, who embarks on a quest to uncover the messy truth of things, Percy actually holds up a mirror to the aspects of our politics and society that we least want to observe: the deadly effects of our radical individualism and quest for perfect autonomy.

Continuing the examination of Percy's later works, Micah Mattix explores the role of scientism in Percy's thought, specifically focusing on his last novel, *The Thanatos Syndrome*. Mattix argues that Percy's diagnosis of a living death in American society is best understood as originating in our incapacity to understand ourselves rightly. Percy's recurring motif of words having lost all meaning, being "used up," bears special importance in his novels because without those words, the characters cannot even name the evils they face, let alone understand them. Mattix points us to Percy's partial solution in *Thanatos*: the return to an understanding of man as more than merely reducible to stimuli and responses, but rather as a creature whose capacity for speech and understanding transcends all attempts at scientific reductionism.

Turning our attention to the nature of the South in Percy's writings, Richard M. Reinsch II observes that Percy intimated in several addresses and essays his belief that the South is, in certain respects, capable of teaching the rest of the United States enduring truths of man's nature and being. Reinsch argues that the South's evangelicalism might help reawaken the region's distinctive culture and demonstrate an alternative to the highly secular model blue states present. This is not to say that Percy maintained no misgivings about Protestant thought—his skepticism toward effusively emotional faith remained. But Reinsch argues he may have overlooked the deeper spiritual claims Protestants make—ones that rival those of Catholics. As a practical fact, evangelicals continue to maintain the South as a bastion of Christian faith and provide strong theological support to traditional marriage and family life. Reinsch turns to *Love in the Ruins,* and specifically the images of love and marriage it presents, to show how southern evangelicalism resists the desiccated and desiccating understanding of marriage posited by therapeutic liberalism. This complicates the picture of Percy as a specifically and narrowly Roman Catholic novelist, and demonstrates some of the ways his Kierkegaardian influences bear out in his writings.

Brian A. Smith's essay explores the politics and psychology of *Love in the Ruins.* He argues that Percy's value to political philosophers lies in the way he depicts the failures of modern morals and culture to recognize human imperfection. Percy suggests that while strong communities and religious beliefs once moderated our self-destructive tendencies, our culture has undermined these defenses. Percy develops a compelling account of how we might find our way back to a better sort of life together. In *Love in the Ruins,* Percy holds our way of life to a mirror and shows that the future we have to fear is not Nietzsche's docile last man, but rather the danger that we might become trapped in the extremes of human life: at one extreme, we aspire to live like angels, abstracted from ordinary human cares; at the other, we immerse ourselves in bodily existence and lose sight of consciousness itself. If Americans become "last men," Percy seems to observe, we will do so in strikingly different ways that always betray the possibility of hope.

Brendan P. Purdy and Janice Daurio aim at uncovering the philosophical background to Percy's political engagement with segregation by looking closely at what they see as Percy's three deepest intellectual influences: semiotics, Kierkegaard, and Catholicism. Purdy and Daurio show how Percy's work in these three areas demanded he take a more consistent stand on the issues of his day. They relate his ideas to those of others in the history of philosophy, painting a picture of Percy's intellectual journey and his likely influences along the way, and show that Percy's peculiar combination of a consistently Catholic moral vision, his quest for a realist theory of language, and his intellectual relationship with Kierkegaard demanded he accept the moral principle of equality and embrace integration in the South.

Finally, Peter Augustine Lawler locates Percy's thought, with the help of Alexis de Tocqueville, as a southern and Stoic criticism of American Cartesianism and a Catholic criticism of southern Stoicism. The result is the kind of aristocratic Christianity Tocqueville recommends as the way to reconcile proud experiences of great personal worth with the egalitarian and charitable truth about the singular greatness of each and every particular human being. The southern Stoicism Walker Percy learned from the philosopher-poet who raised him, William Alexander Percy, shows us that Tocqueville was right that Americans, to learn the truth that they're more than techno-beings with interests, have to be elevated by the experiences of ruling oneself and others found in the magnanimous and generous literature of the classical Greeks and Romans. Tocqueville, of course, didn't know what the Percys did: that the aristocratic antidote to America's Cartesian excesses flourished for a while in the South. But that Stoic antidote itself, Percy adds, was flawed by injustice and a lonely indifference to the ordinary reality of personal love. So American Thomism emerges as a Christian criticism of the self-deception of pagan magnanimity, and as magnanimous criticism of the self-absorbed yet self-deceived pettiness and even trashiness of democratic materialism.

In these essays, we hope to convince our readers that Walker Percy's peculiar synthesis of ideas in philosophy and fiction does more than illuminate our predicament—he shows us a way to think and talk about politics and society that will lead us out of today's confusions. In many ways, Percy is vital for understanding the American present, and he can help show us ways to avert an enervating future. He can lead us away from the stale debates of contemporary conservative and liberal thought and back into considering the proper politics and community for human beings understood as wayfarers in the world and strangers to ourselves.

Walker Percy

A Brief Biography

Ralph C. Wood

William Buckley once wittily remarked that all future presidents should be made to take a double oath of office. They should swear not only to uphold the Constitution of the United States of America but also promise to read, mark, learn, and inwardly digest Walker Percy's novel of 1971, *Love in the Ruins*. "It's all there in that one book," Buckley declared, "what's happening to us and why."[1] Such extravagant praise is meant to echo the extravagance of Percy's satire. Yet the outrageousness of such an accolade, far from silencing further consideration of Percy, prompts us to ask what kind of man stands behind such a book. Much of what follows is not original with me but a précis of Jay Tolson's fine biography, *Pilgrim in the Ruins*, but will serve to orient the reader to the chapters that follow mine.[2]

Walker Percy was born in Birmingham, Alabama, on May 28, 1916, to a very distinguished family. He had French Catholic ancestors on his mother's (Martha Susan Phinizy) side, and on his father's side the family could trace its ancestry back to the Percys of Northumberland, who appear in Shakespeare's plays. Funeral monuments honoring the Percy family can still be seen in the cathedral at Beverley in Humberside. Walker Percy's father, Leroy Pratt Percy, had graduated from Princeton University and Harvard Law School with honors, and he had taken up a career as an attorney and general counsel for Tennessee Coal, Iron and Railroad. Birmingham was known as the "Magic City" because it had grown so rapidly and prosperously since its founding in 1870. Yet the Percys were not newcomers to Birmingham. In fact, Walker Percy's grandfather (also named Walker) had settled there in

1886 after graduating from the University of the South ("Sewanee") as well as the University of Virginia Law School. Thus did the Percys rise rapidly to social and civic prominence in the raw and bustling city. Yet theirs was not a typical southern milieu but a decidedly multicultural place, with a large population of Jews, Greeks, Italians, and Russians coming to operate the new coal mines, steel mills, businesses.

Walker Percy's father, like his forebears, had been imbued with the ancient ideal of noblesse oblige, a secular version of the biblical claim that "to whom much is given, of him will much be required" (Luke 12:48). The Percy family believed that the "nobility" who have achieved great material and social success are not meant to live in idle luxury; they are obliged, instead, to devote themselves to the commonweal. Thus were the Birmingham Percys active in various civic clubs, even as they were vigorous opponents of bigotry and narrow-mindedness, especially when it was directed against Catholics, Jews, and Negroes. They were also members of the Independent Presbyterian Church, a congregation whose pastor had been ousted from an older Presbyterian church because he was a humanist who denied the existence of miracles and the divinity of Jesus. (Such moralistic Presbyterianism is satirized, by the way, in the figure of Ellen Oglethorpe in *Love in the Ruins*.)

Walker Percy described his Birmingham childhood as having many occasions for happiness. Together with his two younger brothers, he enjoyed hunting and fishing with a black caretaker named Elijah Collier ("Lije"), and the Percy brothers spent theirs summers at boys' camps in cool Wisconsin. The three Percys attended a small, select academy called Birmingham University School, where Walker was known as quiet and studious, but also as somewhat sickly, since he was afflicted with allergies. Though he was a much better student than athlete—excelling chiefly in Latin and math but also sending off short stories to various boys' magazines—he was not an insufferable little egghead. On the contrary, nearly everyone found him funny. Yet nearly everyone also noticed something distant and aloof about young Walker, as if he were too vulnerable and frail a creature to be suited for the rough-and-tumble of ordinary life. In this regard Percy very much resembled his mother, who was also rather delicate and remote—indeed, an almost otherworldly figure. The boys were never close to her.

In 1924 the Percys left the Five Points neighborhood at the commercial hub of Birmingham for a new suburban life. They moved over Red Mountain to a grand new home next to the Mountain Brook Country Club.

It was an elaborate mansion that would later become the model for the Vaughts' "castle" in *The Last Gentleman*. Yet not all was well in the prosperous Percy household. Leroy Percy was given to violent mood swings. At first he would be warm and cheerful, then suddenly angry and downcast. He was a brilliant, driven man who made exhaustive annotations in his Bible and who read the fiction of Joseph Conrad obsessively. He was obsessive about other things as well, especially gambling and golfing and hunting. He also seemed strangely determined to create rivalries among his sons, pitting them against each other, for example, in gun-shooting contests. They, in turn, came to dread the evening ordeal at the dinner table with a depressive father made edgy by alcohol. It seems that Leroy Percy's misery may also have been complicated by an unconsummated love affair. As one of the Percy brothers later confessed, "It just wasn't a happy family."[3] The father's depression worsened, as did his maddening insomnia, until on July 9, 1929, the forty-year-old Percy went to the attic and blew his brains out. His funeral was held before Walker and his brothers could get back to Birmingham from their camp in Wisconsin. They were aged thirteen, twelve, and seven.

The world's violent volcanic core had erupted into Walker Percy's seemingly tranquil existence. He later admitted that he had spent his entire life and work trying to answer a single question: "I guess the central mystery of my life will always be why my father killed himself."[4] The answer may be genetic no less than spiritual. "Melancholy and suicide," writes Tolson, "have a prominent place in the Percy family saga."[5] The very first Percy to arrive in America, a Natchez planter named Charles, tied a sugar kettle to his neck, walked into an icy Mississippi creek, and drowned himself in January 1794. Walker Percy's own grandfather had also killed himself in 1917 after a long battle with depression. Thanks to the psychiatric help now available, Walker and subsequent generations of Percys have staved off the deadliest effects of melancholy. Yet the Percy urge to suicidal self-doubt is not only a biological tendency. The Percy men of this century have also been haunted by the high honor that their ancestors once achieved but that none of them has quite lived up to—at least in the political sense of becoming public movers and shakers. Their Mississippi forebears were men of action who carved prosperity out of the American wilderness, who rose to public prominence, who built strong levees to prevent the flooding of their native city of Greenville, who often stood down the Ku Klux Klan. Their twentieth-century epigoni, by contrast, have become mainly men of thought rather than action, and thus are they haunted by a sense of failed honor.

As if Percyesque melancholy, unlike lightning, could indeed strike twice in the same place, Walker and his brothers were dealt a second deathblow in the spring of 1932. They and their mother, Mattie Sue, had come to live in Greenville, the ancestral Percy home in the Mississippi Delta. Taking a ride in the countryside with her ten-year-old son Phin on an April afternoon, Mrs. Percy drove her Buick off a wooden bridge and into a bayou. The screaming son grabbed his mother as the car began to fill with water. She squeezed his hand in response, but she neither spoke nor moved. Frantically he managed to make his way out a rear window, unable to drag his mother with him. No one knows whether Mrs. Percy veered off the bridge after suffering a heart attack or whether she in fact committed suicide, seeking to take her "baby" out of this sad world with her. In either case, the three Percy brothers were made orphans. Walker's sense of loneliness and homelessness, already acute, would now become permanent and incurable. In fact, Percy would later assent to Albert Camus's contention that suicide is the major philosophical problem of the twentieth century: in a world which seems devoid of ultimate order and meaning and worth, why should one not do away with oneself?

The sixteen-year-old Walker Percy received a startling answer to this question not first by way of philosophical or religious argument but rather by ethical action. To the surprise of nearly everyone, he and his two brothers were adopted and raised by their father's forty-four-year-old bachelor first cousin, William Alexander Percy. Walker was later to say of "Uncle Will," as the boys came affectionately to call him, "that he was the most extraordinary man I have ever known and that I owe him a debt which cannot be paid."[6] Such praise is not too strong. Will Percy was a veritable Renaissance man who embodied all the virtues of the Old South. He was a distinguished poet who wrote both English and Latin verse, a heroic soldier of the First World War, a onetime teacher of literature at Sewanee, a friend of William Faulkner and other literary luminaries, the proprietor of the Percy family's large cotton plantation outside Greenville, and a graduate of Harvard Law School—though his legal career was of less moment than his civic work. He openly opposed the Ku Klux Klan, even carrying a pistol to protect himself, and he organized aid for local Negroes whose homes were ravaged by the floods of the 1920s before the Tennessee Valley Authority helped control them. Thanks largely to efforts of such public-spirited citizens as Will Percy, Greenville became one of the most enlightened and progressive towns in an often benighted and repressive state. The local white high school, for example, was academically rigorous. Percy received a first-rate education there, contributing stories and editorials to the school newspaper edited by a buddy who was to become his best friend, his fellow writer, and also his lifelong antagonist: the relentlessly agnostic Shelby Foote.

Uncle Will raised Walker and his two brothers to be men of culture. He took them to New Orleans to see the opera, he read Shakespeare and the romantic poets to them aloud, he helped them appreciate the music of major composers from Bach to Stravinsky (especially Brahms), he taught them to read Plato and the Stoics, and he inspired them to follow one of the classic professions: medicine, education, the military, or the law. It is noteworthy that ministry was not on the list. Uncle Will was in fact a deeply religious man who had been raised as a Catholic and who as a youth had considered the priesthood. But during his undergraduate years at Sewanee he gave up not only his Catholicism but also his Christianity, choosing instead to become a religious humanist. "No priest could absolve me," he wrote about his loss of faith, "no church could direct my life or my judgement." From then on, he declared, "I would be living with my own self."[7] Yet Will Percy was no crusading anti-Christian; on the contrary, he loved the elegant English of the Book of Common Prayer, and he supported the church as one of the pillars of society, a necessary institution for maintaining social order and dignity. Even so, his beliefs were far more Stoic than Christian. For him the cosmos forms a massive closed cycle of beautiful repetitions and regularities, and our human purpose is to put ourselves in accord with the fundamental patterns of nature. Though the universe came from nowhere and is going nowhere, it is not a meaningless realm. For in accepting the finality of death and defeat, we can still attain a certain tragic, if also lonely, nobility. Uncle Will's plangent autobiography, *Lanterns on the Levee: Recollections of a Planter's Son* (1941), is his memorable account of his Stoic life and outlook. It offers a powerful lament over the loss of southern grace and virtue with the rise of what William Faulkner called the Snopeses, the cultureless money-grubbers who care nothing for the permanent things. That Will Percy was a closeted homosexual may have also contributed to his melancholy life, which ended in exhaustion at age fifty-seven.

At first Walker Percy seemed to be a disciple of Uncle Will's Stoic philosophy. It is certain, in any case, that the Percy who matriculated at the University of North Carolina at Chapel Hill in 1933 was no Christian. He had been inspired by Sinclair Lewis's novel *Arrowsmith* to become a medical doctor, thus fulfilling Uncle Will's wish that his adopted sons contribute to the human good. Yet young Percy was not a moral idealist so much as a social pessimist. Here he followed in his adopted father's train. Percy scorned the newly elected Roosevelt, for example, on the grounds that the human lot could not be improved by social legislation. Percy also held to the materialist conviction that human existence could be understood almost entirely in physical terms, and that it could be improved only through medical advances and environmental changes. Here he had been much influenced by the work of Julian A. Huxley and H. G. Wells. He had learned from their book *The Science of Life* that the scientific method will eventually solve the world's mysteries. Hence Percy's own decision to take an undergraduate degree in chemistry—a major whose intellectual impersonality echoed Percy's own personal aloofness. Though he was a popular fraternity member and ladies' man, the youthful Percy always held himself apart, never letting anyone get too close, women least of all. There was indeed a fatalistic streak in Percy that made him doubt the good that anyone could do. He became, in fact, something of a misanthrope who looked upon his fellow creatures and did not like what he saw. His favorite Dostoyevsky character was Ivan Karamazov, the atheist who believes in nothing but science.

Yet there was also a romantic and literary side to Percy's existence that manifested itself during his Chapel Hill years. He took courses not only in chemistry, biology, and the other sciences; he also read Schopenhauer and Nietzsche, and he became especially adept at German. Percy began less than auspiciously in English. He flunked the entrance exam and was remanded to remedial freshman composition for writing a convoluted description of the Mississippi River in imitation of Faulkner's style in *The Sound and the Fury!* Yet Percy did well in the humanities, and he served as the movie reviewer for the *Daily Tarheel*, the campus newspaper. Moviegoing would become a lifelong Percy practice, a means of escape from the madding world—even if he would also make a devastating critique of the film world in his first novel, *The Moviegoer* (1961). The romantic state of Percy's soul was even more plainly revealed in the summer tour of Germany that he took with his German professor in 1934. To his later shame, Percy found himself greatly impressed by the Hitler Youth—their moral seriousness, their impressive uniforms, their motto of *Blut und Ehre* (blood and honor), their willingness to die for the sake of their country and their cause. That they supported the Nazi cause mattered less to Percy than that they belonged to what Tolson calls "the oldest strain of Teutonic romanticism, the *Lebenstod* (love of death) that runs from the oldest German sagas, through the romances, Wagnerian opera, and Weimar culture before erupting in the mythology and symbolism of Nazism."[8] It is also a troubling fact that neither Walker Percy nor his brother Roy resigned from their University of North Carolina fraternity when Shelby Foote, their friend and fellow Greenvillean, was blackballed from membership because of his partially Jewish background. Percy was elected to Phi Beta Kappa during his junior year, and he was graduated with honors in chemistry in 1937. Yet he was not tapped for the highest social honor—membership in Chapel Hill's most prestigious secret society, the Golden Fleece. He was also rejected by the Harvard Medical School. Though seemingly minor defeats, they rankled Percy for the rest of his life.

Yet Percy was hardly doomed to mediocrity. Instead, he attended the highly regarded College of Physicians and Surgeons at Columbia University in New York City, where again he did outstanding work. There at Columbia Percy became ever more enamored of the scientific worldview: its elegance, its order, even its strange logic in the mechanism of diseases. It was a world that Percy could so easily master that he was not often seen studying his science books but reading novels and magazines. When the time came for him to choose a specialty, he elected pathology, perhaps because it allowed him to retain his personal aloofness: he would not be required to have firsthand dealings with patients. Yet Percy was also drawn to psychiatry. The reason seems clear: for all of his seeming suavity and easygoing manner, he was a very troubled man. Percy was losing much of his earlier enthusiasm for medicine, and he spent a good deal of his time at Columbia visiting Uncle Will's New York friends, many of whom were either latently or openly homosexual. Moreover, when other students would be burrowing into books and lab work, Percy was slipping downtown for his weekly appointment with an analyst, Dr. Janet Brioche. She was a neo-Freudian whose foremost concern was not with elaborate psychiatric theories but with the welfare of her analysands. Patiently she helped Percy deal with his many perplexities—his father's suicide, his own loneliness and sadness, his uncertain sexuality and his even more uncertain future, his obsession with familial honor, and (not least of all) his anger at never having known a mother's love. In Percy's case, the Freudian method of "transference" actually worked, as he gained such confidence and trust in Dr. Brioche that he was able to transfer many of his fantasies and feelings about his dead parents to this surrogate mother. But while Dr. Brioche could soothe Percy's spiritual ache, she could not cure it. As he would later observe, "In my own experience the most valuable lesson of psychoanalysis was learning what it could not do."[9] No sooner, in fact, had Percy finished his medical degree at Columbia in 1941 than he lost his surrogate father. Will Percy died in January 1942, shortly after America's entry into the Second World War. Percy's world was falling apart in nearly every imaginable way.

Percy had elected to do his residency in pathology at Bellevue Hospital in New York City, where he performed autopsies on unclaimed bodies from Skid Row. Careless about wearing masks and gloves, Percy and three of his fellow internists (on a team of twelve) contracted tuberculosis from bacilli still alive in the cadavers of these derelicts. Though the physical causes of the disease had been discovered in 1882, still in 1942 it was thought also to be the result of moral defection—a product of corrupt character or weak will. Percy often wondered if this superstition were perhaps true. Before the discovery of streptomycin in 1946, the only known cures for consumption, as it was then called, were an optimistic attitude and an extended rest amid salubrious air. To ensure the latter, Percy was sent to the famous Trudeau Sanatorium on Lake Saranac in the Adirondack Mountains of upstate New York. Expense was no concern, since Uncle Will had left the Percy brothers a very generous estate. Yet if optimism were the key to Percy's cure, his odds were not good. He was filled, on the contrary, with self-doubt and self-disgust as he lay in indolent ease while his two brothers went off to the war. Yet the convalescent Percy found that he did not miss medicine, and his illness also meant that he was saved from the grave choices he was dreading—decisions about marriage and career and what to do with himself in a world that seemed to make ever less sense. During his two years at the sanatorium, Percy became known as a cynical and nihilistic figure, a quick-witted but morose loner. Percy was later to write his first book—an unpublished novel called "The Gramercy Winner," in imitation of Thomas Mann's *Magic Mountain*—about the decadence of life at a sanatorium. As a world with "no sweat, no love, no exercise, no injury," it was a metaphor of our own moral decadence in a world that has also come to live amid moral indolence and ease.[10]

Why, then, did Percy later describe his disease as a stroke of good fortune? The immediate answer is that it freed him from continuing the medical career for which he had lost all interest. More deeply it meant that, there on Lake Saranac, Percy began to find his spiritual life no less than to recover his bodily health. It was during these crucial months that Percy began to turn away not only from his scientific materialism but also from the Stoic humanism of Uncle Will. He was now in search of more substantial answers to the ache that gnawed at his soul. Percy spent much of his time in the sanatorium reading. He burrowed deeply into Tolstoy and Dostoyevsky, Franz Kafka and Thomas Mann. But he also read theologians, including Augustine and Aquinas and Søren Kierkegaard.

Percy got well enough to return to New York City in late 1944, where he enjoyed (thanks to the inheritance he had received at Uncle Will's death) the carefree life of a young bachelor who had no intention of returning to medicine. Yet Percy suffered a relapse in mid-1945, and he was forced to convalesce again at a sanatorium in New Haven, Connecticut, where the playwright Eugene O'Neill had been a patient thirty years earlier. There Percy found himself strangely reborn, largely through re-reading Dostoyevsky's *Notes from the Underground*. This angry and satirical book, with its powerful critique of nineteenth-century determinism, awakened Percy to his own true vocation: to be a writer. At last he knew what he really wanted to do: to write about twentieth-century man as also a creature in extremis.

Percy returned to Mississippi in 1946 to approach his thirtieth birthday not only joyfully but also fearfully. He had answered the great question of what to do with himself, but many other questions remained unanswered: to write in what setting, in what literary genres, about what subjects, and with what (if any) other human beings as his companions? There in Greenville and at Brinkwood, the family's mountain retreat in Sewanee, Tennessee, Percy dated a series of local women. But as soon as the relationships would grow serious—even reaching the point of marriage—he would coldly abandon these women, leaving them crushed and causing them to regard Percy as a cad. It seems clear that Percy was toying with personal possibilities. Possibility, he had learned from Kierkegaard, can serve as both the ultimate temptation and the ultimate threat. The open-ended liberty to create one's own life tempts one either to godlike pride in choosing whatever one wants, or else it threatens one with the demonic despair of finding nothing worth doing. The outward and visible locus of such pure possibility, Percy believed, is the American West. And so in 1947 Percy persuaded his old Greenville friend Shelby Foote to join him on a trip to New Mexico. Both of these young bachelors were aspiring writers, and yet neither of them had shown much more than promise. Perhaps they would find what they were supposed to do out there on those barren mountains and under the gigantic sky, where there were no complications of family and region and history.

It is also noteworthy that, at about this same time, Percy purchased the German Luger that his father had brought back from Europe but had later sold to a nephew. That Percy not only purchased this gun but also kept it near at hand makes one wonder: was he filled with a self-loathing that caused him to consider the act that his father had committed? It is not an idle question. In *The Last Gentleman,* suicide in the New Mexico desert looms large and, in *The Second Coming,* suicide with a German Luger becomes an awful possibility. Yet Percy knew that the true possibility is not death but life. Percy was not just jesting when he declared that the chief question of his life was whether he would kill himself.

He knew that, if he were not to commit self-murder, he would have to seek a radical newness of life that would produce radical ethical action. To Foote's tremendous surprise, therefore, Percy announced that he was leaving Santa Fe and returning to New Orleans to marry Mary Bernice ("Bunt") Townsend. It wasn't an arbitrary decision. Percy had met her several summers earlier while he was working at a Greenville hospital where she was working as a nurse. Percy had been smitten by Bunt because she wasn't the proverbial southern belle, the fluttery coquette playing the ritual game of romance. She was straightforward in her manner, self-supporting in her work, and competent to do almost anything she turned her hand to. Bunt, in turn, was impressed with Walker's almost painful modesty about his prominent family's mystique. Because she was the only woman in whose presence he was completely comfortable, Percy felt not only eros but also philia toward her. Bunt was no mere prospective sexual partner but also a woman who could become his best friend. Yet Percy was extremely shy at social gatherings, and he dreaded a wedding that would serve as a huge familial event. But he didn't put their courtship on hold. Bunt and Walker began dating again in October 1947, and they were married on November 6. With only a few friends gathered as witnesses, the ceremony was performed at the First Baptist Church of New Orleans. The pastor, Dr. J. D. Grey, urged the couple to make their love as pure as the gold in their wedding rings. Shelby Foote, Percy's best man, stifled his giggles because he knew that the ring he had just handed the minister was made of platinum.

The newlyweds lived at first in Sewanee and New Orleans, as Percy continued to read and write. He was also pondering his religious no less than his literary future. One of the figures whom Percy had first read at the Saranac sanatorium was the great Danish Protestant thinker of the nineteenth century, Søren Kierkegaard. Again Percy turned to Kierkegaard's little essay called "On the Difference between a Genius and an Apostle." There Kierkegaard argues that the genius outstrips the ordinary run of women and men by his superior intelligence and insight, by the sheer brilliance of his mind and the sheer inventiveness of his imagination. Shakespeare, Michelangelo, Beethoven, Einstein (to supply obvious examples) are all geniuses whose work the world seeks to fathom. Yet eventually someone will do it, says Kierkegaard. Someone will completely comprehend their work, fathoming it fully, so that another genius will have to create yet a new masterwork of science or art. Sad to say, even the work of this new genius will finally be outstripped. The reason is not far to find. The humanist world of the genius, Kierkegaard contends, is a beautiful but sad world because it is confined within the realm of *immanence*. The genius discovers possibilities that are latent within the human condition. He brings to birth, like a midwife, what is already potential within us. The apostle, by contrast, works within the sphere of *transcendence*. Though perhaps undistinguished by intelligence or eloquence or learning—indeed, he may be an illiterate fisherman or a humble tentmaker!—the apostle announces News from beyond the walls of the world: deliverance to the captives, sight to the blind, hearing to the deaf—indeed, salvation to and for all. The apostle thus speaks with an authority not his own. He is called to announce Tidings that he has not himself discovered or invented. And there are only two responses to this apostolic Word. It cannot be declared merely interesting or made the object of further study: it must be either heeded or howled at.

"Here I am," Percy later wrote, "a Catholic living in Louisiana, and the man to whom I owe the greatest debt is this great Protestant thinker." "I suppose the great bombshell for me," Percy also wrote, "was the famous passage of Kierkegaard describing Hegel as the philosopher who explained everything under the sun except one small detail: what it means to be a man who lives in the world and who must die."[11] No small lack, this! Kierkegaard also wittily remarked that, after constructing the world's largest philosophical system, Hegel had then to figure out how to draw his next breath. Hegel was a thinker, said Kierkegaard, who was forced to live in a shack outside the great crystal palace of his own philosophy. Percy saw that Kierkegaard was exactly right: while it possible to invent systems of *thought,* it is not possible to create a system of *existence.* Living is not systematic. We live by fits and starts, by backing and filling, by inching forward and falling back yet again.

While there is indeed a tremendous legacy of human wisdom, it cannot be transmitted progressively, so that each generation advances further than the previous. On the contrary, said Kierkegaard, each person and each age must begin over again at the beginning. Yet for all of Kierkegaard's brilliant insight, Percy was troubled by the great Dane's solitariness and sadness, and especially by his notion that faith is finally an absurd leap into the void. Even Kierkegaard regarded himself as a corrective rather than a cure. Percy was drawn, instead, to Catholicism because it offered him a theology that reconciled faith and reason. As a satirist who wanted to sting his audience out of spiritual torpor, Percy the Catholic would have not only a Kierkegaardian diagnostic tool for detecting the nature of our modern sickness; he would also have the authoritative and communal remedy to it. Percy thus came to believe, as he would later have his crazy character Dr. Thomas More confess, "the whole Thing, God Jews Christ Church."[12]

Yet Percy's conversion was not entirely an affair of the mind. It's as if he and Bunt were renewing the Catholic cord that Uncle Will had snapped at Sewanee many years earlier when he gave up the faith. It's also noteworthy that Percy the young agnostic had acquired a grudging respect for Catholics. One his best friends at Chapel Hill had been Harry Stoval, a Catholic who rolled out of bed every Sunday for Mass while Percy and his roommates were still three sheets to the wind. When they complained about his disturbing their sleep in order to observe meaningless rites, Stoval replied: "Your religions may not mean anything to you, but you sure as hell better not trifle with mine."[13] Again at Columbia, Percy found himself drawn to Frank Hardart, another unapologetic Catholic. Once more, at the Trudeau Sanatorium, Percy was impressed with a New Jersey Catholic named Art Fortugno. Percy noticed that all these Catholic friends were imbued with certainty and serenity, with a clear sense of their difference and their distance from ordinary American values. Fortugno was also a man whose keen theological arguments forced Percy to read Thomas Aquinas for the first time. Percy was impressed with the clarity and depth of Aquinas's thought. He saw that Catholicism offered him a theological system altogether as impressive as modern science in its range and completeness and consistency—yet without the reductionist pretense of modern scientism.

Walker and Bunt Percy did not seek instruction in the Catholic faith from a professional theologian or professor but from a practical-minded parish priest (rather like Father Rinaldo Smith in *Love in the Ruins*). They were baptized at the Holy Name Church in New Orleans on Saturday, December 13, 1947. Rather than dreading his first confession, Percy eagerly awaited it: "This is one of the main reasons I've become a Catholic," he admitted.[14] Together with three hundred schoolchildren, they were confirmed on Easter in the spring of 1948. When the priest insisted that, as the only two adult converts among all of these young confirmands, they lead the procession into the church, the Percys politely refused. They marched, instead, at the end of the line. That they were thus made to seem like spiritual babes was no obstacle; on the contrary, they saw themselves as fellow pilgrims and wayfarers with all other Catholics and Christians, whether young or old, naïve or wise. They also sought to live a quiet and modest life, away from the decadence of the French Quarter on the one hand, but also from the affectation of the Garden District on the other. They chose, instead, to live in the rather nondescript town of Covington, across Lake Pontchartrain from New Orleans. Drawing on the inheritance left by Uncle Will, they built a lovely home near a tributary of the Bogue Falaya. St. Joseph's Benedictine Abbey was also located nearby, and the Percys would often worship in the great abbey church on high holy days, when the Mass would be chanted in Gregorian fashion.

They also became involved in local school and civic affairs. Percy the former segregationist took seriously the social teachings of the Gospel, especially as they were embodied by such Catholics as Dorothy Day in her work among the poor of New York City and Father Louis Twomey in his concern for the civil rights of Negroes. Though never an activist himself, Percy became unapologetic in his support for the desegregation of the local schools. He denounced the local White Citizens' Councils, formed to keep blacks out of the formerly all-white schools, calling them "uptown" versions of the Ku Klux Klan. He also helped local blacks open their own savings and loan association, so they could secure credit that the white banks would not grant them because they lacked the wherewithal to make down payments in purchasing homes. He also defended Archbishop Rummel of New Orleans when, in a pastoral letter, the bishop declared segregation to be sinful. He also argued that the Confederate flag could no longer represent anything other than "segregation, white supremacy, and racism."[15] Yet Percy was no righteous scourge of the racists. He admired the Baptist minister Will Campbell not only for his defense of black people against discrimination, but also for admitting that rednecks were still his brothers and sisters in Christ. Percy would write important essays on the race question for *Commonweal* and *Harper's* as well as for the radical Protestant journal *Katallagete*. As a political centrist, Percy opposed the Catholic radicalism of violent Vietnam War protesters such as Daniel and Philip Berrigan. He also lamented the support that certain fellow Catholics gave to the Sandinistas in Central America.

Yet Percy sought primarily to live and work as a novelist, not as a social commentator. Soon he established the routine that he would follow for the remaining forty years of his life. He would read and write all morning, then have lunch and take a nap, then work again in his home study or town office, before breaking either for a walk, bird-watching, or a swim in the river. Yet Percy was no stay-at-home writer like Eudora Welty and Flannery O'Connor. He and his wife were eager travelers. Percy found that travel invigorated his imagination. As a pathologist no longer working with a microscope but now with words, he was always looking for telltale symptoms of the human ailment. He also sought to invigorate his work by subjecting it to the critique of others. He showed his fiction not only to the anti-Catholic aesthete Shelby Foote, but also to fellow Catholic converts Allen Tate and Caroline Gordon (and later to Thomas Merton). They offered both praise and criticism.

Yet Percy's progress as a novelist remained agonizingly slow. He finally gave up on a 942-page work called "The Charterhouse"—a novel about conversion—and burned it. He completed "The Gramercy Winner"—a novel about baptism—but no publisher would take it. Yet these failures were essential to Percy's apprenticeship as a novelist, and he would keep returning to his early concerns. Still, Percy's promise as a writer had not yet borne fruit. For eight years he had travailed in his reading and his writing, but he had almost nothing to show for it. He was now forty, and he was beginning to get desperate about his future.

Percy decided to try a new tack. He had been reading not only literary but also philosophical works during these years—Sartre, Camus, Heidegger, and Jaspers among non-Christian existentialists; Maritain, Marcel, Aquinas, and Kierkegaard among Christian thinkers; Whitehead, Russell, Cassirer, Husserl, and Carnap among strict philosophers; and especially the aesthetician Suzanne Langer. Seeking to put his own outlook into clear focus, Percy began to write philosophical essays, mainly about the relation of words to things, and whether their relation depends on a transcendent third reality: the person who uses words to refer to things, and the God whose own triune life makes such references real rather than arbitrary. Percy argued that language is our unique human faculty, that symbol use is the single capacity differentiating us from the other animals.

To his surprise, these essays were readily accepted by various philosophical journals. Many years later, in 1975, they were collected into a volume called *The Message in the Bottle.* Percy's philosophical concern about the nature of language also had surprising personal relevance. In 1948 the Percys had adopted a ten-month-old girl whom they had baptized as Mary Pratt. When in 1954 their biological daughter, Ann, was born, it soon became evident that she was stone deaf. The Percys were not daunted. Instead, they employed a speech teacher named Doris Mirrilees, a woman cut from the same cloth as Helen Keller's Annie Sullivan. The Percys wanted to ensure that Ann not only learn to use sign language but also to speak. Much of Percy's later interest in semiotics—the science of signs—derives from his many hours spent teaching Ann to sound out the most fundamental words.

The real breakthrough essay for Percy was entitled "The Man on the Train: Three Existential Modes." It was published in a 1956 issue of *Partisan Review,* and it dealt with the modern problem of alienation—with the urban commuter who is a seeming success in the world, but who is personally miserable, yet who is utterly unaware of the fact, much less the cause, of his alienation. Percy explores the various means for diagnosing such alienation, how one seeks to escape from it, and yet how finally there is no avoiding the enigma of one's own selfhood. It was as if, having got clear about the fundamental problem that he wanted to explore philosophically, Percy could also write about it novelistically. Percy would later make the following remarkable (if somewhat overheated) confession in a letter to Caroline Gordon: "Actually I do not consider myself a novelist but a moralist or a propagandist. My spiritual father is Pascal (and/or Kierkegaard). And if I also kneel before the altar of Lawrence and Joyce and Faulkner, it is not because I wish to do what they did, even if I could. What I really want to do is to tell people *what they must do and what they must believe if they want to live.*"¹⁶ Now that Percy at last had his philosophical and religious bearings, Shelby Foote suggested that he use New Orleans, a city that Percy knew intimately, as the setting for the fledgling novel he was trying to get off the ground. Though it took four painstaking years of writing and revising, *The Moviegoer* was finally published in 1961. Its popular sales were modest, but the critics liked it so much that it won the National Book Award (NBA) for fiction, the highest American literary prize. *The Moviegoer* is, among other things, a novel about Binx Bolling's conversion—but also, and not least of all, Percy's own metanoia. Because he was a great enthusiast for the presidency of John Kennedy, the event of November 22, 1963, threw him off track for an entire year, as he sought without success to write about it. Yet in 1967 he came forth with *The Last Gentleman,* a runner-up for the National Book Award. It too is a story about conversion—only in this case a pilgrimage in reverse, and it ends with an extremely ironic and marvelous kind of baptism. *Love in the Ruins* followed in 1971, and it again won the chief prize. Though not Percy's best literary achievement, it is surely his funniest and perhaps his most prophetic work. *Lancelot,* Percy's angriest but also one of his finest-crafted novels, was published in 1977. *The Second Coming* followed in 1980, and *The Thanatos Syndrome* in 1987. Neither of them lives up to the high standards set in Percy's earlier work. Two more volumes of essays were issued: *Lost in the Cosmos: The Last Self-Help Book* in 1983, and *Signposts in a Strange Land* posthumously in 1991.

This is hardly to say that, once he had made his literary breakthrough, Percy passed swimmingly through the world. On the contrary, he remained a troubled man, even as his troubles also fed his fiction. What Tolson observes of the first novel is true of Percy's work as a whole: "The drama of his life was less a story of events than an internal struggle—psychological but ultimately spiritual—to find a ground of certainty and security, a struggle to find an essential self, a soul. Percy had finally learned how to project this internal quest upon a believable fictive world."¹⁷ Afflicted with inveterate insomnia, Percy joked that he tried not to lose too much sleep over it. He also suffered from other psychosomatic illnesses, including chronic diverticulitis as well as bipolar disorder. About the latter, Percy quipped that his wife would like to see more of the manic highs and fewer of the depressive lows. There were dark periods in Percy's life when he found refuge in women other than his wife, especially graduate students at Louisiana State University when he was teaching there. He could also be unspeakably coarse and curt, even toward his dear Bunt. There is also the indisputable fact of Percy's dependence on alcohol to help quiet his demons. Thus did he both begin and end as a man whose spleen injured himself and others even as it inspired much of his art.

Yet these personal failings cannot cancel Percy's courage and generosity. He was almost entirely responsible for the publication of John Kennedy Toole's hilarious novel *A Confederacy of Dunces*—after the manuscript had been foisted on him by the suicide of Toole's importunate mother. Percy was also an unabashed opponent of abortion. He argued that we might as well kill the aged, infirm, and unproductive on similar grounds. It is no surprise that Percy should have become a staunch advocate of John Paul II's Christian witness to our "culture of death," as the pope called it. In a letter that the *New York Times* refused to publish, Percy sought to startle his fellow Americans by saying that we are now faced with a stark choice: "It's either the Pope or Los Angeles."[18] Percy also became overt in his own personal witness, reminding Shelby Foote and other agnostic friends that they should not let their lives end without giving themselves to Jesus Christ.

When Percy contracted prostate cancer, he volunteered for his doctors at the Mayo Clinic to use experimental medicines, in the hope that they might learn how to cure others even if he himself were not healed. He also joined a Benedictine lay confraternity in order to be buried among the monks at St. Joseph's Abbey, located not far from his home in Covington. When death came, as it did near the end of his seventy-fourth year, Percy the pilgrim had reached his shrine and Percy the writer had finished his work. His grave marker declares simply: "Walker Percy, May 28, 1916–May 10, 1990."

Notes

1. William Buckley, *Firing Line*, December 12, 1972.

2. Jay Tolson, *Pilgrim in the Ruins: A Life of Walker Percy* (New York: Simon and Schuster, 1992).

3. Ibid., 42.

4. Ibid., 396.

5. Ibid., 51.

6. Walker Percy, *Signposts in a Strange Land*, ed. Patrick Samway, S.J. (New York: Farrar, Straus, and Giroux, 1991), 62.

7. William Alexander Percy, *Lanterns on the Levee: Recollections of a Planter's Son* (Baton Rouge: Louisiana State University Press, 1988), 95.

8. Tolson, *Pilgrim in the Ruins*, 118.

9. Quoted in ibid., 333.

10. Quoted in ibid., 172.

11. Percy, *Conversations with Walker Percy*, ed. Lewis A. Lawson and Victor Kramer (Jackson: University Press of Mississippi, 1985), 127.

12. Percy, *Love in the Ruins* (New York: Farrar, Straus, and Giroux, 1971), 106.

13. Tolson, *Pilgrim in the Ruins*, 127.

14. Ibid., 204.

15. Ibid., 353.

16. Cited in Jan Nordby Gretlund and Karl-Heinz Westarp, eds., *Walker Percy: Novelist and Philosopher* (Jackson: University Press of Mississippi, 1991), 169.

17. Tolson, *Pilgrim in the Ruins*, 302.

18. Percy, *Signposts in a Strange Land*, 350.

The Moviegoer's Cartesian Theater
Moviegoing as Walker Percy's Metaphor for the Cartesian Mind

Woods Nash

Binx Bolling is the moviegoing protagonist of *The Moviegoer* (1961), Walker Percy's first published novel. In an interview, Percy once referred to Binx as a "victim" of Descartes, to whom Percy attributed "many of the troubles of the modern world."[1] Did Percy intend some connection between Binx's moviegoing and his unfortunate Cartesian heritage? In this essay, I argue that Percy used Binx's moviegoing as a metaphor for his having a Cartesian mind. As Percy knew, many Descartes scholars regard the Cartesian self as a purely thinking thing whose mind is like a theater. Seated in that theater, the self entertains ideas, or mental objects, which stand like a screen between the self and the nonmental world. It is consistent with the two most widely held readings of Descartes on the nature of an idea to regard ideas as mental objects, as I note below. I then argue that there is ample evidence to support our seeing Binx's moviegoing as a metaphor for his having a Cartesian mind. Next, I describe how our reading *The Moviegoer* in this way might enrich our understanding of this novel, Percy's other work, and Percy himself. I conclude with some brief reflections on the implications of my reading for Percy's regarding modern society, individual character, and contemporary culture as Cartesian.

Before I can elicit the various connections that the novel makes between Binx's moviegoing and Descartes, I must first briefly discuss Descartes' view of the nature of an idea. Only after considering Descartes' view will we be in a position to appreciate the nuances of Percy's portrayal of Binx-the-moviegoer as a Cartesian specter and spectator.

Descartes on the Nature of an Idea: Two Interpretations

In his *Meditations*, Descartes famously concluded, from the mere fact that he thinks, that he could be certain of his own existence. It was impossible for him to be deceived in the belief that he, a thinking thing, exists, for, Descartes reasoned, to be deceived, there still must be *something* that is deceived and some *thought* about which that thing is deceived. Thus, Descartes achieved certainty about this: There is at least one thing in the world—namely, him, a thing that thinks. But what is it to think? To think, Descartes held, always involves having ideas. I take all of this to be a fairly uncontroversial reading of Descartes. What is a bit more contentious, however, is this issue: How should we understand Descartes' conception of an idea? An answer to this question is important, for if the Cartesian self is characterized by thinking, and if thinking involves having ideas, then Descartes' conception of an idea informed his view of the self. Furthermore, if, as I will argue, Percy suggested that Binx has a Cartesian mind, then, to a great extent, Binx has a Cartesian self.

In the "preface to the reader" of his *Meditations*, Descartes commented that the word *idea* is ambiguous. "Idea," Descartes told us, can be taken materially and refer to an operation of the intellect, or a mental act. However, "idea" also "can be taken objectively, as the thing represented by that operation; and this thing, even if it is not regarded as existing outside the intellect, can still, in virtue of its essence, be more perfect than myself."[2] Thus, in this passage, Descartes identified at least two senses of *idea*— "idea" as a mental act and "idea" as a mental object. Given this ambiguity, we might ask: Did Descartes intend to use "idea" in one or both of these senses? Or did he hold some other conception of an idea—for example, "idea" as some combination of both mental act and mental object? Fortunately, according to the argument that I wish to make, the way in which Percy used moviegoing as a metaphor for the Cartesian mind could be supported by either of the two most plausible readings of Descartes on the nature of an idea. Those readings are (1) every idea is some combination of both a mental act and a mental object;[3] and (2) every idea is only a mental object.[4] On both of these readings, *the self, in thought, first encounters mental objects.* That is, in thought, mental objects are likened to a screen that separates the self from nonmental reality. For Descartes, that screen of mental objects is in place, so to speak, whether or not the self attains knowledge of any nonmental reality. The self, in thought, has no immediate access to nonmental reality.

Moviegoing as Metaphor for the Cartesian Mind

The novel's title renders it obvious that readers are to think of Binx as a moviegoer.[5] And this is not hard to do: in the course of the story, Binx attends several movies, and he often refers to films, actresses, and actors. When he leaves work at his uncle's brokerage firm, it is his "custom" on summer evenings, he tells us, "to take a shower, put on shirt and pants and stroll over to the deserted playground and there sit on the ocean wave, spread out the movie page of the *Times-Picayune* on one side, phone book on the other, and a city map in my lap" (10). Choosing a theater in some remote neighborhood of the city, he plots a route to it.

Yet, beyond the literal sense in which Binx is a moviegoer, I wish to argue that Binx is a moviegoer in a metaphorical sense—that is, his literal moviegoing is a metaphor for his having a Cartesian mind. There is, I think, ample evidence to support this thesis. First, the novel suggests that a person can be a moviegoer in a nonliteral sense of that term. Second, Percy was aware that Descartes scholars have likened the Cartesian mind to an inner theater. Third, the novel alludes to Descartes when Binx refers to Archimedes' "secret leverage point" (82)—a "point" that, as ghostly and nowhere, involves the sort of detached perspective that Binx maintains for most of the novel, especially in his moviegoing. Fourth, Binx often thinks of his life situations as if they were scenes in a film. In doing so, he allows his thoughts of movies to stand between himself and the world, just as, for Descartes, mental objects stand like a screen between the self and the nonmental world. When these points are seen cumulatively, it becomes likely that Percy used moviegoing in this specific, metaphorical sense.

Nonliteral Moviegoing in **The Moviegoer**

First, let us note that the novel suggests that a person can be a moviegoer without literally going to movies. On the bus from Chicago to New Orleans, Binx talks with a young "romantic," of whom he observes: "He is a moviegoer, though of course he does not go to movies" (216). If not in the literal sense, in what sense is this young man a moviegoer? Binx hints at an answer to that question, I think, in these musings: "Two things I am curious about. How does he sit? Immediately graceful and not aware of it or *mediately graceful and aware of it?* How does he read *The Charterhouse of Parma?* Immediately as a man who is in the world and who has an appetite for the book as he might have an appetite for peaches, or mediately as one who finds himself under the necessity of sticking himself into the world in a certain fashion, of slumping in an acceptable slump, of reading an acceptable book on an acceptable bus?" (214–15; my emphasis). Binx concludes that the young man reads and slumps *mediately:* "He is a romantic. His posture is the first clue: it is too good to be true, this distillation of all graceful slumps" (215). The young man's actions are accompanied by his entertaining ideas of acceptable actions—ideas that mediate whatever contact with the world the young man achieves. He is not immediately immersed in, or engaged with, the world. Instead, holding in his mind an image of the distillation of all graceful slumps, he slumps. In short, this "romantic" is a Cartesian whose mental self is separated from the physical world by ideas—or mental objects—such as images.[6] All of this is consonant with the two dominant interpretations of a Cartesian idea as—or, at least, as involving—a mental object. So, in the case of the young man on the bus, we might say that Percy used the label "moviegoer" as a metaphor for the young man's having a Cartesian mind. We should also note that Binx seems to have an intimate understanding of the young man's predicament—perhaps because Binx sees a bit of himself in this romantic (214–16).

The "Common Image" of the Cartesian Mind as an Inner Theater

Admittedly, this single example is, at best, scant evidence that Percy intended to use moviegoing in any metaphorical sense *throughout* the novel. As further evidence, consider that Percy read closely Jacques Maritain's *The Dream of Descartes* several years before he began writing *The Moviegoer.*[7] In Maritain's work, Percy would have found a reference to Cartesian ideas as "pictures" that thought "discovers in itself." Maritain wrote: "Locke's formula: *ideas are the immediate objects of thought,* is a pure Cartesian formula. *Idea-pictures, idea-screens.* In short, we know only our ideas; thought has direct contact only with itself."[8] If the Cartesian self achieves any contact with the world, that contact is mediated by ideas. It is quite plausible that, for a faithful moviegoer (as Percy was), Maritain's characterization of Cartesian ideas as "pictures" and "screens" would elicit thoughts of the movies—or "picture shows," as they were often called.

Furthermore, Percy was familiar with Arnold Toynbee's *The Growths of Civilizations*, in which Toynbee compared the wall-watching experience of the people in Plato's allegory of the cave to moviegoing.[9] Though it is, of course, quite a stretch from Platonic to Cartesian metaphysics, Toynbee's comparison might at least have set Percy to ponder moviegoing as an experience that could be used as a metaphor for other philosophical views.

Finally, in his commentary on Descartes, Jorge Secada drew on what he called a "common image" when he characterized the Cartesian mind as a theater "in which are displayed all the immediate objects of awareness. Keeping to the analogy, this inner theatre includes not only the stage but also the stalls, for the direct objects of the soul include both its formally existing acts of thought [that is, mental acts] and the objectively existing objects of these acts [that is, mental objects]."[10] Given Percy's interest in Descartes, it would not be surprising to learn that Percy was familiar with this "common image" of the Cartesian mind as an inner theater and that, in *The Moviegoer*, he replaced Descartes' theater with the modern movie cinema.

Descartes and Moviegoing in the Novel: Moviegoer as Detached, Ghostly, and Nowhere

Alongside Binx's encounter with the young romantic on the bus, there is another passage in the novel that seems to connect Descartes and moviegoing. Binx and Kate have just emerged from a cinema and are wandering across a university campus. Kate asks Binx about his "vertical search," which is the search that he undertook years before he embarked on his current "horizontal" search. Earlier in the novel, Binx described his vertical search in these terms:

> During those years I stood outside the universe and sought to understand it. I lived in my room as an Anyone living Anywhere and read fundamental books. . . . Certainly it did not matter to me where I was when I read such a book as *The Expanding Universe*. The greatest success of this enterprise . . . came one night when I sat in a hotel room in Birmingham and read a book called *The Chemistry of Life*. When I finished it, it seemed to me that the main goals of

my search were reached or were in principle reachable. . . . The only difficulty was that though the universe had been disposed of, I myself was left over. There I lay in my hotel room with my search over yet still obliged to draw one breath and then the next. (69–70)

Now, outside the cinema, when Kate asks Binx about his vertical search, Binx explains that the search was exciting because "as you get deeper into the search, you unify. You understand more and more specimens by fewer and fewer formulae. . . . Of course you are always after the big one, the new key, *the secret leverage point,* and that is the best of it" (82; my emphasis).

Commenting on this passage, Lewis A. Lawson noted that "that 'secret leverage point,' the Archimedean fulcrum to use in moving the world, is far, far outside the world, *so that one must look at the world as if it were a movie.*"[11] Furthermore, Lawson observed: "That 'leverage point' was sought, as Percy well knows, by Rene Descartes."[12] Lawson went on to cite Norman Kemp Smith's version of Descartes' Second Meditation, where Descartes wrote: "Archimedes, that he might displace the whole earth, required only that there might be some one point, fixed and immovable, to serve in leverage; so likewise I shall be entitled to entertain high hopes if I am fortunate to find some one thing that is certain and indubitable."[13] Thus, we have this further association between Descartes and moviegoing: in pursuing the vertical search, Binx had sought an Archimedean-Cartesian point—a perspective "outside the world" from which he could understand the world, viewing it "as if it were a movie," as Lawson wrote.[14] Furthermore, even though Binx claims to have abandoned his vertical search years ago, he remains drawn to the Cartesian ideal of an extraterrestrial vantage point. As Howland put it: "*For most of the novel,* Binx clings to his objective-transcendent viewpoint. He assumes that he can look at his life from the outside, as if he were Descartes's disembodied cogito, cut off from the world it would know."[15] Like the stereotypical Cartesian, Binx is "prone to taking a detached observer's stance toward the world, to formulating experience reductively, and to abstracting and categorizing others—a form of alienation."[16] Here, it is also worth noting that, at the end of the novel, Binx appears to have abandoned both moviegoing and his former posture of Cartesian detachment. In this way, the novel's association between Cartesianism and moviegoing is further strengthened. Below, I will return to this last point.

Finally, Percy paired the Cartesian mind and moviegoing by showing that Binx, in moviegoing, risks being nowhere, just as, for Descartes, there is a sense in which the self, or mind, is nowhere. To be sure, insofar as a mind and a body are "intermingled"—to use Descartes' term from the *Meditations* (81)—a mind might be connected to, or associated with, the location of a particular body. However, when that mind is considered by itself as a substance whose essence is thinking, that mind is neither temporal nor spatially extended or located. In short, the Cartesian mind is ghoulish. Witness Binx's moviegoing during his vertical search: he tells us that, for him, there was "a danger of *slipping clean out of space and time.* It is *possible to become a ghost* and not know whether one is in downtown Loews in Denver or suburban Bijou in Jacksonville. So it was with me" (75; my emphasis). Binx also describes this danger in terms of his being "lost, cut loose metaphysically speaking," for he might be "seeing one copy of a film which might be shown anywhere and at any time" (75). Thus, Binx acknowledges that he is tempted to watch movies in a way that, paradoxically, positions him nowhere, just as the Cartesian mind is nowhere.

Furthermore, while Percy here used ghost imagery to suggest the dislocation of the Cartesian mind, elsewhere Percy employed ghost imagery to characterize the movie theater itself. When Binx, Sharon, and Lonnie see *Fort Dobbs,* Binx describes the Moonlite Drive-In as "this ghost of a theater" (144). Percy's image of the ghost for both Cartesian person and theater echoes Gilbert Ryle's famous and abusive description of the Cartesian mind as "the Ghost in the Machine."[17] Five years before Ryle's book was first published in 1949, Maritain, in *The Dream of Descartes,* referred to the Cartesian mind as "an angel inhabiting a machine."[18] As already noted, Percy was familiar with this work of Maritain. Given his interest in contemporary philosophy, it is likely that Percy was also familiar with Ryle's book. So, it seems that, from Descartes, Percy borrowed the image of a mind that haunts the Newtonian world—which includes the body—and he refashioned that image as a moviegoer transfixed in an enveloping theater. Together in the dark, spectator and screen might suffer a ghostly dislocation from the machinations of their anonymous surroundings.

Movies as the Screen That Mediates Binx's Life Situations

I have come to my fourth and final bit of evidence that Percy used moviegoing as a metaphor for the Cartesian mind: Binx often thinks of his life situations as if they were scenes in a film. In doing so, he allows his thoughts of movies to stand between himself and the world, just as, for Descartes, mental objects stand like a screen between the self and the nonmental world.

Binx's propensity to think of his life as if it were a movie began early. When Binx was a boy and his brother died, his Aunt Emily commissioned him to "act" like a soldier—a word that Binx understood in its movie-related sense of "take on a role," for, just after Binx relates that childhood conversation with his aunt, he tells us that he became a soldier in Korea (10). "I could easily act like a soldier. Was that all I had to do?" (4). Below, I consider several examples of Binx's frequent film-related references.

Besides Binx's desire to "act," the movies also intervene in his life by giving him "memorable moments." "Other people, so I have read, treasure memorable moments in their lives: the time one climbed the Parthenon at sunrise, the summer night one met a lonely girl in Central Park and achieved with her a sweet and natural relationship, as they say in books. I too once met a girl in Central Park, but it is not much to remember. What I remember is the time John Wayne killed three men with a carbine as he was falling to the dusty street in *Stagecoach*, and the time the kitten found Orson Welles in the doorway in *The Third Man*" (7). Later, when Binx eyes an attractive woman sitting near him on the bus, it occurs to him that, if this were a scene in a movie, he would only have to wait and a perfect opportunity to meet her would arise: "The bus would get lost or the city would be bombed and she and I would tend the wounded. As it is, I may as well stop thinking about her" (12–13). Additionally, Binx says that he carefully maintains "a Gregory Peckish sort of distance" from Sharon (68). Binx later compares Sharon's appearance to "snapshots of Ava Gardner when she was a high school girl in North Carolina" (93). All told, Binx references at least twelve films, thirty-seven actors, and eight actresses in the novel.[19] By assuming a role or imagining himself in a scene or letting movies constitute his memorable moments, Binx is divorced from his immediate, physical surroundings. His life situations are mediated to him by film-related references—as, for Descartes, mental objects might mediate nonmental reality.

Furthermore, as I briefly noted above, the mental objects that a Cartesian self entertains do not guarantee that person any knowledge of the nonmental world. When this point is considered alongside my thesis, it is not surprising to find that Binx senses the danger of his separation from the physical world: "What is the malaise? you ask. The malaise is the pain of loss. The world is lost to you, the world and the people in it, and there remains only you and the world and you no more able to be in the world than Banquo's ghost" (120). For Binx, the screen of Cartesian ideas is a nearly impenetrable divide. Everyday objects—like the collection of his wallet, keys, handkerchief, and pencil on his dresser—are often lost to him: "A man can look at this little pile on his bureau for thirty years and never once see it. It is as invisible as his own hand" (11). So, it is not difficult to see a connection between Binx's experience of separation, or losing the world, and his moviegoing, at which times he is in danger of being "lost, cut loose metaphysically speaking" (75)—like a ghost, as we saw above. Howland made that connection in these terms: "Moviegoing is one stratagem that Binx uses to orient himself: while he is in the theater, all life is reduced to the image on the screen, and 'real' life [outside the theater] is temporarily suspended."[20]

Finally, outside the theater, "Binx adopts the fictive world of the cinema, impersonating the gestures and expressions of screen stars who, like William Holden, seem to have a 'peculiar reality' that he lacks."[21] Here, Howland invoked a passage in which Binx refers to the "resplendent" and "heightened reality" that movie stars possess *when they are encountered in the flesh*, which Binx contrasts with the "shadowy and precarious existence" of persons, like himself, who are sunk in everydayness (15–17). That contrast is, I think, reminiscent of Descartes' contention that the objective being that ideas possess is "much less perfect than [the formal being] possessed by things which exist outside the intellect" (103). In other words, because Binx is a self long accustomed to entertaining a mere screen of ideas, it is not surprising that he would regard his own existence as "shadowy and precarious" when compared to the glorious and cool 3-D formality of a screen star come to life. Merely to behold William Holden on the screen is fine enough, but to meet him incarnate in the French Quarter is surpassingly better.

In light of all of the evidence mustered in this section, I conclude that it is very plausible that Percy used Binx's moviegoing as a metaphor for his having a Cartesian mind. Percy, it seems, deployed that metaphor in an astute way, for he focused on the point at which there has come to be scholarly consensus regarding the nature of Cartesian ideas—namely, that a Cartesian idea is, at least, a mental object that stands like a partitioning screen between a mental self and the nonmental world. Granting the plausibility of this reading of *The Moviegoer*, one still might wonder: How might this reading enrich our understanding of the novel, how does it position *The Moviegoer* in relationship to Percy's other work, and what does it tell us about Percy himself? I will address these questions now in the final section.

Walker Percy and *The Moviegoer:* Rampant Disease in the Theater of Mind

When, to everyone's surprise, *The Moviegoer* won the 1962 National Book Award for fiction, Percy commented in his acceptance speech that "it is perhaps not too farfetched" to compare his novel "with the science of pathology." He continued:

> Its posture is the posture of the pathologist with his suspicion that something is wrong. There is time for me to say only this: that the pathology in this case had to do with the loss of individuality and the loss of identity at the very time when words like the "dignity of the individual" and "self-realization" are being heard more frequently than ever. Yet the patient is not mortally ill. . . . In short, the book attempts a modest restatement of the Judeo-Christian notion that man is more than an organism in an environment, more than an integrated personality, more even than a mature and creative individual, as the phrase goes. He is a wayfarer and a pilgrim.[22]

Yet, even as his book began to reach a wider audience, Percy was disappointed that most readers did not find in the novel's ending the suggestion that Binx becomes a Christian. That suggestion might be seen, for example, in Binx's invocation of Kierkegaard—"As for my search. . . . I have not the authority, as the great Danish philosopher declared, to speak of such matters in any way other than the edifying" (237)—and in his reassuring his half siblings that Lonnie, their dying brother, will not be disabled when he is resurrected (240). "Somewhat melodramatically," Jay Tolson wrote, Percy "concluded that his novel was unsuccessful, 'since it apparently failed of its primary purpose: that it was meant to be a novel of hope in the midst of pagan despair.'"[23] Percy vowed that his next novel would "be mainly given to ass-kicking for Jesus' sake."[24]

I want to suggest, first, that my reading of the novel is important because it helps to explain Percy's urgency to have readers see that Binx's search culminates in Christian faith. Percy's urgency is related to the severity of

Binx's predicament and to Percy's belief that that predicament is both deep and wide in Western culture. In arguing that Percy accused Descartes, I am far from the first, of course, to frame Binx's peculiar pathogenesis in categories provided by modern philosophy. Quite often, Binx's predicament is defined somewhat narrowly in Kierkegaardian language: Binx longs for certification, it is said. Binx is an aesthete pursuing endless diversions. Binx is foundering at a stage lower than the religious. And so on. Surely, all of this is on target, and none of it is good news for Binx. But this standard Kierkegaardian diagnosis falls short, I think, in that it fails to see the popular prevalence of Binx's predicament, its depth (that is, reaching to the very core of the modern self), and that both prevalence and depth have specific roots in Western culture—namely, in Descartes.

But neither am I the first to think of Binx as afflicted with a Cartesian malady. Patricia Lewis Poteat, in particular, noted that "Binx's predicament . . . bears the unmistakable mark of our culture's tacit and wholesale adherence to the Cartesian picture of the self."[25] In her comments on the passage in which Binx says that the malaise renders him as insubstantial as "Banquo's ghost," Poteat said that Binx is experiencing

> the plight of modern man exiled from the world, ironically, by the very science which has transformed that world for his benefit and comfort. As one who feels that exile keenly, Binx speaks right to the heart of the dilemma. Indeed, his definition of the malaise might equally be described as a concise statement of what it is like to live as though the Cartesian picture of the self upheld by modern science were exhaustively true; as though the "I" were synonymous with a discarnate mind reluctantly inhabiting an insensate body and loosed upon a world of equally insensate and hostile objects.[26]

By describing several ways in which that "Cartesian picture of the self" is manifested metaphorically in Binx's moviegoing, my reading of the novel points to our culture's lens-dependence as symptomatic of our scientifically minded, Cartesian selves. (I use the phrase "lens-dependence" because, quite often, the screen and the lens go hand in hand, as they do in filming, editing, projecting, and watching movies.) We need the lens. It reinforces who we are—disembodied eyes that are given license to watch the world at a remove, to see without being seen. The Cartesian picture of the self consoles us as seers and knowers who have privileged access to the objects of our knowledge. And that picture of the self is deeply embedded in our lens-dependent practices. By pointing to that depth in Binx's affinity for the movies, my reading of *The Moviegoer* sheds light on the moral and spiritual urgency that Percy brought to having readers see that Binx, through both Christian faith and his engagement with Kate, eventually escapes the Cartesian theater. That theater is a lonely place. There is very little community there.[27] Because Percy wanted us to see that, at the end of the novel, Binx has experienced a conversion, it should also come as no surprise that, in the epilogue, Binx does not mention the movies. He is no longer a moviegoer. He is no longer Cartesian.

Furthermore, my reading of the novel is important in that it brings together two aspects of many of Percy's other works—(1) his antipathy for Descartes; and (2) the prevalence of our culture's lens-dependence—that other commentators on *The Moviegoer* have not combined. Percy noted our fascination with both the lens and the screen in many of his works. Movie cameras appear repeatedly in *Lancelot*. In *Love in the Ruins*, the Love Clinic is equipped with a lenslike mirror through which ecstatic subjects can be observed. In *The Last Gentleman*, Binx's father's telescope resurfaces in the hands of Will Barrett, Forney Aiken conceals a tiny camera in his necktie, and Uncle Fannin and Merriam are transported as they watch Captain Kangaroo on TV. So, like the lens of the projector that makes Binx's view of the movie screen possible, Percy put these screens and lenses to uses that evince a desire to see without being seen—to assume, that is, the perspective of a ghost.[28]

Searching Percy's other works, we also need not look far to find evidence of his hostility toward Descartes. This example, from *Lost in the Cosmos*, connects neatly with Binx's predicament: "The Self since the time of Descartes has been stranded, split off from everything else in the Cosmos, a mind which professes to understand bodies and galaxies but is by the very act of understanding marooned in the Cosmos, with which it has no connection. It therefore needs to exercise every option in order to reassure itself that it is not a ghost but is rather a self among other selves. One such option is a sexual encounter. Another is war."[29] Binx tried war, and heaven knows he tried sexual encounter. Yet, more subtly, we might notice that Binx, like the Cartesian self, is "stranded" and "marooned": "This morning . . . I felt as if I had come to myself on a strange island. And what does such a castaway do? Why, he pokes around the neighborhood and he doesn't miss a trick" (13). Later, Binx tells us that, because he has awakened "to the possibility of a search," to pass a Jew in the street "is like Robinson Crusoe seeing the footprint on the beach" (89).

In this section, I have argued that my reading of *The Moviegoer* illuminates Percy's hope that readers both notice Binx's conversion and see it as a salve, for Percy believed that the poisonous roots of Binx's Cartesian predicament are both deep and widespread in Western culture. Furthermore, I have argued that my reading melds two aspects of Percy's other works that other commentators on *The Moviegoer* have not combined. Those two aspects are Percy's aversion for Descartes and our culture's fascination with both the screen and the lens. I want to conclude, now, by suggesting that my reading of *The Moviegoer* reveals that novel to be more autobiographical than we had previously thought.

Like Binx, Percy was once an avid moviegoer. Also like Binx, Percy was once mesmerized by the wonders of science and prone to depend on a lens.[30] As a medical student, Percy chose to specialize in pathology because, as he later put it, it was where "medicine came closest to being the science it should be. . . . Under the microscope, in the test tube, in the colorimeter, one could actually see the beautiful theater of disease."[31] Thus, in Binx's moviegoing and in his scientific distance, the novel invests Binx with the same posture of Cartesian detachment that Percy had assumed in his youth. Furthermore, in the brevity of the novel's epilogue, it is easy to overlook the fact that Binx is going to medical school, as Percy once did. This detail suggests that, converted though he may be, Binx is not yet out of danger, for, in studying medicine, Binx is moving toward yet other lenses (for example, ophthalmoscope, otoscope) and other screens (for example, computer monitor, ultrasound machine), and he remains at risk of taking up research.

Cartesian Society, Cartesian Character, and Screen Culture

I want to conclude by suggesting that Percy's portrayal of Binx as having a Cartesian mind has both moral and social implications for Percy's understanding of many contemporary persons as latter-day heirs of Descartes. Furthermore, I wonder whether that portrayal might help us understand more about the Cartesian origins of our infatuation with screens.

When Percy gave Binx Bolling to be read, he was, of course, giving readers a fictional someone with whom he thought many of them would identify. Percy, it seems, thought of Binx as representative of a condition that was—and might be still—more or less widespread in the United States and perhaps elsewhere. More than twenty years after the novel was published, Lawson wrote: "It is by now pretty generally agreed that the theme of Walker Percy's *The Moviegoer* (1961) is contemporary man's experience of alienation."[32] On Percy's view, Binx is not alone in his estrangement. As noted earlier, he regarded both Binx's "pathology" and its real, rampant equivalent as having "to do with the loss of individuality and the loss of identity at the very time when words like the 'dignity of the individual' and 'self-realization' are being heard more frequently than ever." Now, if I have been correct to contend that, according to Percy, the pathogenesis is Cartesian, what does that tell us about Percy's view of society? As evidenced by other chapters in this volume, there are many ways to address that question. Here, briefly, is just one of them: Percy's Cartesian depiction of Binx tells us that he thought that we, like Binx, are prone to social detachment and isolation. We want to distance ourselves from others, to sit alone in our mental cinemas. Like Binx, we—to recycle an earlier quotation from Desmond—are "prone to taking a detached observer's stance toward the world, to formulating experience reductively, and to abstracting and categorizing others." Typing in my stall, I have not spoken with my colleagues all day—and it is late afternoon. I find their chatter and laughter in the hallway an annoyance because they interrupt my *thoughts*. Given to disconnecting ourselves in such ways, we might be sick indeed, and perhaps we caught it from Descartes.

In addition to its social implications, what might my reading tell us about Percy's moral—and, as he would have added, spiritual—view of persons? If Percy wished for us to see Binx as having a Cartesian mind, then it is plausible to suppose that Percy also wished for us to see Binx as a Cartesian self deeply invested with Cartesian *character*. So, my reading opens up a new approach to this question: How might Percy have regarded Binx's character as morally deficient or praiseworthy? Through a close scrutiny of Binx, perhaps we could articulate whatever virtues and vices are, on Percy's view, most at home in a Cartesian character or disposition. As we do so, we might disclose Percy's view of the moral traits with which Descartes' contemporary children are invested and learn something more about the human estate that Percy thought in need of conversion.

Finally, if my argument has been persuasive, Percy was, to my knowledge, the first thinker to trace to Descartes the roots of our culture's love affair with the screen. Thus, my reading of the novel also breaks new ground by posing this question: How might our Cartesian intellectual heritage have prepared us to attend so closely to the reality of, and to confer value on, screens? My reading of *The Moviegoer* depends on a somewhat simple structural similarity between the movie theater and the Cartesian mind. These days, it is no secret that many of us are, like Binx, often absorbed in, and transported by, screens. With regard to that experience, are there ways—beyond those specified by my reading—in which Descartes might be the patriarch of our times?

Notes

Originally published in *Perspectives on Political Science* 40, no. 3 (2011). Reprinted by permission of Taylor and Francis Group.

    1. *More Conversations with Walker Percy*, ed. Lewis A. Lawson and Victor A. Kramer (Jackson: University Press of Mississippi, 1993), 160.

    2. René Descartes, *The Philosophical Writings of Descartes*, vol. 2, translated by John Cottingham, Robert Stoothoff, and Dugald Murdoch (New York: Cambridge University Press, 1988). The Adam and Tannery notation for this passage is AT VII, 8. In citing Descartes below, I will use notations, inserted parenthetically in the text, that refer readers to the relevant places in volume 7 of the twelve-volume edition of Descartes' works by Adam and Tannery. Quotations are from Cottingham et al.'s translation.

    3. Vere Chappell has argued that, for Descartes, every idea is some combination of both a mental act and a mental object. While a mental act is an event "that occurs in the mind," a mental object is something in the mind "upon which the mind is directed." See his "The Theory of Ideas," in *Essays on Descartes' Meditations*, ed. Amelie O. Rorty (Los Angeles: University of California Press, 1986), 178. Agreeing with Chappell, Lilli Alanen summarized their view in this way: All Cartesian ideas "are complex mental phenomena or processes of which act and object are merely different aspects which . . . always occur together." See her "Sensory Ideas, Objective Reality, and Material Falsity," in *Reason, Will, and Sensation: Studies in Descartes's Metaphysics*, ed. John Cottingham (New York: Oxford University Press, 1994), 231.

    4. This reading was defended by Norman Kemp Smith. On Smith's view, Descartes regarded images as paradigm cases of ideas. In reaching this conclusion, the key passage for Smith was this portion of the Third Meditation: "Some of my thoughts are as it were images of things, *and it is only in these cases that the term*

"*idea" is strictly appropriate*—for example, when I think of a man, or a chimera, or the sky, or an angel, or God" (37; my emphasis). See Smith's *New Studies in the Philosophy of Descartes: Descartes as Pioneer* (London: Macmillan, 1953).

5. Walker Percy, *The Moviegoer* (New York: Vintage International, 1998). Below, all page references to *The Moviegoer* will be cited parenthetically.

6. The fact that Percy labels the young man a "romantic" should not, I think, dissuade us from concluding that he is also Cartesian. Earlier in the novel, Binx made this note to himself: "Explore connection between romanticism and scientific objectivity. Does a scientifically minded person become a romantic because he is a left-over from his own science?" (88). Mary Deems Howland articulated Percy's view of the romantic-scientist relationship in this way: "The romantic looks at life from a transcendent remove while the scientist studies the world from a position above it." See Mary Deems Howland, *The Gift of the Other: Gabriel Marcel's Concept of Intersubjectivity in Walker Percy's Novels* (Pittsburgh: Duquesne University Press, 1990), 30. Thus, the "romantic" and the Cartesian share the presumption that they can attain an objective detachment from life situations.

7. Jay Tolson, *Pilgrim in the Ruins: A Life of Walker Percy* (New York: Simon and Schuster, 1992), 237.

8. Jacques Maritain, *The Dream of Descartes* (New York: F. Hubner, 1944), 169; my emphasis on "Idea-pictures, idea-screens."

9. Lewis A. Lawson, "Walker Percy's *The Moviegoer*: The Cinema as Cave," in *Following Percy: Essays on Walker Percy's Work* (Troy, NY: Whitston, 1988), 88–89, 105.

10. Jorge Secada, *Cartesian Metaphysics: The Late Scholastic Origins of Modern Philosophy* (New York: Cambridge University Press, 2000), 110.

11. Lawson, "Cinema as Cave," 92; my emphasis.

12. Ibid., 105–6.

13. Ibid., 106.

14. Ibid., 92.

15. Howland, *Gift of the Other*, 26; my emphasis.

16. John F. Desmond, *Walker Percy's Search for Community* (Athens: University of Georgia Press, 2004), 42.

17. Gilbert Ryle, *The Concept of Mind* (New York: Barnes and Noble, 1963), 15–16.

18. Maritain, *Dream of Descartes*, 179.

19. Lewis A. Lawson, "Moviegoing in *The Moviegoer*," *Southern Quarterly* 18, no. 3 (1980): 26.

20. Howland, *Gift of the Other*, 28.

21. Ibid.

22. Tolson, *Pilgrim in the Ruins*, 297.

23. Ibid., 300.

24. Ibid., 301.

25. Patricia Lewis Poteat, *Walker Percy and the Old Modern Age: Reflections on Language, Argument, and the Telling of Stories* (Baton Rouge: Louisiana State University Press, 1985), 60.

26. Ibid., 60–61.

27. Binx's inching toward community with Kate might be seen in the way that they watch movies together. Early in the novel, when Binx and Kate see *Panic in the Streets,* Binx narrates: "There is a scene which shows the very neighborhood of the theater. Kate gives me a look—it is understood that we do not speak during the movie" (63). Late in the novel, in Chicago, when they see *The Young Philadelphians*—a well-chosen title—Binx tells us: "Kate holds my hand tightly in the dark" (211).

28. As Lawson wrote, in Percy's fiction, "there is a recurrent character who thinks that by putting a 'scope—microscope, telescope, lapsometer—between himself and the extended world he can draw it nearer. But the character discovers that, on the contrary, such technology pushes the world away, so that it resembles a movie screen; the 'moviegoer' is Percy's brilliant image of the modern man who is alienated by the very scientific-empirical, 'spectator' method that he has embraced." See "Walker Percy's Physicians and Patients," in *Following Percy,* 230.

29. Walker Percy, *Lost in the Cosmos: The Last Self-Help Book* (New York: Picador, 1983), 44.

30. See, for example, Tolson, *Pilgrim in the Ruins,* 109.

31. Ibid., 148.

32. Lewis A. Lawson, "English Romanticism . . . and 1930 Science in *The Moviegoer,*" in *Following Percy,* 123.

Walker Percy's Critique of the Pursuit of Happiness in *The Moviegoer, Lost in the Cosmos: The Last Self-Help Book*, and *The Thanatos Syndrome*

Elizabeth Amato

Americans have exercised magnificently the right to pursue happiness. Americans enjoy, on the whole, comfortable lives and unprecedented political and personal freedom, but, as happiness studies show, not much happier lives. While happiness studies indicate that happiness levels remain flat, happiness researchers are optimistic that their research on the causes and correlates of well-being can be used as the basis of domestic and international policy to increase human happiness.[1] Although many of these researchers have been highly critical of how most people identify the pursuit of wealth as nearly identical to the pursuit of happiness, they do not question the validity of the pursuit of happiness per se; they merely suggest that the pursuit of happiness be carried on by more effective means. In contrast, Walker Percy observes that the pursuit of happiness causes us to flee unhappiness rather than look into what our lingering discontent may indicate about ourselves. Our unhappiness, according to Percy, can either lead us to search for more sophisticated diversions or, as he hopes, guide us to understand ourselves as lost beings in need of each other.

Instead of treating unhappiness like a problem to be solved, Walker Percy explains that we must consider what our unhappiness reveals about ourselves. Unhappiness proves to be a fortunate starting point for self-reflective inquiry into why the self is unhappy—or the search, as Percy calls it. As Percy shows, the individual's search to understand the discontent of being a self points him toward recognizing others as fellow searchers with whom he can share his search and thus experience, if not happiness itself, then at least the beginnings of it. Our search is not meant to be unpleasant or lonely. It depends on our recognition of others as fellow searchers with whom the search can be shared.

As will be shown in *The Moviegoer, Lost in the Cosmos,* and *The Thanatos Syndrome,* Percy repeatedly shows his characters rejecting the pursuit of happiness, embarking on a search, and discovering their need for others. Percy's critique of the failure of the pursuit of happiness to satisfy the needs of the human person as a social being remains constant through his novels. *The Moviegoer* plainly illustrates how the diversions of the pursuit of happiness only fill time without fulfilling the individual and isolate the individual from others. In *Lost in the Cosmos* and *The Thanatos Syndrome,* Percy focuses on how the pursuit of happiness risks leading us away from political life toward rule by experts and destruction of the self in the name of increasing well-being.

The Moviegoer

In *The Moviegoer,* Percy presents the search as an alternative to the pursuit of happiness, which he identifies as the way of life sponsored by liberalism. *The Moviegoer* is the story of a young man, John Bickerson "Binx" Bolling, who is called upon by his formidable Aunt Emily to decide what to do with his life. At nearly thirty years old, Binx has had an undistinguished career as a failed researcher, a veteran of the Korean War, and currently as a prosperous but banal stockbroker. Aunt Emily, however, aspires for her nephew to reject the mean, low way of American bourgeois life, to pursue greatness and nobility, and to accept his duty to make a meaningful contribution to humanity, such as a career in medicine.[2] Binx does not feel under any such obligation. Instead of great ambitions, Binx carefully cultivates the "ordinary life" or, as he also calls it, his "Little Way" (9, 99).[3] Binx claims that he is "a model tenant and a model citizen and takes pleasure in doing all that is expected of [him]" as a typical American everyman (6). In addition to honoring customarily American concerns for security and comfort, Binx whiles away his time seducing his secretaries and going to the movies.

Too reflective and self-conscious of his role-playing as the anonymous everyman, Binx knows that his dreary happiness is "the worst kind of self-deception" (18). The search, an alternative to Emily's plan and Binx's "ordinary life," is heralded by "clues." These "clues," like the contents of his pockets which, although familiar objects, are suddenly strange and wondrous, remind Binx to "pursue the search" (11). Binx struggles to follow his search's clues, and his efforts are unsteady until he realizes that his cousin, Kate, is a fellow searcher who can bring steadiness and a kind of happiness to their joint search.

Binx associates the pursuit of happiness with "everydayness," which he characterizes as the immersion of the self into the role of a consumer of goods, services, hobbies, and expert advice (13). In *The Moviegoer*, the chief representatives of everydayness are Nell and Eddie Lovell. Binx comments that Eddie "understands everything out there and everything out there is something to be understood" (19). For the Lovells, the world is "something to be categorized and explained, then dismissed" as they occupy themselves pursuing happiness.[4] The pursuit of happiness disconnects them from seeking to understand the world and their place within it. They have outsourced examination of the world to experts and so are "free" to pursue happiness as they please. The Lovells give themselves over to consumer immanence through products and prepackaged experiences and hobbies. As Percy makes clear, the pursuit of happiness does not succeed in bringing the Lovells contentment; instead, it serves to distract them from undertaking their peculiarly human task to seek an answer to the discontent they feel.

For the most part, the liberal pursuit of happiness is the attempt to make the self happy by the possession of goods. The individual believes he can make himself happy by possessing the things that are supposed to constitute the happy life. Percy's insight is that the liberal formulation of happiness—primarily understood as security, control, and comfort—defines the objects of the individual's pursuit and, in so doing, prevents the individual from being open to consider other goods and conditions for human happiness. In distinction, Binx's search is characterized by clues that point to an unknown final end—"to be aware of the possibility of the search is to be onto something" (13). Binx finds "clues," but he and we readers do not know to what the clues point. Binx's search remains open-ended. The importance of defining the ultimate end of the search recedes from view and instead the way in which one searches with others assumes more significance.

The pursuer of happiness views other individuals as goods, or objects, to be possessed for the sake of a happy life. The individual does not need others to help or join him in his pursuit of happiness. This is why, for Percy, the pursuit of happiness is a nonstarter. Individuals, according to Percy, are not self-sufficient but rather are dependent and in need of each other to live well. The stumbling block to the pursuit of happiness is that it is a lonely pursuit that isolates one from others. Despite the modern exaltation of autonomy, dependency and need are not negative qualities. Instead, for Binx, they become happy, or fortunate, conditions for individuals to gain the help they need from each other. As long as the individual persists in doggedly pursuing happiness by himself, he cannot become or be happy. But, as Percy emphasizes especially in *Lost in the Cosmos* and *The Thanatos Syndrome,* the danger does not end here—it cannot be contained within the private life of the unhappy individual pursuer of happiness, but will cancerously spread to the social and political body. The lonely pursuer of happiness, overcome with despair, may turn to violence and self-destruction. Fortunately for Binx, the sight of Kate looking for him stops him from descending into despair. Binx realizes that Kate is like himself—a being who is also troubled and in need of help to live well. The search can be shared and unites individuals in a common activity that brings felicity although it is not focused on happiness. Kate and he find their way to happiness not by looking for it, but by finding each other.

Through Binx, Percy shows us that the self's dependency, which draws us to others, is a happier circumstance than pretending that the self is self-sufficient. The Lovells believe they can find happiness by playing the role, or part, of a consumer. The Lovells play a part, but Binx realizes that he *is* a part in need of another. Being a part is better than playing a part. The pursuer of happiness denies his partiality and so experiences much uneasiness and unhappiness as a result. Percy's search presents the possibility of some relief and respite from our unhappiness and loneliness when we realize our need for others. Rather than being a step down from self-sufficiency, being a part, needing others, becomes the occasion for greater happiness. Binx experiences gladness in finding in Kate another fellow wayfarer with whom he can share his life. Binx and Kate's marriage represents not the resolution or end of the search but the way in which the two will continue searching together.

Lost in the Cosmos: The Last Self-Help Book

In *Lost in the Cosmos: The Last Self-Help Book*, Percy playfully mocks the American desire for self-reliant, step-by-step techniques for well-being. Armed with self-help manuals, Americans believe they do not need anyone else to help them, because they can help themselves. It is do-it-yourself happiness. However, Percy's mockery is limited. First, the popularity of self-help books points to a broadly felt desire for self-knowledge and guidance that indicates some awareness that the self needs help. This differs somewhat from *The Moviegoer*. Everydayness is nearly impenetrable as described in *The Moviegoer*. *Lost in the Cosmos* shows that everydayness obscures and misdirects, but cannot suppress that Americans are searchers who look for help, if not always in the right places. Despite how little we may know about ourselves, yet it remains that we are knowers and so capable of coming to a fuller understanding of the self.

Second, in *Lost in the Cosmos*, Percy turns his attention more explicitly to ordering society and political bodies toward the highest goals of human life. For Percy, to answer how we should live in political communities, it is necessary to consider what is good for human beings and how those goals can be furthered collectively and individually. It is no surprise that the main action in *Lost in the Cosmos* is a political decision that Captain Schuyler must make for the sake of himself and the human race. *Lost in the Cosmos* ends with two alternative space odysseys in which World War III devastates Earth and a spaceship is sent to look for alien life. In the first space odyssey, the spaceship find aliens, but the aliens refuse to help the humans. The aliens do not help because it is not in their self-interest to help and they only risk disordering themselves by interacting with the spaceship. In the second space odyssey, the spaceship does not find aliens, and so returns to war-devastated Earth. With no possibility of help from alien life in the second space odyssey, the survivors must look to each other and deliberate about how best to live. Two options are set forth for the captain of the space crew—one that virtually ensures the continuation of the species and secures its well-being and one that proves riskier from the perspective of species survival and security but is better for fulfilling the human desire for happiness. Percy does not reveal the captain's decision, but instead shows what would happen in either case.

Captain Marcus Aurelius Schuyler is an Air Force Academy graduate who studied astronomy at MIT and has a background in history. NASA selects him to pilot a spaceship to investigate a possible signal from aliens. The slender hope is that aliens may be able to save humanity from its self-destructive warfare. Captain Schuyler takes after his Stoic namesake with respect to his "dark view of the human condition" and his penchant to "t[ake] his pleasure in acting well even though he knew it probably would not avail and that things would end badly."[5] With his ancient perspective, Captain Schuyler is aptly suited to this mission as an individual ready to do what is necessary under bleak circumstances. The three women crew members are Tiffany, an astrophysicist-psychotherapist, Kimberly, a linguist-semioticist, and Jane, the ship's doctor. Jane is also a religious minority affirmative-action choice, as required by recent Supreme Court rulings. A Methodist, Jane represents the small Christian minority lingering in America. On the outward journey, she refuses to have sex with Captain Schuyler until he, in his capacity as captain of the ship, marries them. Twelve children are born to the space travelers.

Finding no aliens, the spaceship returns to Earth. Upon arriving in the Utah desert, they find Earth devastated by war, with but a few survivors. Aristarchus Jones, a loner astronomer who calculated when and where the spaceship would return, and Abbot Leibowitz, the abbot of a Benedictine monastery who leads a small community of monks and misbegotten children, greet the spaceship. Radiation has contributed to birth defects and caused increasing sterility. The arrival of the spaceship with the crew and their healthy children present a chance that the human race might yet survive and thrive. Returning from space, the space travelers are like "aliens." With their spaceship and healthy and fertile children, they represent the only hope for humanity. It is an undetermined hope. It is not clear what course of action would be best for humanity, because it is not settled what ends are best for human life.

Aristarchus and the abbot present the captain with two alternatives: either go to Europa, a habitable moon of Jupiter, or take their chances on Earth in Lost Cove, Tennessee. Aristarchus Jones argues that the human race cannot survive on Earth—it faces too much radiation and sterility. Colonizing Europa presents a bright opportunity to make a new start. Civilization can be based on "reason and science" like ancient Ionia, free from the mistakes of Plato and religion (246). On the other hand, Abbot Leibowitz says that he does not know whether human life is finished on

Earth and gives a Christian account of humans as fallen beings, redeemed through the birth, Passion, and Resurrection of Christ, and waiting for the promised return of Christ. Abbot Leibowitz believes he may be the only person alive who can consecrate priests and so says that he will "stay here in case the human race survives and needs priests" (249).

Percy first shows what would happen if Captain Schuyler decides in favor of Aristarchus's plan; he leaves nuclear war–ravaged Earth for Europa to realize Aristarchus's utopian society. Named in honor of the original birthplace of science, New Ionia is "operated on the principles of Skinner's Walden II modified by Jungian self-analysis, with suitable rewards for friendly social behavior and punishment, even exile, for aggression, jealous, hostile, solitary, mystical, or other anti-social behavior" (256). Instead of government, the New Ionians have daily group sessions "of self-criticism and honest appraisal of others," in which they practice a new golden rule of "honesty, absolute honesty" (257). Furthermore, New Ionia is ostensibly free from pain and deformity (the deformed children were left behind on Earth). There is no political or ethnic conflict, and sex is free from inhibitions. Much, however, of the group's contentment and cooperation is drug induced. The air is much thinner on Europa and to compensate the New Ionians are given daily rations of cocaine. To encourage proper social behavior, they are daily expected to participate in *dewalis* sessions where they smoke dried lichen that "induce[s] a mild euphoria." After many years, New Ionia becomes a "peaceful agricultural-fishing society" (256).

In New Ionia, the Captain sits outside his cave reading *Henry IV* and replays an old recording of Mozart's fourteenth string quartet. Captain Schuyler is ironic about the utopian society and considers the group sessions akin to AA meetings. Jane and he are no longer married and Jane sulks in her cave by herself; she knows New Ionia does not tolerate sulking in the open. Two extraordinarily beautiful young women, Candace and Rima, attend to him and invite him to sleep with them. He agrees, but he is little moved by the prospect of sex.

If Captain Schuyler decides in favor of Abbot Leibowitz, he stays on postapocalyptic Earth and goes to Lost Cove, Tennessee. The community members grow traditional local crops like collards; they trap rabbits, enjoy tobacco, and drink whiskey. Radiation levels persist and sperm count varies. Even so, Lost Cove increases in numbers both from pregnancies and from other survivors. These survivors include "Southerners, white and Anglo-

Saxon, and blacks, with a sprinkling of Hispanics, Jews, and Northern ethnics" (258). Both the physically sound and deformed children flourish. Unlike in New Ionia, the Lost Cove community has room for many types of individuals. To be sure, Lost Cove does not suit everyone. Some of the hippies voluntarily decide to leave and "move on" from Lost Cove (261). Presumably, they form or join a community elsewhere.

In addition to ethic and racial groups, many social and religious groups flourish in Lost Cove. On the Sunday that Percy shows us, some are at Mass, others are at Protestant services, and others, the nonbelievers, are "gathered companionably." The captain enjoys sitting on a hillside just above the cave where he is joined by other "unbelievers—non-church-goers and dissidents of one sort and another" (259). It is an eclectic crowd of mountain men, former Atlanta businessmen, feminists, hippies, and vagabonds. The Sunday morning hillside nonbelievers debate about agricultural and political subjects such as corn co-ops and what Lost Cove ought to do about the violent (and snake-handling) community in old Carolina. The captain serves as the community's leader and negotiates with an emissary from the violent Carolina community, which wishes to reignite old ethic and religious conflicts.

From the perspective of survival, the human race will be best served by going to Europa. Aristarchus Jones, however, promises more than survival. He promises that New Ionia will be a happy new beginning for human civilization. Free from the errors of the past and from biological defects, its colonizers build New Ionia on scientific insights into human sociability and well-being. To a great extent, New Ionia succeeds. As theirs is a fishing community, the New Ionians enjoy much leisure, apparently free from backbreaking labor of procuring food and securing settlements. No other peoples on Europa exist to threaten them and so there is no need to defend New Ionia. In the absence of such basic concerns, New Ionia can focus on the group's well-being. Life in New Ionia appears comfortable, secure, leisurely, and peaceful.

Despite its appearance, New Ionia falls short of the utopian promise. To be clear, New Ionia is not an Orwellian political dystopia but a scientific, nonpolitical attempt to construct a society conducive to human well-being. New Ionia succeeds insofar as well-being is concerned, but it lacks the richer, robust feelings associated with happiness. Much as in *Brave New World*'s World State, life is so well managed in New Ionia that its inhabitants have little to do. Captain Schuyler is like a man in exile, with only his books and music to relieve somewhat his old longings for action and decision. One commentator observes that Captain Schuyler reads *Henry IV*, Shakespeare's play about leadership, but New Ionia needs no leadership.[6] Since individuals have little need of each other, they do not enjoy the hearty relationships that contribute to happiness. Captain Schuyler does not talk, discuss, debate, or bicker with the inhabitants in New Ionia. He has sex with the younger New Ionians—New Ionia is not unpleasant—but sex is a poor surrogate for the more "complex courtship" he enjoyed with the three women crew members on the outward journey to find alien life (235).[7] New Ionia's postpolitical society does not need a man of action, and so the captain retreats to the Stoic's inner sanctuary. In this respect, Captain Schuyler experiences lingering aches for action and complex human relationships.

In New Ionia, public displays of unhappiness are not permitted. Jane sulks in her cave, because she knows she would not be allowed to sulk in public. In this respect, Percy shows that Aristarchus Jones's plan to do without political life and the errors of the past by imposing honesty—transparency—as the reigning virtue and key to happiness does not succeed. In fact, these so-called demands for honesty aim to suppress voices that question and disagree with the reigning ideology. In addition, group sessions aim to reduce difference among individuals, or "otherness," so as to minimize social discord. New Ionia succeeds in keeping the peace, but New Ionia's honesty policy prevents individuals from sharing their lives with others through private relationships. No spousal pairs, no families, no friends, no political parties, clubs, or other private associations smaller than New Ionia itself exist. Smaller private associations are treated with suspicion, because individuals may keep secrets with each other. Group sessions relentlessly aim to bring to light the internal feelings of its members. Those individuals who display behavior or sentiments antithetical to New Ionia's founding principle can be exiled. It is unclear by whom or by what decision-making body or process dissenters are punished, but exile from New Ionia is surely the equivalent of a death sentence. No other communities exist on Europa to harbor dissenters, and there is little chance of any others coming into being.

It is unlikely that the captain is greatly moved by Aristarchus Jones's modern enthusiasm for science's ability to create a perfect society or by the abbot's concern that the human race needs priests. It is worth considering, then, why Percy gives this choice to a Stoic and how might the captain be swayed to make his decision in favor of Lost Cove—the choice for the complex and varied human relationships necessary for happiness. As a Stoic, Captain Schuyler possesses admirable qualities for leadership. He is resolute and confident in bleak circumstances. He is a leader and capable of making political decisions for the sake of those in his care. Despite his fondness for lost causes, Percy cheats the captain out of his lost cause and compels him to put his virtues in the service of the future and of the survivors. Captain Schuyler had enjoyed thinking he lived at the end of an age but, quite unexpectedly, he finds himself in the position of being the founder of one.

If the captain follows his preference for lost causes, he will choose New Ionia. Unlike Aristarchus, Captain Schuyler knows that New Ionia will be another failed attempt to escape the past and the self by relocating, just as the Puritans tried in the New World. With resignation, the captain would accept it as humanity's fate to chase after new beginnings and happiness and end up disappointed. In New Ionia, Captain Schuyler would retreat, with his books and music, and live with thin contentment as he relied on his own internal resources for his happiness with scant regard for anyone else.

If Captain Schuyler chooses the Abbot Leibowitz's plan, he is choosing in favor of being with Jane. The captain learns to include himself among the survivors—to make decisions as one of them, not on behalf of them. His original mission was a search for alien life, but instead, Captain Schuyler and Jane find each other on the journey. While on the way back to Earth, the crew members look forward to their return and eagerly chat about what they will do and where they will go when they arrive. Jane asks the captain if he would prefer to come to Tennessee with her, to which he responds that he would. Captain Schuyler's preference for Jane indicates a reform in his Stoicism away from internal self-sufficiency and toward realizing that he needs other people and is not simply needed by them. The captain does not have to accept the abbot's account of man as a fallen being awaiting the second coming of Christ to choose Lost Cove. The space mission with Jane revealed to him the possibilities of sharing his life searching with someone else.

Furthermore, as the pilot of the ship, Captain Schuyler enjoys a position of leadership. To choose New Ionia would be to choose against himself, because New Ionia does not need his fortitude, confidence, and protection.[8] Decisions in New Ionia affecting the group will be managed according to scientific-behavioral theories; once the appropriate conditions are set in place, there will be little room for individual intervention. In New Ionia, the captain is a relic (perhaps useful only as a fertile male), but in Lost Cove, he has much to do for the community's political life. With respect to political life, Abbot Leibowitz's plan is incomplete or partial. Political life is left up to the captain and the other members of Lost Cove. Through a hopeful prudence, Percy presents a practical demonstration in *Lost in the Cosmos* that New Ionia may promise happiness, but in Lost Cove there are happier people. Lost Cove is the choice for individuals making their way in life guided by particular human relationships.

Although he set forth the plan for New Ionia, Aristarchus Jones does not appear in either alternative future. In New Ionia, presumably, he wields the unseen power that directs the community. In Lost Cove, perhaps Jones withdraws from society to resume research, or perhaps he moves on to live elsewhere. Percy treats Aristarchus Jones rather kindly. Jones is a searcher, though clueless about his own existence as a searcher. He uncovered the old records about the spaceship's scheduled return and, having faith that it would return, he traveled on horseback to the Utah desert in expectation of its arrival. However, the sense of a higher purpose, which justifies Aristarchus Jones's slight regard for the particularity of human life, leading him to recommend leaving behind on Earth the misbegotten children and all the other survivors, comes under closer scrutiny in *The Thanatos Syndrome,* as does his confidence that science can find a solution to human unhappiness.

The Thanatos Syndrome

In *The Thanatos Syndrome,* Percy more forcefully illustrates how the scientific approach to pursuing happiness sacrifices our capacity for happiness, our consciousness, in the name of promoting animalistic well-being. Feliciana parish is threatened by a utopian social engineering conspiracy that tries to re-create society free from the causes of human misery and unhappiness. The problem is not that the scientists fail and produce a dystopia, but rather that they succeed to a remarkable degree to alleviate social problems. Their "solution" extracts heavy costs. Members of Feliciana parish risk losing their self-awareness, humanity, life, and liberty. Percy defends unhappiness—not in itself good—but as part of the predicament of being a conscious self and so as a clue to self-understanding that promises a greater and more fulfilling happiness. Unhappiness can direct us to a greater good of being in community with others that makes unhappiness seem less terrible and provides real relief from the restless pursuit of happiness.

Set in the near future, *The Thanatos Syndrome* begins as a mystery. Not quite a murder mystery or a medical mystery, but a psychological mystery. Dr. Tom More, a psychiatrist, "stumbled onto something" amiss with his patients.[9] He sees clues and slight differences that point toward a peculiar sickness or loss of self among the inhabitants. His former patients do not exhibit their "old terrors" but appear to be cured of them. Instead of anxiety and discontent, they display "a mild vacancy, a species of unfocused animal good spirits" (21). His patients, while freed of their old fears, can barely communicate, and though they appear contented, they sometimes exhibit remarkable brutality and odd sexual behavior. More knows that unhappiness is a part of being a self, but also that we are happily situated to search with others by talking and listening. With the help of an eclectic group, More puts together the clues to uncovering who and what is behind the community's loss of self.

More discovers that Bob Comeaux and John Van Dorn have been adding heavy sodium to the water supply as part of a project (called Blue Boy) to decrease crime and misery and increase well-being and happiness. The Blue Boy project enjoys significant and remarkable success. It reduces many social evils, such as crime, unemployment, suicide, violence, domestic abuse, teenage pregnancies, the spread of AIDS, drug use, depression, anxiety, and suicide. Moreover, it improves IQ scores. Although it decreases verbal and communication skills, heavy sodium improves mental recall and computations. For example, individuals cannot link together words and sentences to tell a story, but they can recall information and make calculations much like a savant.

Although Comeaux and Van Dorn work together, they have appreciably different visions regarding the origin of social ills and how to correct them. Comeaux believes that evolution gave human beings unnecessarily large brains, which led to the superego's excessive ability to inhibit ego. Evolution's mistake can be corrected through the right therapeutic drugs. Release the ego from the superego's hold over it and people are happier, less prone to the cares and anxieties that lead to most social problems. Comeaux's co-conspirator, Van Dorn, thinks Comeaux has shortsighted goals for society and regards Blue Boy as just the first phase in the restoration of society and the promotion of human excellence. Van Dorn has contempt for Comeaux as a "technologist" and argues that "you don't treat human ills by creaming the human cortex" (217). Van Dorn recognizes that human beings have to remain human "enough to achieve the ultimate goals of being human" (219). Van Dorn blames society for inhibiting the sexual energy that motivates the greatest achievements of artists and scientists. Proper education—intellectual, physical, and sexual—can release those energies. At Belle Ame Academy, which is "founded on Greek ideals of virtue," Van Dorn employs "the tough old European Gymnasium-Hochschule treatment" (214, 219). According to him, this rigorous method releases the repressed sexual energy necessary for "sexual geniuses" like Mozart and Einstein to achieve excellence in the arts and sciences (220). The Belle Ame teachers engage in pedophilic acts with the children as part of their educational training in excellence.

Blue Boy is an unauthorized project and Comeaux and Van Dorn know that releasing heavy sodium without consent is a politically dubious maneuver. Yet, Comeaux and Van Dorn reasonably expect that when they reveal the positive statistics to the public, their project will be embraced by the current presidential administration. Comeaux and Van Dorn fear that More will expose Blue Boy to the public without the appropriate public relations that would lead to its acceptance, so they attempt to compel More to join their project.

More dislikes Comeaux and Van Dorn's methods, but initially seems impressed with their results. He flounders to provide a counterargument to Comeaux and Van Dorn's claim that their methods have superseded his own. More visits Father Smith, who sees through the scientists' claims and links their abstracted love of humanity and eugenic policies to the Third Reich. In an impassioned speech, Father Smith explains that "tenderness" is a "disguise" and leads "to the gas chamber" (128).[10] More finally decides to thwart Comeaux and Van Dorn's project. Blue Boy is shut down and the people of Feliciana recover their former, troubled selves, but Van Dorn and Comeaux escape punishment.

One criticism of the novel is that Tom More cannot give an adequate explanation why the scientists' project to improve the quality of human life and increase well-being is misguided. Although Tom More may be the ostensible protagonist of the story, many commentators believe the irascible

Father Smith is Percy's true spokesman and, as one critic claims, "represents Percy's most uncompromising attack on science."[11] Representative of this view, Mary Deems Howland observes with disapproval that More consistently fails to counter directly Comeaux's argument that they share the same basic goal: to improve the human lot. Howland comments that "when More fails to tell Comeaux that what he is doing is wrong, the reader feels compelled to jump into the void left by Tom and confront Bob's ideas directly."[12] Howland finds Father Smith's uncompromising condemnation and refutation of Comeaux and Van Dorn's project more satisfying. Whereas More is compromised by his breakthrough research on heavy sodium that made Blue Boy possible and his own ambivalent sympathies with Comeaux's goal to reduce human suffering and improve the human lot (a carryover of his sentiments in *Love in the Ruins*), Father Smith remains staunchly and adamantly opposed.

Howland is right insofar as she observes that More consistently fails to confront Comeaux with a counterargument in the style of Father Smith's impassioned defense of the dignity of the human person against Comeaux and Van Dorn's devaluation of individual life. Father Smith's argument is attractive because he is so uncompromisingly opposed to the scientists and has no doubt that every human being has dignity based on being a creature of God, created in his image and called to fulfill his vocation toward beatitude. But Father Smith's argument convinces only if one already agrees with him. Instead, Percy opts to give a practical demonstration of the mutual help human beings may give to each other. More never directly confirms Father Smith's metaphysical account of fallen human nature redeemable only through God's grace. By his example, More defends the search with others against Comeaux and Van Dorn, who would do away with the unhappiness that leads individuals to seek to understand themselves through the aid of others. More does not defeat Comeaux and Van Dorn by theoretical argumentation. Instead, after foiling their conspiracy, instead of punishing or killing them, he offers to help them—an offer they refuse.

Percy sets *The Thanatos Syndrome* slightly in the future, in which he may suppose fictional but plausible political circumstances in which groups of individuals deemed of limited social utility are disposed of for the sake of improving the well-being of the whole. It is believed that individuals who possess limited personal autonomy suffer a compromised quality of life that renders their life not worth living. Although Blue Boy is unauthorized, Percy shows that given the public policies already in operation at the start of the novel, the American doctrine of rights does not sufficiently protect individual life and liberty. The pursuit of happiness, instead of being the reason *for* life and liberty, becomes the justification to deprive individuals *of* life and liberty. Socially vulnerable groups, such as AIDS patients, children with severe mental and physical impairments, and the elderly, are already marginalized and deprived of life and liberty through ordinary political procedures. Congress cuts funding for Medicare but continues to fund the Qualitarian centers where the euthanasia of impaired and unwanted children and seniors is routine. By federal regulation, AIDS patients and children born with AIDS live under quarantine—a great deprivation of personal liberty. The Supreme Court creates a "Right to Death provision" through a series of rulings that support euthanasia of children and the elderly (199).

Comeaux and Van Dorn correctly see their project as a continuation of these public policies. The Supreme Court grounded its decision in favor of euthanizing unwanted or severely deformed or mentally impaired children on the proper respect for the family, the opinions of experts, and due concern for children who may otherwise lead intolerable lives of abuse or suffering. In consideration of the euthanasia of the elderly, the Court reasoned that life primarily characterized and prized for its autonomy must be pro-choice toward death with a view to preserving individual independence. No doubt these are the reasonable considerations the Court would balance in its judgment. Percy takes care to add this detail to make the Court's ruling plausible to the reader and thereby make the danger real.

In this way, Percy highlights deficiencies in current American public discourse that stem from flaws within our political order's understanding of the human person. The doctrine of rights, because it is incomplete, does not sufficiently protect individuals who are considered lacking in self-sufficiency from oppression. Our public discourse relies too heavily on an abstract concept of the individual as an independent, self-sufficient being in whom autonomy is the essential characteristic. Giving primacy to the preservation of individual autonomy mistakes the autonomous self, a theoretical creation, for the good of the whole person. When public judicial and legislative deliberations focus on quality of life and dignity to preserve individual autonomy, they obscure the extent to which human beings are needy beings who need each other to live and to form the social relationships that contribute to the search for self-understanding. Comeaux confidently expects that just as the courts have consistently upheld the addition of fluoride to drinking water—for the mere but tangible benefit of improving the public's teeth—they will uphold the addition of heavy sodium in the water supply as a true political and social panacea.[13]

The main objection More musters against the scientists' plot is that they are "assaulting the cortex of an individual" without informed consent (193). More's argument rests on familiar liberal grounds regarding the principles of consent. By depicting More voicing this argument, Percy shows the weakness of solely liberal foundations to protect individuals from the kind of scientific manipulation conducted by Comeaux. Comeaux belittles the question of informed consent, calling it a "philosophical question"; he claims that the "real" question is whether human misery is caused by evolving unnecessarily large brains (194).[14] Comeaux replaces a political question of consent that entails theories about social contract, rights, duties, and personhood in favor of a much simpler empirical, material question. He rejects political discourse regarding rights and consent as so much metaphysical nonsense that has overlooked the real or the material problem behind social problems that can be solved more effectively through chemical therapy. Without a stronger foundation than consent for the dignity of the human person, Percy underscores how precarious and unstable our political protection is against projects like Blue Boy, which promise and seem to deliver results that increase human well-being.

Turning the tables on More, Comeaux claims that he protects society from the real assaulters—criminal malefactors like murderers, robbers, and rapists. Blue Boy virtually eliminates those violent social malfeasants. By bypassing the usual political concerns for consent and rights, Comeaux and Van Dorn believe they achieve what the political process could not. Divisive political debates can be transcended by scientific solutions. As a case in point, Comeaux cites the rise in youthful pregnancies, which entails contentious debates on "contraceptives in schools, abortion, [and] child abuse" (196). By adding a hormone that changes the female reproduction cycle from menstrual to estrus to school cafeteria lunches, youthful pregnancies virtually disappear in the test high school. With that simple biological alteration, intractable and endless arguments about abortion are bypassed, the state saves money, families stay together, and so "family life is improved" (197).

Such palpable results as Blue Boy's appear to overcome objections based on rights and consent, because heavy sodium achieves the social concord and individual well-being that the doctrine of rights and politics failed to produce. Given the desperate and bleak situation of rampant crime and unhappiness, the public may well embrace Blue Boy, willing to do anything for the sake of a cure. Not only are our governing institutions unable to uphold individual life and liberty, it seems that the public itself may have lost the will to defend individual life and liberty. The ends of liberalism and even the pursuit of happiness can be better accomplished by other means. Blue Boy accomplishes what the political process has failed to do. Social ills are overcome, but lost is the individual freedom to answer the question "how to live" both for oneself and as a participating member of society.

Consequently, Blue Boy's brilliant statistical success hides how these so-called social improvements come at the expense of the groups traditionally and historically marginalized in American society. The spread of AIDS is reduced primarily because heavy sodium decreases the desire for drugs (fewer needle transmissions) and reduces homosexual tendencies. Comeaux proudly says that voluntarily the Gay and Lesbian Club at Louisiana State University disbanded, gay bars closed, and the sale of homosexual videos dropped. Crime rates have dropped. "Young punks" who used to menace the streets are "of their own accord" learning trades in occupations like plumbing and the service industry (198). The most dramatic presentation of the effects of heavy sodium is the image of the prison inmates in the fields—the men bare chested, the women wearing "colorful kerchiefs"—singing old hymns ("Swing low, sweet chariot") and picking cotton (266). Comeaux says that they are content and do not want to leave. Although he claims that he is "just a guy out to improve a little bit the quality of life for all Americans," he has re-created society according to his own liking (200). Comeaux suppresses homosexuality to eliminate AIDS, gains control over women's reproduction systems, channels troubled youths to service industry jobs, and converts prisoners (mostly black) into virtual slaves working the fields.

In contrast to that of the Blue Boy scientists, More's approach to treatment is less like a cure and more, as one commentator describes it, "a process involving mutuality and reciprocity between physician and patient."[15] More seeks to help his patients and also hopes to be helped by them. For example, although More is concerned about Father Smith's mental and physical health, he seeks Father Smith's advice about how to respond to Comeaux's job offer and the heavy sodium in the water. Unlike the scientists, More "understand[s] himself as related to, and dependent upon others."[16] More calls this his "best therapy," in which he is "asking for help and helping by asking" (234).[17]

Tom More brings people together and unites them, usually by showing them how they can help each other. More explains that where movies and TV stories "go wrong" is that "you don't shoot X for what he did to Y, even though he deserves shooting" (332). More knows that killing Comeaux and Van Dorn will not remove the human longing for death and self-destruction. The Comeauxs and Van Dorns of the world cannot be defeated entirely, nor can the impulse toward death be located within specific individuals whose disposal will set the world aright. Instead, More says, "you allow X a way out so he can help Y" (332). More's strategy is not to convince someone that he is in need of someone else, but to show him how he can help another person. Individuals, perhaps most of all liberal individuals who value autonomy, enjoy thinking of themselves as benefactors rather than beneficiaries. More knows that this tendency is a matter of individual vanity and reluctance to admit the need of another. As a practical matter, when one individual helps another, the action is not simply external but also operates internally on the doer and so brings about good to the doer as well as the recipient. An individual is simultaneously a benefactor and a beneficiary. Needing and helping another person creates a relation to someone as another self and not an object to be manipulated. More sees the possibility of this full, comprehensive good, but it is impossible in Comeaux and Van Dorn's envisioned society, where human freedom is enjoyed only by the few—the scientists. The scientists, by excluding themselves from the treatments they give to others, reveal a different hierarchy of values applied to themselves—they implicitly value their freedom more than mere animal well-being.

More is remarkably successful at rehabilitating many of the lesser participants in the scientists' scheme. But there is a limit to rehabilitation. Van Dorn returns to his "old self, his charming, grandiose, slightly phony Confederate self," writes a splashy best seller, and becomes a regular on TV talk shows (344). Comeaux quietly disappears—rumor has it—to China to assist in its one-child-per-family policy. Despite More's best efforts, Van Dorn and Comeaux refuse to be helped. *The Thanatos Syndrome* does not end with a perfect resolution. The project to add heavy sodium to the water supply is an example, even a crude example, not the real source of the impulse toward death and self-destruction. As Percy shows, "happily ever after" is a misguided ending, even for the "good guys," who are also troubled and lost selves. Percy presents neither total triumph nor utter defeat, but shows that by searching with others for hope the self does not have to succumb to self-destruction.

In *The Thanatos Syndrome*, More wonders: if a drug can "turn a haunted soul into a bustling little body, why take on such a quixotic quest as pursuing the secret of one's very self?" (13). If a pill can relieve the self of its cares and burdens, engaging in the task of searching the self seems self-indulgent and perverse. Although as a psychiatrist More can prescribe psycho-pharmaceuticals, he mentions that he rarely does so. The patient will feel better, he says, but "they'll never find out what the terror is trying to tell them" (6). More points to the Enlightenment as the source of a distinctive type of modern anxiety and unhappiness: "This is not the Age of Enlightenment but the Age of Not Knowing What to Do" (75). Consequently, pursuing happiness is "an odd pursuit," because it is trying to be something that you are not, which is like trying to have another eye color than the one you have. The deep problem with the pursuit of happiness is that the manner in which people pursue happiness blinds them from recognizing that their pursuit is precisely what keeps them from being relieved of their anxiety. More's message to his patients who seek a cure is that there is no cure: "Maybe a cure is knowing there is no cure" (76). More does not cure his patients of their anxiety, he cures them of their expectation that they ought to be cured and helps them think of anxiety as a clue to self-understanding.

Likewise, through *The Moviegoer* and *Lost in the Cosmos*, Percy brings his readers to consider unhappiness as a starting place for joint searches. Unhappiness draws us together because it points us toward understanding how we need each other and how we may help each other. The liberal pursuit of happiness does not properly understand the human being as a needy, dependent being who, above all, needs other people to live well. Percy does not point to our dependency as good in itself but as a fortunate, even happy, circumstance. According to Percy, liberalism mistakenly exaggerates human autonomy or self-sufficiency. Yet humans are not helpless beings; they are able to help and be helped by each other. Through our capacity to help and be helped, our lives achieve greater well-being and contentment than we could know as pursuers of happiness. Percy reminds us of our common existential predicament and restores to us the fundamental question "What shall I do?" that the pursuit of happiness implicitly tries to answer. In his quest to answer this question, Percy points to the search with our fellow wayfarers as the means for us to find peaceful respite now, in company and conversation with others and living in hope of happiness.

Notes

1. See, for example, Joseph E. Stiglitz, Amartya Sen, and Jean-Paul Fitoussi, *Mis-measuring Our Lives: Why GDP Doesn't Add Up* (New York: New Press, 2010); Derek Bok, *The Politics of Happiness: What Government Can Learn from the New Research on Well-Being* (Princeton, NJ: Princeton University Press, 2010); Richard Layard, *Happiness: Lessons from a New Science* (New York: Penguin Books, 2005); and Carol Nickerson, Norbert Schwarz, Ed Diener, and Daniel Kahneman, "Zeroing in on the Dark Side of the American Dream: A Closer Look at the Negative Consequences of the Goal for Financial Success," *Psychological Science* 14, no. 6 (2003): 531–36.

2. Emily asks him, "Don't you feel obliged to use your brain and to make a contribution?" Walker Percy, *The Moviegoer* (New York: Vintage International, 1998), 53. Subsequent page references to this work will be given parenthetically in the text.

3. Terrye Newkirk notes that by using "Little Way" to describe his life, Binx "burlesques" St. Thérèse's "Little Way of spiritual childhood," in which her goal is "to live everyday life with great heroism" in "*Via Negativa* and the Little Way: The Hidden God of *The Moviegoer*," *Renascence* 44, no. 3 (1992): 190, 191. In contrast to St. Thérèse's "Little Way," Binx's "Little Way" intentionally avoids any hint of heroism. Binx's "Little Way" uses ordinary life as a shield to hide from his aunt's hopes for glorious and grand deeds. It diminishes ordinary life for the sake of living an undistinguished life, in contrast to how St. Thérèse's "Little Way" elevates ordinary life.

4. Barbara Filippidis, "Vision and the Journey to Selfhood in Walker Percy's *The Moviegoer*," *Renascence* 33, no. 1 (1980): 13.

5. Walker Percy, *Lost in the Cosmos: The Last Self-Help Book* (New York: Picador, 1983), 229. Subsequent page references to this work will be given parenthetically in the text.

6. Michael A. Mikolajczak, "'A Home That Is Hope': Lost Cove, Tennessee," *Renascence* 50, nos. 3–4 (1998): 313.

7. The captain had fun "playing the unflappable captain" and "doing his job, and lounging at his ease" in such a way as to please the women, which in turn pleased him (228, 235).

8. The captain's last name, Schuyler, in Dutch means "protector" or "scholar."

9. Walker Percy, *The Thanatos Syndrome* (New York: Picador, 1987), 4. Subsequent page references to this work will be given parenthetically in the text.

10. After his hospice closes, Father Simon Smith starts living in a fire tower, much like St. Simeon Stylite, a Desert Father ascetic who lived on top of a pillar. Father Smith explains the modern attraction to death by telling More about an episode in his youth when he was visiting relatives in Germany. In his contempt for both the religion of his mother and the romanticism of his father, he had been deeply attracted to the readiness, willingness, and determination of his cousin, Helmut, to die for his country as an SS officer cadet. Father Smith admits that if he had been a German youth, he would have joined Helmut. Father Smith's point is that everyone is sick with the thanatos syndrome, not just the scientists behind Blue Boy.

11. Robert Hughes, "Walker Percy's Comedy and *The Thanatos Syndrome*," *Southern Literary Journal* 22, no. 1 (1989): 6. See also John F. Desmond, "Walker Percy, Flannery O'Connor, and the Holocaust," in *At the Crossroads: Ethical and Religious Themes in the Writings of Walker Percy* (Troy, NY: Whitson, 1997), 94–101; Gary M. Ciuba, *Walker Percy: Books of Revelations* (Athens: University of Georgia Press, 1991), 270–83; Patricia Lewis Poteat, "Pilgrim's Progress; or, A Few Night Thoughts on Tenderness and the Will to Power," in *Walker Percy: Novelist and Philosopher*, ed. Jan Nordby Gretlund and Karl-Heinz Westarp (Jackson: University Press of Mississippi, 1991), 208–24; and Sue Michell Crowley, "*The Thanatos Syndrome:* Walker Percy's Tribute to Flannery O'Connor," in Gretlund and Westarp, *Walker Percy*, 225–37.

12. Mary Deems Howland, *The Gift of the Other: Gabriel Marcel's Concept of Intersubjectivity in Walker Percy's Novels* (Pittsburgh: Duquesne University Press, 1990), 137. Howland refers to an incident after the Qualitarian center is closed in which Comeaux tells More, "What people don't know but what you and I know is that we're both after the same thing—such as reducing the suffering in the world and making criminals behave themselves. . . . *You can't give me one good reason why what I am doing is wrong.* The only difference between us is that you're in good taste and I'm not" (347). Comeaux leaves before More has a chance to respond.

13. It appears that Percy paints a harsh portrait of the future of American politics, depicting our political institutions failing utterly to protect life and liberty. Later in the novel, Percy reveals that the Supreme Court's ruling was more ambiguous with regard to interpretation and implementation. After More foils the conspiracy, he asks Max Gottlieb to have all infant candidates for pedeuthanasia to be sent to the hospice. Gottlieb objects that he cannot, because it would violate the Supreme Court case *Doe v. Dade*, which determined that personhood does not begin until eighteen months of age. More counters that the court ruling did not require

pedeuthanasia; it "only permits it under certain circumstances" (334). It makes a difference whether the ruling is interpreted broadly, to require euthanasia, or narrowly, to permit it conditionally. By More's narrow interpretation, the Supreme Court's ruling appears more reasonable and circumspect. It appears that doctors, like Comeaux, interpret the ruling to support their eugenic purposes, whereas it is possible to interpret it narrowly to apply only to exceptional cases.

14. Part of the human brain and consciousness is, as Comeaux explains, "not only an aberration of evolution but is also the scourge and curse of life on this earth, the source of wars, insanities, perversions—in short, those very pathologies which are peculiar to *Homo sapiens*" (195). In Freudian terms, Comeaux explains that heavy sodium suppresses the superego and bolsters the ego by releasing natural feel-good chemicals, endorphins.

15. Jon Young, "Walker Percy on the Cartesian Ideal of Knowing," *Renascence* 42, no. 3 (1990): 134.

16. Ibid., 129.

17. To be clear, More does not pretend to need help for the sake of boosting the confidence of his patients. More describes how Ella, a patient who feared failure, discovered that she and he had attended the same high school and university and gave him two yearbooks. Giving More the yearbooks allowed Ella to remind her doctor about himself and his past. Ella helped More in a small but nonetheless real way.

On Dealing with Man

James V. Schall, S.J.

> I've always held that art and even novels were just as valid as science, just as cognitive. . . . Science will bring you to a certain point and then no further; it can say nothing about what a man is or what he must do. And then the question is, *how do you deal with man?*
> —Walker Percy, interview with John Carr, 1971

> Scientists are more interested in teaching apes to talk than in finding out why people talk.
> —Walker Percy, "Questions They Never Asked Me," 1977

> Why is it that the look of another person looking at you is different from everything else in the Cosmos? . . . And why is it that one can look at a lion or a planet or an owl or at someone's finger as long as one pleases, but looking into the eyes of another person is, if prolonged past a second, a perilous affair?"
> —Walker Percy, *Lost in the Cosmos,* 1983

Aristotle often compares the quest for happiness with the quest for health. With his medical background (a background Aristotle also seems to have shared with his own father), Walker Percy was quite aware of the difference between what a doctor does and what a novelist does. The one describes what exactly is the condition of this human body; the other depicts what precisely is the condition of this human soul. Both are equally "scientific." They both must know and state *what is,* and, indeed, what ought to be in the context of what is there. What we are and what we ought to be come together in the exact person *that is*. We live with the consequences of the health or lack thereof both of body and of soul. They both relate to our free accepting or rejecting of *what we already are*.

A doctor, qua doctor, Aristotle tells us, is concerned with the restoration to health of this particular person. It is John or Sally Smith, lying there before him, not a "case" in a medical book. This restoration to health of this particular person is his end and the action directed to it. Whatever his intentions, if the health of this person is not his end, he is not a true doctor. The doctor, like all students of human biology, is also concerned in general with what it is for a human being, as opposed to an animal, to be healthy. The respective "what it is to be healthy" in a human being and an animal are both goods but of differing kinds. What it is to be a healthy horse is analogous, not identical, to what it is to be a healthy human being. The two differ according to the end or purpose of the being itself.

A doctor is useful to us individually when we are not healthy. His purpose is fulfilled when this particular patient becomes healthy. The doctor is not concerned about medicine in general but with Sally or John as lacking health. His end is what is needed to restore health. Nor does the doctor as such "heal" the patient. The operative nature present in this particular patient does the healing. The doctor aids, removes, and helps (or sometimes hinders) this process. The doctor does not "invent" what it is to be healthy. He aids in its accomplishment.

Once a patient is healthy, the doctor, as doctor, has nothing further to say to the patient, except perhaps some advice on how to remain healthy. The free activities of the healthy man fall under the realms of ethics, politics, art, metaphysics, and theology. They concern "living well," not just living. One strives to live and to live well, but merely being alive is not what human life is about, though it is its presupposition. *Prius est esse*—first it is necessary to be alive as this being before this being can do what it is for.

Plato and Aristotle both note that the doctor, who can do us the most good where our health is concerned, can also do us the most harm. He knows better what can damage us. This caveat is why we do not go to a doctor who is our enemy or hates us. This is also why we do not go to an incompetent doctor. Moreover, the patient participates in the doctor's prescriptions. The doctor can do little for the uncooperative patient. Plato had already noticed this. If the doctor tells the patient to take a certain medicine or perform specific kinds of exercises, it is still up to the patient to do them. The doctor cannot force him. If he does not do as the doctor recommends, the doctor can no longer treat the patient according to his art. The patient becomes his own doctor.

And not all doctors know what this particular patient needs here and now. This is why we have specialists. And if all efforts fail, we have death, which comes eventually to all men. No doctor or scientist can keep us alive forever in this world, though more and more are trying. They think that it is a good thing. It isn't.

The causes of death are investigated by pathology. But what death is concerns philosophy and revelation. The doctor pronounces us dead; he does not explain what death as such is, though we know it is the cessation of this human life. He merely declares that we are dead, if we are. Philosophy, Socrates said, is preparing to die. He was not speaking as a doctor. He was more important than a doctor. His jailer explained to Socrates, in a basic medical way, how the poison would kill him. He did not answer Socrates' other question in the *Apology* about whether death was an evil. Socrates said that he knew that doing wrong was evil. But he did not know whether death was. Death was better than doing wrong. It is better to die than to do wrong. Our civilization is, or was, based on this fundamental distinction.

Plato even has a character who spends his whole life worrying about his own health and keeping himself alive. The man had no time, Plato thought, to live a human life. A full human life, properly speaking, begins when we are no longer concerned exclusively with our health. Real life begins, as it were, when we no longer think of our health. We just have it. The healthiest person thinks least about health. He pursues the activities that are properly human, the activities of health, as Aristotle called them.

But what are the activities of a healthy person? The activities of health are not the concern of the doctor, except insofar as he has his own healthy life to live. What is it, then, that we do when we are healthy? We are to live as human beings and live well. And living well means that we acquire and practice the virtues that are indicative of what we are—the practical and the theoretical virtues. Yet, we might have the virtues but not be using them. Happiness is using them. And we use the virtues in order that we might be what we are. Being is an activity, not just a state. When we discover what we are, we find, paradoxically, that we are not much concerned with ourselves.

The purpose of the virtues is not to "discover" ourselves, as if to say that we do not already know what we are, who we are, or that we are. It turns out that we ourselves are not the primary object of our own existence. We do not make ourselves to be what we are. Our existence always faces *ad alium*, toward someone else. We are not "self-sufficient." Our mind does not first think itself. It first thinks the *what is* that is not ourselves. To be what we are, we have to be more than ourselves, without ceasing to be what we are. We exist as a being to be completed, not as one already complete.

"The quest of the self is probably self-defeating," Walker Percy said in an interview with Charles Bunting, "I mean if religion has any validity at all, then the quest for the self is nonsense, you know. It's the quest for God, or as Kierkegaard, I think, said: the only way the self can become self is by becoming itself transparently before God. . . . I suppose a good deal of my novel-writing could be a satire on the theme of the so-called quest for the self, or self-fulfillment. . . . A great deal of bad novel writing is about searching for one's self."[1] These are remarkable words.

Paradoxically, we will never find ourselves if we spend our lives seeking ourselves. We spend our lives seeking what is not ourselves, as Augustine said. If by living we find only ourselves, we imitate the loneliness of Aristotle's divinity, who evidently had no friends. It is the wonder of the Trinitarian revelation that God is not lonely. It is the wonder of good novels that we discover that we, ultimately, are not lonely either, both because we live and love others of our kind and because of our "transparency before God," as Percy put it. Ultimately the only lonely beings in the universe are those who choose themselves as *all that is*.

In Walker Percy's *Message in the Bottle*, we find him concerned with how science can prevent us from having the primary experiences of seeing, hearing, or smelling things as they are. These are experiences, as Aristotle said, that we would want even if they brought us no pleasure. Yet, they are delightful in themselves. Percy speaks of our having "access to being" and the "recovery of being."[2] He is getting at something basic here. Do we need something called "science" to stand between ourselves and reality? If we do, can we really know anything that is not ourselves? In spite of our actual experiences, do we need "experts" to verify for us whether our experience of reality is real or not? Can we rely on our given capacities and powers?

We can have this problem because many scientific theories tell us about what we are, but only one "me" deals with it all. Early in *Lost in the Cosmos*, Percy amusingly asks: "Can you explain why it is that there are, at last count, sixteen schools of psychotherapy with sixteen theories of the personality and its disorders and that patients treated in one school seem to do as well or as badly as patients treated in any other—while there is only one generally accepted theory of the cause and cure of pneumococcal pneumonia and only one generally accepted theory of the orbits of the plants and the gravitational attraction of our galaxy and the galaxy M31 in Andromeda?"[3] The obvious conclusion is that, if a theory is in fact true, it will eliminate those opinions that are not true. The reaching an agreed-upon, logical conclusion is a perfection of knowledge, not a denial of freedom.

This conclusion is simply common sense, the kind Aristotle is said to have possessed when he wrote: "We must, however, not only state the true view, but also explain the false view; for an explanation of that promotes confidence. For when we have an apparently reasonable explanation of why a false view appears true, that makes us more confident of the true view" (*Nicomachean Ethics* 1154a23–26). We know false views exist alongside of true ones. We can tell the difference.

One of the most amusing experiences in reading Percy is what I might call "coming across scientific theories that cannot be true." The passage from his famous "self-interview," cited above, with regard to teaching apes to talk rather than understanding why human beings speak makes this point in an epigrammatic way. Percy, even though he respected science properly understood, thought that something was wrong with much of the whole modern movement. But he often approached the problem by its popular effects. Wrong theories of mind will disrupt the world of ordinary men.

In *Lost in the Cosmos,* we find the famous parody sequence called "The Last Donahue Show." Phil Donahue is largely forgotten today, but at one time his was a very popular TV show. Donahue would open up his show to popular thought on a variety of current issues. Percy's satire of this show falls within the method of *Lost in the Cosmos* itself. It examines whether what is presented as popular makes sense. Percy calls this process a "thought experiment." The very title of the chapter, "The *Last* Donahue Show," implied that the format had simply become so silly that most normal people could see its absurdities. People often need to have humor to see truth.

Percy imagines a show, with Donahue as host, composed of four persons before the camera. One is an active homosexual male from San Francisco. He is said to have had five hundred random "contacts." This statistic is balanced nicely by a prosperous married businessman. He seems to spend his lunchtime making about as many heterosexual contacts as the homosexual makes male contacts. The third member is a fourteen-year-old girl who is pregnant by the time-tested methods. Finally, we find a female sex therapist who runs a talk show on her specialty, how to cure sexual problems.[4]

Percy, of course, has great fun with this situation, which is both absurd and close to reality, as life often is. The sequence brings out the fact that natural law itself is revealed in the laughter or reaction of the audience to the "reasons" given by the interviewees to justify their activities. Each justification represents a separate moral disorder of soul that is now said to be "normal" and often a "right."

The fourteen-year-old girl, paradoxically, seems in fact to be the most sensible of the group. The reason that she gives for her pregnancy is simply that she wants the baby. The therapist is appalled at this response. She immediately blames the situation on the schools for not teaching sex education and how to prevent conception. She reckons with everything but the girl before her, who is not influenced by such strange theories.

Much to the older woman's consternation, the pregnant girl tells the therapist that she (the girl) has been thoroughly indoctrinated in the schools about all the means available for preventing pregnancy, including abortion, the getting rid of failures to prevent. The girl knows that she is pregnant. She knows how she got that way. She is savvy. She knows that pregnancies produce human babies, nothing else. In this case, it will produce hers. She simply wants the baby because it is, well, something she wants, something good. Naturally, this response of the girl undermines the whole theory behind modern sex education. What is prevented is what normal people want because of what it is. We have to conclude either the girl is nuts or that she sees something that the theorists and politicians do not see, namely, her baby.

Now, I cite this famous "thought experiment" because it comes up again in an equally amusing interview of Percy with Jo Gulledge, which originally appeared in the *Southern Review*. Gulledge wants to discuss *Lost in the Cosmos* with Percy. She sees that the book is "half-serious and half-satirical." Percy responds: "I wrote it as a primer and in a light tone to make it accessible and to avoid academic portentousness. Readers, I have discovered, are not much interested in heavy works on semiotics. Nobody reads academic semiotics but semioticists, and I sometimes wonder if they do."[5] Obviously, Percy himself was not overwhelmed by academia or its influence.

Gulledge then turns to this academic reception of *Lost in the Cosmos*. "A major criticism seems to be what your reviewers called a hard line approach on homosexuality. . . . Do you think you are going to get any feedback from that?" What interests me here is how Percy dealt with this question, which implied some bias on his part, a major academic fault these days, no doubt. Percy responds that he does not see how he is any more critical of homosexuals than of heterosexuals. Both follow disordered agendas. He treated them both fairly on the basis of what they said of themselves about their activities. We begin with the truth that each stated what he did.

Percy asks the interviewer if she is thinking of the scene in *Lost in the Cosmos* where the San Francisco man describes in detail what he does in city parks and why he does it. Homosexuals, like the heterosexual businessman, can be very "promiscuous, amazingly so." He was only reporting what each man said he did. Anybody could understand that something abnormal (the five hundred) was going on here. The audience members had no trouble comprehending that the businessman, who said that he was married and had his wife's approval for his philandering, was out of order. They immediately "booed" him for thinking nothing was wrong with his frequent lunchtime activities.

In *Lost in the Cosmos,* Percy continues his examination of what follows from separating sex from personality and responsibility. Two heterosexual Nobel Prize winners, by opening their own sperm bank with their own presumably high level of offerings, propose to "benefit millions of women." The two generous "scientists" think that millions of women are of inferior intellectual stock. But by using their sperm (not that of their husbands or lovers), they could improve the "quality" of the race. This assumption, no doubt, lets us know what these scientists think of themselves and their own intelligence. This path obviously would obviate the need of husbands except perhaps as caretakers for the supposedly higher-level sons and daughters now begotten thanks to the sperm of the elite scientists, who become evidently fathers of thousands of sons and daughters. Much of this was in Plato.

Percy thus affirms that he was no more critical of homosexuals than of Nobel Prize Laureates or businessmen.[6] So what's the beef? Percy's point all the way through, however, was that normal people could see quite clearly, when they are amusingly spelled out, the aberrations in such activities and see through claims that they are simply neutral or even good for everyone involved. Most of such activities and proposals, seen as "thought experiments" in Percy's time, are now the subject of legislation whereby they are legitimated by positive law. The "thought experiment" has appeared aboveground. We are now doing what we recently only imagined.

Percy's writings are filled with scientists who cannot make contact with their own souls, with novelists and artists who find that science and scientists have little to say about what a human being is. In a letter to Shelby Foote, Percy wrote:

> What do you mean, what are we to the French and the French to us! A great deal to both of us and in entirely different ways—all going back to the old Cartesian split, a typical Frenchman who perpetuated a typical French disaster from which we have been suffering ever since—with of course exciting consequences—with you on one side of the split and me on the other. The French are ideologues, i.e. madmen, and yet without them, we'd sink into a torpor. The mind-body split, locked-in ghost in the machine on one side, structure and world on the other, me with the former, you with the latter.[7]

Contrary to what we might expect, however, Percy does not think that the resolution of this problem is to arrive at a mutual understanding between science and literary culture. Speaking in his own capacity as a scientist, Percy thinks that the proper solution lies within science itself. Basically, if the scientist and the novelist are both dealing with reality, what is their point of contact?

In his 1989 Jefferson Lecture at the National Endowment for the Humanities, Walker Percy addressed the question of the place of science and arts in society. Percy begins the lecture in this striking way: "I wish to offer two propositions for your consideration. One is that our view of the world, which we get consciously or unconsciously from modern science, is radically incoherent. A corollary of this proposition is that modern science is itself radically incoherent, not when it seeks to understand things and subhuman organisms and the cosmos itself, but when it seeks to understand man, not man's physiology or neurology or his bloodstream, but man *qua* man, man when he is peculiarly human. In short, the sciences of man are incoherent."[8] Percy argues that this issue is really located in the Cartesian split between a world of things and a world of thought. The whole modern question is: How are these two worlds related to each other?

As Percy points out in a number of ways, he has no problem with science if it is describing and analyzing the bloodstream, his or anyone else's. We can look at a man's finger as long as we wish, as I cited Percy in the beginning. The fact is that there is something in man that cannot be measured by scientific methods, which presuppose matter of some sort as their objects. Reductionism means that only that which can be measured by scientific method is real. Percy rather proposes the realism of the American philosopher Charles Peirce. Peirce affirms this uniqueness of man. Yet this same man has a real connection with the world that science investigates. This connection is seen in man's capacity to name and understand things. He can distinguish between things. He can identify them as different.

"Precisely that which is distinctive in human behavior, language, art, thought itself is not accounted for by the standard scientific paradigm which has been sovereign for three hundred years, that indeed, science as we know it cannot utter a single word about what it is to be born a human individual, to live and to die."[9] This realism, Percy knows, is connected with the Aristotelian and Thomist tradition in which the mind is itself ordered precisely to the truth of existing things. The perfection of the mind is to state this truth as known. This affirmation can only be made if there is a reality in which both *what is* and our knowing converge in the same order.[10]

Those who are accustomed to reading Plato will be familiar with Percy's arguments that lead us to the notion of the spirituality of things because we know them. Percy does not, to be sure, come up with a doctrine of forms. But he does offer a sophisticated argument, following both Peirce and Percy's own experience of watching children learn to speak. Knowing what a thing is, that this word relates to that thing known, that that thing known is this kind of a thing, not that kind, indicates a spiritual power already in existence. It needs only the opportunity to manifest itself.

The world of physical reality and the world of literature are not two different worlds. They belong to the same world and belong to each other. But there is only one being within that world that combines both in his very being. We cannot teach apes to think. But babies do learn to know, to speak, to identify. That is, they put things together—words, things, and their expanding knowledge of the relationship between them. This knowing too exists in the same world, not as separate but as distinguished.

Percy argues that the "thing," whatever we call it within us that enables us to perform this knowing activity, is a natural phenomenon. It is already there. It is not something put there by human power. It is a human power in action. This power in us is "real as a cabbage or a king, but it is not material. No material structure of neurons, however complex, and however intimately it may be related to the triadic event, can itself assert anything. ... A material substance cannot name or assert a proposition. The initiation of a speech act is an act—or, that is, an agent. The agent is not material."[11] Truth only exists when the agent knows the thing, himself, and the relation of his knowing to the thing known.

What is the significance of this analysis of the existence of a power usually called the soul? It exists and can be identified by our reflexive powers in analyzing how we know and what we know. In his interview with John Carr, Percy remarked that the key question is "How do we deal with man?" Does the scientist who examines him by methods that exclude this spiritual side know anything about him, about what he really is? Does not the novelist know more about man than the scientist? Percy has no intention of not going to the doctor to find out what ails him, even if he himself has decided to practice another kind of medicine. But because of this relation of language and world centered only in the human soul and mind, can we hold together the two worlds split apart by the "madness of Frenchmen"?

A reason can be found about why we cannot look into the eyes of another human being for longer than ten seconds, whereas we can look into the eyes of a lion as long as we wish. The reason is that what lies behind the eyes of our friend is another person, not just another thing. When we look into the eyes and soul of another, they are looking back at our soul. The proper way to learn about that other person is to engage in those spiritual and human enterprises whereby we know one another in freedom and friendship, where we discuss the highest things to indicate how it is that we ourselves live.

Percy has always been fascinated with language as well as by the place where he lives, in Covington, Louisiana, to be exact. Aristotle had already observed that man is the animal that speaks. His reason and speech are directly consequent on each other. We find in the same world "two worlds." One exists out there; the other one is "spoken" on the basis of what is already out there. The speaking world is to state what the objective world is. Neither world is complete without the other. Thing leads to word, word back to thing.

In his amusing and insightful self-interview, "Questions They Never Asked Me," Percy writes:

> I have discovered from experience that even if anyone has the ultimate solution to the mystery of language, no one would pay the slightest attention. In fact, most people don't even know there is a mystery. Here is an astounding fact. . . . The use of symbols between creatures, the use of language in particular, appears to be the one unique phenomenon in the universe, is certainly the single behavior that most clearly sets man apart form the beasts, is also the one activity in which humans engage most of the time. . . . And yet it is the least understood of all phenomena.[12]

But once we establish the fact that we can speak, can speak of *what is*, what follows asks, more in detail: What do we speak about?

In his essay "Naming and Being," Percy remarks that the fact that we can "name" a being is every bit as much a mystery as the fact that the being is there to be named. "If we must speak of a 'need' in connection with human behavior, let us speak of it as Heidegger does: 'The need is: to preserve the truth of Being no matter what may happen to man and everything that "is." Freed from all constraint, because born of the abyss of freedom, this sacrifice is the expense of our human being for the preservation of the truth of Being in respect of what-is.'"[13] Percy was more interested in metaphysics, the science of being as being, than he was of the nature of politics. Yet at the same time, Percy did focus on how our modern world seems ready to fall apart.

Percy is often considered an apocalyptic writer. Certainly *The Thanatos Syndrome* or other surreal atmospheres that we find in *Love in the Ruins* make it appear that he made up a world that is not familiar to us. This approach seems to be the reason why Patrick Samway chose the following passage from Percy's "Notes for a Novel about the End of the World" to introduce his collection of Percy essays. Percy probably knew Robert Hugh Benson's 1910 novel, *The Lord of the World*, a book that shows the same sort of concerns that Percy manifested in his essays and novels.

Percy wrote: "Instead of constructing a plot and creating a case of characters from a world familiar to everybody, he [the novelist] is more apt to set forth with a *stranger in a strange land* where the signposts are enigmatic and which he sets out to explain nevertheless."[14] What does this comment have to do with "the end of the world"? Obviously, it refers to those passages in Scripture, in the book of Daniel or the end of the Gospel of Matthew, about the signs of the last days and their not being recognized. The novelist, at his best, relates the life of his characters not only within the ordinary situations of ordinary life, but within the whole purpose of human life in this world and the next. This account of each life reflects the particular purpose of each human person in the universe, which provides the scene of his deciding what he shall be.

In this sense, Percy is rather like Flannery O'Connor, whom he knew. She said that her apparently exaggerated, if not deranged, southern characters were necessary to enable us to see what is normal. Our culture is itself so distorted that we need to be shocked by what appears to us to be abnormal to see just how abnormal our chosen everyday life has become. The only way we can see the disorder of our souls is to stretch them out, make them bigger than life, even make them to seem like monsters.

The signposts point to what is really important in our lives. Thus, we cannot be surprised that O'Connor gave her stories and novels Scripture-sounding titles like *The Violent Bear It Away*. Percy has a similar kind of title, *The Second Coming*. As a novelist, Percy stands in judgment of his culture through the lives of characters so affected by the derangement of our times that either they cannot see themselves, or they cannot help living a life that is attached to some transcendent purpose whereby these purposeful people can see *what is* in a way obscure or closed off to the citizens of our time.

Percy's novel *The Thanatos Syndrome* is but another form of what John Paul II called the culture of death. This connection between apocalypse and politics is always present in Percy. When he is not acting as a novelist but as a social critic, he spells out themes that appear in his novels in sometimes preposterous forms. The very title *Lost in the Cosmos* is also a guide to where Percy thinks we are. Rational beings, according to our own understanding of ourselves, presumably have become more and more intelligent due to science and modern folkways. But, at the same time, do we really know what or who we are? The cosmos itself is not lost. The cosmos does not know that it is a cosmos, let alone why it exists or why anything in it feels lost. Intelligence is the personal property of man. Its only source is ultimately the source of intelligence itself. Intelligence is not something that the cosmos can inaugurate. It properly belongs to what is itself mind.

The only way we can get lost in the cosmos is not to know what the cosmos is in its relation to us. We are lost because we have rejected the explanations of what we are that were found in reason and revelation. We have made ourselves lost, curiously, because we did not want to live in the universe as it was explained and given to us, a universe in which we were central, but not as its creators. Each of us had a purpose to our lives that was given to us in our very creation. We had freely to complete ourselves, granted the fact that we already were human beings, not turtles, from our actual beginnings. It was this latter realization that Percy thought was the reason why novels themselves only arise in a Christian culture.

"Judeo-Christianity is about pilgrims who have something wrong with them and are embarked on a search to find a way out. This is also what novels are about," Percy wrote.[15] Why modern political philosophy differs from this view is that, as Eric Voegelin said, it is an effort to "immanentize the eschaton."[16] That is, it attempts to cure this thing wrong with human nature by reforming politics and economics by human means, not by wisdom, grace, and sacrifice, which are looked upon as alienating. "Thus, it is no accident that the novel has never flourished in the Eastern tradition," Percy continued. "If Buddhism and Hinduism believe that the self is illusory, that ordinary life is misery, that ordinary things have no sacramental value and that reality itself is concealed by the veil of *maya*, how can any importance be attached to or any pleasure be taken in novels about selves and happenings and things in an ordinary world?"[17]

Yet, Percy's novels and essays reinforce each other as we notice in them that the denial of God and natural law leaves modern understanding of the world subject to no norms other than what we put there. Once freed from any relation to a free acceptance of human nature that guides him to *what he is*, the new civic man builds himself on the rejection of the basic things that made man to be man. What happens in Percy's novels is that the new self-made man becomes more and more of a monster. He not only defines himself, but he builds a new man in direct opposition to the kind of man offered in nature, the nature that was given with human being in the first place.

In *Signposts*, we find printed a letter to the editor to the *New York Times* on January 22, 1988. If we wonder what the *New York Times* is, its refusal to publish this letter by a prominent novelist on the fifteenth anniversary of *Roe v. Wade* is a good indicator of the deepest sort of dishonesty of soul. This was the annual "Right-to-Life" day designed to call attention to the unnaturalness of this Supreme Court decision allowing legal abortions for any reason. I cite this letter, in particular, because it indicated the degree to which our media will not permit a full discussion of what is at stake. But Percy clearly joins together the disorder of the public world, apocalyptic themes, and the clearest reasoning about the logic of erroneous positions.

"While it may indeed be argued that in terms of Judaeo-Christian values individual human life is sacred and may not be destroyed," Percy writes in his unpublished letter, "and while it is also true that modern medical evidence shows ever more clearly that there is no qualitative difference between an unborn human infant and a born human infant, the argument is persuasive only to those who adopt such values and such evidence." If these positions are rejected, for whatever reason, it follows that the pro-abortion logic is valid. The human infant is not a baby but a "produce of conception," merely part of the woman's body.[18]

Percy wants to give grounds why this impasse may not be definitive. What he does is stretch out the consequences that follow when we accept the position that the "destruction of human life" can be accepted in any way.[19] History is instructive to us, as Percy thinks. He examines the eugenic laws that were passed in Germany in the Weimar Republic, before the Nazis were in power. These laws in no way were the cause of the Nazi position, though, contrariwise, they may have rather been instructive to the latter's views.

What Percy suggests is that "once a line is crossed, once the principle gains acceptance—juridically, medically, socially—innocent human life can be destroyed for whatever reason, for the most admirable socioeconomic, medical, or social reasons—then it does not take a prophet to predict what will happen next, or, if not next, then sooner or later."[20] What Percy predicted has now happened with the advance of biotechnology and expansion of "designer" concepts of family and life by the same logic. But it is not merely a dismantling of the family. It is a replacing of it with scientific devices designed to free women or to improve the genes or to lengthen life or to produce children outside of intercourse or to retract the need of a child for the mother and father that begot him.

Percy, who sees the logic of these proposals and techniques, tells us that "a warning is in order," a warning almost identically repeated by Benedict twenty years later in his encyclical *Spe Salvi*. What Percy adds is the political dimension that is intrinsic in the logic of denying a natural order that does not depend on man's will, except for choosing to recognize it: "Depending on the disposition of the majority and the opinion polls—now in favor of allowing women to get rid of unborn and unwanted babies—it is not difficult to imagine an electorate or a court ten years, fifty years from now, who would favor getting rid of useless old people, retarded children, anti-social blacks, illegal Hispanics, gypsies, Jews. . . . Why not?—if that is what is wanted by the majority, the polled opinion, the polity of the time."[21] It is now more than twenty years since Percy wrote these lines. These positions, originally devised in the democratic Weimar Republic, now appear in all modern republics, including ours. They have been carried out. Each of these propositions Percy has foreseen is either proposed or is in effect. They are in the logic of his argument.

I have entitled these reflections on Walker Percy, using one of his own expressions, "On Dealing with Man." He asked about man because he saw that the answer to this question was beyond the competence of what are normally called the sciences. Man cannot be "dealt with" from the outside, at least not the man who is free and understands that he and his fellows must involve themselves in any improvement—and of any degeneration, for that matter. Man is not an object to be improved by something outside himself.

As Plato said, the only way to improve the polity is to improve the soul. No doubt things about man can be known to be disordered. But to improve him, he needs his own input. He needs the virtues. He needs to understand that he must participate in his own improvement, his own happiness, even if he does not create himself in what this happiness consists. He participates only in whether he will choose what he ought to do.

Students of Descartes, which Percy is, have, like Jacques Maritain, often thought that Descartes' theory of knowledge was like the angels. Unlike human knowledge in Aristotle or Aquinas, Cartesian knowledge required no body, to which it is the form, with which it in particular might contact the world. Souls with bodies were not unlike Augustine's Manicheanism, theories that enabled us to do whatever we wanted with the body on the grounds that we were untouched by it in our moral lives. This was a strange kind of freedom, quite opposed to that freedom exemplified in Aristotle's theory of virtue that told us that to reach the contemplative truth, we needed to discipline ourselves so that we were free of the attachments that caused us to use our minds to justify whatever it was we wanted to do. The body was to become the servant of the mind in their mutual understanding of the world *that is*.

In a very short essay, written in 1969 and entitled "Eudora Welty in Jackson," Percy brought up this angelism question. It seems to be a feature of modern writers that they are "alienated" from their city or their families or the cosmos itself, in which they are lost. Why Percy speaks in this context of Eudora Welty is because she was a very good writer who lived her life in her home. "What is most valuable about Eudora Welty is not that she is one of the best living short-story writers. . . . No, what is valuable is that she has done it in a place."[22] She knew her hometown of Jackson, Mississippi. She knew its complexities and the stories of the people who lived there because she lived there. Percy found this living at home characteristic also of another philosopher he much admires, namely, Kierkegaard in Copenhagen.

One is reminded here of the Christian theme that its founder lived most of his life in a small town, yet in a place where he was no prophet among his family. The ordinary folks around him did not recognize him, nor did the leaders of his land. And yet, Percy finds that there is a connection between this angelism and the need to recapture the normalcy of body and spirit that is found in the Aristotelian tradition. "It is at least possible to live as one imagines Eudora Welty lives in Jackson, practice letters—differently from a banker banking but not altogether differently—and sustain a relation with one's town and fellow townsmen which is as complex as you please, even ambivalent, but life giving."[23]

Whether in Nazareth, Copenhagen, or Jackson, the place of full human and unique existence can be recognized as local. "The time is coming when the American novelist will tire of his angelism—of which obsessive genital sexuality is the most urgent symptom, the reaching out for the flesh which has been shucked—will wonder how to get back into a body, live in a place, at a street address. Eudora Welty will be a valuable clue."[24] Likewise is Walker Percy. The body cannot just be "shucked"; we are not Manicheans, the first heretics, who believe the body is evil. The soul that does not know its normal relation to its body, with which it is one person, seeks shocking things to prove to itself that it exists.

"How do you deal with man?" Not really by studying apes or even the whole cosmos. You deal with man by knowing what he is and the drama of his existence, which is not completed in this life, but which is neither completed without his body. The resurrection remains the connection that man most hopes for. All of our literature somehow tells us that we seek the face of another. What is the reason why we can only gaze into the eyes of another, even someone we love, for only a few seconds? It is not because we find nothing there. Rather, it is because we find another there who, like us, is made for God, and neither will find rest in anything less.

In "Questions They Never Asked Me," Percy's "self-interview" puts the final seal on those who think his reasoning, his plots, his doctrines are, well, silly. He is asked (that is, asks himself): "Q. *Are you a dogmatic Catholic or an open-minded Catholic?* A. I don't know what that means, either. Do you mean do I believe in the dogma that the Catholic Church proposes for belief? Q. *Yes.* A. Yes. Q. *How is such a belief possible in this day and age?* A. What else is there?"[25]

In the end, amusingly, probably Percy would say that, for his part, this is "how he deals with man." None of the dogmatic alternatives that Percy carefully spells out in his novels and studies deals half so well as this one with the actual inhabitants of Nazareth, Copenhagen, Jackson, Mississippi, or, I suspect, Covington, Louisiana, his hometown. In such towns of this world, the residents are neither angels nor bodies, but imperfect, fascinating human persons, possessing both. Each is on his journey that his very being sets before him.

Each person is intended for glory. The drama of human existence, best seen perhaps by a novelist like Percy, is whether and how each one finds this glory through loves and hatreds of others. No one is, finally, lost, either in the cosmos or in everlastingness, except through his own choices. This is the truth of our existence that makes the novel possible among the cities of men composed of living human persons.

Notes

1. Charles T. Bunting, "An Afternoon with Walker Percy," in *Conversations with Walker Percy*, ed. Lewis A. Lawson and Victor A. Kramer (Jackson: University Press of Mississippi, 1985), 49.

2. Walker Percy, *The Message in a Bottle: How Queer Man Is, How Queer Language Is, and What One Has to Do with the Other* (New York: Farrar, Straus, and Giroux, 1975), 51.

3. Walker Percy, *Lost in the Cosmos: The Last Self-Help Book* (New York: Washington Square, 1983), 11.

4. Ibid., 48–59.

5. Jo Gulledge, "The Reentry Option: An Interview with Walker Percy," in Lawson and Kramer, *Conversations*, 285.

6. Ibid., 286.

7. *The Correspondence of Shelby Foote and Walker Percy*, ed. Jay Tolson (New York: Norton, 1998), letter of March 4, 1978, 238.

8. Walker Percy, "The Fateful Rift: The San Andreas Fault in the Modern Mind," in *Signposts in a Strange Land*, ed. Patrick Samway, S.J. (New York: Farrar, Straus and Giroux, 1991), 271.

9. Ibid., 288.

10. Walker Percy, "Naming and Being," in *Signposts*, 130–38.

11. Percy, "The Fateful Rift," 287. See Robert Sokolowski, *The Phenomenology of the Human Person* (New York: Cambridge University Press, 2008).

12. Walker Percy, "Questions They Never Asked Me," in *Signposts*, 419.

13. Percy, "Naming and Being," 137–38.

14. Percy, *Signposts*, frontispiece.

15. Walker Percy, "Another Message in the Bottle," in *Signposts*, 366.

16. Eric Voegelin, *Science, Politics, and Gnosticism* (Chicago: Gateway, 1969), 89.

17. Percy, "Another Message," 366.

18. Walker Percy, "An Unpublished Letter to the *Times*," in *Signposts*, 349.

19. Ibid.

20. Ibid., 350–51.

21. Ibid., 351.

22. Walker Percy, "Eudora Welty in Jackson," in *Signposts*, 222.

23. Ibid., 223.

24. Ibid.

25. Percy, "Questions They Never Asked Me," 416.

Walker Percy's "Theory of Man" and the Elimination of Virtue

Nathan P. Carson

It is no overstatement to say that throughout his entire authorship, the critique of our current cultural anthropology, together with the formulation of a new "theory of man," was Walker Percy's central concern. In many of his earliest essays, most of which predate his first and highly acclaimed novel, *The Moviegoer,* Percy outlines what he sees as the currently fractured state of our theory of humanity and emphasizes the need for an empirically demonstrable consensus view regarding what human beings most distinctively are. Throughout his career, Percy repeatedly attempts to articulate just what such a consensus view could be, for without it, modern human beings (in his view) remain lost to themselves amid the ruins of modernity.[1]

In this chapter, I examine Percy's theory of human nature, with a particular emphasis on what an ideal person in Percy's economy might be like, including the virtues such a person must possess. In focusing on Percy's anthropology, with its empirically evident and natural ground for virtues, I do not attend to Percy's political thought as such. Rather, I will examine Percy's account of our distinctive proper function as human beings, for it is a function that grounds political community and the virtues that sustain it and provides its teleological and hence normative dimensions. My ultimate aim is to determine how successfully Percy's anthropology performs this task.

In this essay, then, after summarizing Percy's critique of our incoherent Darwinian and Cartesian conceptions of humanity, I examine Percy's view that symbolic representation is the unique capacity that makes us human. Then, I elucidate his claim that unlike everything else in our world, we humans are "unsignifiable" and cannot be captured under the auspices of symbolic predication. I show that for Percy, unsignifiability entails an ineradicable and God-given anxiety, making both our self-placement in the world and transcendent orientation unavoidable. Then, after examining the necessity and normativity of our relatedness to other signifying selves, I conclude my exposition by examining what an ideal self-placement in the world might look like, including its ecstatic orientation toward the world, others, and God. Next, in the constructive portion of the chapter, I offer extended speculation regarding what virtues might be proper to the kind of beings that Percy thinks we are, and how such virtues positively sustain human inquiry, interpersonal communion, and the goods of community that undergird the human polis. Finally, however, I argue that Percy's commitment to human unsignifiability radically undermines most of these positive prospects. For this unsignifiability, which preserves for Percy our proper orientation toward the world, others, and God, is deeply incompatible with either virtue predication or virtue possession.

Present Anthropological Incoherence

Percy claims that, on the one hand, many people in the post-Enlightenment age see the human being as merely an "organism in an environment," an anthropology built on the developments of Darwinian science and B. F. Skinner's condition-response behaviorist theories. Percy exerts single-minded persistence in demonstrating how inadequately the "organism-in-environment" theory explains humanity. He argues that one cannot simply take "this or that laboratory hypothesis—say, learning theory as applied to organisms in a laboratory environment—and by verbal sleight-of-hand stick the label onto man." For those in this Darwinian-behaviorist camp, says Percy, it may be "quite natural to think of man as you think of rats or chimpanzees, as an organism, a biological energy system, not qualitatively different from other such energy systems." On this view, Percy adds, any *unique* characteristic of human beings is seen as "yet another evolutionary stratagem" for adapting to or conquering an environment. Yet if human beings are mere organisms, Percy queries, how can it be that they are unhappy even in the most perfect environment? Even if we grant such qualities as abstract thinking, art, culture, and the use of tools as mere results of evolutionary progress, this theory still is unable to account for many things. What other organism makes war against its own species, commits suicide, or is vulnerable to manifold self-psychoses?[2]

However, what is the alternative? Here Percy notes that many people seem to know that humanity has unique properties that must be accounted for, and so they fill this gap by holding on to an anthropology—"implicit in Western civilization itself"—comprised of the leftovers of a burned-out Judeo-Christianity that includes such vague ideas as "freedom," "mind," the "sacredness of the individual," and the like.[3] Percy says that most people, while holding the organism theory in one hand, hold these "traditional" Greek and Judeo-Christian dualist teachings about the nature of human beings in the other. However, for Percy, this traditional view of the human self as an "intermediate being," as a composite or synthesis of body and soul (for example), is unhelpful precisely because it is held incoherently in tandem with the "organism-in-environment" view and because the terms of traditional Judeo-Christian definitions no longer hold any meaning for the average Western person.[4]

What is more, the traditional Judeo-Christian "intermediate" view of humanity as both angel and beast suffers from a cultural Cartesianism that renders it deformed and unintelligible. For example, Percy situates many of his critiques of the intermediate view in the context of Cartesian dualism that split the consciousness of Western humanity into "body and mind," a "strange Janus monster" that has subsequently been methodologically presupposed in the natural and psychological sciences. In Percy's view, then, we are incoherently positioned between the reductionistic organism theory of humans as Darwinian beasts and the unintelligible theory of humans as Cartesian angels, most of us holding to both without knowing exactly how the two hang together.[5]

Attempting to move beyond this predicament, Percy seeks an empirically accessible anthropological theory, one that overcomes the incoherence and limitations of either the Darwinian beast view, the Cartesian angel view, or their awkward Frankensteinian marriage. As they presently stand, says Percy, none of these approaches is of any help scientifically; they are even a hindrance if we think they offer a comprehensive anthropological theory. As an alternative, Percy seeks something within science itself that can account for both humanity's creatureliness and its intermediate uniqueness.[6] So, he searches for an empirical insight that could offer a coherent, empirically accessible, and experientially validated view of human beings, offering a way out of our present anthropological incoherence.

The Symbol-Mongering Being

To make a start at pinpointing such an insight, Percy says, "When man doesn't know whether he is an organism or a soul or both, and if both how he can be both, it is good to start with what he does know."[7] What we do know, says Percy, is that human begins talk. Here is a starting point that everyone, theologians and scientists alike, can agree upon. For Percy, language (and the symbolic representation behind it) is the unique marker of human being, but also fully empirically evident and hence something that may bring disparate theories together into a cohesive whole.[8]

The human phenomenon of language is no evolutionary advancement or adaptation, according to Percy. The appearance of a symbol-mongering being in the evolutionary record is, he argues, "as sudden as biblical creation." The human brain, Percy continues, increased in weight by as much as 54 percent in a few thousand years, "much of this increase occurring in the cortex," especially "around the Sylvan fissure implicated in the perception and production of speech." Taking his cue from writers, linguists, psycholinguists, and semioticians such as Charles Sanders Peirce, Suzanne Langer, Ernst Cassirer, and Noam Chomsky, Percy sees this breakthrough into the "daylight of language" as an "all-or-none threshold" and "a spectacular quantum jump that made man human," such that we now live in a whole new world. Hence, Percy claims, "so sweepingly has his [humanity's] life and his world been transformed by his discovery of symbols that it seems more accurate to call man not Homo sapiens—because man's folly is at least as characteristic as his wisdom—but Homo symbolificus, man the symbol-mongerer, or Homo loquens, man the talker." Here Percy suggests that if human beings are truly unique in this capacity and acquisition, then "surely a good place to look for a minimum consensus view of man is as languaged creature, not man the mind-body composite."[9]

In his examination of man the symbol-mongerer, Percy turns to the semiotic work of pragmatist Charles Sanders Peirce and his distinction between the only two kinds of natural interactions in the cosmos: those involving "dyadic relations" and those involving "triadic relations." The latter, Percy argues, is unique to human beings and different in *kind* from all other physical or biological interactions that happen. A *dyadic* event may be briefly described as a cause-effect relation or a stimulus-response occurrence such as subatomic particle collision or a man's response to female pheromones. For Percy, human transaction with symbols is the only kind of natural event that we know of that cannot be reduced to such a dyadic relation or causal interaction. Following Peirce, Percy calls such symbolic activity "triadic" due to this fundamental irreducibility between symbol (signifier), the object (signified), and the mind of the symbol user itself.[10]

Percy himself was struck by the uniqueness and importance of this aspect of being human while reading the story of Helen Keller's breakthrough into the symbolic world. For the first seven years of her life, Keller seemed to operate in dyads, as, for instance, when her teacher, Miss Sullivan, "spelled C-A-K-E into Helen's hand and Helen went to look for cake—like one of Skinner's pigeons." The qualitative leap between the "dyadic" Helen of those first seven years and the "triadic" person she becomes after April 5, 1887, captivated Percy and fueled much of his anthropological theory. The significant occurrence happened as Miss Sullivan placed one of Helen's hands under the running water at a well-house pump and spelled W-A-T-E-R in the other. In that moment, Helen, for the first time, understood the word *water* to *be* the substance running over her hand. She broke through the threshold of symbol and language when she finally made the connection between *naming* and *being*.[11]

With regard to this triadic breakthrough, Percy notes that "man's capacity for symbol-mongering in general and language in particular is so part and parcel of his being human, of his perceiving and knowing, of his very consciousness itself, that it is all but impossible for him to focus on the magic prism through which he sees everything else."[12] Given her age, Keller's case is valuable because her breakthrough is simply more discernible as the amazing "quantum leap" that it actually is. This leap, though a precondition for myriad human maladies, is for Percy nothing less than the entrance of the child into full humanness. It is "the discovery of the world and the coming to oneself as a person" and involves "the secret of knowing what the world is and of becoming a person in the world."[13]

The Human Task: Communion through Symbolic Naming

The connection Percy draws between triadic language, "discovery of the world," and the task of "becoming a person in the world" is crucial. By virtue of our own nature as symbol-mongering creatures, we are saddled with the ineradicable and twofold task of naming the world, on the one hand, and of achieving selfhood by rightly positioning ourselves in the world, on the other. I will examine each of these tasks, beginning with the task of naming.

In Percy's view, *Homo symbolificus* (or man the symbol-mongerer) not only has and responds to the cosmic environment, as do other organisms, he also has a *world*. The sign-user goes around making signs, naming things around him, and creating a symbolic world of meaning within the physical world of the cosmos. Here, everything has a place, is accounted for, and named. Percy claims, "It is of the nature of the symbol-mongering consciousness to delineate and transform all sensory data into intentional symbolic forms. The whole objectizing act of the mind is to render all things . . . formulable." Moreover, since the act of naming is a fundamental aspect of human consciousness, the symbolic rendering of all things formulable grants the sign-user epistemic access to the world around her. For Percy, triadic symbolization is a necessary condition for knowing or cognizing something as an object, since without a sign, precisely nothing is known or so cognized.[14]

So, for Percy's triadic self, everything encountered must be known *as* something, or else it is not known at all: "Once it dawns upon one, whether deaf-mute or not, that *this is water*, then the first question is *What is that*, and so on, toward the end that *everything is something*. There has come into existence an all-construing mode of cognition in which everything must be formulated symbolically and known intentionally *as* something." In order that a particular bird be "known and affirmed," a "*pairing* is required: the laying of *symbol* alongside *thing*" (for example, that *bird* is a *robin*). In this way, naming moves the namer beyond mere biological orientation to an *ontological* orientation toward being, providing us with access to being such that the world may be discovered, unveiled, and celebrated with joy. Notably, the symbolizing activity in question here is "a means of *knowing* . . . not in the sense of possessing 'facts' but in the Thomistic and existential sense of connatural identification of the knower with the object known."[15]

Here we reach the first significant point about Percy's view of human selfhood as *task*, as I began to discuss above. One telos of this task of naming is the achievement of symbolic *communion* of the symbolizing self with everything other in the symbolic order, as the other is "fixed and formulated by the symbol."[16] Now, Percy holds that we can engage in this activity in better or worse ways, but our task of knowing by naming ideally opens up the created order, inviting it into a communion between knower and known; and it is a task that can occasion wonder and joy in the namers themselves.

I now turn to a second crucial aspect of the human task, occasioned by our encounter with things we either do not or cannot know. This, as I stated above, is the task of human self-placement in the symbolic world. Given our ubiquitous need for symbolically formulating our world, Percy contends that the *absence* of knowledge through symbolic communion may occasion helplessness or acute anxiety for the symbol-mongering self in the face of the unnameable and unknowable. And, as it so happens, Percy argues that the symbol-mongering creature himself can never be symbolically captured; she is utterly immune to any "stable symbolic transformation" or semiotic closure of being. Percy puts it this way: "It is the requirement of consciousness that everything *be* something and willy-nilly everything *is* something—*with one tremendous exception!* The one thing in the world which by its very nature is not susceptible of a stable symbolic transformation is *myself!* I, who symbolize the world in order to know it, am destined to remain forever unknown to myself."[17]

To myself, the sign-maker, all significations apply, yet none of them apply. I cannot capture myself and pin myself down; I am a slippery being that is always, maddeningly, *becoming*. The selfhood of the symbol-mongerer amounts to an inexhaustible subjectivity that refuses the solidity and reduction that an accompanying symbol would entail. Percy famously depicts this view in *Lost in the Cosmos:*

> Semiotically, the self is literally unspeakable to itself. One cannot speak or hear a word which signifies oneself, as one can speak or hear a word signifying anything else, e.g. *apple, Canada, 7-Up.*
>
> The self of the sign-user can never be grasped, because, once the self locates itself at the dead center of its world, there is no signified to which a signifier can be joined to make a sign. The self has no sign of itself. No signifier applies. All signifiers apply equally.
>
> You are Ralph to me and I am Walker to you, but you are not Ralph to you and I am not Walker to me. . . . For me, certain signifiers fit you, and not others. For me, all signifiers fit me, one as well as another. I am rascal, hero, craven, brave, treacherous, loyal, at once the secret hero and asshole of the Cosmos.
>
> You are not a sign in your world. Unlike other signifiers in your world

which form more or less stable units with the perceived world-things they signify, the signifier of yourself is mobile, freed up, and operating on a sliding scale. . . .

The signified of the self is loose and caroms around the Cosmos like an unguided missile.[18]

Percy calls this unsignifiability "the symbolic predicament of the self." Nonetheless, says Percy, such "problematic" self-unnameability is precisely that which grounds the human being in the task of human becoming. It is indeed a creational given that roots the human self in relation to "other," but only *becomes* "problematic" when, as Percy so aptly demonstrates in his fictional characters, a person attempts to grasp himself as an autonomous subject apart from such relationality. The symbolic and hence *relational* character of epistemology means that the self cannot know itself as "something" apart from relational pairing of itself with the "other."[19]

This brings us to our next problem, which further illumines the nature of the self's task. If the self is unnameable to itself, then the issue of *self-placement* within one's own symbolic world arises. Percy argues, "As soon as the self becomes self-conscious—that is, aware of its own unformulability in its world of signs—from that moment forward, it cannot escape the predicament of its placement in the world." For Percy, *placing* oneself in one's world is inescapable, yet also highly problematic:

> Please note that once the symbol-mongering organism has a world, he must place himself in this world. He has no choice. He cannot not do it. If he refuses to make a choice, then he will experience himself placed in this world as one who has not made a choice. He is not like a dog or a cat who, when deprived of all stimuli, goes to sleep. Unlike an organism in an environment, a man in a world has the unique capacity for being delighted with the world and himself and his place in the world, or being bored with it, anxious about it, or depressed about it. He can exploit it, celebrate it, be a stranger in it, or be at home in it.[20]

Why does Percy take the task of placing the unsignifiable self in a world of signs to be an unavoidable predicament? Self-unsignifiability is one part of the answer. However, the answer also involves recognizing Percy's explicit debt to Søren Kierkegaard's *The Concept of Anxiety*, in which objectless anxiety (over "nothing") is an ineradicable and God-given emotion that reveals to people their transcendent orientation and inescapable freedom and task to become selves before God.[21] Unlike Kierkegaard, however, Percy treats anxiety as a necessary consequence of our nature as self-unsignifiable symbol-mongering beings: "The being of the namer slips through the fingers of naming. If he tries to construe himself in the same mode by which he construes the rest of the world, he must necessarily construe himself as a nothing, as Sartre's characters do. But this is not to say that I am nothing; this is only to say that I am that which I cannot name. I am rather a person, a namer and a hearer of names."[22]

Here, borrowing from while altering Kierkegaard, Percy claims that self-unsignifiability and the attendant problem of self-placement in the symbolic world cause anxiety over "nothing." Unlike object-based anxiety, says Percy, "the anxiety which follows upon symbolization is ambiguous" because it is anxiety over the "nothing" that is the unsignifiable self. As it is the native ability of the symbol-mongerer to name and place things in her world, when faced with herself as the unnameable, anxiety over nothing settles in. Since this situation is, for Percy, part of the very nature of what it means to be *Homo symbolificus,* we can conclude that for Percy, as for Kierkegaard, anxiety is a given and inescapable characteristic of human nature. The catastrophic *fall* into a self-absorbed "suck of self," shame, despair, and myriad inauthentic symbolic identifications of the self with either God or things in the world only occurs, it would seem, as a result of the sign-user freely "turning from the concelebration of the world to a solitary absorption with self."[23]

This is further verified by Percy's arguments, in "The Coming Crisis in Psychiatry," against those in the human sciences who treat anxiety as purely pathological, since it is biologically counterproductive. If human beings are mere organisms in an environment, as many in the human sciences presuppose, asks Percy, then why do human beings seem to be the *only* organism in the cosmos capable of pure self-imposed misery in a perfect environment? Given their reductively biological view of humanity, says Percy, the social sciences *must* treat biologically useless anxiety as pathological. However, in doing so, these sciences render themselves "unable to take account of the predicament of modern man."[24]

In opposition to this, Percy affirms Erich Fromm's view that anxiety may be an *"appropriate"* reaction "for the man who confronts himself and discovers—nothing." Thus does Percy suggest that "anxiety may be quite the reverse of a symptom" which, together with our symbol-mongering and self-unsignifiability, point us toward "goals beyond the biological," a "true estate" of human being involving "a concept of human nature and what is proper to it." Indeed, Percy claims that anxiety marks an "incurable God-directedness" or transcendence in human beings. It is *not* merely the consequence of living in a consumerist age of biological needs satisfaction, though this surely makes its occurrence more acute.[25] Rather, Percy holds that anxiety, an ineradicable indicator of our transcendent orientation, is ultimately entailed by our symbol-mongering nature and inability to fix ourselves under a stable signifier. The perennial character of this condition is further verified by Percy's endorsement of the existentialist insight that anxiety reveals to us our *freedom* and task of becoming a self. Hence Percy comments that "anxiety may be quite the reverse of a symptom. It may be the call of the self to the self, in Kierkegaard's words: the discovery of the possibility of freedom to become a self."[26] As mentioned above, anxiety only becomes pathological (and hence a form of despair), when the self encounters its own unsignifiability in a world of signs and responds with a self-conscious, narcissistic inward collapse, grasping to make of itself, in Cartesian fashion, a reified *something* in the world of signified things.

In *The Second Coming*, for example, Will Barrett runs into just such unsignifiability and task of self-placement, and his response is terribly misguided:

> He gazed at himself in the bathroom mirror, turned his head, touched his cheek like a man testing whether to shave. Presently his face canceled itself out. The bright-faceted forehead went dark, the deep-set eyes began to glow, the shadowed pocked cheek grew bright. The mirror, he noticed, did not reflect accurately. It missed the slight bulge of forehead, the hollowing of temple which showed in photographs. Even when he turned his head, his nose did not look snoutish as it did in a double mirror.
>
> Something stirred in him. He looked at his watch. In three minutes Kitty would slip out into the cloud. When he thought of her standing in the summerhouse, hugging herself, wrapped in fog, he smiled. She would sit on the damp bench, straddling slightly, her thighs broadening and filling the creamy linen skirt. Yes, it was in her, not in a mirror, he would find himself. Entering her, he would be answered, responded to, delineated. His life would be proved by her. She would echo him, print him out, trace his shape like radar. He could read himself in her.
>
> His heart gave a big pump. Did Kitty want what she appeared to want?

> Did she want him to fuck her in the summerhouse? Yes! And it was Kitty's ass he wanted. Yes![27]

Here, Will is looking for himself, but finds nothing. The mirror signifies some things, but it fails to pin Will down in his own symbolic world. In the mirror's reflection, Will's face "canceled itself out" as the mirror "missed" him and "did not reflect accurately." He is stuck with the problem of self-placement in his own world and, disappointed by the mirror's inability to signify him or give him such a place, he turns excitedly to another mode of self-placement. Illicit sex with Kitty Vaught may be just what Will needs to be "delineated," printed out, traced like radar.

While this passage appears to deal with anything *but* anxiety, anxiety is nonetheless the chief matter at hand, especially when we consider the implicit connection here between anxiety and desire, a pairing that becomes explicit later in the novel. For Percy, nonpathological anxiety is precisely a form of desire and longing that attracts and repels as it coaxes the self out of its present state toward its telos of resting transparently under God in consciousness of itself as a self. Will Barrett, by contrast, responds to his own unsignifiability with despair. His creational "anxiety over nothing"—the anxious longing for signification that marks the "God-directedness" in Will and compels *some* kind of placement in the world—is transmuted into a compulsive and inordinate sexual desire. Will plans to place himself in the world by "entering" Kitty Vaught.

In the forgoing discussion I have tried to show why, for Percy, the human task of self-placement in the world is unavoidable. If, as Percy supposes, anxiety indicates an "incurable God-directedness" that is mutually entailed by our symbol-mongering nature and our own unsignifiability, and if such anxiety reveals our inescapable freedom, then human beings are stuck with the predicament of placing themselves, unsignified, in a world of signs.

Proper Self-Placement in the World

I now want to turn to Percy's constructive vision for what it means to be rightly placed in the world as an unsignifiable and nonpathologically anxious human person. While Percy is undeniably a comic master at depicting and diagnosing *mis*-placements, I will focus strictly on his positive vision and ultimately on the virtues that might be needed to sustain this vision. To understand Percy's notion of proper self-placement, we must first grasp his view about social consciousness and co-signification. Along the way, Percy's view of proper placement in the world will come clear, amounting also to a serious critique of the individualist or hyperautonomous Cartesian and Kantian ego. These points will also figure prominently in my later discussion of Percian virtues.

Earlier I examined Percy's view of the symbol as epistemic need, which is the view that without triadic-symbolic representation, human beings neither have nor know a world. A relation to the "other" that is my symbolically ordered world is an essential element in the constitution of the symbol-making self, and communion with that other is one of its goals. However, Percy expands this position to a far more ambitious one: the notion that representational acts are irreducibly *social,* and indeed that consciousness itself is irreducibly social or intersubjective in character.

Put briefly, Percy claims that consciousness is not a psychological "state" of one sort or another, but rather a *con scio,* a "knowing with" or relation that occurs within the shared symbolic world of triadic co-signification. I am conscious that "this is a robin" not because I have conjured up a unique sign in my own private language, but because it is a robin "for you and me." Reminiscent of Wittgenstein's theory of meaning as use in a social form of life, Percy borrows the view from George H. Mead that *consciousness* is "a phenomenon arising from the social matrix through language," and hence meaning as well. Thus not only Descartes but the phenomenologist and the existentialist tell only half of the story, because awareness is symbolic in character, and such symbols are irreducibly intersubjective in character: "I am not only conscious *of* something; I am conscious of it as being what it is for you and me."[28]

Hence, Percy flatly rejects any theoretical or normative conception of the human being as an autonomous subject, or even as a form of the phenomenologist's prereflective transcendental ego. Percy contends that the "prime reality of human consciousness" is not the Cartesian cogito ("I am conscious of this chair"), nor the Sartrean prereflective and impersonal *cognito* ("There is consciousness of this chair"), since both of these approaches *presuppose* consciousness. Rather, for Percy, the proper construal of the "originary act of consciousness is the joint affirmation that the object is there for you and me," a co-designation by means of symbol that "*is itself* the constituent act of consciousness" ("This *is* a chair for you and me"). This, says Percy, offers a "symbolic corrective" to both Anglo-American empiricism and existentialism in their attempts to defeat both the Cartesian cogito and the Kantian transcendental ego. "The decisive stroke against the myth of the autonomous Kantian subject," says Percy, "is the intersubjective constitution of consciousness. There is a mutuality between the I and the Thou and the object which is in itself prime and irreducible."[29]

This means, among others things, that Percy envisions human beings as irreducibly in need of one another for that which makes them distinctively human. Regarding the self that unavoidably must operate within a symbolic world, Percy says, "You—Betty, Dick—are like other items in my world—cats, dogs, and apples. But you have a unique property. You are also a co-namer, co-discoverer, co-sustainer of my world—whether you are Kafka whom I read or Betty who reads this. Without you—Franz, Betty—I would have no world."[30] To have no symbolic world is to be subhuman, or potentially human at best. For Percy, then, inasmuch as the symbol is humanly requisite for epistemology, and shared meaning is a necessary condition of consciousness, symbol-mongering persons are irreducibly dependent on others for their very status as conscious human beings. Indeed, Percy claims that "it is inconceivable that a human being raised apart from other humans should ever discover symbolization."[31]

From this social view of the nature of consciousness, Percy advances further, moving toward a normative conception of human relationality and intersubjective communion. Percy grounds this conception in the empirical reality of symbolic exchange between human beings. Moving beyond his initial Peircian triad—symbol-maker, symbol, and object—Percy pairs two triadic sign-transactions into his "symbol tetrad," bringing the "utterer" and "receiver" together. He thus forms an integrated account and normative construal of consciousness that includes Marcel's intersubjectivity, Buber's authentic "I-Thou" relation (and the possibility for "I-it" inauthentic relation), and Mead's social construal of consciousness:[32]

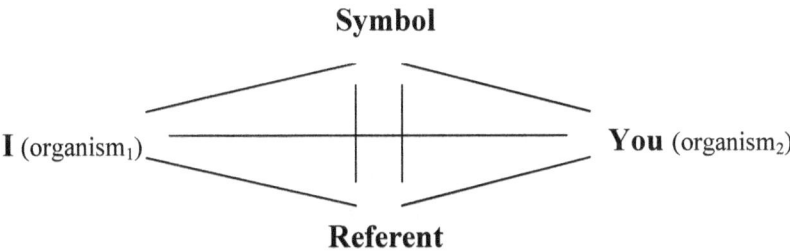

This "tetrad" adds new dimensions to C. S. Peirce's triad, and it illustrates that for Percy, without a symbolic meaning that is intersubjectively shared and co-affirmed, the symbol-mongerer has no world. However, it also clarifies that the "I-Thou" interpersonal relation is not only "the very condition of being and knowing and feeling in a human way," as Percy claims, but that this relation also includes an inescapably normative dimension. Hence, Percy says, "The Thou is at once the source of my consciousness, the companion and co-celebrant of my discovery of being—and the sole threat to my unauthentic constitution of myself." In a reversal of Sartre's aggressively objectifying stare, Percy claims that the "look" of the other can disturbingly expose my inauthentic modes of self-placement, for what the look "discovers" and affirms about me is my literal "unspeakableness" (unsignifiability). Rather than affirming my unauthentic self-construal as an autonomous something or an object in its world, the truly intersubjective look of the Thou exposes me "not as a something" but as "*nothing*." Moreover, when both the "I" and "Thou" mutually share this affirmation of unsignifiability, the mutual gaze turns from aggressive "exposure" to "love in the communion of selves."[33]

Where authentic love occurs in such intersubjective communion, anxiety over one's own unsignifiability turns outward into a direct desire for the other, and ultimately into an anxious longing for the transcendent source of that love, of which the love itself is a sign. Toward the close of *The Second Coming*, for example, Will Barrett comes to realize that Allie, and the love they share, is a gift and hence "a sign of a giver."[34] Thus, Percy does not bring Will through his entire pilgrimage simply to fall in love with a girl. There is indeed a "God-directedness" at the core of Will's anxious longing, and Allie serves as a horizontal, sacramental sign, a message in a bottle pointing him to a vertical relation to God. For Percy, the experience of intersubjective communion between Allie and Will is not a tetradic end in itself, a closed system of human intersubjectivity. Rather, it is a relation that is, like Kierkegaard's self-as-relation, a "derived, established relation" that finds its telos only in God.

Percy's understanding of human nature and proper self-placement is further clarified by the one sustained moment in which he speculates on the nature of unfallen symbol-mongering beings. We catch glimpses of this in the novels, of course, but these glimpses are often intermingled with the intractable personal pathologies of Percy's fictional characters.

Percy's clearest speculation on unfallen symbol-mongering beings takes the form of a discussion about aliens, in which he reflects on the possibility that other intelligences in the cosmos could also have broken through the dyadic barrier into self-consciousness and the symbolic world, but without falling into the inauthenticity of grasping for themselves as autonomous, solitary *somethings*. Percy queries, "Might they not have achieved the world of signs without succumbing to the terrible penalty? Might there not exist preternatural [prelapsarian] intelligences who do not necessarily share the shadow-life of the earth-self?"[35] If so, what does this Edenic life look like?

In the first of his two "Space Odyssey" short stories, toward the end of *Lost in the Cosmos*, Percy describes an imagined conversation between humans and another race of intelligent, sentient beings who seem to have retained their unfallen state. Claiming that their race possesses an unfallen "C_1 consciousness," the alien spokesman describes their "preternatural" state:

> [It is] something like the consciousness of a child grown mature and sophisticated but maintaining its innocence permanently and avoiding the malformations of self-consciousness, enjoying the beauty of our planet and each other and our science and art without weariness, boredom, fear, guilt, or shame. Like what you call the Helen Keller phenomenon . . . [which is] the joy of consciousness and the discovery of the Cosmos through the mediation of symbols and the cooperation of others and the preservation of this joy against the incursions of boredom, fear, anger, despair, shame, and the love of war and death and the secret desire for the misfortune of others.

To this, Percy adds that "a C_1 consciousness is selfless . . . unaware of self, because it is looking out, seeing things, and symbolizing through intersubjective transactions with others."[36]

With these unfallen aliens in mind, together with our analysis above, we may safely formulate Percy's ideal conception of human nature, leading to fruitful reflection on the virtues of beings with such a nature. Although we are indeed intermediate "angel-beasts" and in some sense organisms, the chief unique human ability is triadic symbolization expressed in language, and this makes human beings fundamentally relational and capable of intersubjective tetradic communion. Normatively, then, the ideal self is one that refuses, in its anxiety, to grasp for the "nothing" of autonomous being. Rather, it bypasses the narcissistic "fall" into solitary subjectivity occasioned by its unsignifiability, and turns instead to *place* itself outward toward the world of signs, toward other signifying selves, and through that communion, toward the *Sign-Giver.*

The Virtues of the Symbol-Mongering Self

With a robust grasp of Percy's theory of human nature and its proper function and tasks, we may now move to a speculative discussion about the sorts of virtues that such beings might need to possess. As stated above, such reflection is a necessary propaedeutic to Percy's politics proper. For, through it we gain an initial understanding of how Percy's "theory of man" and its complementary virtues both sustain and provide normative standards for the individual goods, communal goods, and practices that undergird the human polis. After some extended reflection on the positive virtue-ethical prospects in Percy's economy, I will then argue, in the final section of this chapter, that Percy's rather central notion of "unsignifiability" undermines most (if not all) of these positive prospects.

Intellectual Virtues

Some virtue and vice categories appear unavoidable in Percy's economy. First, there are the intellectual virtues associated with our native task of signifying and so knowing and discovering the world as well as the wonder, delight, and *communio entium* that can result from this. This is an activity in which we symbol-mongers can engage either excellently or not, and hence requires any number of intellectual virtues such as intellectual courage, integrity, deliberative excellence, scientific knowledge, understanding, and intellectual equity.

More significantly, however, the *communio entium* brought about by the exercise of these virtues is finally nothing less than a *communio personarum,* since we are irreducibly in need of one another in this task that is ultimately a co-naming of the world and placing ourselves in a life-giving, concelebratory orientation toward it. Here there appears a possibility for scientific practice, and the virtues belonging to it, that avoids the scientific self-abstraction of "angelism" Percy is so worried about. For the scientist can be rooted in a community of inquirers who together take delight in the open-handed intersection of naming and being. Central to this "angelism" corrective is Percy's clear emphasis on the *emotional* dimension of the activity of naming, where the inquiry itself issues not in a theory abstracted from the inquirer herself, but in one that is intimately connected with her ordinary human passions and loves, as well as those of the others in her community of inquiry. This underscores the plausible and appealing supposition that the finest excellences or virtues of human naming are excellences of the *whole* person. An understanding construed as a purely cognitive and perceptual grasp of a body of knowledge is, in Percy's economy, an impoverished sort of understanding compared to one that involves *appreciation,* or attunement to the evaluative dimensions of what is known, where such appreciation is partly constituted by the affective and motivational dimensions characteristic of human love, joy, delight, and wonder.

Virtues of Acknowledged Dependence

A second group of virtues (and related vices) that appears categorically unavoidable in Percy's world consists in what Alasdair MacIntyre calls the "virtues of acknowledged dependence."[37] For MacIntyre, these virtues include gratitude, humility, compassion, generosity, kindness, and gentleness. Moreover, he approaches virtues of dependence by claiming that our human dependence and fragility are best understood by considering what we have in *common* with nonhuman animals, often at the biological level.[38] In striking contrast to this approach, Percy bases the need for virtues of acknowledged dependence on our qualitative uniqueness as human beings; these are the very traits of ours and correlative needs that *cannot* be reduced to the biological. Our own capacity for symbolic representation (for example), our ability to have a world, is fundamentally dependent on others at the level of consciousness and nonreducible to the biological sphere. Moreover, both the activity of naming and the ability to *enjoy* our symbolic order at the intersection of naming and being are fundamentally dependent on the co-naming and co-celebration of other signifiers. Ultimately, that which makes me distinctively human—my triadic ability to name the world and celebrate it—could never occur apart from the existence and naming activity of other persons.

More important, perhaps, the virtues of acknowledged dependence are crucially needed for avoiding what Percy calls the great "suck of self." This is Percy's equivalent of the "fall" for human beings who, when becoming self-consciously aware of their own unsignifiability in a world of signs, freely fall into a narcissistic self-absorption that includes construing oneself as an autonomous subject to which stable predicates may be applied. The "I-Thou" exchange of intersubjectivity is critical here for, as we have noted, Percy holds that we are fundamentally dependent on others not only for co-validating our symbolic enterprise in the world as namers and knowers, but also for the sort of communion that can expose our inauthenticity and reaffirm the truth of our unsignifiability. Both the very fact of our unsignifiability and the anxiety this produces and the fact of our fallen inauthentic modes of selfhood that deny such unsignifiability underscore the irreducible place of the other in preserving with us a proper orientation toward ourselves and the world.[39]

This becomes crystal clear when we consider Percy's critique of the pagan Stoic code of honor in the aristocratic ideals of the American South. *This* virtue ethics—exemplified so well by Emily Cutrer of Percy's *The Moviegoer* and the Compson family in Faulkner's *The Sound and the Fury*—elevates personal, self-absorbed autonomy and self-sufficiency as the highest achievement in virtue. It is marked by a *self-conscious* and dignified protection of one's own virtue, and it is this reflective and egoistic eudaimonism that motivates the concern for virtues like a sense of duty, generosity, nobility of soul, honor, and the like. Percy considered this sort of Stoicism, especially in its individualistic pop-Cartesian form in the South, as the perfect recipe for suicide, as demonstrated in the case of Quentin Compson. By contrast, Percy's view that self-consciousness is *pathological* (excepting awareness of oneself as unsignifiable), consciousness is irreducibly social, and that communal intersubjectivity is central to the naming project, constitutes a counterideal to this Stoic "wintry kingdom of the self," as he calls it.[40] There is little place in Percy's economy of virtues for such self-sufficient and self-reflective Stoicism, or indeed for an Aristotelian *megalopsuchos* or Nietzchean Übermensch who enjoys his self-sufficiency and benevolence while disdaining dependence on others.[41]

What virtues of acknowledged dependence, then, might be compatible with Percy's vision? First, given that my only knowledge of the cosmos is mediated through triadic language, and given also that my symbolic world is essentially dependent on the co-signification of others (I *have* no independent and self-sufficient consciousness), it would seem that the virtue of humility finds a natural home in Percy's account, especially the virtue of epistemic humility. Recall that at least one case of madness in Percy's novels involves Will Barrett's descent into his Cartesian cave by virtue of a lust for epistemic certainty about God's existence. Note also the absence of this lust at the close of the novel, when it is chastened by the interrogative: "Is she [Alison Huger] a gift and therefore a sign of a giver?"[42]

Other-Regarding and Communal Virtues

Second, given Percy's emphasis on the maladies of acute self-consciousness as well as our native orientation outward toward the world, others, and God, it would seem that other-regarding virtues are crucial in Percy's economy, some of which are also virtues of acknowledged dependence. These virtues include, among others, gratitude, compassion, generosity, kindness, and gentleness. When the other is God, especially in light of our anxiously acknowledged unsignifiability and consequent transcendent orientation, the theological virtues of faith and hope have an ineradicable place as well. In a moment of Kierkegaardian comparison, for instance, we could say that nonpathological anxiety over the "nothing" of unsignifiable selfhood can and should drive us toward transparent faith in the God who constituted us with this restless task of becoming a self.

Third, the virtues that sustain the goods internal to communities seem rather central, given Percy's emphasis on both intersubjectivity and authentic "I-Thou" human community. Although some of these virtues aren't directly forms of acknowledged dependence, they operate within a broader context of acknowledged dependence in that their expression in action exhibits a tacit appreciation of the value of the communities that sustain us. Here, I have in mind the virtues of collegiality, conscientiousness, appreciative regard and respect for persons, love, and the disposition to be forgiving.

Expanding on this, a community-sustaining (and other-regarding) virtue that *might* be especially apt in light of Percy's project is, in my view, the virtue of being disposed to be attentive to the good-making characteristics of others. The expression of this virtue in the activity of focused and *just* attention, expounded so ably by Iris Murdoch, is an explicit counter to what she calls the "gravity" of our self-centered egoism, whose chief characteristic is the unimaginative reification of other persons under a limited set of signifiers. Illustrating the attentive counter to this, Murdoch imagines a case in which a mother-in-law ("M") views her daughter-in-law ("D") as "positively rude [and] tiresomely juvenile" as well as "vulgar." However, M is self-critical enough to look again, giving "careful and just *attention*" to that which confronts her, resulting in her *discovery* that D is "not vulgar but refreshingly simple, not undignified but spontaneous," and so on.[43] This Murdochian vision seems at least compatible with Percy's ideal for "I-Thou" intersubjective communion. For the parties to a Percian community lovingly and attentively resist closure of predication, but instead seek new and ever-deepening appreciation of one another's qualities, affirming the inexhaustibility of signifiers assignable to the being and personhood of the other.

The Problem of Virtue Predication and Possession

Up to this point I have discussed a number of virtue categories that we humans might need in order to flourish in light of our native and natural capacity for triadic language, the task of naming and knowing productive of communion, the interdependent character of consciousness and signifying activity, and self-unsignifiability. From intellectual virtues and virtues of dependence to community-sustaining virtues and Murdochian attentiveness, Percy's account of human uniqueness appears to offer a rich storehouse of virtues and their communal flourishing. However, there is good reason to think that, given Percy's account, the storehouse is quite bare.

Here I want to focus on a special problem arising from Percy's unsignifiability claim which, as I have shown, is indispensably central to his account of human nature, our intersubjective communion, and our transcendent orientation. The general worry I have is this. Most traditional conceptions of virtue, from at least Aristotle on, hold that virtue is a *hexis*, a *settled* state or diachronically stable disposition of character such that it can be predicated of a whole person, rather than simply of his activities or actions in circumscribed roles or contexts.[44] Now, given human unsignifiability, *can* virtue truly be predicated of a person? It would appear that the answer is no. However, if virtue cannot be truly predicated of an unsignifiable self, then it follows that one could never be truly praised or blamed for possession or nonpossession of a virtue. We then arrive at the very un-Percian conclusion that no matter *how* we place ourselves in the world, we cannot be morally or personally criticized for it. If I happen to place myself in the world like Binx Bolling, with a new MG and the thigh of a secretary to cure my malaise, then I cannot be criticized, for the predicate "inauthentic" cannot be applied to me.

Now, all of this depends on what Percy really *means* by the unsignifiability of the self. One obvious response to the above problem is to say that the unsignifiability of selfhood applies only to the first-personal standpoint, whereas it is perfectly possible and desirable for *others* to predicate certain virtue or vice terms of me, and especially authenticity or its lack. This reply could be drawn from the passage cited earlier:

> Semiotically, the self is literally unspeakable *to itself*. . . . The self of the sign-user can never be grasped, because, once the self locates itself at the dead center of its world, there is no signified to which a signifier can be joined to make a sign. The self has no sign of itself. No signifier applies. All signifiers apply equally.
>
> You are Ralph to me and I am Walker to you, but you are not Ralph to you and I am not Walker to me. . . . For me, certain signifiers fit you, and not others. For me, all signifiers fit me, one as well as another. I am rascal, hero, craven, brave, treacherous, loyal, at once the secret hero and asshole of the Cosmos.[45]

Here Percy predicates of himself both the virtue of courage and the vice of cravenness, while suggesting that a host of other contradictory predicates could apply, although he is ultimately *stuck* with none of them. For he himself stands at the center of his own signifying universe, looking out.

So, perhaps the point is that *in the case of self-signification*, it is necessarily the case that we cannot predicate virtue of ourselves, and this might helpfully preclude virtue-ethical egoism or fastidiously Stoic preoccupation with one's own virtue or flourishing. Notably, though, Percy also claims that others *can* both assign and rule out predicates in my case. So, the solution to the worry above might be this: *I* cannot truly predicate virtue of myself but *you*, as my co-namer and communicant, can engage in such predication. However, here we encounter another problem: Percy doesn't think co-namers ought to be doing this.

For instance, elsewhere, Percy is absolutely clear that in the *best* cases of "I-Thou" communion, the communicants do not pin each other down with determinate and stable predicates, unlike the case of Murdochian attentiveness. Rather, as I've noted above, the best cases of intersubjective communion are those in which the *look* of the other reveals to me my unformulability and unsignifiability, and so offers a corrective for any inauthentic modes of self-placement I may have adopted whereby I identify myself with some *thing* in the world, like a new car. It is only a nonloving or perverted

Sartrean stare that objectifies and so shames the other by reducing him to a *thing,* like an "ink pot on the table."[46]

The *Second Coming* provides an excellent example of this. As Alison Huger is treating Will Barrett's wounds after his fall into her greenhouse, the narrator comments, "It was no trouble handling him until he came to and looked at her. She could do anything if nobody watched her. But the moment a pair of eyes focused on her, she was a beetle stuck on a pin, arms and legs beating the air. There was no purchase. It was an impalement and a derailment." However, when Will does look at Allie for the first time, "Her back felt looks," but his "looks did not dart or pierce or impale. They did not control her. They were shyer than she and gave way before her, like the light touch of a child's hand in the dark."[47]

For Percy, while the other "can be objectized and relegated to the order of the stable configuration," this is a fundamental falsification of intersubjective community and of the being of the persons involved. Hence he says, "The look is of the order of pure intersubjectivity without the mediation of the symbol," and that what is revealed to me in "the *discovering* look of the other, is literally my *unspeakableness* (unformulability). To be taken for a nature, an ink pot, would be the purest happiness. No. I am exposed—as what? not as a something—as *nothing,* as that which unlike everything else in the world cannot be rendered *darstellbar.*"[48] In other words, what the other *discovers* and affirms about me, in the best cases of intersubjective communion, is my unsignifiability. So, my unsignifiability cannot be limited merely to my own subjective self-consciousness; it is affirmed and discovered by the look of the other. The difference, perhaps, is that while I am *necessarily* unspeakable to myself, it is merely possible that you recognize my unsignifiability, and this is what the best cases of human communion require. Why is this required? Because, for Percy, such appreciation of unsignifiability is authentically *just;* it gets at the truth of the matter about human beings. The truth is *not* that I *am* a "nothing" in the hypostasized Sartrean sense, but rather, as Percy says, "I am that which I cannot name. I am rather a person, a namer and a hearer of names."[49]

This last quotation raises a new response to my worry. Doesn't Percy simply object to codifying the human person in the same way that we codify beetles on pins or ink pots? Isn't he just pointing out the truth of the existentialist insight that the being of persons is qualitatively different than the being of things in the world? For he clearly thinks that *some* stable predicates or names apply to us, none of which is clearly predicable of nonhuman things. This list includes, for example, *namer, hearer of names, talker, symbol-mongerer, person,* and *child of God.*

This response is certainly on target. However, the problem is that these signifiers only isolate the sort of beings that humans are, and not the character traits or virtues that might be proper to such beings. As Percy himself notes, the realities of language, self-consciousness, and unsignifiability introduce for us "a concept of human nature and what is proper to it."[50] But the moment we begin *talking* about the excellences proper to such a being, where the excellences in question are stable character predicates like *generous, just,* or *charitable,* then it seems that we've contradicted Percy's claim that "the one thing in the world which by its very nature is not susceptible of a stable symbolic transformation is *myself!*"[51] The objection that the inability to give stable (or any) predication applies only to the first-personal perspective fails, for we have already noted that the truth discovered in ideal cases of second-personal "I-Thou" communion is, for Percy, the same. Appreciation of the "Thou," if it is *just,* does not assign virtue or vice as a stable disposition of character to the other ("Walker *is* generous"), but simply appreciates the kind of being that the other is: unnameable, a namer, a person, and so on. While we could predicate virtue of others, we *should not*, for such predication somehow limits or falsifies the unsignifiable being of the other.[52]

While this seems damaging enough, the problem also moves beyond mere speech and predication to the level of ontology. If, ontologically speaking, we are truly unsignifiable beings, then there appears to be a deep contradiction between the sort of beings that we are (unsusceptible of stable signification) and what the virtues of such a being would have to be, in order to count as virtues (relatively stable dispositions of character). If I *do* happen to have a virtue, an excellence that is a stable disposition of my character, then it runs ontologically counter to that unsignifiability that makes me anxious, aware of my freedom, and directed toward world, others, and God. In a very real sense, then, either virtue predication or virtue *possession* runs counter to that which makes me most deeply human. Put simply, if virtue *predication* limits or falsifies, then a fortiori (in Percy's economy) genuine virtue *possession* does so as well. Given unsignifiability, human beings cannot coherently possess virtues.

I have not discussed every aspect of Percy's thoughts on unsignifiability. So there may be some other promising way of reconciling it with both predication and possession of virtues that are proper to beings like us, such that our ecstatic orientation toward the world, others, and God is retained. At this point, however, I don't see how. Given the unsignifiable sort of beings that we are, it would seem that virtues either cannot or should not be predicated or possessed. However, surely we (and Percy) want to say that in the best cases of intersubjective appreciation, we can and should predicate stable virtue characteristics of others when they in fact possess them. Perhaps I am *in fact* generous, kind, cruel, or niggardly. A just appreciation, while not reducing my being as a person to those characteristics, should recognize that those character traits are *mine* and, in a real and stable sense, are truthful ontological characteristics of *me* as a whole person.

At the end of the day, perhaps we should charitably note that Percy himself humbly called his anthropological theory "nothing more than a few trails blazed through a dark wood, most dead-ended. I should consider it worthwhile even if it established no more than that there is such a wood—for not even that much is known now—and that it is very dark indeed."[53] Percy's trailblazing, even if not systematically coherent, remains a rich storehouse of reflection on what it is to be truly human amid the ruins of post-Cartesian modernity.

In this chapter I have tried to articulate Percy's critique of our current cultural anthropology together with his formulation of a new "theory of man" from the empirical starting point of human language. I have tried to show that Percy's account—including the sociality of consciousness, self-unsignifiability, anxiety, and intersubjective communion—offers substantial resources for reflection on the human virtues. His conjunction of the ontological joys of scientific and philosophical inquiry, on the one hand, and radical dependence, other-regard, and community, on the other, is a refreshing and rare combination. Indeed, this pairing forms a particularly apt prescription for our time in which, all too often, the activity of discovery in the sciences and the goods of interpersonal communities are seen as opposed at worst or irrelevant to one another at best. And although I have found some reasons to worry about whether we can genuinely predicate or possess such virtues, his critique of the modern malaise, articulation of the unavoidability of self-placement, and ability to pinpoint human teloi beyond the biological remain profoundly important achievements for our age of the lost self.

Notes

1. I must note here, as I do toward the end of this essay, that Percy himself never thought he had achieved a comprehensive anthropology. In the opening pages of *Message in the Bottle*, Percy's most mature anthropological text, he writes this overly humble yet revealing disclaimer: "It [his theory of man] . . . is nothing more than a few trails blazed through a dark wood, most dead-ended. I should consider it worthwhile even if it established no more than that there is such a wood—for not even that much is known now—and that it is very dark indeed." Walker Percy, "The Delta Factor," in *The Message in the Bottle: How Queer Man Is, How Queer Language Is, and What One Has to Do with the Other* (New York: Farrar, Straus, and Giroux, 1975), 10. Hereafter I will cite this work as *MB*, followed by article title and page number(s).

2. Walker Percy, "Is a Theory of Man Possible?" in *Signposts in a Strange Land*, ed. Patrick Samway, S.J. (New York: Farrar, Straus, and Giroux, 1991), 112–14. Subsequent references will be cited as *SP*, followed by the title of the article and page number.

3. *MB*, "The Delta Factor," 9, 20.

4. *SP*, "Theory of Man," 111–12. Clearly, what Percy refers to here as "the traditional Judeo-Christian teaching" is less Judeo-Christian than it is Hellenistic and Platonic. This may be due in part to Percy's (self-admitted) oversimplification of the categories, wherein on several occasions he lumps "Greek and Judeo-Christian teachings" together to represent the same anthropological view (ibid., 111, 113). As far as I can tell, however, Percy does not hold this extreme dualism to be the proper Christian position, as ample evidence throughout his novels and other writings makes clear (cf. his sacramental realism and emphasis on the unity of the "angel-beast" wayfaring person). In the context of some of these "traditional" comments, then, Percy appears to be referring to Descartes' "strange Janus monster," the anthropology that has the trappings of Christianity but is responsible for "the fateful rift," that "San Andreas Fault" between body and mind (*SP*, "Fateful Rift," 271). For Percy's more orthodox and Thomistic characterizations of "the Judeo-Christian tradition," which affirm human possession of a soul and our place "between the beasts and angels," see *MB*, "The Delta Factor," 18, 23–24. Cf. also Walker Percy, *Lost in the Cosmos: The Last Self-Help Book* (New York: Farrar, Straus, and Giroux, 1983), 208–12. Subsequent references will be cited as *LC*, followed by the page number.

5. Percy does not reject every aspect of each of these two theories. He comments that he scientifically "subscribes" to the "Darwinian naturalistic concept of man." Also, however, he theologically subscribes to the Judeo-Christian view that we have a soul. So Percy does indeed view the human person as an "intermediate

being," a synthesis or composite entity composed of elements like body and soul. *SP*, "Theory of Man," 113–15. Cf. also *SP*, "Rediscovering *A Canticle for Leibowitz*," 228. Cf. also Walker Percy, "An Interview with Walker Percy," interview by John C. Carr (*Georgia Review* 25 [Fall 1971]), in *Conversations with Walker Percy*, ed. Lewis A. Lawson and Victor A. Kramer (Jackson: University Press of Mississippi, 1985), 63–64. Also, note Percy's frequent fictional portrayals of the organic *unity* of the categories "angel" and "beast" as a return to the Edenic creational ideal, as in *Love in the Ruins*. In this novel the protagonist, Tom More, expresses his ideal for his psychiatric patients: "What if man could reenter paradise, so to speak, and live there as both man and spirit, whole and intact man-spirit, as solid flesh as a speckled trout, a dappled thing, yet aware of itself as a self!" Walker Percy, *Love in the Ruins* (New York: Dell, 1971), 35.

6. For instance, Percy says that "the source of the incoherence lies within science itself, as it is presently practiced, and the solution of the difficulty is not to be found in something extra scientific, not in the humanities or in religion, but within science itself. When I say science, I mean science in the root sense of the word, as the discovery and knowing of something which can be demonstrated and verified within a community" (*SP*, "Fateful Rift," 271–72). The sciences he has in mind include psychology, psychiatry, linguistics, developmental anthropology, and sociology. Cf. *SP*, "Fateful Rift," 272–73.

7. *MB*, "The Delta Factor," 9. Cf. also *MB*, "Symbol as Hermeneutic in Existentialism," 279.

8. *MB*, "The Delta Factor," 7; *SP*, "Theory of Man," 122.

9. *SP*, "Theory of Man," 118–20, 122.

10. *MB*, "The Message in the Bottle," 126. Cf. also *MB*, "Toward a Triadic Theory of Meaning," 161–62. Percy writes, "From the beginning and for the most of fifteen billion years of life in the Cosmos, there was only one kind of event. It was particles hitting particles, chemical reactions, energy exchanges, gravitational attractions between masses, field forces, and so on." The same dyadic exchange also characterizes all biological organism interactions on our planet. However, even those attempts by scientists to get chimpanzees involved in linguistic exchange with each other, or B. F. Skinner's stimulus-response experiments with rats and "symbolic communication" exercises with pigeons, are simply dyadic interactions, though more complex. *LC*, 85, 90, 92–94, 100. Cf. also *SP*, "Theory of Man," 120–21.

11. *LC*, 95, 98.

12. *MB*, "The Delta Factor," 29.

13. *SP*, "Naming and Being," 130–31.

14. *MB*, "Symbol as Hermeneutic in Existentialism," 283, and cf. "Symbol as Need" in *MB*, 288–97. For instance, Percy says that a "symbol is the vehicle for the

conception of an object . . . the vehicle by which we are able to speak and perhaps to think about something." *MB*, "Symbol as Hermeneutic in Existentialism," 280. The "perhaps" here may be important, for otherwise, Percy's view might implausibly preclude pre-triadic symbol-making children from cognizing anything as an object through some sort of pre-linguistic mental representation.

15. *MB*, "Symbol as Hermeneutic in Existentialism," 281; *SP*, "Naming and Being," 134; *MB*, "Symbol as Need," 296–97.

16. For Percy, such a "fixing" or "formulating" carries an inherent risk. In its ideal employment, the symbol or the name assigned to something brings about—for the namer—"a new orientation toward the world" whereby—in Heideggerian fashion—*being* itself is revealed or unveiled, discovered, and celebrated. However, the symbol or name may also ossify rather than unveil freshness of being: "the selfsame symbol which discloses being may be the means by which being is concealed and lost." In the case of the above example, if a wonderful bird is "known" and "named" as a "robin," eventually the wonderment of that creature is emptied out; it is relegated to the domain of the commonplace: that bird is *only* a robin. When such "words no longer signify," as Percy's fictional characters so often point out, freshness of being must be recovered through renewed deployment of symbols (*SP*, "Naming and Being," 134–35).

17. *MB*, "Symbol as Hermeneutic in Existentialism," 283. In his article "Is a Theory of Man Possible?" Percy puts it another way: "Semiotics would call attention to the strange position of the symbolizing self in the world which it discovers. In a word, the self can perceive, formulate, symbolize everything under the sun except itself. A self stands in the dead center of its universe, looking out. The paradox of consciousness is that the stranger we meet on the street and glance at for a second or two we see more clearly than we shall ever see ourselves." *SP*, "Theory of Man," 127. On anxiety in the face of the unnameable, see *MB*, "Symbol as Hermeneutic in Existentialism," 281.

18. *LC*, 106–7. Here Percy jumps directly from this unsignifiability into a description of fallen people in despair, "lost in the cosmos." Given his other texts and comments on the reality of unsignifiability as a creational aspect of human constitution, we must not interpret this text in *LC* to mean that the unnameability of the self is *only* a fallen predicament. Certainly for Percy, unsignifiability is a huge postlapsarian problem. However, the reality that "the being of the namer slips through the fingers of naming" is a creational reality, tied as it is to the very makeup of triadic consciousness and being. And it is this unsignifiability that forever binds human beings to the "flux of becoming." Hence human beings are, in Percy's view, always tied to the task of human becoming. Cf. *SP*, "Naming and Being," 136.

19. *MB*, "Symbol as Hermeneutic in Existentialism," 282.

20. *SP*, "Theory of Man," 127. Cf. *LC*, 109–10.

21. For a thorough treatment of the parallels between Kierkegaard's *The Concept of Anxiety* and Percy's project as a whole, see my unpublished Th.M. thesis, "At the Heart of Anthropology: Søren Kierkegaard and Walker Percy on the Nature and Shape of Creational Selfhood" (Regent College, 2007).

22. *SP*, "Naming and Being," 136–37.

23. Ibid., 135; *LC*, 108–9. For Kierkegaard's treatment of the "ambiguous" and yet revelatory character of "anxiety over nothing," see Søren Aabye Kierkegaard, *The Concept of Anxiety: A Simple Psychologically Orienting Deliberation on the Dogmatic Issue of Hereditary Sin*, trans. and ed. Reidar Thomte, in collaboration with Albert B. Anderson (Princeton, NJ: Princeton University Press, 1980), 41–45. Subsequent citations to this work will be given as *CA*.

24. *SP*, "The Coming Crisis in Psychiatry," 251–62. In this article Percy draws from Erich Fromm's *The Sane Society* (1955), in which Fromm argues that in humanity there exists a "pathology of normalcy," such that people who otherwise are considered "normal" by typical social standards are actually pathology ridden and desperately alienated from themselves.

25. Ibid., 252, 254–57. Note also the direct connection to Kierkegaard's comments in *CA*: "What effect does nothing have? It begets anxiety" (42). In addition, throughout "The Coming Crisis," Percy treats the loss of self or the "nothing" of the self and its estrangement from its own being as a result of a society that defines human beings as isolated subjects and organisms in environments. This, of course, would prevent us from interpreting anxiety as a constituent element of human nature, since it would turn out to be a predicament brought about by pathological cultural factors. However, in the midst of his attack on the present maladies of this age, Percy also makes it clear that anxiety points us to a "transcendence" or "incurable God-directedness" that is "in man's nature" and is no less than "the one distinguishing mark of human existence." Thus, even though (here and elsewhere) Percy argues against the cultural factors that bring about "the loss of the creature"—much in the same way that Kierkegaard takes issue with the loss of the individual in the Hegelian Christendom of Denmark—there is plentiful evidence that Percy views the creational self as *necessarily* marked by anxiety in light of semiotic unsignifiability, as I have demonstrated above. *SP*, "The Coming Crisis in Psychiatry," 260–61. For further evidence supporting this view, see *LC*, 109–11.

26. *LC*, 255. Elsewhere Percy speaks of anxiety as the agent of "a summons to authentic existence, to be heeded at any cost" (*SP*, "The Coming Crisis in Psychiatry," 259). In his supposition that anxiety is a mark of transcendence, Percy aligns quite explicitly with the existentialists, noting how they too "view man's plight . . . as the perennial condition of human existence, a condition necessarily entailed by man's freedom." In the context of these comments on anxiety, Percy further states that ex-

istentialists, theistic or atheistic, agree "that transcendence is the one distinguishing mark of human existence" that amounts to humanity's "incurable God-directedness."

27. Walker Percy, *The Second Coming* (New York: Farrar, Straus, and Giroux, 1980), 171–72. Subsequent citations to this work will be given as *SC*.

28. *SP*, "Theory of Man," 124; *MB*, "Symbol, Consciousness, and Intersubjectivity," 266, 268, 274. Although Percy affirms Mead's socially constructed consciousness, he argues that Mead's thesis fails precisely at the point at which he treats human beings as dyadic creatures engaged in stimulus-response behaviors.

29. *MB*, "Symbol as Hermeneutic in Existentialism," 282–83.

30. *LC*, 101. To avoid confusion, we must note here that for Percy the *presence* of another human being is not a necessary condition for the existence of symbolic and socially constructed consciousness. Percy's assertion that "all such triadic behavior is *social* in origin" (ibid., 96) is described in more detail in *MB*, "The Symbolic Structure of Interpersonal Process," 200, where he states, "The second person is required as an element not merely in the genetic event of learning language but as the *indispensable and enduring condition of all symbolic behavior.* The very act of symbolic formulation, whether it be language, logic, art, or even thinking, is of its very nature a formulation for a *someone else*. Even Robinson Crusoe, writing in his journal after twenty years on the island, is nevertheless performing a through-and-through social and intersubjective act."

31. *MB*, "Symbol, Consciousness, and Intersubjectivity," 270, 272.

32. This diagram is a combination of two that Percy draws up. *SP*, "Is a Theory of Man Possible?" 124; *MB*, "The Symbolic Structure of Interpersonal Process," 200.

33. *SP*, "Theory of Man," 127; *MB*, "Symbol as Hermeneutic in Existentialism," 285.

34. *SC*, 360.

35. *LC*, 109.

36. Ibid., 208, 211. A contrast between this Edenic C_1 self and the fallen C_2 self is helpful here: "A C_2 consciousness is a consciousness which passes through a C_1 stage and then for some reason falls into the pit of self. . . . In some evolving civilizations, for reasons which we don't entirely understand, the evolution of consciousness is attended by a disaster of some sort which occurs shortly after the Sy [symbolic] breakthrough. It has something to do with the discovery of the self and the incapacity to deal with it, the consciousness becoming self-conscious but not knowing what to do with the self, not even knowing what the self is, and so ending by being that which it is not, saying that which is not, doing that which is not, and making others what they are not. . . . A C_2 consciousness . . . looks out, sees, and symbolizes but has also become self-conscious. But the self is literally inconceivable—unlike a tree or a star or you, it cannot be conceived under the auspices of a symbol—and is referentially mobile." Ibid., 211–12.

37. Alasdair MacIntyre, *Dependent Rational Animals: Why Human Beings Need the Virtues* (Chicago: Open Court, 1999).

38. With MacIntyre, however, it is not clear *why* our dependence is supposed to issue from our commonality with other animals, since we appear to be far *more* dependent and fragile, in many ways, than they. Moreover, acknowledged animality does not always lead to acknowledged dependence, as is clear in Aristotle, whose thoroughgoing acknowledgment of animality is quite compatible with an ethics that elevates human self-sufficiency.

39. For the best description of Percy's "fall," see *LC*, 107–9. For intersubjective exposure of inauthenticity, see *MB*, "Symbol as Hermeneutic in Existentialism," 285.

40. *SP*, "Stoicism in the South," 83–89.

41. The obvious legitimacy of this critique of Nietzsche is perhaps less obvious in the case of Aristotle, for whom self-sufficiency figures less prominently in ethics than it does in the Stoics, for example. Here MacIntyre helpfully notes how it is that Aristotle throws up barriers to understanding human fragility and dependency: (1) in his ethical and political inquiry he systematically refrains from consulting women, slaves, and laborers ("for whom the facts of affliction and dependence are most likely to be undeniable"); (2) he says that manliness entails not wanting others to share our grief; and (3) that the magnanimous man likes to confer benefits, as this is the mark of a superior person, but does not like to acknowledge benefits received. All of these deficits appear to stem from Aristotle's preoccupation with self-sufficiency. MacIntyre, *Dependent Rational Animals*, 6.

42. *SC*, 360.

43. Iris Murdoch, "The Idea of Perfection," in *The Sovereignty of Good* (London: Routledge, 2001), 16–17.

44. This is of course only the traditional view. In the contemporary virtue ethics literature, a number of views affirm the "modularity" of virtues, that is, that they are limited to contexts and domains with which their possessor has adequate life experience. If I possess the virtue of courage on the battlefield, I may lack that virtue when suddenly faced with the realities of becoming a father for the first time. Much of the literature pursuing this treatment of virtue must, of course, either deny or mitigate the traditional thesis of the unity of the virtues. As far as Percy is concerned, it does not ultimately matter whether we take the traditional mutual entailment view or go with a modular view of virtues. For either approach requires predicating a stable virtue of a person; it is only the scope of the predicate domain that is different.

45. *LC*, 106–7 (for the phrase *"to itself,"* emphasis is mine).

46. *MB*, "Symbol as Hermeneutic in Existentialism," 284–85.

47. *SC*, 233, 236.

48. *MB*, "Symbol as Hermeneutic in Existentialism," 286 (my emphasis on the word "discovering").

49. *SP*, "Naming and Being," 136–37.

50. *SP*, "The Coming Crisis in Psychiatry," 257.

51. *MB*, "Symbol as Hermeneutic in Existentialism," 283.

52. Percy's worry appears to be the reductive character of such a predication. Saying that "Walker Percy *is* generous" seems to amount, in his view, to a kind of wholesale identity claim. So perhaps Percy's view is that for any predicate P assigned to any given person S (including the predicate "nothing"), it is not the case that $P = S$ in the sense of *exhaustively* capturing S's identity. But why does Percy worry about this? The copula *is* doesn't perform this hypostasizing function in the case of anything else, so why should it in the case of persons? When I say, "That *is* a robin," there is always the danger of reductively and absurdly claiming "That is *only* a robin." But of course a robin is also a bird, a winged creature, a mother (in some cases), and *Turdus migratorius*. In the case of persons, the claim that "Walker *is* generous" is perfectly compatible with the claim that "Walker *is* kind" or "Walker *is* witty," and so on. We're simply adding noncontradictory predications to the original one.

53. *MB*, "The Delta Factor," 10.

Confessing the Horrors of Radical Individualism in *Lancelot*

Percy, Dostoyevsky, Poe

Farrell O'Gorman

Lancelot is Percy's richest and most challenging novel. It is challenging because its narrator is so beguiling and intelligent, so clearly right about many of the shortcomings of his society, and yet at the same time deadly wrong. To a degree the same might be said of Percy's two other first-person narrators, Binx Bolling and Tom More. But by comparison with either, Lance Lamar is at once more seemingly sure of himself and more extravagantly flawed. At the same time, his tale ends more cryptically, lacking the brief but hopeful family interludes that close *The Moviegoer, Love in the Ruins,* and *The Thanatos Syndrome* alike. *The Last Gentleman* is the only one of Percy's fictions to end anywhere near as ambiguously as *Lancelot*, but this effect is greatly heightened in the latter novel by the obviously problematic nature of its narrator.

Properly understanding that narrator depends upon properly understanding *Lancelot*'s particular genre, which is likewise the key to understanding its fundamental concern with the pervasive influence of radical individualism in the late modern West. Furthermore, the richness of *Lancelot* might be viewed as a subtle function of—or better yet, response to—that concern. For this is the most substantively allusive of Percy's novels, written as if to highlight T. S. Eliot's argument in "Tradition and the Individual Talent" that great works of literature, like individual human beings, necessarily come into being only in relationship to a constellation of predecessors.

As Percy himself put it, the "strange paradox about writing novels" is "simply this: there's no occupation in the universe that is lonelier and that at the same time depends more radically on a community, a commonwealth of other writers."[1] *Lancelot* is written in such a way as to intentionally highlight such relationship, despite the fact that the literary works to which it alludes are generally concerned with the plight of the isolated and alienated individual. My claim here is arguably true of the Arthurian legends' accounts of the fallen Lancelot himself (though the written accounts of such legends vary widely). It is inarguably true of the many works of modern literature alluded to in the novel, the Shakespearean play whose protagonist is often deemed the first modern man—*Hamlet*—being one of the most subtly pervasive examples.[2] Here I am concerned only with identifying the most crucial of those works.

I will argue that *Lancelot* is best understood as a problematically "confessional" and Gothic novel that is most fruitfully read in relation to two distinct sources: one a short novel, Fyodor Dostoyevsky's *Notes from Underground,* and the other a broad tradition of Anglo-American Gothic fiction particularly well represented in the work of Edgar Allan Poe. Percy's general indebtedness to Dostoyevsky is well documented, and *Notes from Underground* was the one novel by the Russian master that he chose to teach in his Literature of Alienation seminar, but its startlingly close relationship to *Lancelot* in particular has never been explored.[3] Both *Notes* and *Lancelot* were created by authors who embrace traditional Christianity but utilize obsessive and intentionally offensive post-Christian narrators who simultaneously critique and personify what the authors see as the horrors of the radical individualism engendered by modernity.[4] *Notes* was not only the first of Dostoyevsky's great Christian novels, but also the first to show subtle signs of his familiarity with the Anglo-American Gothic "tale of terror."[5] Indeed, the Russian novelist particularly admired the Gothic fiction of his American near contemporary Poe, whose name is quite conspicuously inserted into the text of *Lancelot*—a novel which upon publication was immediately recognized as being so indebted to Poe as to openly invite the subtitle "The Fall of the House of Lamar," after Poe's famous story "The Fall of the House of Usher."[6] In the second part of this essay I will examine Poe and the Anglo-American Gothic tradition at length, arguing that understanding it is crucial to understanding *Lancelot*. But I begin with Dostoyevsky because his moral perspective with regard to the unnamed narrator of *Notes* fundamentally resembles that of Percy with regard to Lance. That perspective is clearly rooted in an ancient Christian tradition that predates—and is in some respects only problematically related to—the literature of the United States.

Notes from Underground: Confessing from the "Mousehole" of Modernity

> In general, I could never stand saying "Sorry, Papa, I'll never do it again."
> —Fyodor Dostoyevsky's Underground Man, *Notes from Underground*

What Percy most admired about *Notes from Underground* "was Dostoyevsky's weaving of cultural criticism with his fictional characterization of a man in extremis."[7] He read the novel repeatedly throughout his life, and its influence was noticeable as early as *The Moviegoer*. One contemporary reviewer, Brainard Cheney, correctly emphasized that both novels are narrated by individuals who identify and sense the limitations of "scientific humanism" even though they themselves, to varying degrees, remain trapped within those limitations.[8]

This broad observation is only strengthened when one notes the differences in the specific cultural circumstances in which the two men wrote. Dostoyevsky lived a century and a hemisphere away from Percy. During his early association with the Petrashevsky Circle, a group of intellectuals attracted to the utopian socialism of Charles Fourier and to Western European liberalism generally, Dostoyevsky wrote his first novel, *Poor Folk*, as a reformer with seemingly clear political intent. But he soon took a radically different course. After his 1849 arrest by tsarist authorities and subsequent imprisonment in Siberia, Dostoyevsky reclaimed his inherited Orthodox faith and mounted a vehement critique of modern Western ideologies in his major novels *Crime and Punishment, The Idiot, The Possessed,* and *The Brothers Karamazov*. *Notes from Underground*, published in 1864, "initiates the exploration of human separation from God" that dominates these mature works." Furthermore, *Notes* arguably remains Dostoyevsky's "most profound statement of the human need for Christ."[9]

That statement is far from explicit. The text is in the form of a journal that the narrator claims will never be published but that nonetheless addresses—and insults—the reader at length. Most of the first part of *Notes* reads as if it were straightforward polemic against the scientism and utopianism current among the narrator's educated contemporaries, but the second moves inevitably toward a resentful and half-retracted "confession" of the narrator's own general loathsomeness—and of his horrific abuse of a fallen woman who finally offers him love. *Notes* generally resembles *Lancelot* in these respects and also in that the text itself masquerades as a dialogue with the reader (in *Lancelot* Percival doubles for the reader, to a degree) yet is on the most obvious level a monologue—that is, the narrator is speaking primarily to himself. Other important parallels are clear from the beginning. *Lancelot* opens in a cell with a notably limited view, a hospital room wherein the narrator has previously been visited only by noxious therapeutic experts; likewise, the first part of *Notes from Underground* is pointedly titled "The Mousehole," in which the narrator expounds at length from his cramped apartment on his sensation of being "walled in" by theories current in St. Petersburg, the most Western of Russian cities and also "the most abstract and premeditated city on earth."[10] Hostile to the virtual worship of science and medicine current among his peers, he begins by stating, "I'm a sick man," a self-diagnosis that soon seems plausible enough—except for the fact that he immediately qualifies it with a mockingly reductive assertion: "I think there's something wrong with my liver." Yet both out of a desire to declare his independence and "out of spite," the narrator refuses "to ask for the doctors' help. So my liver hurts? Good, let it hurt even more!" (84–85). The reader of *Notes* therefore has the immediate sensation of being locked in a small room with an intelligent but also angry and destructively self-reliant theoretician, as is the case in *Lancelot*.

Lance Lamar, too, is "sick," though Percy—who knew the limitations as well as the promise of twentieth-century medicine—would prescribe him no simple course of therapy. Rather, he recognized the complex dynamic between his flawed protagonist and a flawed culture, the same dynamic that shaped *Notes*, in which the narrator "is not only a moral-psychological type whose egoism Dostoyevsky wishes to expose; he is also a social-ideological one, whose psychology must be seen as intimately connected with the ideas he accepts and by which he tries to live."[11] Accordingly, the Underground Man's egoism must be understood in relation to his longtime immersion in the twin currents of rationalism and romanticism emanating from Western Europe in the wake of the Enlightenment—currents he now longs to escape, though he ultimately finds himself unable to do so alone. His narrative is therefore neatly divided into part 1, which forthrightly attacks the reductive excuses for "metaphysics and ethics" current in Russian intellectual circles and the "rational egoism" of the utopian Nikolai Chernyshevsky in particular, and part 2, which recalls the narrator's life in St. Petersburg in the 1840s even as it satirizes that era's "sentimental Social Romanticism"— a romanticism that allegedly cultivated "a sense of spiritual noblesse" and "emphasis on *individual* moral responsibility" on behalf of the oppressed, but is revealed in *Notes* to be essentially "egoistic" in that it encourages its practitioner to see himself as a godlike savior.[12] The common source of these two currents, then, is egoism: the solitary self, whether by thinking or by feeling, becomes the focal point of existence, the sole arbiter of what is moral and indeed of what is real. The irony that the Underground Man becomes keenly aware of is that a narrowly empiricist reason may convince the self that it does not even exist, or at least that it is not free, and that unchecked romanticism inevitably leads the self to an entrapping solipsism.

Lance is caught in these twin currents as well. He habitually attempts to maintain some control over the narrative of his life by posturing as a detached and hyperrational scientist or detective. This habit is clearly exemplified in his early desire to explain all sexual activity as merely a matter of "the touch of one membrane against another," of "molecules encountering molecules and little bursts of electrons along tiny nerves—no different in kind" from those involved in houseflies scrubbing their wings (*Lancelot* 17, 89). Yet Lance is simultaneously prone to a self-glorifying and isolating romanticism. That romanticism is inherently bound up with the utopian vision manifested both in his formerly progressive politics (his 1960s roughly correspond to the Underground Man's 1840s) and in his current fixation on founding his own postapocalyptic Camelot in the Shenandoah Valley.

I will explore these characteristics of Lance below in relation to Percy's specifically Anglo-American milieu and to Poe. But it is important to stress now that while Poe also wrote "confessional" narratives of a sort, he, unlike Dostoyevsky and Percy, steadfastly conceived of literature as essentially amoral—as concerned primarily with "Beauty," not with "Truth."[13] To say that Dostoyevsky differs from Poe in this regard is not to say that the Russian writer's work is merely didactic, of course; without discounting Dostoyevsky's clear Christian commitment, Mikhail Bakhtin has famously analyzed the complex "polyphony" of voices present in his novels.[14] A general understanding of how those voices function in *Notes from Underground* is essential to understanding the model of confession Percy ultimately draws on in *Lancelot*.

Dostoyevsky had in fact considered giving the novel that became *Notes* the title *Confessions,* intending it in part as a satirical response to Rousseau's self-celebrating autobiography of the same name. But when Dostoyevsky's novel is read in relation to the larger European literary tradition, it is also properly seen as akin to a much older and quite different *Confessions:* his Underground Man is finally "a composite of Rousseau and Augustine, a Rousseauvian narrator struggling mightily to escape from the trap of Rousseauvian form—with its implicit values—and to gain the high ground of the Augustinian confession that would make him whole."[15] Such confession would, of course, ultimately have to be directed to God and to recognize not only specific individual sins but also original sin. The Underground Man's bondage to original sin is arguably the deepest source of his sense of being entrapped or enclosed, but his own "secular, rational world view will not allow him to identify this as the root cause of his crisis" and so he constantly remains tempted to refer to "it as a disease, using the clichés of medicine, which, together with the other sciences, usurped religion in the 1860s."[16]

Accordingly, the Underground Man never enters into explicitly Christian confession in the text itself. He resembles Lance in that and in that finally "in spite of himself he bears the potential for religious salvation; it lies in his refusal to accept a cheap version of reality, one in which salvation can be gained through mere human activity in an exclusively material world or through empty Romantic dreaming."[17] That refusal is intriguingly grounded by the Underground Man in his closing paragraph. Having recounted his affair with and cruel emotional abuse of the prostitute Liza, he attempts to steer clear of overt remorse for his own actions and return to the mode of general theorizing that he favored in part 1. But his own developing thoughts begin to indict his previous embodied actions: "Why, today we don't even know where real life is, what it is, or what it's called!" he exclaims. "We even find it painful to be men—real men of flesh and blood, with *our own private bodies;* we're ashamed of it, and we long to turn ourselves into something hypothetical called the average man. . . . Soon we'll invent a way to be begotten by ideas altogether" (195). The narrator has earlier critiqued a reductive materialism that ultimately explains away human identity, but here he begins to intuit that the body—not merely the mind or spirit—may in fact be a proper key to approaching the real.

The narrator begins to intuit, in other words, the traditional Christian anthropology that Dostoyevsky ultimately shared with Percy. It is worth noting, however, that these final lines can also be read in historical context as Dostoyevsky's implication "that the only hope" for the narrator and his contemporary readers is to reject all "bookish, foreign, artificial Western ideologies, and to return to the Russian 'soil' with its spontaneous incorporation of the Christian ideal of unselfish love." The issue for Dostoyevsky, in other words, was not only modernity's pernicious influence on Christianity; it was godless theoretical Europe's pernicious influence on holy peasant Russia. Dostoyevsky's tendencies toward "Slavophile messianism" likely strike the contemporary reader as either a laughably quaint or a disturbingly nationalistic feature of his particular version of Orthodox faith.[18] What is most important for our purposes is to note that Percy finally saw no such solution for Lance within his own national mythos, no quintessentially American embodiment of "the Christian ideal of unselfish love." Yet for Percy, too, the body—if not any particular soil—was somehow essential both to apprehending the real and undermining the ideology of radical individualism. In order to fully understand this claim, we must consider *Lancelot* in relation to the Anglo-American Gothic tradition.

Poe's Legacy: Individualism and the Gothic Tradition

> The thousand injuries of Fortunato I had borne as best I could, but when he ventured upon insult I vowed revenge.
> —Edgar Allan Poe, "The Cask of Amontillado"

Gothic literature is defined most broadly as the literature of terror or horror, often featuring supernatural or apparently supernatural events. It is most famously exemplified by nineteenth-century fictions such as *Frankenstein, Dracula,* and the tales of Poe. For some readers, to be sure, such fictions may seem excessively fantastical, melodramatic, or sensationalistic. Most of Percy's fiction does not fit into this mold. But *Lancelot* does, insistently so, as it features an imprisoned and mentally unstable criminal narrator, graphic scenes of orgiastic sex and violence, and even some seeming elements of the supernatural in the extended hallucinatory sequences leading up to the climactic explosion of the Lamar mansion. In crafting such a narrative, Percy was well aware that his native region had fostered the long-established genre (if not cliché) of "Southern Gothic" literature, generally characterized by "grotesque characters, explorations of abnormal psychological states, dark humor, and a sense of alienation or futility." Indeed, in some respects *Lancelot* almost perfectly exemplifies a distinctly upper-class mode of the Southern Gothic, resembling works such as William Faulkner's *The Sound and the Fury* and Tennessee Williams's *A Streetcar Named Desire* insofar as it features the legacy of a "patriarchal plantation aristocracy, built upon and haunted by a racist ethic, besieged by civilization and democracy, and ultimately defeated as much by its own intransigence as by external forces."[19]

Yet Percy would balk at the categorization of *Lancelot* as merely a Southern Gothic fiction, and rightly so.[20] He followed Dostoyevsky's model once again insofar as he intuited how his predecessor had "transformed the thematic and scenic commonplaces" of the Gothic so that they posed more profound "metaphysical riddles"; both authors ultimately revised a popular and potentially only titillating genre so as to demonstrate how "the language of the Gothic novel and its themes," if given a "strong moral cast," can offer "a powerful rhetoric for describing modern man's predicament."[21] Dostoyevsky aside, however, *Lancelot* is indeed properly read as responding to a peculiarly Anglo-American Gothic tradition—not necessarily a "Southern" one—that had its roots in an eighteenth-century British culture wherein hopes and anxieties regarding modernity often took shape in relation to the Roman Catholic past. This British tradition was communicated to Percy largely through the work of Poe, whose American revisions of it he in a sense completed, becoming a forthright Catholic critic of some of the fruits of the modern individualism that the earliest British Gothic fictions had implicitly touted.

Such dimensions of the Gothic have not always been fully appreciated. But prominent scholars have begun to reread the early British Gothic with regard to religion in ways that also illuminate the Anglo-American Gothic. Diane Long Hoeveler explains why the genre originated precisely in the late eighteenth century: "The killing of Catholicism in England took more than two hundred years, and the gothic charts that murder in all its convoluted moves. Killing the king becomes in the gothic the killing of a corrupt duke or monk, while the rationality so highly prized by Protestant individualism and Enlightenment ideology moves to center stage, creating a new cultural ideal that chastised idolatry, superstition, hierarchy, and popery in all its forms." This new cultural ideal was envisioned as essentially bodiless, representing "Enlightenment beliefs in the self as unitary, reasonable, and located somewhere above and beyond the body," but also was figured as "capitalist" and "male"—that is, autonomous and unfettered.[22]

The British Gothic, then, came into being at a time when a modern England that increasingly valued a self-reliant and essentially disembodied but figuratively masculine rationality sought in effect to exorcise its Catholic past—as manifested in prototypical Gothic novels such as Horace Walpole's *The Castle of Otranto* (1764) and Matthew Lewis's *The Monk* (1796), which are set in medieval Italy and in Spain, respectively. Such titles alone suggest the tendency of first English and then Anglo-American culture to associate Catholicism with threatening enclosures.[23] If the Reformation and Enlightenment had offered enterprising Anglo-American individuals apparent liberation from the medieval past—room to breathe in, open space—then Catholicism might seem to threaten to lock them back up: in castles and cathedrals, monasteries and abbeys, dungeons and confessional booths—figurative coffins all.

Among major American antebellum writers, Poe most obviously played on such stock Gothic images, which seemed safe reading to most early U.S. citizens: like the radical Calvinists who had originally settled New England, they could believe or at least hope that such evils properly belonged on the other side of the Atlantic, not in their new Canaan. Accordingly, Poe's "The Masque of the Red Death" is a tale of moral and bodily corruption that features doomed aristocrats who lock themselves up in order to avoid a bloody plague that is killing their subjects—and the setting is not Poe's own U.S. Atlantic seaboard, but rather an abbey conjured up out of the medieval past, an abbey wherein Death himself wears priestly vestments. In "The Black Cat," the narrator kills his wife and walls her corpse up in a cellar "as the monks of the middle ages are recorded to have walled up their victims" (354). In "The Pit and the Pendulum," a victim of the Spanish Inquisition is cast into a tomblike dungeon where he is bound by a "surcingle" (a belt for a clerical cassock) and subjected to "monkish ingenuity in torture." On the walls of his hellish cell he sees painted "all the hideous and repulsive devices to which the charnel superstition of the monks has given rise" (310–11).

The word *charnel* generally refers to a house filled with dead bodies, but it is closely related to the word *carnal,* having to do with the flesh. And this narrator, like so many of Poe's narrators, would finally like to believe that death and perhaps even the corruptible body itself are mere superstitions, figments of the imagination. Accordingly, these would-be disembodied intellects attempt to remove all reminders of the flesh from their field of vision. As we have seen, Hoeveler maintains that such idealization of the disembodied intellect flourished in eighteenth-century England, but conditions existed for it to take even more radical form in the early United States. Alexis de Tocqueville famously characterized early American individualism as inadvertently following the model of Descartes, whose *"cogito ergo sum"* initiated or at least concisely exemplified a major shift in Western thought. It did so not only by clearly valuing isolated individual thought over engagement with community and tradition, but also by equating the individual self with the mind at the expense of the body. As Percy often remarked, such an equation, along with the Cartesian glorification of technology, left the self a mere theorizing ghost in a seemingly mechanistic cosmos—a potentially desperate ghost, one constantly tempted to reassert the reality of its existence via bestial violence or sex.[24]

It is just such violence (though not, significantly, such sex) that will ultimately bring us back to Poe. Philosopher Stanley Cavell has convincingly described both Poe and his contemporary Ralph Waldo Emerson as "odd" but nonetheless somehow legitimate literary and philosophical descendants of Descartes. His case in point with regard to Emerson is the essay "Self-Reliance," a source of well-known exhortations to individualism: for example, "Society everywhere is in conspiracy against the manhood of every one of its members"; "Whoso would be a man must be a nonconformist"; and "Nothing is at last sacred but the integrity of your own mind." Less quotable but striking nonetheless is Emerson's extended assertion, "The nonchalance of boys who are sure of dinner . . . is the healthy attitude of human nature." Emerson's choice of the boy as the "healthy" human being, the "healthy" American, is in keeping with R. W. B. Lewis's classic observation that mid-nineteenth-century American authors developed a literary mythology of the authentic American as a figure of heroic innocence, alone in a new world at the beginning of history—the American Adam. This is a version of Adam before the Fall, and, crucially, of Adam before Eve, a solitary male in a U.S. wilderness figured in the post-Puritan imagination less as a new Canaan than as a new Eden.[25] This, then, is one long-standing vision of what it means to be an American: to be like Adam in the Garden, thinking for oneself without the apparent restraints of tradition or community or family, maybe even without the complications of the body—certainly of the female body. And if Cavell is right, we can draw a line connecting Descartes to Emerson's optimistic equation of ideal American identity with such youthful self-reliant masculinity.

And then—by contrast—we have Poe. Cavell writes: "The sound of Poe's prose, of its incessant and perverse brilliance, is uncannily like the sound of philosophy as established in Descartes," as Descartes himself has "the air of a mad diarist" in works such as his *Meditations*. Yet finally Poe's prose reads as if it "were a parody of [Cartesian] philosophy." So it is that in Poe's many confessional tales, the self-absorbed narrator generally begins as if he is searching "for a proof of his existence," for "a proof . . . that he is alive."[26]

And he does so by killing other people.

This is essentially what happens in "The Tell-Tale Heart," one of Poe's most chilling stories. Here the imprisoned narrator explains how he murdered an old man who shared his house. Strictly speaking, this is not a confession in the legal sense—let alone the Augustinian sense!—for the narrator has already admitted his crime. He speaks because, bizarrely, he wants to establish his sanity as he explains just how methodically, just how rationally he planned and carried out the murder. He supplies only one motive: the old man's diseased eye disturbed him. Why? Because, a close reading of the text reveals, the old man's deteriorating body reminded the narrator of his own embodiment and mortality. As is often the case in Poe's fiction, the two characters are clearly doppelgangers, or at least one sees the other as a reflection of some aspect of himself. Accordingly, the narrator has also imagined that his victim's eye, though diseased, was in fact as powerful as a microscope—just as he emphasizes his own powers of observation in describing his meticulous preparation for the murder, observing the old man nightly by means of a single ray of light from a lantern, focusing on the eye like a surgeon so that the old man himself seems almost to disappear even before the act is committed. Lance Lamar practices a similar scientific detachment and focus before acting out in violence. This pattern begins with his comparison of discovering his daughter's aberrant blood type to an astronomer's analysis of telescopic photography and culminates with the filming of his wife's adultery, which he carefully arranges in the second half of the novel.

"The Tell-Tale Heart" is characteristic of much of Poe's fiction in its isolated, self-absorbed narrator, who seeks to attain the position of an all-transcending intellect by removing the human body from his field of vision, who asserts a kind of hyperrationalism that is inherently bound up with his murderous impulses, and who practices the kind of perverse science openly decried in Poe's poem "Sonnet—to Science," wherein the speaker complains to a personified Science that it "alterest all things with thy peering eyes." He then asks Science accusingly: "Why preyest thou thus upon the poet's heart? Vulture! Whose wings are dull realities" (21). This speaker, then, fears that modern science has claimed a monopoly on explaining reality—presenting us, for example, with the hard cold fact that human bodies are ultimately corpses—and believes that the poet's duty is to create an escape from that reality into the realm of imagination. Both of these traits are characteristic of Poe's romantic milieu and are undergirded by modern assumptions about art, knowledge, and human identity that are not shared by Percy or earlier Catholic artists such as Dante, but that are ultimately relevant to understanding *Lancelot* as well as Poe.

Certainly those assumptions support the tendency of so many of Poe's characters to wish to remove reminders of embodiment from their fields of vision. Generally, those reminders are other human beings; frequently, they are female. In this regard we should finally consider Roderick Usher, who buries his cataleptic twin sister alive in "The Fall of the House of Usher." In doing so Roderick, a hypochondriac intellectual who resolutely avoids all sensual experience, seeks to reject the seemingly "feminine" fate of being enclosed—of dwelling in, and being born via, a bloody body that must inevitably die. He also has some reason to fear science, or at least what is being done to humanity in the name of science. He buries his sister in a vault beneath the ancestral family manor because if he buries her outdoors she will likely be dug up by grave robbers collecting cadavers for medical schools—grave robbers who in Poe's time went by the grim name of "resurrection men," perhaps revealing an increasing fear in the modern West that this is the only kind of resurrection in store for humanity.

All of Poe's fiction is profoundly shaped by the fact that "the medieval idea of the *homo toto*, the whole and indissoluble man, [had been] supplanted during the Enlightenment by the concept of a self that divided at death."[27] Accordingly the house of Usher itself, which strangely resembles a human head, has a pronounced fissure running down its middle—reminiscent of Descartes' mind-body split, corresponding here to the Roderick-Madeline split. This fissure causes the entire structure to collapse at the end of the story, prefiguring the fate of the Lamar house in *Lancelot*. In this regard it is highly significant that the supposedly "feudal" Usher manor has been identified by many critics as suggestive of a "Gothic" plantation house in Poe's native Virginia, and that Roderick Usher bears some resemblance not only to John Randolph of Roanoke but also—in Allen Tate's estimation—to Thomas Jefferson of Monticello.[28]

Tate's reading of Poe is particularly important because it directly influenced Percy, whom he mentored to a degree. But before turning to it I should close my consideration of Poe by again emphasizing the prevalence of dead women in his work—another point of kinship with *Lancelot*, which features the deaths of Lance's first wife, Lucy, his mother, and most crucially Margot. Poe famously wrote in "The Philosophy of Composition" that "the death of a beautiful woman is, unquestionably, the most poetical topic in the world" (680). He might seem to be in excellent company here: Dante and Petrarch wrote about dead women, after all. But in the *Divine Comedy*, Dante's beloved Beatrice—whose voice opens *Lancelot* via the novel's epigraph from *Purgatorio*—is not, of course, merely dead. A member of the communion of saints, she is Dante's active guide to Paradise, where they will ultimately be reunited in company with others in worship of God in body as well as soul. Compare this with the bleak vision of Poe's most famous poem, "The Raven," wherein the lonely male speaker sits mourning the death of his beloved Lenore. He finally, passionately, asks the dark bird that has flown in his window whether or not in some afterlife he will "'clasp a sainted maiden whom the angels name Lenore, / Clasp a rare and radiant maiden whom the angels name Lenore ?' / Quoth the raven, 'Nevermore'" (57).

Here even the speaker's query is deeply perverse, because he knows in advance how it will be answered: "Nevermore" is the only word the bird has uttered all night. And the fundamental *No* that ends this poem could not be more different from the *Yes* that ends *Lancelot*. But we can better understand the subtly affirmative nature of Percy's novel by reading it with Poe's *No,* and his rendering of the Anglo-American Gothic, in mind.

Beyond Individualism: Detecting the Real in *Lancelot*

While the moral shortcomings of Dostoyevsky's confessional narrator in *Notes* are clearly understood when juxtaposed with the author's professed Christian conviction, Poe offers no explicit or implicit moral position from which his protagonists and confessional narrators might be judged (though their frequent criminal insanity is self-evident enough). Even the presumed hero of "The Purloined Letter," the ratiocinative French detective C. Auguste Dupin, bears a striking moral resemblance to the villain whom he finally apprehends. So how is it that Percy—who once described himself to his early mentor Caroline Gordon as inclined to be at least as much "a moralist or propagandist" as he was a novelist—found himself prepared to draw on the morally ambiguous fictions of Poe so profitably in *Lancelot*?[29] He did so in large part via the critical essays of Gordon's husband, the prominent poet and critic Allen Tate.

It was from Tate, that is, that Percy learned to read Poe in the manner I have attempted above, looking beneath the surfaces of his fiction to see how on the most profound level it breaks with the earlier British Gothic model as it chillingly exemplifies the pathology of Cartesian thought and concomitant radical individualism. Tate's provocatively paired essays "The Angelic Imagination: Poe as God" and "The Symbolic Imagination: The Mirrors of Dante" make this point directly and at length.[30] Furthermore, Tate—a 1950 convert to Catholicism who had earlier been one the most prominent of the Vanderbilt Agrarians—helped Percy to see such Cartesian individualism as inherent in his own national and regional milieu. "The Angelic Imagination," which equates the term *angel* with disembodied intellect, briefly describes Poe's antebellum Virginia as "a society committed to the rationalism of Descartes and Locke by that eminent angel of the rationalistic Enlightenment, Thomas Jefferson" (416). Poe's regional identity is also the primary subject of the essay "Our Cousin, Mr. Poe," wherein Tate describes the Richmond native as "a gentleman and a Southerner" whose protagonists are generally "hyperaesthetic egoist[s]," "dehumanized" men who seem to be mere "machines of sensation and will," men whose violent betrayals of their own bodies and their human kin alike would, in Dante's schema, merit "neither Purgatory nor Heaven; and only two stations in Hell" (389, 395). Tate, then, generally disparages Poe's legacy. But as a southern writer of gentlemanly extraction himself, he has a horrified fascination with it: "I confess that his voice is so near to mine that I recoil a little, lest he, Montresor, lead me into the cellar, address me as Fortunato, and wall me up alive" (400). Such self-analysis underlies one of Tate's later essays that helped Percy—as he wrote in a letter to Tate—to understand a certain sort of Confederate romanticizing as strangely bound up with "the narcissism-solipsism of the modern intellectual," a connection he had previously sensed but not fully grasped.[31] That essay, "Narcissus as Narcissus," begins with brief reference to Poe but is in fact Tate's explication of his own poem "Ode to the Confederate Dead"—itself mentioned by Lance in *Lancelot* (47).

In the novel, Lance Lamar's dead father—whose figurative ghost still haunts Lance—most obviously embodies the sort of self-isolating romanticism mentioned in Percy's correspondence with Tate. But all of the foregoing discussion prepares us to understand the horrific character of Lance Lamar as we examine the novel directly in light of Poe and the Anglo-American Gothic tradition, albeit with two qualifications. First, Percy much more directly than Poe ultimately writes of a radical individualism rooted in specifically American contexts. He does so by making Lance not only a somewhat "foreign" Gothic aristocrat but, more profoundly, a modern scientist-detective and finally a violently self-reliant frontiersman—the American Adam with a bowie knife. Second, Dostoyevsky, not Poe, is Percy's ultimate model in writing this problematically "confessional" novel that indirectly diagnoses the true illnesses of his society—though Percy's subtle Catholic prescription, unlike Dostoyevsky's implicit Russian Orthodox one, lacks reductive nationalistic or ethnic undertones. The Eucharist that figures in the final pages of *Lancelot* offers, in the view of Percival and Percy alike, a potential vision and taste of the real and of true community—a vision and taste that Lance has failed to attain throughout the novel, a vision and taste necessarily grounded in the body.

In what sense, then, does the novel read like a Gothic fiction? Poe is both explicitly mentioned and indirectly alluded to throughout *Lancelot*. This first-person narrative opens, like "The Tell-Tale Heart," with a violent man locked in a cell, a man not entirely sure whether he has committed a crime or been diagnosed with a mental illness; and it proceeds in parts along the lines of "The Cask of Amontillado," detailing the narrator's obsessions with honor and vengeance. It also resembles "The Purloined Letter" in that Lance poses as a detective of sorts. But the novel most consistently mirrors "The Fall of the House Of Usher": Lance's first-person narrative stems from a visit *by* his boyhood friend Percival (reversing the narrator's visit *to* his boyhood friend Roderick in Poe's story); the ancestral family house that provides the setting is irrevocably destroyed at the end; and the narrative turns upon fear of and attempts to control not only women but human bodies generally, ultimately playing on and revising earlier Gothic associations of women, entrapping embodiment, and Catholicism—all three of which are violently rejected by Lance.

Despite his protests against the morally depraved world around him, Lance himself is clearly the chief horror in the novel. In certain respects he initially seems to be a stock early Gothic villain: he is aristocratic heir to a manor that, to visiting midwestern tourists, looks "as foreign . . . as Castel Gandolfo," the summer residence of the pope (25); that manor is in overwhelmingly Catholic south Louisiana, which has a faux-feudal history; and he has certain medieval obsessions, notably with his own perverse notion of chivalry. Yet it is crucial to note that he has absorbed his father's admiration not of the real Middle Ages but rather of the Middle Ages imagined by the British Presbyterian novelist Sir Walter Scott. Romantic novels such as Scott's *Ivanhoe*—as Percy wrote elsewhere—featured only "a Christianity which was aestheticized by medieval trappings and a chivalry abstracted from its sacramental setting."[32] In its Arthurian allusions *Lancelot* takes the bright nineteenth-century medievalism of Scott and gives it a dark Gothic face, though it does so in a manner that, as with Poe, ultimately focuses on a modern rather than a medieval horror.

For one thing, Lance himself is insistently post-Christian, and is depicted as a logical descendant of the sort of Virginia gentleman of Poe's era whom Tate described as "a deist by conviction and an Anglican or Presbyterian by habit" (416). Lance's milieu is less genteel than old Virginia, however, and more "Southern Western," as he puts it—that is, closer to the old frontier (92). As Lance's father told it, the Lamars descend from "Tory English colonials" who arrived in "corrupt" colonial Louisiana and fought to build their own "chaste and incorrupt little Anglican chapels" despite being surrounded on all sides by "savage Indians" and "superstitious Romans" alike (14, 116). This formulation of the Lamar family history strangely resembles the captivity narratives of early New England Protestant settlers who routinely conflated hostile Native Americans with enclosing Roman Catholics—narratives that in some respects prefigured Gothic fictions themselves.[33] Lance's father preferred to dream of a Louisiana somehow Anglicized and "suffused by gentle Episcopal rectitude" of the sort he associates with Robert E. Lee, but Lance himself—despite his open aversion to Christianity—at times prefers to posture as a more radical Protestant in the mold of Oliver Cromwell. He is a Puritan of sorts who will launch "a new Reformation" to save a corrupt America by violence (215, 177).

Lance's obsession with the seeming loss of "chivalry" in a United States in the throes of the sexual revolution is, therefore, more complicated than it seems. On one level it is a continuation of his father's merely nostalgic fantasy of a purer past. But Lance becomes a nightmarishly modern figure of a self-reliant rationality that is both strangely puritanical and narrowly dichotomizing. What he calls "chivalry" in fact follows the nineteenth-century American pattern Tate attributed to Poe, whose "exalted idealization of Woman . . . was only a little more humorless, because more intense, than the standard cult of Female Purity in the Old South" (389). That idealization is reflected in Poe's quasi-Cartesian protagonists' habit of professing "an impossibly high love of [woman], one that bypasses the body and moves in upon her spiritual essence" (404). Lance follows suit in his verbal reconstruction of his deceased and virginal wife, Lucy, focusing steadfastly on her "opaque Georgia eyes" in contrast to Margot's "sweet Texas ass": Lucy "was a dream" and all the purer for it, in Lance's eyes (85, 119). It is important to note, however, that Lance does not fear only female sexuality. He ultimately feels trapped by his own body as well, as discussed further below.

Lance's generally Cartesian position of abstraction from his body is reflected in his narrative of his initial research regarding his wife's infidelity, where he presents himself not as medieval knight but as a kind of scientist or detective. Near the novel's beginning he calmly describes his discovery, a year previous, that he was not the father of one of his children. Science not only aids him in this discovery as he notes and researches his daughter's blood type but also seems to offer him some solace as he uncovers increasing evidence of his wife's infidelity. "As a physician," he asks Percival, "wouldn't you say that nothing more is involved [in the act of adultery] than the touch of one membrane against another? Cells touching cells" (16–17). It is highly significant that the priest here is also an M.D. and therefore a true authority on soul and body alike, while Lance is merely a theorizing layman whose technological society has conditioned him to see himself as an all-transcending intellect that properly manipulates physical reality.

Lance's identity as detective is reflected in his reading of Raymond Chandler novels and references to the violent television show *Mannix*, but is best read as yet another nod to Poe, generally credited with inventing detective fiction. *Lancelot* resembles "The Purloined Letter" in that the object of Lance's search—sin—is hidden in plain sight (that is, in himself), and also in that the detective himself is morally tainted. Furthermore,

Lance is a particularly American sort of detective. As he conducts a solitary investigation into his wife's and finally his entire community's sexual degeneracy, he perfectly exemplifies the radical individualism underlying the American detective story in general: the solitary investigator "boring into the center of society to find it rotten . . . constitutes the fundamental drama" of the genre. Furthermore, "the mythology of American individualism" is such that the isolated detective's own "moral heroism is always just a step away from despair. . . . The hero's lonely quest for moral excellence ends in absolute nihilism."[34] No better description exists for Lance's state in the final pages of the novel. Yet this description applies equally well to another archetypal American hero relevant to *Lancelot:* the frontiersman who has left civilization and its seemingly restrictive mores behind.

Lance comes to see himself in this role late in the novel as he persistently recalls how his great-great-grandfather cut a man's throat "from ear to ear" in a savage duel on a Mississippi River sandbar, using not a broadsword but a bowie knife—which Lance himself ultimately uses to kill his wife's lover (155). Lance himself, then, is finally neither medieval knight nor Tory gentleman, but a self-reliant frontiersman who willfully and violently inflicts his abstract designs on nature—here, on human bodies.[35] Here Percy deconstructs his own family's faux-Christian aristocratic heritage and places at the center of American history not Robert E. Lee and other aristocratic figures who might seem "as legendary and mythical as King Arthur and the Round Table," but instead the likes of Daniel Boone or Davy Crockett—the American Adam with a bowie knife (116).[36]

Legends concerning such figures are as close to an autochthonous popular mythology as the United States has produced.[37] Accordingly, whereas Dostoyevsky tended to see Russian "soil" as especially well suited to nurturing Christianity in the nation's common people, Percy—or at least Lance—does not posit American soil or identity in any such light. Indeed, the only character who speaks of values springing from the "soil" is the utterly ungrounded film director Jacoby (114). This is ironic but also fitting, for Percy writes of an America far removed from that envisioned by the Vanderbilt Agrarians or the Jefferson who idealized the yeoman farmer. *Lancelot*'s America is one in which common citizens act "as if they lived out their entire lives in a dim charade, a shadowplay in which they were the shadows" and movie actors were "resplendent larger-than-life beings"; they are prone to believe that their own "reality could only be found in the illusions" of mass media (152). The late twentieth-century ascendance of such media and accompanying blurring of the line between reality and simulacra is a major theme in the novel, one connected to the tendency of Cartesian individualism to transform physical reality "into a mere hall of mirrors for the self-reflecting ego."[38] Indeed, playing roles and designing one's own identity without regard to physical reality or "soil" might itself be seen as quintessentially American.[39] What is finally "American" in Lance's fixation on the violent frontiersman, then, may not be the frontiersman himself so much as Lance's choice to play his role—as opposed to that of his father's preferred Robert E. Lee, or some other figure altogether.

The novel's consistent engagement with the seemingly arbitrary "play" of different identities (and of different texts) in part reflects Percy's postmodern milieu. But Percy cannot be deemed a literary postmodernist. Rather, he was a Christian realist who believed that Christianity itself guaranteed a number of essential "properties of the novel without which there is no novel," among them "the density and linearity of time and the sacramental reality of things."[40] For Percy, there is *a* reality grounded in God's ongoing presence in all Creation, and that reality is more particularly revealed in Christ and the sacraments administered by Christ's Church—without which humans are more prone to self-delusion than they would be otherwise. Lance's relationship to the Church and sacraments, then, is a crucial indicator of his relationship to reality as Percy sees it.[41]

A post-Protestant himself, Lance initially expresses some distant admiration for the Catholic Creoles whom his father saw as merely "superstitious Romans," because despite their apparent moral laxity they—unlike his own family—seem to have found the "secret of leading ordinary lives well" (24). But Lance becomes increasingly angry with the Catholic Church for what he sees as its failure to establish and enforce clear moral dichotomies. The bulk of the narrative is, again, a monologue delivered Poelike in a mental hospital room that doubles as a potential confessional booth. But this stock Gothic element is cast in a new light when Lance expresses his anger at the Church's apparent moral ambiguity: "With you," he tells Percival, "everything seems to get dissolved in a kind of sorrowful solution. Poor weak mankind! The trouble is that in your old tolerant Catholic world-weariness, you lose all distinctions. Love everything" (130–31). "Damn you and your God," he rails later. "Between the two of you, you should have got it straight and had it one way or the other. Either it [that is, sex or any other action] is good or it's bad, but whichever it is, goddamn say so. Only you don't. You fuck off somewhere in between. You want to have it both ways: good, but— bad only if—and so forth" (176). Lance is oddly innocent here, expressing a Manichean preference for seeing the world in black and white. Hence his anger at a Church that, as Percy's coreligionist Flannery O'Connor once put it, is not necessarily composed of "good people"—the Creoles with their lax mores make this obvious to Lance—but "is composed of those who accept what she teaches, whether they are good or bad, and there is a constant struggle through the help of the sacraments to be good."[42] The Church's complexity in this regard may seem too "effeminate" for Lance (note the traditional female pronoun used by O'Connor). Indeed, Lance explicitly blames the Church for "emasculating" the Christ he would prefer to follow, a Christ who would demand immediate moral perfection rather than instituting the sacrament of confession for struggling sinners (178).

Lance is such a sinner himself, in Percy's view. And because Lance is speaking to a priest, *Lancelot* not only echoes Poe's Gothic fiction and the general form of *Notes from Underground* as a confessional novel; here, the actual sacrament of confession is directly relevant to the plot. Furthermore, the sacraments as a whole are crucial to understanding Percy's ultimate revision of the Gothic. For what is finally horrifying in *Lancelot* is not Percival's Catholicism, which via the sacraments stresses the union of body and soul; what is horrifying is Lance's own tendency to deny and distrust the body, to divide body and soul, or—more precisely—body and mind, in two. While he prefers to contemplate his romantic "dream" of Lucy, as noted above, he is simultaneously drawn by animal lust to the physicality of Margot. This tension between romantic idealism and unbridled bodily urges comes to a head when Lance theorizes about and expresses his anger at a God or at least a nature that—his narrow scientific perspective has convinced him—has designed men to be compulsory rapists and women to submit to rape. By the end of the novel it becomes clear that, to Lance, human biology itself finally seems a trap, a limiting enclosure. He articulates this view most clearly using the language of Darwinian "evolution" (222–24). But interestingly, in making this observation Lance begins to directly indict the God he has professed little faith in elsewhere, in a crypto-Gnostic assertion that the natural world as he sees it is simply too evil and entrapping *not* to have some sort of supernatural intelligence behind it.

Elsewhere Lance expresses this conviction in ways that recall the earlier Gothic association of the body with a confining Catholicism. Midway through the novel he compares Margot's body to the "ark" of the covenant and speaks of "eating" that body sexually, as if it were some kind of Eucharistic sacrament (171). Read in context, however, this debased—because merely naturalistic—"sacrament" only serves to place Lance in quasi-Darwinian competition with other sexual predators. The culmination of this pattern is the late scene where Lance secretly approaches Margot and her new lover Jacoby together in bed. The bed itself, he says, looks "like a cathedral, a Gothic bed, posts as thick as trees, carved and fluted and tapering to spires and gargoyles above the canopy. The headboard was as massive and complex as an altar screen. Panels of openwork braced posts and rails like flying buttresses." Lance kneels behind one of these buttresses, listening to his wife and her lover—who seem to be one body—posing himself as "an unconsecrated priest hearing an impenitent confession" (237). This is in fact Lance and Margot's own marriage bed, and therefore an apt symbol of how Lance has come to see marriage and sex itself: not as potentially saving sacraments, but as Gothic enclosures—as further emphasized when he mounts the bed and clasps the two lovers together so tightly as to begin suffocating them.

If this were a tale by Poe, suffocation would be the end of it. But Percy simultaneously offers the reader breathing space and presents a moral quandary by framing the end of the novel with a question. Left quietly despairing in the ruins of his own hyperrationality, Lance finally asks Percival, What are *you* going to do? "So you plan to take a little church in Alabama, Father, preach the gospel, turn bread into flesh, forgive the sins of Buick dealers, give communion to suburban housewives?" (256). Given his solipsistic outrage at society and his distrust of the body as anything other than a useful weapon, nothing could seem more useless to Lance than all these flawed individuals coming together—in the flesh—to confess their sins and receive the word and body of Christ.

To this question, Percy offers the potential beginning of an answer more specific and affirmative than any hinted at even in *Notes from Underground*. For in the last pages of what has been a chilling monologue, the priest begins to speak. In answer to Lance's question about his plans at the parish and broader questions as well, he repeats one simple word: *Yes*. The priest-physician—the Percival who is in part Percy himself—has listened intently, assuming a posture that some critics have seen as "feminine."[43] But he has now emerged in formal priestly garb as a knight in the service of a lady, the Church (163). He begins to speak with authority both in this regard and as a physician who will presumably prescribe to Lance a regimen of charity, the agape-Eucharist that will ground his identity not in disembodied self-reliance but in embodied communion.[44] So the novel ends not with Poe's Gothic isolation or even with the poignantly promising self-reflection that closes *Notes*, but with a real dialogue and therefore the possibility that Lance's encounter with Percival might become a saving confession after all—that via word and sacrament Lance might escape not the body but rather a limiting intellectual inheritance that elevates the self-reliant mind above all else.

It is fitting, then, that the novel itself exists so clearly in communion with earlier fiction—with that "community" or "commonwealth of other writers" upon which Percy saw his own work depending. He understood his larger culture and its capacity for self-understanding in relation to the work of that literary community. Hence Percy once observed that to many modern readers the Good News no longer seems new (or good) in part because the very vocabulary of Christianity seems "worn out," which poses a particular problem for the Christian writer. How might such a writer get around this problem? By using "every ounce of cunning, craft, and guile he can muster.... The fictional use of violence, shock, comedy, insult, the bizarre, are the everyday tools of his trade."[45] *Lancelot* is Percy's most direct attempt at this strategy, and its complex approach to revitalizing a Christian message for his contemporary culture is made all the richer by its relationship to the work of Dostoyevsky and Poe.

Notes

1. Walker Percy, "Herman Melville," in *Signposts in a Strange Land*, ed. Patrick Samway, S.J. (New York: Farrar, Straus, and Giroux, 1991), 199.

2. Like Hamlet, Lance is haunted by the ghost of his father and seeks to avenge a cuckolding, but he must wait until he is absolutely certain. Lance's certainty comes via watching a film, Hamlet's via watching a play.

3. Jay Tolson, *Pilgrim in the Ruins: A Life of Walker Percy* (Simon and Schuster, 1992), 343.

4. Percy did express qualified admiration for a sort of modern Christian individualism, that exemplified by Kierkegaard: "Maybe his extreme individualism, inwardness, subjectivity, was justified by the blandness and overcorporate nature

of Christendom" in the early nineteenth century. Yet Percy simultaneously identified this individualism as Kierkegaard's weakest point. Percy sought to avoid it himself in part by cultivating the "consciously Catholic attitude toward" or view of "nature" as "sacramental" exemplified by Thomas Aquinas and Gerard Manley Hopkins. See *Conversations with Walker Percy,* ed. Lewis A. Lawson and Victor A. Kramer (Jackson: University Press of Mississippi, 1985), 119, 124.

5. Robin Feuer Miller, "Dostoevsky and the Tale of Terror," in *The Russian Novel from Pushkin to Pasternak,* ed. John Garrard (New Haven, CT: Yale University Press, 1983), 103–21.

6. Poe's "The Purloined Letter" is referenced by Lance on page 101 of *Lancelot* (New York: Picador, 1999), which will hereafter be cited parenthetically in the text. For Dostoyevsky's reading of Poe, see Vladimir Astrov, "Dostoievsky on Edgar Allan Poe," *American Literature* 14 (1942): 70–74; and Joseph Frank, *Dostoevsky: The Stir of Liberation, 1860–1865* (Princeton, NJ: Princeton University Press, 1986), 74–75. For assessments of *Lancelot* that briefly note the novel's connection to Poe, see Lewis Lawson, "The Fall of the House of Lamar," in *The Art of Walker Percy: Stratagems for Being,* ed. Panthea R. Broughton (Baton Rouge: Louisiana State University Press, 1979), 219–44; and Patrick Samway, "Another Case of the Purloined Letter (in Walker Percy's *Lancelot*)," *New Orleans Review* 16, no. 4 (1989): 37–44.

7. Tolson, *Pilgrim in the Ruins,* 183.

8. Quoted in ibid., 291. Lewis Lawson observes that Cheney's review "founded Percy criticism" by pointing out *The Moviegoer*'s indebtedness to Dostoyevsky and Camus insofar as it featured "a narrator-hero who reveals himself to be a villain." See "From Tolstoy to Dostoyevsky in *The Moviegoer,*" *Mississippi Quarterly* 56, no. 3 (2003): 413.

9. Carol A. Flath, "Fear of Faith: The Hidden Religious Message of *Notes from Underground,*" *Slavic and East European Journal* 37, no. 4 (1993): 510.

10. Fyodor Dostoevsky, *Notes from Underground,* trans. Andrew R. MacAndrew (New York: Penguin/Signet, 2004), 87. Quotations from this work will hereafter be cited parenthetically in the text.

11. Frank, *Dostoevsky,* 314.

12. Ibid., 333, 345.

13. Edgar Allan Poe, "The Philosophy of Composition," in *The Selected Writings of Edgar Allan Poe,* ed. G. R. Thompson (New York: Norton, 2004), 680. *Selected Writings* is hereafter cited parenthetically in the text.

14. Mikhail Bakhtin, *Problems of Dostoevsky's Poetics,* trans. Caryl Emerson (Minneapolis: University of Minnesota Press, 1984).

15. Rene Fortin, "Responsive Form: Dostoevsky's *Notes from Underground* and the Confessional Tradition," *Providence* 3, no. 1 (1995): 6.

16. Flath, "Fear of Faith," 511.

17. Ibid., 522.

18. Frank, *Dostoevsky,* 345–46.

19. Molly Boyd, "Gothicism," in *Companion to Southern Literature,* ed. Joseph M. Flora and Lucinda H. MacKethan (Baton Rouge: Louisiana State University Press 2002), 311.

20. Indeed, at points the novel seems a parody of the Southern Gothic.

21. Miller, "Dostoevsky and the Tale of Terror," 106, 119.

22. Diane Long Hoeveler, "Inventing the Gothic Subject: Revolution, Secularization, and the Discourse of Suffering," in *Inventing the Individual: Romanticism and the Idea of Individualism,* ed. Larry Peer (Provo, UT: International Conference on Romanticism, 2002), 6–7, 9. The gendered aspect of this ideal on one level exemplifies what Nicholas Boyle deems "the controverted feminine," that is, "a rejection on theological grounds of feminine language and imagery" characteristic of both "the Reformation and early modern period" in much of northern Europe. See his *Sacred and Secular Scriptures: A Catholic Approach to Literature* (Notre Dame, IN: University of Notre Dame Press, 2005), 200. For more on anti-Catholicism and the Gothic, see Chris Baldick and Robert Mighall, "Gothic Criticism," in *A Companion to the Gothic,* ed. David Punter (Oxford: Blackwell, 2000), 209–28.

23. See Jenny Franchot, *Roads to Rome: The Antebellum Protestant Encounter with Catholicism* (Berkeley: University of California Press, 1994).

24. See, for example, ch. 18 of Percy's *Lost in the Cosmos: The Last Self-Help Book* (New York: Farrar, Straus, and Giroux, 1983).

25. R. W. B. Lewis, *The American Adam* (Chicago: University of Chicago Press, 1959).

26. Stanley Cavell, "Being Odd, Getting Even (Descartes, Emerson, Poe)," in *The American Face of Edgar Allan Poe,* ed. Shawn Rosenheim and Stephen Rachman (Baltimore: Johns Hopkins University Press, 1995), 19–20, 33. On Poe's relationship to Descartes, also see Jeffrey Folks, "Poe and the *Cogito,*" *Southern Literary Journal* 42, no. 1 (2009): 57–72.

27. J. Gerald Kennedy, "Phantasms of Death in Poe's Fiction," in *The Haunted Dusk: American Supernatural Fiction, 1820–1920,* ed. Howard Kerr, John W. Crowley, and Charles L. Crow (Athens: University of Georgia Press, 1983), 42.

28. David Leverenz, "Poe and Gentry Virginia," in Rosenheim and Rachman, *American Face of Edgar Allan Poe,* 213, 221. Allen Tate, *Essays of Four Decades* (Chicago: Swallow, 1968), 416. Tate's work is hereafter cited parenthetically in the text.

29. Percy, letter to Caroline Gordon, quoted in Tolson, *Pilgrim in the Ruins,* 300.

30. I discuss Percy's indebtedness to these two essays and to Tate generally in *Peculiar Crossroads* (Baton Rouge: Louisiana State University Press, 2004), 119–24, 134–36.

31. Quoted in Patrick Samway, *Walker Percy: A Life* (Chicago: Loyola, 1999), 228.
32. Percy, "Stoicism in the South," in *Signposts*, 85.
33. Franchot, *Roads to Rome*, 87–89.
34. Robert Bellah et al., *Habits of the Heart: Individualism and Commitment in American Life* (Berkeley: University of California Press, 1996), 145–46.
35. For more on how *Lancelot* mirrors Faulkner's *Absalom, Absalom!* in this regard and in foregrounding the Catholic-Protestant divide along the Louisiana-Mississippi border, see my "Rewriting American Borders: The Southern Gothic, Religion, and U.S. Historical Narrative," forthcoming in *Storytelling, History, and the Postmodern South*, ed. Jason Phillips (Baton Rouge: Louisiana State University Press). That essay presents briefer readings of Poe and *Lancelot* in relation to a broader consideration of the Gothic in the Americas.
36. For Percy's association of Cartesian individualism with the "frontier hero" as depicted in western films, see John Desmond, *Walker Percy's Search for Community* (Athens: University of Georgia Press, 2006), 13–14.
37. See Richard M. Slotkin, *Regeneration through Violence: The Mythology of the American Frontier, 1600–1860* (Middletown, CT: Wesleyan University Press, 1973).
38. Folks, "Poe and the *Cogito*," 58. Gothic fiction's typical concern with illusion and the supernatural blends seamlessly with this aspect of the novel.
39. Ralph Ellison associated American identity with role-playing in his novel *Invisible Man,* which Percy greatly admired. In *Lancelot,* the "fakery" Lance typically attributes to actors and Louisiana alike is in fact more broadly American, as exemplified by Margot's lifelong attempt to act out the archetypal rags-to-riches narrative—poor country girl transformed to grand aristocratic belle (119).
40. Percy, "How to Be an American Novelist in Spite of Being Southern and Catholic," in *Signposts,* 177–78. On Percy as "Christian realist," see O'Gorman, *Peculiar Crossroads,* ch. 3.
41. The presence of an institutional Church as a sign and potential option for the protagonist makes *Lancelot* quite different from *Notes* (where the narrator is oblivious to a Christian tradition that he presumably sees as merely moribund). *Lancelot* perhaps more closely resembles *The Brothers Karamazov* in this regard.
42. Flannery O'Connor, *The Habit of Being* (New York: Farrar, Straus, and Giroux, 1988), 346.
43. See Marie Hebert, "Between Men: Homosocial Desire in Walker Percy's *Lancelot,*" *Mississippi Quarterly* 56, no. 1 (2002–3): 125–45.
44. Desmond has demonstrated how Percy's thought regarding community and language was deeply informed by his understanding of the Eucharist. For Percy,

Christ's "transfigured and glorified body is the final answer to Descartes' mind-body split" and also "the ultimate sign of mystical community, enfleshed in the body and blood in the Eucharist . . . and in the many signs of the spirit that exist in the mystery of the communal, semiotic world" (*Walker Percy's Search for Community*, 257).

45. Percy, "Notes for a Novel about the End of the World," in *The Message in the Bottle: How Queer Man Is, How Queer Language Is, and What One Has to Do with the Other* (New York: Farrar, Straus, and Giroux, 1976), 118. Percy here explicitly references the example of O'Connor as Christian writer—one whom, I would add, has also been described as "Gothic" and who responded to Dostoyevsky and Poe in vital ways herself.

Walker Percy's Alternative to Scientism in *The Thanatos Syndrome*

Micah Mattix

Walker Percy's *The Thanatos Syndrome* is often read, and rightly so, as a critique of scientism. Scientism is the belief that science alone can make truth statements about the world. For Percy, such a perspective always dehumanizes. Because man is viewed as matter, all personal and social ills are ascribed to chemical imbalances in the brain and call for pharmacological solutions. In the novel, the solution is doses of heavy sodium introduced into the water supply. Amazingly, the solution "works." Crime and anxiety disappear and pleasure is maximized through increased promiscuity. The problem, of course, is that this solution "kills" the self. Those who have drunk the contaminated water lose the capacity to use triadic signs, which, for Percy, is what distinguishes humans from animals. While they have been "cured" of "the familiar anxieties, terrors, panics, phobias," they have a "curious flatness of tone," Percy writes, and speak in "two-word chimp utterances."[1] They no longer have the capacity for hermeneutical context, and they mate openly and indiscriminately. They have become primates.

For Percy, the literal loss of the capacity of the characters to use triadic signs in the novel is a symbol for the widespread loss of the self in America in the late twentieth century. Like the doses of heavy sodium that "zap" self-awareness, America's constant production of *immediate dyadic pleasures*—pleasures (like pornography and roller coasters) that produce a direct physiological response—reduces the population's capacity to use triadic signs. Thus, at the end of the novel, when Tom More arrives in Disney World with his recovering wife, he notices that the retired Canadians and Ohioans "are amiable, gregarious, helpful—and at something of a loss" (338–39). They look "somewhat zapped" (339). Like the oblivion produced by the doses of heavy sodium earlier in the novel, these immediate dyadic pleasures also dehumanize.

Thus, the death syndrome that Percy diagnoses in the novel is found at all levels of American society. We live in a culture that, at a theoretical level, reduces man to matter, and in practice, kills our capacity for triadic signification—the source of our sense of self—as a "cure" for psychological suffering. Yet, what alternative is there? One possible critique of Percy is that his project is largely negative. Cleary he is a gifted diagnostician, but what good is it to know that one is dying if there is no cure?

While it is true that Percy tends to focus on diagnosing the modern malaise, he does, in fact, offer a possible "cure," however partial or unreliable. It is found in the recognition that we are more than mere material entities, which is something that human language, particularly of the sort found in novels, always necessarily affirms. To examine this alternative in *The Thanatos Syndrome*, however, we must first retrace his view of language and literature.

Following Charles Sanders Peirce's triadic theory of linguistic signs, Percy argues in "Is a Theory of Man Possible?" that the way humans use signs is qualitatively different from how other animals use them. Primates, such as chimpanzees, can learn to respond to words as stimuli. For example, it is possible to condition a chimpanzee to jump when the word "jump" is spoken by using a system of rewards. However, chimpanzees do not associate the word with the action. Like B. F. Skinner's use of light as an associative *stimulus* in pigeons and Pavlov's use of a bell as an associative *stimulus* in dogs, words, in this instance, are associative stimuli that produce a particular conditioned response in chimpanzees. This is what Peirce and Percy call a dyadic event.[2]

How humans respond to and use language is qualitatively different. Not only can humans respond to the word "jump" by jumping, but they also link the word and the action via a "coupler." We link, furthermore, not discrete instances of jumping with the word "jump" but the characteristic of what we could call "jumpingness" with the word. Thus, the word "ball" signifies not individual balls, but the characteristic of a certain roundness.[3] For Percy, this is why he distinguishes in "The Mystery of Language" between a sign—"something," he writes, "that directs our attention to something else" (in this case, particular instances of jumping)—and a symbol.[4] In the latter case, the word and the idea expressed in it are mashed together—however arbitrarily—and become one. This is what Percy means when he writes: "Naming or symbolization may be defined as the affirmation of the thing as being what it is under the auspice of the symbol."[5] Thus, according to Percy, linguistic symbols are categorically different from signs. Symbols combine a sign (in this case, a phoneme or a script) and the "inescape" of a particular entity or attribute. This "inescape" is real, cognitive, and immaterial, and without it, meaning or signification would be impossible. For Percy, all material objects have an inescape, but so do immaterial attributes and emotions—"things" such as good and evil or the feelings of love and hate. For Percy, these attributes and emotions are no less real than our notion of roundness. They are universal and cannot be reduced to mean nothing more than "good for self-preservation" or "bad for self-preservation," as many social Darwinists would have it.

Thus, the human language is a *testament* of being, and this testament, or knowledge, produces a satisfaction that is more complex and of a higher sort than the merely physiological pleasure of drugs or roller coasters. Again, in "Naming and Being," Percy points out that when a child learns what the word "ball" means, he "will hold the ball and speak its name a thousand times to anyone who will listen, or to no one at all. In doing so, he experiences a joy which has nothing to do with the biological need-satisfactions which have determined all previous joys."[6] This joy, according to Percy, comes from the knowledge of being, the *identity asserted* between the sign ("ball") and being (in this case, "roundness"). This *is* a ball. The pleasure is not produced because of the child's understanding of some sort of natural link between the word and the thing being named. Most signs are arbitrary, according to Percy. In fact, the "scandal" of naming is that the less "natural" the relation between the sign and the thing being named, the greater the pleasure. This is Percy's point in "Metaphor as Mistake." The greater the gap between word and thing, the greater the validation of the thing's ineffable "being" the word asserts:

> *For this ontological pairing, or, if you prefer, "error" of identification of word and thing, is the only possible way in which the apprehended nature of the bird, its inescape, can be validated as being what it is.* This inescape is, after all, otherwise ineffable. I can describe it, make crude approximation by such words as darting, oaring, speed, dive, but none of these will suffice to affirm

> this so distinctive something which I have seen. This is why, as Marcel has observed, when I ask what something is, I am more satisfied to be given a name, even if the name means nothing to me (especially if?), than to be given a scientific classification.[7]

Thus, without espousing a simplistic Cartesian dualism, Percy views human language as a testament to the reality of universal, nonmaterial attributes and emotions, even the human soul.

Percy writes that communication happens when "one person utters a symbol—a word—or draws a painting, whatever—and a second person receives the symbol and understands it—or perhaps misunderstands it—to be about something else, which both persons have experienced."[8] The referent, or the "inescape," that the symbol names becomes the object of both the speakers' attention. Because there is no consciousness without intentionality, according to Percy (who follows John Searle is this respect), and because, he continues, we are not only "conscious of something; we are also conscious of it as something we conceive under the symbol assigned to it, . . . without the symbol, I suggest we would not be conscious of it at all."[9] Thus, consciousness for Percy is "named" experience and unconsciousness "unnamed" experience.

While this is where the post-structuralist wolves begin to circle, Percy himself had little time for the strongly ideological application of Ferdinand de Saussure's distinction between *signifiant* and *signifié* found in the work Lévi-Strauss, Foucault, or Derrida. In a footnote to his semiotic intermezzo in *Lost in the Cosmos*, Percy states: "Whatever the virtues of structuralism as a method of linguistics, ethnology, and criticism, it is the self-proclaimed foe, on what seem to be ideological grounds, of the very concept of the human subject." "I do not feel obliged to speak of the deconstructionists," Percy continues self-assuredly and not without a little wit.[10] For Percy, the stating or writing of a linguistic sign by one person and its reception by another is a functional (if not always infallible) form of communication. This is possible because there is a God external to the cosmos under which the self and all other things are named, and who is a co-namer of the universe. Percy writes in "Semiotic and a Theory of Knowledge":

> The symbol meaning relation may be defined as not merely an intentional but as a cointentional relation of identity. The thing is intended through its symbol which you say and I can repeat, and it is only through this quasi iden-

> tification that it can be conceived at all. Thus it is, I believe, that an empirical and semiotical approach to meaning illumines and confirms in an unexpected manner the realist doctrine of the union of the knower and the thing known. The metaphysical implications of semiotic are clear enough. Knowing is not a causal sequence but an immaterial union. It is a union, however, which is mediated through material entities, the symbol and its object. Nor is it a private phenomenon—rather is it an exercise in intersubjectivity in which the Thou serves as an indispensable colleague.[11]

God is "an indispensable colleague" for Percy because he is external to the named world and can thus be an "objective" interlocutor.

For Percy, great novels and poems "name" the "inescape" not of things but of events or values such as the goodness of justice or the ugliness of selfishness. In "The State of the Novel: Dying Art or New Science?" Percy writes: "Good art tells some home truths about the way things are, the way we are, about the movement or lack of movement of the human heart." "Art," he continues, "is cognitive, as cognitive and affirmable in its own way as science, and . . . in the case of the current novel what it cognizes, discerns, knows and tells is of a unique order which cannot be grasped by the scientific method."[12] In "Metaphor as Mistake," he writes that "poetry validates that which has already been privately apprehended but has gone unformulated for both of us."[13] For Percy, this produces both pleasure and discomfort at the same time. The pleasure one feels when reading a great novel is found in the identification of the moral nature of man that takes place in the novel. This is, in turn, a testament to the reality of such universal, immaterial attributes:

> And does it not still happen with us that when we are reading a great novel or a great poem or seeing a great play or film or even listening to music, that in the best parts we experience this same expansion of consciousness, this same sense of discovery, of affirmation, when the novelist writes of an experience we've had and only vaguely recognized but had not had it pointed out until this moment. The response is an affirmation: "Aha! yes, that's it! Sure enough, that's the way it is! I never thought of it before but"—and so on.[14]

Unlike the cognitive scientist, who points to things such as variety and form as the source of pleasure in a work of art, Percy rightly points to the fact that the pleasure is *ontological* and *moral*. For what is named in a great novel or poem are immaterial things, like the "movement of the human heart," the "order which cannot be grasped," and things "privately apprehended." These are truths not about things per se but about the order of and relation between things, as well as desire, will, peace, and agitation. The more accurate this naming, according to Percy, the greater pleasure one feels when reading a great work.

The discomfort one feels is due to the fact that as one's sense of self increases as these attributes of the unnamable self are defined, so does the sense of anxiety at not being able to name oneself. "Of all the things in the world," Percy writes, "oneself is the only being that cannot be symbolized."[15] (Some higher being needs to name us, as Percy discusses at length in *Lost in the Cosmos*.) Furthermore, as one becomes aware of one's self in the world, the sense that I might, in fact, be lost in what Dante calls a "dark wood . . . savage, dense and harsh" increases. In fact, in Dante's *Inferno*, the poet's realization of his utter perdition comes after he "came to" himself.[16] Be this as it may, Percy suggests in *The Thanatos Syndrome* and elsewhere that this negative consequence of self-knowledge is better than the alternative of either a self-imposed or mandated oblivion.

In *The Thanatos Syndrome,* Percy presents reading and writing as an alternative to the scientism of Bob Comeaux, Max Gottlieb, and John Van Dorn for dealing with the modern malaise and human suffering. We see this alternative, in particular, in Father Smith's "Confession," which is separated typographically from the novel itself and functions, like Shakespeare's "play within the play" in *Hamlet,* as a story within the story. While Smith's confession is presented in the novel as a piece of nonfiction, it has literary elements, like Saint Augustine's *Confessions,* to which it no doubt alludes. In *American Jeremiad,* Sacvan Bercovitch argues that the first literary genre of the American colonies was the jeremiad—a sermon, following the prophet Jeremiah, in which the minister denounces society for its moral failings and calls for it to return to God—and William Rodney Allen has made an interesting case that Father Smith's confession is precisely this sort of sermon.[17] (In fact, Allen goes on to note that Smith's confession closely parallels elements of *Lancelot*.)[18] In either case, while Smith's confession is clearly nonfiction, it is of a rather literary sort (much, it is worth noting, like Percy's own nonfiction). In fact, Smith refers to it as his "tale" (256).

Father Smith himself possesses all of the characteristic traits of the novelist. First, according to Percy, the novelist separates himself from society, which often leads to personal catastrophe. In *Lost in the Cosmos*, Percy notes that the artist "transcends" the world "in his use of signs." He separates himself from his fellow man in order to name them and the order (or disorder) that connects them. The feeling of transcendence is exhilarating but momentary—the artist must always "reenter" society. The results are often catastrophic. Because the transcendence offered by art is one in which the artist "names" if not the self, the attributes of the self and, therefore, participates in the momentary but nevertheless real "salvic effect of art," the return from this momentary sense of salvation are often all the more hellish. Thus, when the artist reenters the mundane world, unable to escape again via art, he becomes a wasted drunk or commits suicide. Thus, Percy writes: "If poets often commit suicide, it is not because their poems are bad but because they are good."[19]

Second, the novelist is both the sanest and craziest of people. In "Novel-Writing in an Apocalyptic Time," Percy writes that in a time of great confusion and fracture, poets and novelists can go crazy (or seem crazy) because they perceive, with great clarity, the insanity of the present world. In times of catastrophe in the past, Percy writes: "Poets and novelists seemed to be possessed by a whole separate coven of witches, demons, terrors, and premonitions, of which the general population seems by and large oblivious. Either one is crazy and the other sane, or the former has gone crazy for reasons which the latter has not yet caught on to." Percy continues: "And, to tell the truth, I am still not sure which is right: whether it is the poet and novelist who, like the man in Allen Tate's definition, is a shaky man trying to reassure himself in a generally sane world, or whether it is the population at large which is slowly going mad and the poet who has the sensibility or vulnerability—thin skin—to notice it." Of course, Percy *does* know, and it is clearly, for him, the latter. Hence, he writes that despite whatever "shakiness" or "fecklessness" he might have, the novelist's duty is to "record what other people, absorbed as they are in their busy and useful lives, may not see."[20] Of course, what they do not see is horrific.

Last and most obviously, the novelist traffics in triadic signs. He uses language. Yet, as Percy remarks in "Notes for a Novel about the End of the World," his language must be unusual. Because everyday language itself is "worn out," and the audience indifferent, the novelist, at least at the end of the twentieth century, must, through the "fictional use of violence, shock, comedy, insult, the bizarre," somehow renew the devalued signs. If he is successful, both "he and his reader may come to themselves," as Dante does at the beginning of *The Inferno*.[21]

As noted above, Father Smith possesses all of these characteristics. Like most artists in the twentieth century, Father Smith has separated himself from society. He lives in a fire tower in Feliciana parish and sees few visitors, except Tom More and the faithful but simple Milton, and his physical separation is a symbol of his internal psychological separation. This separation, however, like the separation of the novelist, is done, at least in part, for the benefit of society. While the women in Father Placide's office invent convoluted theories regarding Father Smith's sudden retreat to the fire tower, Jan Greene, in a snort of common sense, says, "For God's sake. Like Jonah. I mean, really. Has it ever occurred to anybody that he might be up there for a much simpler, more obvious reason? . . . He could be doing vicarious penance for the awful state of the world. It is, after all, good Catholic practice" (112–13). In other words, it could be that Father Smith is suffering, doing penance, in an effort to heal the world, to bring it to itself.

Furthermore, when he lived in society, he exhibited the same self-destructive tendencies that Percy claims artists in the twentieth century develop. When More knew him from Hope Haven, Smith drank heavily and was (as he continues to be) misanthropic—he views people as either "victims or assholes" (243).

Smith, moreover, is both crazy and sane at the same time. When More first sees him, after Father Placide has told him that he cannot decide whether Father Smith is "a nut or a genius," he is perplexed. At first, Smith looks the same as when he knew him in Alabama: "He still looks like an old Ricardo Montalban with a handsome seamed face as tanned as cordovan leather, hair like Brillo," but More quickly notices that something "is different" (115). "Then I see that something is wrong with him. He is standing indecisively, fists in his pockets, brows knitted in a preoccupied expression. He does not look crazy but excessively sane" (116). When More sees him again, he has just had a "spell"—he's as "stiff as a board," according to Milton—and at first he refuses to speak (231). He shakes and possesses the "thin skin" vulnerability that Percy sees as part of the essential character of the novelist.

Last, Smith traffics in triadic signs. He "spots" fires from his tower, calls a second tower, and the location of the fire is "triangulated" (119–21). This is an image of how triadic signs work. Yet, he is preoccupied, as good novelists are, Percy argues, with the lack of signification, meaning, of signs in the modern world. When More first visits Smith, the good father falls into a frenzied explanation of his inability to "preach" (we might say, metaphorically, to write): "Because—it doesn't signify" (117). Words, Father Smith argues, have been emptied of their meaning. They no longer function as symbols, Smith argues, but are mere dyadic signs. This is demonstrated, according to Father Smith, in the fact that Tom More associates certain words—"clouds," "Irish," "Blacks"—not with certain "inescapes" but with the stereotypical connotations. However, the word "Jew," which Smith believes has not been evacuated of meaning, is associated by More with real, living Jews—"Max, Sam, Julius." "Since the Jews were the original chosen people of God," Smith argues, "a tribe of people who are still here, they are a sign of God's presence which cannot be evacuated" (123). For Smith, this unevacuated presence of God has its fullest assurance in the Incarnation of Christ expressed in the Eucharist.

If Father Smith can be thought of as a novelist, and his text is his "Confession," that leaves us Tom More as the reader. He is, first of all, a Freudian psychologist who prefers to allow his patients to talk about their problems rather than practice more highly intrusive forms of therapy. At the beginning of the novel, he is confronted with a textual problem—why are the people of Feliciana parish acting the way they are acting—and, as the novel progresses, he is faced with a moral one. Throughout, he "reads" peoples' actions and words. He notes the changed mannerisms and language of his patients and his wife and, with the help of Lucy Lipscomb, he is able to access the files of the Louisiana Department of Public Health and thus uncovers Comeaux and Van Dorn's secret plan to "cure" the folks of Feliciana parish of the ills of mental disease and crime.

Yet, while More is able to figure out the "textual" or scientific problem—why is it that people in Feliciana parish are acting apelike?—he is confused regarding the morality of the situation. While he seems to recognize innately that what is happening to the people of Feliciana parish is wrong, he is tempted by the ethical reasoning of Comeaux and Van Dorn. In a discussion with Lipscomb before they uncover the atrocities that are taking place at Belle Ame, More explains that he has been offered a job on "the team" and is unsure if he will take it or not (211). Even after the sexual abuse at Belle Ame is discovered, More is still unsure what he will do. When he arrives at Father Smith's a second time, he explains the situation:

> I tell him about my latest discoveries about Dr. Comeaux's and Dr. Van Dorn's Blue Boy project, about their offer of a job, about their threats if I don't take it to send me back to Alabama for parole violation. I mention the incidents of sexual molestation at Belle Ame Academy, but also tell him of Bob Comeaux's impressive evidence of social betterment through the action of the addictive heavy sodium. "I'm not sure what I should do," I tell him, frowning, troubled, but keeping an eye on him. As a matter of act, I do not know what to do. (234)

While Smith was at first unable to "preach," overwhelmed by the fact that words no longer signify, a few lines after More's own mini-confession, Smith overcomes his inability and recounts his story, his "Confession." More at first is unable to understand what Smith wants to tell him, but after he leaves, he makes the right decision (according to the logic of the story), to refuse the offer from Comeaux and Van Dorn.

Smith's "Confession" deals with his time in Nazi Germany and his attachment to a young German soldier, Helmut, and Smith's (now-shocking) longing to join Helmut and participate in what he saw as the SS's heroic cult of death. On this score, it is interesting to note that Smith's confession uses one of the tools Percy suggests novelists writing "in an Apocalyptic age" should use—shocking moral dilemmas and violence. Smith tells of his early disdain of "what my mother called religion" and of his "father's fecklessness and his everlasting talk about the loftier things in life, Truth, Beauty, Freedom, Art, the Soaring of the Spirit in the Realm of Music," which is contrasted with his deep attraction to the sense of duty at the SS expressed in Helmut. Quoting Churchill, he states: "There is nothing they would not do or dare; no sacrifice of life, limb or liberty they would not do for love of country" (242, 249). "This is my confession," Father Smith continues. "If I had been German not American, I would have joined him. I would not have joined the distinguished Weimar professors. I would not have joined the ruffian Sturmabteilung. I would not have matriculated at the University of Tübingen or Heidelberg. I would not have matriculated at Tulane, as I did, and joined the D.K.E.s. I would have gone to Junkerschule, sworn the solemn oath of the Teutonic knights at Marienberg, and joined the Schutzstaffel" (248–49). Following this confession, Smith tells More of his arrival as an American soldier at the famous hospital Eglfing-Haar after its liberation. He asks the nurse about Dr. Jäger, one of the "more humane" members of the group of Weimar intellectuals, who believed that euthanasia should be used only to eliminate those who suffered, not those who were useless "to themselves [and] to the state" (246). The nurse tells Smith of how Jäger would take disturbed children—children "in bad shape," Smith tells us, "though nothing like what I saw at Dachau"—to a room called the "special department" to kill them. Smith concludes his confession and footnote: "It was a matter of some interest. Soldiers are interested, not horrified. Only later was I horrified. We've got it wrong about horror. It doesn't come naturally but takes some effort" (254).

At the conclusion of Smith's "Confession," More remarks, "I'm not sure I understand what you're trying to tell me—about your memory of—about Germany" (256). However, it is after hearing this story that More decides decisively, as noted above, to refuse Comeaux and Van Dorn. More's eventual decision to do the right thing after his encounter with Father Smith is presented as an alternative to the efforts of Comeaux and Van Dorn to cure man's psychological and moral problems by medication. Smith's story has reaffirmed More's moral bearing. It has done the difficult work of naming horrible actions *horrible* and distinguishing between *good* intentions and *right* actions. At first, More does not *recognize* Smith's naming. He asks questions in order to process the significance—"What happened to Dr. Jäger?" "What happened to the others you met?" "Are you trying to tell me that the Nazis were not to blame?" "Are you suggesting that it was the psychiatrists who were villains?" "Are you saying that there is a fatal flaw peculiar to the Germans, something demonic?" (254–56). Note that these questions begin with the basic details of the story itself—common questions about characters and plot—but move quickly to *moral* questions. Here we see More's moral development. He senses that the naming that took place in the tale was a moral one, but perhaps because of his own moral failings, his lack of practice in naming the moral world, he at first struggles to recognize what Smith is saying. While Percy is too clever a novelist to provide us with a simplistic "aha" moment, it is clear that More, in the end, is able to determine the moral significance of the tale. Smith concludes his conversation with More: "In the end one must choose—given the chance." More responds: "Choose what?" The answer: "Life or death. What else?" (257). After this, More decides to turn Comeaux and Van Dorn in (though, at this point in the novel, it is far from clear whether he will in fact be successful).

At the conclusion of the work, we find More reunited with his wife, who has recovered her regular oddness. While the world is far from perfect at the conclusion of *The Thanatos Syndrome*, Percy's final description of the various characters and scenes has a recognizable humanity to it. Ellen gives up "tournament bridge" and converts, first to the Episcopal Church and then to Pentecostalism. While she seems unhealthily attached to a TV evangelist, More states: "She's happy, so I'll settle for it" (353). The children now attend a Christian school that "teaches that the world is six thousand years old and won't have *Huckleberry Finn* or the *Catcher in the Rye* in the library" but, More states, "it's better than Belle Ame, and the kids seem happy and healthy" (354). The hospice is reopened, though Father Smith is unwell and becomes a patient at the hospice himself, and More begins his practice again, choosing it over the low-paying directorship of the hospice. These scenes can be contrasted with animal depictions of Mickey and Ellen earlier in the novel, or the depictions of wide-eyed abused children at Belle Ame. The contrast is the contrast of Percy's view of humans as composite beings and the reductive materialist view of humans as matter alone. The former is clearly messier, more complicated, but an accurate depiction of who we are, the latter inhumane and horrific. This is not to make a commonsense argument, but rather to say that we recognize, empirically, our own human nature in the characters represented at the close of the novel as we recognize ourselves in a mirror.

Both Smith's story and Percy's *Thanatos Syndrome* have named the moral world, and this naming is both a testament to its existence and a call to affirm it in our actions. Although Ralph C. Wood criticized the novel in the *Christian Century* after it was first published for lacking any sympathetic characters and being merely "an angry and admonitory novel," there is an element of hope presented in the work.[22] Percy holds out the hope that, through reading and writing, ethical and moral "triangulation" can still happen. People are still able to "do justice," even at the end of the twentieth century, and the truth expressed in language and literature regarding who we are and what justice is facilitates this.

Notes

Originally published in *Perspectives on Political Science* 40, no. 3 (2011). Reprinted by permission of Taylor and Francis Group.

1. Walker Percy, *The Thanatos Syndrome* (New York: Picador, 1987), 68–69. Hereafter, page references for this work will be cited parenthetically in the text.

2. Walker Percy, *Signposts in a Strange Land,* ed. Patrick Samway, S.J. (New York: Picador, 1991), 120–21.

3. Ibid., 122–23.

4. Walker Percy, *The Message in the Bottle: How Queer Man Is, How Queer Language Is, and What One Has to Do with the Other* (New York: Picador, 1975), 153.

5. Percy, *Signposts,* 133.

6. Ibid., 131.

7. Percy, *Message in the Bottle,* 72.

8. Percy, *Signposts,* 123.

9. Ibid., 124.

10. Walker Percy, *Lost in the Cosmos: The Last Self-Help Book* (New York: Picador, 1983), 87.

11. Percy, *Message in the Bottle,* 263–64.

12. Percy, *Signposts,* 140, 150–51.

13. Percy, *Message in the Bottle,* 72.

14. Percy, *Signposts,* 125.

15. Ibid., 136.

16. Dante Alighieri, *Inferno,* trans. Robert Hollander and Jean (New York: Anchor, 2002), 1.2–5.

17. Sacvan Bercovitch, *American Jeremiad* (Madison: University of Wisconsin Press, 1978); William Rodney Allen, "'Father Smith's Confession' in *The Thanatos Syndrome,*" in *Walker Percy: Novelist and Philosopher,* ed. Jan Nordby Gretlund and Karl-Heinz Westarp (Jackson: University Press of Mississippi, 1991), 189–91.

18. Ibid., 192–93.

19. Percy, *Lost in the Cosmos,* 119–20, 121.

20. Percy, *Signposts,* 157, 162.

21. Percy, *Message in the Bottle,* 119, 118.

22. Ralph C. Wood, "*The Thanatos Syndrome:* Exciting, Horrifying, Disappointing," *Christian Century,* October 7, 1987, 857.

Love and Marriage among the Ruins

Richard M. Reinsch II

Walker Percy intimated in several addresses and essays his belief that the South was strangely capable of teaching the United States enduring truths of man's nature and being.[1] Separated from the larger country since the 1830s by political rebellion, racial oppression, and economic torpidity, the South of the late twentieth century, Percy argued, was now liberated and needed in a new quest to save the Union. As Percy stated:

> I come from the Deep South. I mention this only to call your attention to a remarkable event that has occurred in the last year or two, which has the most far-reaching consequences, and which has gone all but unnoticed. It is the fact that for the first time in a hundred and fifty years the South is off the hook and once again free to help save the Union. It's not that the South has got rid of its ancient stigma and is out of trouble. It's rather that the rest of the country is now also stigmatized and is in even deeper trouble.[2]

The maladies of America, Percy observed, went beyond the conventional list of various social, political, and economic inequalities, instead consisting in the "weariness, boredom, and cynicism" that threatened to rob humane democratic life of meaning in the late modern era.[3] Of course, these existential problems constantly plague democratic government precisely because democratic authority depends on the human person for legitimacy. However, a democratic age bereft of a solid commitment to transcendental meaning and a belief in reason's ability to discern certain truths of man's dignity surely brings these perennial troubles to an acute stage.

Stimulating Percy's historically unorthodox argument was the phenomenon of economic growth and the shattering of de jure segregation in the South. Speaking in 1978 at the University of Georgia, Percy cannily observed: "Undoubtedly then, the lower Mississippi between Baton Rouge and New Orleans will become, is already becoming, the American equivalent of the Ruhr Valley. In the year 2000, Peachtree Street may have replaced Madison Avenue. I find these possibilities quite likely but not terribly interesting and certainly not decisive as the real issues of the future are concerned. They represent economic inevitabilities, more or less what was bound to happen once the South with its advantages in climate, resources, and energy got past the historic disaster which befell it."[4] Having retained a closer affinity relative to states in other regions of the country with smaller government, lower taxes, freedom of contract, and general common sense, the South received renewed business investment from corporations across the nation and also the world. However, the deployment of capital, brains, jobs, and the economic progress this represented was not, in Percy's estimation, the ultimate measure of a changing South. Likewise, the end of segregation, which helped usher much of the continental business activity into the South—the region now safe for democratic capitalism—was not the final word on the region's progress. This, of course, does not slight these very real achievements of civil rights and higher standards of living. Percy approved of the crushing blow that had been delivered to the cruelty and lawlessness of the South by passage of civil rights legislation. The author noted that the post–civil rights South, replete with air-conditioners and enforced rights for its black citizens, was superior to the political-social order that had preceded it. The practical import for Percy was in desegregation's closing of the deep separation between the South and the rest of the nation. Percy asserted, "Southern slavery or Southern racial segregation either to defend or attack" would no longer preoccupy the region's leaders or its detractors.[5]

The merging of the distinct South with the rest of America was by no means an unqualified moment of approbation for Percy. In coming to look like the rest of America, the South might forget or lose its best qualities while assuming the worst of late twentieth-century America. On this score Percy struck a pessimistic note: "What else to do in a Sunbelt South increasingly informed by a flatulent Christendom and Yankee money-grubbing? For the danger is that we are going to end up with the worst of both worlds, the worst of Southern Christendom—that is, an inflated media Christendom without the old Southern pieties—and the worst of Northern materialism—

a kind of mindless money-sports Vegas culture without stern secular saints like Thoreau, Emerson, Melville, Hawthorne."[6] A rather mindless progress, Percy feared, would inform the South. Thus, having achieved its liberation from the burdens of race and widespread poverty, the South would forego its unique capacities and be unable to speak in its original voice to the larger republic. The generational reserves of the region's *caritas* (the theological virtue of charity) would be marginalized by the seemingly endless possibilities of an encompassing commercialism. Percy's fiction is no less forgiving, conversing as it does with the lost self of the secular democratic age. Percy's writing confronts us with our wondering wander, and how one might live in an age that Percy believed was authoritatively inauthentic. Racial tolerance and the growth of commerce were all fine things, but man's formal occupation was always with the self and its relation with God and others.

In many respects, Percy's predictions for the South have come true. The habits and practices of personal, family, and communal virtues that the Old South excelled in have largely receded as organizing elements of behavior. The most popular contributions made by the South might be summed up as NASCAR, Southeastern Conference Football, and country music. Its great cities are now known almost exclusively for their robust business activity. Surely the rise of great poets and saints—persons whom Percy believed were essential in defining and making a culture—will not likely emerge in the business of this situation. For while the Mississippi of the early twentieth century may have scored abysmally low on indices of income and general welfare, it did produce William Faulkner, Eudora Welty, and Walker Percy. Percy teased that literature professors teaching at schools in New England and the upper Midwest may have been raised in superior circumstances as measured by sociological categories, but their academic careers largely consisted of both teaching and writing books about the books that Faulkner and Welty wrote. In short, is there even a culture that can still be shaped by the poet or saint in the contemporary South?

Implicit in a culture and political order almost exclusively defined by making and doing is a lost thickness of soul. The corresponding loss to personal relations from this fact is deeply experienced as the self is cut off from being and engages in the never-ending quest of self-definition, a process that inexorably informs one's most intimate and sacred bonds. The persons within these orders no longer understand their being as grounded in the thought and will of God. Hence, their very person is defined or left undefined by their activity and their making, which becomes furious in light of their sempiternal quest. Man finds himself in the condition of a great freedom, but without corresponding authority and responsibility in the guidance and measurement of his choices. He thus comes to deny the givenness of his being, defining it exclusively by will and desire. From this perspective the question can be phrased as follows: Is the South still capable of acknowledging man as a being grounded in the creative reason of God and thus able to embark on Percy's quest to save the Union?

Complementing Percy's reawakened South was and remains its burgeoning evangelical Christianity. Returning to Percy's broader observations on the dreariness of life where all material needs are met and yet a crushing boredom remains, one might posit that the South's evolved, muscular Protestantism provides a foreboding challenge to the almost intractable problems Percy identified in the thin intellectual commitments of democratic America. While Percy was somewhat skeptical of effusive evangelical religion, he may have overlooked the spiritual provision it makes, in a sense, for the unchanging aspects of man's being. This point seems vindicated by evangelicalism's sustained growth in a philosophically materialistic culture. Moreover, evangelical Protestantism has maintained in certain respects the enduring religiosity of the South and, with it, a compelling theological narrative of marriage and family life.

The quixotic quest that Percy defined for the South will emerge, if it does, from its philosophical and spiritual contact with *being*, of what is authentic about man. Produced by the philosophical and anthropological failures that Percy believed were inherent in Cartesian reductionism, or in the wholesale subscriptions to Darwin, Marx, Freud, and other latter-day theorists, are the larger failures in the human relationships of marriage and family. The distinctive capacity of the person to intimately love the other for the other's own good is displaced, if not eliminated, by theorists who narrow man to a this-worldly preoccupation while simultaneously denying his unique aspects.

One injured element, broached by Percy in his novels *The Second Coming* and *Love in the Ruins,* is the shared love of the domestic family, which becomes misconceived and misshaped in an age no longer conversant with the sacramental significance of man. Percy's discerning observations in these novels afford a unique purchase on the institution's diminishment in the midst of a humanistic age. The failure of this basic and complex love is one of the most deeply and painfully felt consequences achieved by the intrapersonal splits that have resulted from the age of theorist-consumerism. From man's failures to move beyond ideology and theory emerge his inability to even understand love's connection with his existence. Defining reality from the inside out, as an attempt to endlessly accommodate the self, he is unable to make the self-gift of his love to the other. He is hobbled by and remains within his own chosen theory.

Love in the Ruins

Percy's thoughts on the contorted reality of marriage in the present age emerge from the troubled character of Dr. Thomas More in the apocalyptic tale *Love in the Ruins*. Much is decaying in the grand United States of America; as Tom wonders at the outset, "Is it that God has at last removed his blessing from the U.S.A. and what we feel now is just the clank of the old historical machinery, the sudden jerking ahead of the roller coaster cars as the chain catches hold and carries us back into history with its ordinary catastrophes, carries us out and up toward the brink from the felicitous and privileged siding . . . that now the blessing or the luck is over, the machinery clanks, the chain catches hold, and the cars jerk forward?"[7] Elsewhere, the reader learns that wolves freely roam the streets of Cleveland. Tom's town and neighborhood face the return of barbarian Bantus and their incipient cousins: American hippies. Decay, Percy notes in the novel, is very much with Tom More and the denizens of the fading American age.

The failed marriage of Tom More and his wife, Doris, hints at the institution's thoroughgoing dissolution at the hands of the "theorist-consumer" complex. The marriage's ultimate end is heightened by the illness and death of the couple's daughter Samantha. Tom More, however, intimately understands that this particular tragedy was not the real doom of his marriage. It was rather in Tom and Doris's refusal to forgive one another and the type of consolation each sought in the aftermath of Samantha's death.

Doris, More informs us, sought a Gnostic cure: "Books matter. My poor wife, Doris, was ruined by books, by books and a heathen Englishman, not by dirty books but by clean books, not by depraved books but by spiritual books. . . . My wife, who began life as a cheerful Episcopalian from Virginia, became a priestess of the high places. But books ruined her. Beware of Episcopal women who take up with Ayn Rand and the Buddha and Dr. Rhine formerly of Duke University." Percy's notion of the theorist-consumer is concretely revealed here in Doris's "Gnostic pride" and her "yearning for esoteric doctrines." Doris seeks after spiritual theory to end her mounting gloom. Rejecting her native Episcopal faith long before her daughter's death, Doris sought liberation in Eastern spirituality, warmly baked by self-actualization psychology. Doris's Gnostic pride emerges from her acquisition of a peculiar knowledge that soothes her inbuilt anxiety and alienation, most keenly experienced in the wake of Samantha's death. As Doris exclaims, "I must go somewhere and recover myself. To the lake isle of Innisfree."[8] The answers for Doris to the realities of man's frailties, painfully revealed by her child's death and the alcoholic and somewhat cretinous response of her husband, Tom, are found in an excarnated spirituality and an accompanying belief in man's essential goodness. For what Doris truly seeks is to be freed from the failures of man—the soul-body composite—and to seek instead man as the angelic being succoring on the spiritual hosts provided by the latest Western "rotation" of Eastern religion.

Tom More takes a lower road that puts him in the dyadic response of creature to external stimuli. More lucidly observes: "What happened was that Samantha died and I started drinking and stayed drunk for a year—and not even for sorrow's sake. Samantha's death was as good an excuse as any to drink. I could have been just as sorry without drinking. What happened was that Doris and I chose not to forgive each other. It was as casual a decision as my drinking."[9] More submerges himself into the meaninglessness of sensual experience and a rather primitive interacting with his wife. Thus More's lower road forgoes the unique givenness of the human person's creative and purposeful interacting with his *welt*. In addition to More failing his wife, his dyadic responses obscure and diminish his vast scientific capabilities, which he recovers in the novel during periods of a more middling peace. From More's subsequent clarity emerges the following observation, "She [Doris] took the high road and I took the low. She said I was like a Polack miner coming up out of the earth every night with no thought but to fill his belly and hump his wife." Inverse to Doris, Tom has sought to lose himself in the apparent vitality of fleshly experience. As Doris explains to More, "You know the trouble with you, Tom? You don't understand a purely spiritual relationship."[10] True, Tom senses, but as Percy explicates in the novel, no one is capable of such an understanding.

Percy's analysis of the failed marriage in *Love in the Ruins* critiques the theorist-consumer age for its inability to make provision for married love. Percy's conception of the theorist-consumer evokes the fundamental corruptions that have emerged and accumulated on the backside of the Continental Enlightenment's projection of geometric certainty in human reasoning. Man has furiously sought to perfect his abode on earth through an imperial reason and will. The theorist-consumer, in Percy's designation, rebukes a receptive posture toward the world and to the knowledge of his own nature. Rather than seeing himself engaged in more moderate habits of being, which include reflection, a qualified reasoning, attempts at virtue, and appeals to divinity arising from preternatural anxiety, man now becomes the giant suck of self. In this posture man demands transformation, if not completion, by the seemingly limitless programs of modern ideological existence. Reality must be defined by a program that compresses it into a tightly honed package of propositions willed by the theorist. The consumptive element is best seen in man's frenetic devouring of ideology. In contorted fashion these willed propositions feed the undeniable and indefinable spiritual part of man.

The effectual truth of Percy's theorist-consumer is his profound loss of self-sovereignty, which is willingly handed over to the claimed theorists and experts of the day. Man's former consciousness of his being as gift and mystery, a sign pointing toward transcendent reality, is radically denied and transformed by this loss. Percy also explained the age of theorist-consumerism as an outcropping of the scientific worldview applied to phenomena beyond its competency:

> But we miss the point if we say that the Western world and the life of Western man has simply been transformed by scientific technology. This is true enough, but what has also happened is that the consciousness of Western man, the layman in particular, has been transformed by a curious misapprehension of the scientific method. One is tempted to use the term "idolatry." This misapprehension, which is not the fault of science, but rather the inevitable consequence of the victory of the scientific worldview accompanied as it is by all the dazzling credentials of scientific progress. It, the misapprehension, takes the form, I believe, of a radical and paradoxical loss of sovereignty by the layman and of a radical impoverishment of human relations—paradoxical, I say, because it occurs in the very face of his technological mastery of the world and his richness as a consumer of the world's goods.[11]

Percy here lays bare his high criticism of "scientism" and its forgetfulness of the Aristotelian understanding that one cannot expect more from a method of knowledge than it can bear. The hubris described by Percy results from a belief that true knowing implies empirical certainty in diagnosis and remediation of all the complicating elements of man's experiences. Moreover, the application of physical laws and properties to man's ailments is viewed as the only method for gaining leverage on his peculiar mental disabilities and shocking behavioral propensities. Seeking to displace the insights and deep-seated wisdom of premodern philosophical knowing and religiously grounded anthropology and ethics, scientism seeks to become the "all-encompassing world view."[12]

Problems with this methodological imperialism emerge immediately at the level of personal experience. Not filled by theory and ideology, whether it be Karl Marx, Charles Darwin, Sigmund Freud, or any other claimant, is the self, which remains the odd leftover. The leftover self is for Percy the sign of ideology's radical insufficiency as applied to *homo viator*. "Darwin, Newton, and Freud were theorists. They pursued truth more or less successfully by theory—from which, however, they themselves were exempt. You will look in vain in Darwin's *Origin of the Species* for an explanation of Darwin's behavior in writing *Origin of the Species*."[13] The culmination of Percy's observation on human life surrendered to universal theory was the striking loss of personal integrity and freedom. On this point Percy argued, "What I do suggest is that a radical loss of sovereignty has occurred when a person comes to believe that his very self is also the appropriate domain of 'them'; that is, the appropriate experts of the self."[14] Man is fully excarnated in Percy's indictment; the ghostly self floats above the body and mind, awaiting its healing or transformation by the other, the expert. Unable to comprehend himself in his entirety, the person is interminably split. The result is a loss of freedom owing to the resignation of one's sovereignty.

If the scientistic therapeutic approach to being—or, for that matter, any psychological or political theory—can never encompass the entire self, then, Percy states, sadness and distress will surely accompany the self who adheres to it.[15] The leftover self nags the theoretical self by rubbing it with its implacable eccentricities and anxieties. Those who have consumed the ideological realm, or who have sought to placate the self in all manner of goods and services, realize their central problem of contemplating and placing the self has not been solved. Messages from the leftover self hint at the paradoxical condition that an age specifically designed by human will to please and comfort the self is in fact the source of the self's most disorienting and alienating experiences. As Percy noted, "Accordingly, the self finds itself ever more conspicuously without a place in the modern world, which is perfectly understood by theorizing."[16] The sadness and anxiety of the theorist-consumer age is for Percy an important sign. Signified by the agonized displacement of the theorist-consumer is man's unique existence, which is also the source of his profound wonder. From such sadness, man regains his desire to inhabit the self and renew his quest for more enduring signs and clues to understand his tragic being and "where it belongs."

This disorientation of the self that Percy diagnoses in these "dread latter days of the old violent beloved U.S.A. and of the Christ-forgetting Christ-haunted death-dealing Western world" portends even more dramatic consequences for marriage. The false surrender of the self results "in a radical impoverishment of human relations," because the gift of the self to another becomes enfeebled.[17] Paradoxically, the particulars of human experience—marriage, family, work, and community—become the abstract features of life. An existence lived without the possibility of a freedom led by higher loves morphs into a whirling vortex of perfection seeking among the airy heights. The common aspects of shared love, daily work, and child rearing come to be redefined in light of a universal, unending, and ultimately defeated quest for temporal meaning. How, then, can one understand a sustaining *eros* in an age where all experience must translate into the comfort and affirmation of the self?

The terrible irruption is that the goods of marriage, prized as love, fidelity, companionship, reproduction, even concupiscence, move beyond the grasp of husband and wife. Though highly prized by virtually everyone, these elements escape man's comprehension if married love is conceived as a part of the theoretical fulfillment of the self. Marriage itself becomes increasingly extraneous and displaced in an age that seems unable to summon the honor and courage, much less love, to achieve the union of the complementary man and woman. Is the age of ideology and now postideology, which is better described as boredom, able to even contemplate the sacramental love concealed within this most difficult and most necessary of institutions?

Treated by Percy in the experiences of Tom More, and of Will Barrett in an earlier novel, *The Second Coming*, is a sacramental grounding for marriage exemplified in the multilayered communicability of persons. Curiously, Tom senses this directly in his joy that spontaneously erupts from the reception of properly ordered loves. In short, his marriage with Doris once worked because of his transcendent loves. A reception of an ultimate love makes possible his particular love for Doris. Tom states:

> The best of times were after mass on summer evenings when Samantha and I would walk home in the violet dusk, we having received Communion and I rejoicing afterwards, caring nought for my fellow Catholics but only for myself and Samantha and Christ swallowed, remembering what he promised me for eating him, that I would have life in me, and I did, feeling so good that I'd sing and cut the fool all the way home like King David before the Ark. Once home, light up the charcoal briquets out under the TV transmitter, which lofted its red light next to Venus like a ruby and a diamond in the plum velvet sky. Snug down Samantha with the *Wonderful World of Color* in the den (the picture better than life, having traveled only one hundred feet straight down), back to the briquets, take four, five, six long pulls from the quart of Early Times, shout with joy for the beauty of the world, sing "Finch 'han dal vino" from *Don Giovanni* and "Holy God We Praise Thy Name," conceive a great heart-leaping desire for Doris, whose lip would curl at my proposal but who was nonetheless willing, who in fact now that she thought of it was as lusty as could be, her old self once again, a lusty Shenandoah Valley girl, Apple Queen of the Apple Blossom Festival in Winchester.[18]

Prominently featured in Tom's observation is the Catholic understanding of the Eucharist and the grace it both signifies and offers to the communicant. The gratuity of the teaching and its practice, which for Tom and Samantha was in a neighborhood church adjacent to their affluent neighborhood, marked the joy that accompanied it. The delight Tom finds in preparing dinner, singing hymns, drinking bourbon, and reveling in the love of his wife is enabled by the total gift of sacramental religious practice. In recognizing the pure gift of being and, even more, God's rapturous concern with man, Tom is left foolish. Tom's delight points toward his reception of being, of locating it through and under God and also in Doris's being, their love peculiarly opened to both of them through the hybridized transcendence of the Catholic Eucharist.

The grounding of Tom's being in the reception of the Eucharist returns the discussion to Percy's diagnosis of the self's interior disloyalty in the theorist-consumer age. Tom's joy points directly to a transcendent God intimately acquainted with his personal destiny. Thus he is liberated from the false transcendence of the scientistic approach to being and its unnecessary reduction of the human person to a quantifiable monad unable to place his loves, anxieties, hatreds, and eternal longings. Tom's fullest appreciation emerges in one of his final recollections of his former marriage. Here, Tom relates a sacramentality of common life existing, paradoxically, in the attempts of geographical escape he and Doris periodically attempted:

> Sunday mornings I'd leave her and go to mass. Now here was the strangest exercise of all! Leaving the coordinate of the motel at the intersection of the interstates, leaving the motel with standard doors and carpets and plumbing, leaving the interstates extending infinitely in all directions, abscissa and ordinate, descending through a moonscape countryside to a—town! Where people had been living all these years, and to some forlorn little Catholic church up a side street just in time for the ten-thirty mass, stepping up on the porch as if I had been doing it every year for some twenty years, and here comes the stove-up bemused priest with his cup (what am I doing out here? says his dazed expression) upon whose head hands had been laid and upon this other head other hands and so on, for here off I-51 I touched the thread in the labyrinth, and the priest announced the turkey raffle and Wednesday bingo and preached the Gospel and fed me Christ—Back to the motel then, exhilarated by—what? By eating Christ or by the secret discovery of the singular thread in this the unlikeliest of places, this geometry of Holiday Inns and interstates? Back to lie with Doris all rosy-fleshed and creased of cheek and slack and heavy limbed with sleep, cracking one eye and opening her arms and smiling. "My God, what is it you do in church?"
>
> What she didn't understand, she being spiritual and seeing religion as spirit, was that it took religion to save me from the spirit world, from orbiting the earth like Lucifer and the angels, that it took nothing less than touching the thread off the misty interstates and eating Christ himself to make me mortal man again and let me inhabit my own flesh and love her in the morning.[19]

The recovery of his self in Mass makes life possible for Tom in its most fundamental form. Percy's reference to "orbiting the earth like Lucifer and the angels" touches upon the split persona inherent to the scientistic turn in human understanding. The scientist necessarily abstracts from his composite being in performing his exacting work of observation and measurement. He transcends, as it were, the particular existence in order to push further in his scientific work. Freed from the limitations of concrete existence, the scientist understands and makes known his conclusions while existing as an ersatz spirit. The problem for the modern scientist and for the general modern is not the process of abstraction that necessarily accompanies the knowing scientist, but the worldview that seeks to make this process a universal condition. The self, however, remains leftover and hovering, seeking its means of reentry with the physical matter of existence. The scientistic worldview is unable to understand this necessary movement, its purpose, and its signs. Thus, it fails to comprehend alienation and the available remedies. In embracing scientism's stunted depiction of the person, the ordinary man is doomed to replicate its errors and sadness.

Tom's reception of the Eucharist and his ensuing joy in the common goods of life transcend the reductionism of the scientific view. These extraordinary and common graces locate the self within time, in a place situated with other selves who now are comprehensible, even lovable. Thus the sheer commonality and limitations of everyday living stand revealed in their hopeful beauty and truth to the communicant Tom. To believe is to grasp in acute form the full measure of reality and man's place within it. Self-consciousness ceases being an unending burden of anxiety and fear and instead becomes the medium of delight in the ordinary run of a man's life. In stark contrast to this ameliorating reality, Tom becomes unable to place himself in the aftermath of Samantha's death. Deserting his religious practice, Tom fades into a lesser existence. Untethered from his religion and ignoring his scientific acumen, Tom loses direction, groping forward as something of a drunk and a less than able physician.

The Second Coming

In *The Second Coming* Percy provides yet another avenue into the difficulties of married love that arise from existential disorder. Will Barrett, a lonely, rich widower who barely stays this side of suicide, ventures into a cave to pursue his own Pascalian wager. Barrett will leave the cave only upon proof of God's existence and, failing this, he will stay in Sourwood Mountain until his death, the waiting eased by sleeping medication. Barrett, of course, is not really in search of God as the meaning and guarantor of his existence. Rather, he searches for God as one seeking Gnostic certainty. Barrett's experiment is to move beyond faith and possess the knowledge of God that will relieve his personal torment and the crippling memories of childhood, his father, his confused marriage to his now-deceased wife, and his failed relationship with his daughter. In so doing, Barrett seeks to transcend the theological triad of faith, hope, and love and move toward certainty.

Barrett's waiting God out ends not from any direct revelation or lack thereof but from an abscessed tooth, which drives him from the cave, vomiting in pain. In the very attempt to move beyond the limitations of his creatureliness and gain surety, Barrett is incapacitated by his physical weaknesses. The departure from the cave, however, brings Barrett falling, literally, into the arms of another searcher, Allison Huger, the daughter of his decades-old former love interest, Kitty Vaught. Barrett does not ascend from the cave like Dante's pilgrim. Instead, he gets lost and falls into Allie's greenhouse.

Allie is somewhat lost, an escapee of a sanatorium; her primordial aim is to reconnect with reality through language.[20] Her attempts are fitful and incomplete in effectuating this object. Allie, however, does not despair. From the solitude of her greenhouse, which is protected and maintained by the natural rhythms of Sourwood Mountain, Allie stumbles upon her stratagem of being and arrives at her own sacrament of the ordinary: "All this time she had made a mistake. She had thought (and her mother had expected) that she must do something extraordinary, be somebody extraordinary. Whereas the trick lay in leading the most ordinary life imaginable, get an ordinary job, in itself a joy in its very ordinariness, and then be as extraordinary or ordinary as one pleased. That was the secret."[21] If, in Percy's rendering, the disease of late modernity is a crushing existential disloyalty—man's refusal to face his immutable nature and the obligations and ends it gives to man—then Allie, who has spent years in a mental facility, is the wayfaring pilgrim, desperately seeking the prospect of an existence where words and lives touch indispensable meaning.

After his descent into Allie's cave-side home, Barrett's recovery of his self-understanding and identity proceeds apace. A man unable to endure himself, caught between the abyss of suicide or the sterilized existence achieved by a psychotropic drug regimen, he begins his recovery in Allie's care. Both are searchers. Allie's quest is to grasp reality through language, which she does, at best, incompletely. Barrett desires to finally cut through his memories, his fugues, fits of falling, and deep periods of depression and thus answer the question of his own being. Strangely, their meeting one another provides the logos of meaning both require. Allie and Barrett have emerged from their own separate Platonic caves where therapeutic shadows flickered on the walls attempting to erase the real pains of personal confusion and depression. They now see themselves clearly. To be self-knowing for the first time in a long time is the authentic liberation.

In her newfound freedom Allie notices a nagging inconsolability that sets upon her in late afternoons. The ravening particles that surround her appear to take ferocious delight in terrorizing her loneliness. "Time became separated into good times and bad times. The nights and mornings were good times. Then along comes late afternoon—four o'clock? Five o'clock? She didn't know because she had no clock and lived by forest time—but a time which she thought of as yellow spent time because if time is to be filled or spent by working, sleeping, eating, what do you do when you finish and there is time left over?"[22] Revealed to Allie is the irreplaceable need for the other. Precisely who this person is or what she is to do for him remains unclear. Cataloguing prior romantic relationships leaves her even more remote from the prospects of a complete and final giving of her self. Love is an experience somewhat foreign to Allie, not just because of rather meaningless attempts with other men, but owing most prominently to the detraction dealt to Allie by the decisions of her parents. Allie gathers that her mother, Kitty, had preferred ensconcing her in a distant sanatorium rather than personally squaring with Allie's difficulties. The abstracted manner of her mother's care resulted from the daughter's failure to be happy, adjusted, and pleased with self amid the other pleased selves. This had rendered Allie incomprehensible to her mother.

Will Barrett, or the stranger, as Allie understands him in their initial days together, has an immense need of her. Her first interaction is to "hoist" him from the ground after he tumbles into her home. Barrett is one who frequently falls, physically and existentially. Allie intuits that her irreplaceable contribution to Barrett is the careful and loving hoisting of his person from the earth. In short, she is the Archimedean lift and life that collects Barrett and enables him to live without the constant terrors that have enfeebled him. Allie proclaims to a local townsman, "I can do two things. . . . Sing and hoist. . . . With block-and-tackle, differential gears, endless-chain gears, double and triple blocks, I can hoist anything if I have a fixed point and time to figure."[23] Allie's slow repairing of things around her is finally sensed by Barrett after another fall and Allie's puzzlement, "Why didn't you get up? . . . I mean either I am not understanding something or something is not understandable." Barrett replies, "I blacked out . . . I tend to fall down."

Allie responds, "I am a good hoister. When you fall down, I'll pick you up."[24] If Barrett is drenched in too much reality, then Allie is too far from it. Her insufficient memory and general forgetfulness are compensated by Barrett's obsessiveness. Thus does their love find its function and its completion in their own natural and passing strange complementarities.

Percy's depiction of Barrett and Allie ends with Barrett divesting himself of his deceased wife's fortune, emerging from retirement and practicing law, and intending to raise his children from his marriage to Allie amid the community rather than in his robust mountain estate or in an alienating high-rise condominium in Manhattan where his elder daughter was raised. The sacrament of the ordinary, of delight in labor, home, and in his wife and children, marks a new promise for Barrett at novel's end. Dispensed from isolation and therapeutic control, Allie also appears committed to a shared life lived on the renewed terms of a properly ordered and placed self. Percy set a similar theme in the ending to *Love in the Ruins* with Tom's marriage to Ellen Oglethorpe, his dutiful clinic nurse and friend. Here, too, we are witness to marriage, the arrival of children, and life lived in more humble and thoughtful circumstances. Both settings witness the return of religious faith, if incompletely, to Barrett and Tom. Tom returns to sacramental practice and even takes to public penance at the end of the novel in reparation for former sins, the practice having been reintroduced by the novel's fictional pope, John XXIV.

Percy hints that the absence of great wealth, mansions, and servants has liberated the characters, bringing them to an ease with their very selves that was obscured in former times. Tom reflects, "Here's one difference between this age and the last. Now while you work, you also watch and listen and wait. In the last age we planned projects and cast ahead of ourselves. We set out to 'reach goals.' We listened to the minutes of the previous meeting. Between times we took vacations."[25] To be sure, Percy is not proposing an anti-progress theme. The clarity experienced by More and Barrett does not result solely from material humility. The heights that they reached were possible because of a confrontation both men made with death and God. The searching of More and Barrett has led to attempted suicides, to an awareness of their death-in-life, and has also produced thick answers to the questions of why and how one should live. The leftover self, and its gaping difficulties with peaceful existence, has been the ultimate sign for each man, pointing to a reality that transcends the human will. The irrepressible fact of *eros*, present even in the middle age of men who live in profound woe and self-displacement, is another sign of man's incompleteness. Thus, the taking of more humble work, of marrying and having children, of living in modesty, enjoying early mornings on the bayou, reflectively understood through religion, are the mundane and profound clues left the reader of these two novels.

The Long Recovery

Percy may not be entirely at sea in his pronouncement on the larger existential crises moving in contemporary American life. Thinking through Percy's presentation of the acute difficulties of marriage in the theorist-consumer age leads one back to his initial prescription of a southern remedy for a late modern disease that vigorously burns in America. For what could be more fundamental to the flourishing of American civilization and its many achievements than the recovery of the self and, in turn, the domestic family? Moreover, his engagement of these issues through the personal maladies and marital disconnects of Tom More and Will Barrett connects with his broader observations on the redemptive capacity of the South for the rest of the nation.

The larger connection between the health of civilization and its families is too seldom noted. The issue, however, is now joined by powerful, if not unpleasant, realities that press on America from several sides because of its familial failures. Percy's underscoring of the severe loss to personal relations from the displaced self now issues into an acute traumatic stage.

Writing in the middle of the last century, sociologist Carl Zimmerman warned that the onset of the atomistic family which, he noted, emerged fully in the nineteenth century, would slowly drain the energy and resources of the West. Zimmerman's thesis hinges on past historical episodes of atomistic familism, that is, marriage understood through shifting contracts and interests, which he locates chiefly in the decline of the Greek city-state period and the last two centuries of the Roman Empire.[26] Zimmerman's understanding of atomistic familism connects, in a sense, with the misunderstanding self of Percy's writing. The alienation and displacement of the person in the theorist-consumer age leads directly to the tenuous condition of marriage.

Of interest are Zimmerman's observations on the revival of these declining family fortunes in prior ages. The revival that occurred in the aftermath of Roman decline was the commitment of the rising church and its most prominent theologians to *fides* (loyalty), *proles* (children), and *sacramentum* (indissolvable unity of man and wife).[27] In later reflection on this trinity of familial virtues, James Kurth observed, "This meant faith in one's God, faithfulness in one's marriage, and faith in the future of one's next generations. In other words, at that most fundamental of bases of family and civilization was that most intangible of human motives—faith."[28] This movement of the spirit transcended the terribly short horizons that had shrouded moral action in the decayed and now collapsed Roman Empire. Eyes lifted to God, men found new meaning in the Christian language of an eternal destiny. Zimmerman documented the rise of the "trustee family" out of the ashes of Rome, which then slowly evolved into the full flowering of the domestic family in the Middle Ages.

If religious faith and the power of its upward pull on the soul of a civilization is able to overcome the more limited and compromised moralities of the current order, then the South may be, as Percy sensed, able "to help save the Union." Outside the old Confederacy the only state with similar, if not higher, religious observance is Utah, a state whose family demographics resemble those of the American 1950s. In the region's receptivity to a religion committed to the unchanging nature and requirements of the person emerges its capacity to revivify the domestic family.

From the basic failure of marriage emerges the activist and tutelary state that is necessary to manage the unintegrated neediness of persons bereft of familial formation and care. More pressing is the basic inability, in light of familial failure, to even have civil society. Ultimately, the institutions of civil society are built by and minister to the needs of young and growing families. These intermediate institutions slowly lose their way as the contexts of self-government dissipate underneath the weight of the greater dissipation of the family.

The religion of the South, largely evangelical, although with pockets of revivalist Catholicism, is still able to speak restorative truths to the rest of the nation. The prescription of an evangelical South with significant elements of its population still widely actuated by the claims of the New Testament is hard to deny. From the prosperous suburbs of its "Ruhr Valley(s)" in Atlanta, Houston, Dallas, and now Charlotte, among other cities, to its still more static areas, there hover the spirits of a biblical Christianity that are in great tension with the disloyalty to the human person that Percy identified. The central task that Percy anticipates is the need to mount beyond the platitudes of modern rights and face the problem of the intrinsic disorder of the modern self and its career of ruin imposed on personal relations.

Loyalty to man as the measured being finds hope not in the second reality of endless emancipations but in the contemplation of a completeness so thorough that man is driven by his self-consciousness to mount upward. This is not to deny the inroads made by cheaper and distorted understandings of human love, worth, and self-giving that are surely present in the South as in any other part of the country. However, the vessel of authentic understanding remains and can still carry, if properly formed, the profound understanding of marriage offered by St. Paul and St. Augustine in the early Church. It is an understanding of human love that has proved to have remarkable staying power and a hold on nobler spirits even in distressing times. Perhaps the love that the finite and limited person senses between him and the eternal God proves ultimately too significant for the immediate interests of time-conditioned ideologies and pleasures. Thus does man seek to instantiate this love through his marriage and realize its fruits before his own eyes. The exercise of this twofold love between man and God and husband and wife is now the South's unique task to communicate to the rest of the nation.

Notes

Originally published in *Perspectives on Political Science* 40, no. 3 (2011). Reprinted by permission of Taylor and Francis Group.

1. Walker Percy, "Going Back to Georgia," "Mississippi: The Fallen Paradise," "The Southern Moderate," "How to Be an American Novelist in Spite of Being Southern and Catholic," and "Concerning Love in the Ruins," in *Signposts in a Strange Land,* ed. Patrick Samway, S.J. (New York: Farrar, Straus, and Giroux, 1991), 26–38, 39–52, 94–101, 168–85, 247–50.

2. "Concerning Love in the Ruins," 250.

3. "Diagnosing the Modern Malaise," in *Signposts in a Strange Land,* 206.

4. "Going Back to Georgia," 32.

5. Ibid., 33.

6. "How to Be an American Novelist in Spite of Being Southern and Catholic," 182.

7. Walker Percy, *Love in the Ruins* (New York: Dell, 1971), 3–4.
8. Ibid., 61–62, 65–69.
9. Ibid., 259.
10. Ibid., 63–64, 68–69.
11. "Diagnosing the Modern Malaise," 210.
12. Ibid., 211.
13. "Why Are You Catholic?" in *Signposts in a Strange Land*, 309–10.
14. "Diagnosing the Modern Malaise," 210.
15. "Why Are You Catholic?" 311.
16. Ibid., 312.
17. *Love in the Ruins*, 3–4; "Diagnosing the Modern Malaise," 210.
18. *Love in the Ruins*, 12–13.
19. Ibid., 241–42.
20. In Allie's attempt to connect with objective reality through language, the reader senses Percy's rebuke of much of the modern philosophical project, chiefly in Kant, Locke, et al., which tends toward shutting man within the ideas of his own mind, unable to move beyond thought itself.
21. Walker Percy, *The Second Coming* (New York: Farrar, Straus, and Giroux, 1980), 247.
22. Ibid., 317. Allie similarly observes, "Is one supposed to do such-and-so with another person in order to be happy? Must one have a plan for the pursuit of happiness? If so, is there a place where one looks up what one is supposed to do or is there perhaps an agency which one consults? Who says? Who is doing the supposing? Why not live alone if it is people who bother me? Why not live in a world of books and brooks but no looks?" (241).
23. Ibid., 252.
24. Ibid., 256.
25. *Love in the Ruins*, 359. On his renewed disposition Tom comments, "My practice is small. But my health is better. Fewer shakes and depressions and unnatural exaltations. Rise at six every morning and run my trotline across the bayou. Water is the difference! Water is the mystical element!" (360). Elsewhere: "Strange: I am older, yet there seems to be more time, time for watching and waiting and thinking and working. All any man needs is time and desire and the sense of his own sovereignty" (360).
26. Carl Zimmerman, *Family and Civilization* (Wilmington, DE: ISI Books, 2008), 21–57. Zimmerman discourses on other acute instances of challenge offered in the French Revolution, statist ideologies, and the rise of individualism, but locates the Greek and Roman periods as paramount instances of atomistic families.
27. Ibid., 57–58. Zimmerman notes that Augustine developed this theory of the

family from St. Paul, and that it deepened and transcended the understanding of marriage and family in Roman society.

28. James Kurth, "Demography Is Destiny: The Fate of the Western Family and Western Civilization," in Zimmerman, *Family and Civilization*, 318.

Walker Percy's Last Men

Love in the Ruins as a Fable of American Decline

Brian A. Smith

Walker Percy set out to write novels that examined both obvious and latent maladies in our public life. Laden with allusions to philosophy and addressing the gamut of modernity's political and social quandaries, Percy's novels present images of our existence as wayfarers in a profoundly disturbed world. They also stand as near-apocalyptic warnings of where we as a people might soon go. In an essay on the role of the storyteller in modernity, he observed that a

> serious novel about the destruction of the United States and the end of the world should perform the function of prophecy in reverse. The novelist writes about the coming end in order to warn about present ills and so avert the end. Not being called by God to be a prophet, he nevertheless pretends to a certain prescience. . . . The novelist is less like a prophet than he is like the canary that coal miners used to take down into the shaft to test the air. When the canary gets unhappy, utters plaintive cries, and collapses, it may be time for the miners to surface and think things over.[1]

This mandate transforms the novelist into something like a physician, looking to diagnose our society's moral, political, and spiritual diseases before they consume us. Following his own description of this role, rather than simply foretelling the future, Percy hopes to jar us out of our complacency so that his "prophecy in reverse" will not come to pass.[2]

Given the way Percy's writings looked ahead to what are now contemporary cultural trends, the amount of critical commentary on the political and social aspects of his work remains relatively small.[3] In *Love in the Ruins*, he paints a particularly stark picture of a near-future America's descent into apparent chaos and ruin. In this effort, he provides us with an alternative to the commonly cited liberal End of History, and suggests a very different image of the "last man" to complement it, a vision that emphasizes our forgetfulness regarding the Fall.[4]

This essay explores the politics and psychology of *Love in the Ruins* and argues that Percy's value to political philosophers lies in the way he traces out modernity's warping effects upon our already fallen nature, and the consequences this has on our ability to resist self-destructive beliefs and actions in times of crisis. Where human community and sincere religious belief once restrained the extremes of human action, Percy develops a striking account of the way people unmoored from the old order lose their way and, perhaps more important, cannot develop a self-understanding that might lead them into a coherent, healthy life. Because we oscillate between the angelic and the bestial, our peril stems not so much from Nietzschean quiescence but from our alternating extremes of thought and behavior.[5]

Love in the Ruins presents the reader with a few days in the life of Dr. Tom More, an alcoholic psychiatrist living in Louisiana and "a bad Catholic at a time near the end of the world" (title page). More works and lives in Feliciana parish, a little corner of America torn by political, racial, intellectual, and theological passions. The parish is dominated by the federal medical research facility where More serves and once had himself committed as a mental patient. More's claim to the fame he desires rests with his invention of a device he dubs the Ontological Lapsometer, a sort of stethoscope capable of diagnosing and later treating the myriad diseases found in the human soul. Although the lapsometer is the means by which More hopes to make men whole again, its use is fraught with peril. While capable of temporarily manipulating the brain's chemistry to seemingly "heal" the human condition, the device threatens More's community and the wider world with disaster.

Exaggerated as they are, Percy hoped his characters would jar us into a renewed recognition of the dangers we face. While at times he endorses elements of Nietzsche's assessment of how emotionally stilted, uninspiring, and risk-averse souls could grow to dominate our world, this forms only one part of Percy's multifaceted diagnosis. Instead of a Nietzschean depiction of bourgeois mass men merely growing flat souled and increasingly alike, in *Love in the Ruins* Percy provides a rich exploration of the last men who inhabit a profoundly fractured American future.

Early in *Thus Spoke Zarathustra,* Nietzsche describes a sort of spiritual death among the world's content bourgeois. Contrasting them to his human ideal in the "overman," Nietzsche saw their failure to maintain great longings, inability to live with randomness and contingency, and love of comfort as portents of a world where men would slowly abolish danger and passion. Instead of political life, Nietzsche's last man chooses that of quiet private existence where every man insensibly becomes more alike: "No shepherd and one herd! Everybody wants the same, everybody is the same: whoever feels different goes voluntarily into a madhouse." These last men claim to have invented happiness, he observes, "and they blink" when told of the things they miss in their pursuit of egalitarian pleasure.[6] I argue that Percy's account of these last men carries far more nuance and complication, not least because of the way he explores the extremes of even the ordinary human condition.

Dr. More's America

At the outset of *Love in the Ruins,* Percy envisions a bleak future for the United States. He suggests that if a single, unified American ideal ever existed, that bond dissolved some time ago. A variety of competing visions emerged out of the old, fractured center of civic life and as a result, "our beloved old U.S.A. is in a bad way." Neighbors turn upon one another, "race against race, right against left, believer against heathen" (17).[7] Percy blends his characters' beliefs and allegiances together in intriguing ways, for with these Americans politics and theology—or its replacement in a secular scientism or humanism—become hopelessly intertwined. Throughout the novel, More asserts in Pauline fashion that "principalities and powers are everywhere victorious"; Percy uses him to show a variety of ways that our theoretical misunderstandings undergird malevolent political tendencies (5).[8]

In More's America, both major political parties have changed their names, adopting epithets devised by their opponents. On the right, the Republicans acquire the label "Knothead" and print banners proclaiming, "No Man Can Be Too Knotheaded in the Service of His Country." They totally unite religion and politics and cannot see the distortions their faith causes in society, and as a result, mindless defenses of patriotism and property reign among them (17–18). Continuing the long American tradition of allowing their enemies to name them, the Democratic Party adopts "a derisive acronym that the Right made up and the Left accepted," which Percy tells us stood for "Liberty, Equality, Fraternity, The Pill, Atheism, Pot, Anti-Pollution, Sex, Abortion Now, Euthanasia" and was shortened to "Leftpapa," and then simply to "the Left" (18). The Lefts celebrate removing "In God We Trust" from currency (19) and, having removed the "metaphysical baggage" surrounding life, they reduce the debate over euthanasia to one "curious squabble": "Should a man have the right merely to self-stimulation, pressing the button that delivers bliss precisely until the blissful thumb relaxes and lets go the button? Or does he not also have the right to throw a switch that stays on, inducing a permanent joy—no meals, no sleep, and a happy death in a week or so? The button *vs.* the switch" (122). Sparing neither party, Percy maximizes the story's effect by exaggerating all the most divisive issues in our political life—this forms one element of his "prophesy in reverse."[9]

Percy sets the story in Feliciana parish, a small niche where both Left and Knothead live in relative peace and harmony. More resides in an overwhelmingly white neighborhood called Paradise Estates, where both parties peacefully coexist. He divides his days between the solidly Knothead former hometown he serves, "a refuge for all manner of conservative folk ... patriotic chiropractors, two officials of the National Rifle Association, and six conservative proctologists," and the massive government scientific research complex known as "Fedville," where he conducts his research alongside an assortment of mostly Left doctors and scientists. A vast swamp adjoins all of these places, and "the dropouts from and castoffs of and rebels against our society" call it home. The swamp's residents include the African American "Bantu" guerillas that play a key role in the novel's events (14–17).

More's little corner of America serves as a microcosm of the wider world, yet he goes further and contrasts the relatively pleasant disorder of Feliciana parish with a vision of even more widespread political violence. More mentions in passing that his mother "predicted four out of the last five assassinations." Yet her role as "seer and prophetess" bears greater importance in his mind than the horrifying presence of such frequent political murder on the national scene (177). Not entirely oblivious, More sees the outbreaks of violence as a broader symptom of deeper concerns, but most characters find only the most extraordinary moments of butchery remarkable, attributing them to madness without looking deeper. Amid the spectacle of domestic mayhem, More's America also finds itself embroiled in another Vietnam-style intervention. This ongoing fifteen-year war (in which More served with the First Air Cavalry Division) takes place in Ecuador, a nation split between a Communist dictatorship in the north and a Catholic oligarchy in the south (19–20). While Left and Knothead each support their ideological brethren, Percy's characters hardly acknowledge the ongoing war. Ignoring current events and news, they all betray the desire to simply forget about their wider world.

While Knotheads remain nominally religious but deeply enmeshed in worldly concerns, the Lefts embrace scientific materialism and pantheism with an equal fervor. Speaking radically incommensurable languages, neither party easily comprehends the depth of their disagreement, and largely retreats from any point where they might achieve compromise. Many of Percy's creations remain two-dimensional; his use of them as archetypes or embodied ideas sharpens the novel's objectives. He fills More's world with a collection of people who lost sight of what it means to be truly human by embracing extremes instead of any more moderate course. Through them, we can see our own failures in understanding.[10]

A lapsed Catholic who flouts the Church's moral teaching without remorse but nonetheless affirms its dogmas, More finds himself adrift within a Church divided into three parts, with the old Roman believers "a remnant, a tiny scattered flock with no place to go." The majority either left for a Dutch schismatic wing "who believe in relevance but not God" or turned to an almost pagan American Catholic Church that plays "The Star-Spangled Banner" at Mass and upholds a civic religion of "property rights and the integrity of neighborhoods" over any genuine theological doctrine (5–6). Dividing his imaginary Church between liberals and conservatives, "who somehow felt that segregation was part of orthodoxy," Percy hopes to show the danger in subsuming faith into politics, a peril that exacerbates the alienation of men from one another within already fragmented communities.[11] Throughout these snapshots of life, Percy depicts the extreme possibilities of Tocqueville's American individualist, who "gladly leaves the greater society to look after itself" and in time finds himself "forever thrown back on himself alone," facing the "danger that he may be shut up in the solitude of his own heart."[12]

Amid this social unraveling, More encounters a myriad of strange behaviors. Throughout the novel, Percy depicts the hapless doctor's attempt to grapple with what the novelist saw as the distinctively human difficulty of being divided souls—creatures neither able to transcend our bodies nor capable of evading the alienation imposed by the Fall. While all people share this condition, Percy implies that what makes More's world so prone to crisis stems from the way man's notions about himself provide no means of naming or articulating the anxiety alienated consciousness presents. Lacking a language within which we can comprehend our place in the universe, we remain ignorant of our real situation. More's attempts to "solve" this dilemma in Percy's last men form the subject of the next section.

Defining the Cartesian Self

Throughout *Love in the Ruins,* More obsesses over the nature of the modern soul. He makes for a curious investigator: his Catholic beliefs lead him to seize upon what his friends term "metaphysical" notions, such as the divided soul; in his role as scientist and medical doctor, he seeks means to measure and treat his neighbors not as embodied souls but rather as organisms that respond to stimuli.[13] More strikes upon an idea that at least superficially seems to unify both concerns. Knowing he can measure electrical impulses in the brain, he asks a question: Given a machine that can read the location and strength of these changes, "could the readings then be correlated with the manifold woes of the western world, its terrors and rages and murderous impulses?" (28–29). Because nothing avails "in science unless you can measure it," More knows how important just such a device might become in saving Americans from their peculiar discontents—if he can link it to a treatment (106).

More dubs his discovery the "Qualitative Quantitative Ontological Lapsometer." As "the first caliper of the soul," More's device allows him to correlate our varied emotional states with particular neurological readings, and after being modified by a shadowy government representative named Art Immelman, it later allows More to temporarily treat himself and his patients (107). In comparing various forms of life, More notes that the brain activities of animals never show the complex marks of full consciousness. Percy suggests that true human consciousness appears neurologically in our ability to be more than our nature. When More used his lapsometer on a monkey, attempting to measure its pineal activity, "its self, that is to say, coincides with itself." By this, Percy suggests through More that monkeys and other lower animals have no real consciousness. Instead, "only in man do you find a discrepancy. . . . Only in man does the self miss itself, *fall from itself* (hence *lap*someter!)" (36). More's device records and names the failure of the human person to be at home with itself. Humanity's blessing and curse flows from consciousness. Percy's writing emphasizes the ways that our simultaneously reasonable and passionate natures allow us to act in myriad ways that miss the truth about our lives. But More's effort to reunify mind and body leads him into a hubristic fantasy; he becomes convinced he might undo the effects of the Fall itself.

Thus, until the end of the novel, More remains convinced he could bridge the gap between our inner and outer selves through technology. His hope rests in the idea that he might "hit on the right dosage and weld the broken self whole" so that man might "reenter paradise, so to speak, and live there both as man and spirit, whole and intact man-spirit, as solid flesh as a speckled trout . . . yet aware of itself as a self!" (36). Percy depicts a doctor frustrated with those who use science to treat irreducibly human things as mere objects fit for manipulation via the behaviorist stimulus-response model, yet this same physician wishes to use that same science to manipulate the self back into a prelapsarian state. Admitting the theological nature of his ambition, More refers to himself as "the new Christ, the spotted Christ, the maculate Christ, the sinful Christ" who will finally reconcile man to himself (153).[14] Percy highlights the irony that this machine, designed to measure the degree of fallenness, would be responsible for a more profound fall.

More attempts to reconcile human beings to their situation, but in doing so ultimately drives them away from their true nature. By driving away unpleasant feelings—our natural warning signs—the device allows its subject to defer or ignore the partial reconciliation that human community and faith allow us. In his blending of science and soulcraft, More's theological beliefs and vain aspirations lead him in wildly different directions.[15] Beaming ions into the patient's brain, the lapsometer does cause a temporary improvement in the subject's psychological condition: More soothes others' rages and stabilizes his own shaky nerves, but in every case this evades what always remain principally spiritual and social crises. In merely treating symptoms rather than the source of pain, the lapsometer allows him to sidestep our distress and thereby makes us unaware of our own disorders and sin.

However delusive his ambition to "heal" fallenness, More nevertheless understands something about the human condition: that alienation always exists alongside true self-consciousness, and that this causes us to fall away from ourselves in a way that reinforces our separation from God.[16] In Percy's imagined world and in his understanding of our own situation, we face a complicated dilemma in that our alienation manifests itself in unexpected ways.[17] Through More's narration, Percy traces the modern disaster back to Descartes, who inaugurated the "dread chasm between body and mind that has sundered the soul of Western man for five hundred years" (90).[18] Where Aristotle wrote that any man capable of living apart from the polis could only be a beast or a god, what haunts Percy and his literary creation is that human beings simultaneously exhibit the characteristics of *both* animal and deity.[19] We live in such a way that no other creature could endure: "No animal would, for he is pure organism. No angel would, for he is pure spirit" (212). While the Fall imposes this basic situation upon us, the modern condition exacerbates these extreme tendencies.

This division of the whole person and the inability to comprehend our real situation as fallen creatures commonly pushes us to vary between diametrically opposed modes of understanding the world. More terms this condition "angelism-bestialism." Neither situation allows us to be merely human. Bestialism forms the simpler phenomenon of the two extremes. More sees it as a reduction of the human person to existence oriented around "adjustment to the environment," as nothing more than a creature conditioned to respond to stimuli in predetermined ways (27). Percy's images of bestialism center on love and sex. In both cases, More fears how his colleagues and neighbors reduce human relations to merely *biological* interactions. Unable to see love as anything more profound than the outworking of an evolutionary imperative, the doctors at Fedville view couples having difficulty with sex as suffering from a "hangup" rather than any deeper source in their relationship (131–32). The danger here comes in the way human beings cannot live without recognizing or creating some meaning in their relationships beyond the physical connection. Having helped destroy the idea that love bears any mystery, the scientists and those who follow them find themselves falling prey to inhuman ideologies purporting to provide meaning to their lives.

Angelism forms the more complicated of the two extremes, and we can differentiate at least two different varieties of it in More's world: active and passive.[20] Both work to *reason* man out of his limitations and ordinary existence. First and more consciously, active angelism creates a situation where man has "so abstracted himself from himself and from the world around him, seeing things as theories and himself as a shadow, that he cannot, so to speak, reenter the ordinary lovely world. Instead he orbits the earth and himself. Such a person, and there are millions, is destined to haunt the human condition like the Flying Dutchman" (34). More discovers many instances of this phenomenon, but many of the cases appear in those most invested in scientific or political theories. Thus, those possessed by this sort of angelism tend to view the world as little more than an experiment. So long as such abstracted scientists make progress in their research, they consider any and all means legitimate. For Immelman and those like him, the promise of "healing" the human condition through social and psychological engineering leads directly into accepting monstrous sacrifices, as long as they serve progress. In a heated exchange with Immelman, More sums up how such angelism leads into horror: "If people cut each others' throats meanwhile, it's not your fault" for creating the conditions that led men there (363).

More observes that people suffering from angelism often reach that disposition as a direct result of their lofty ambitions and "higher" ideals. More's wife, Doris, who left him to go "in search" of herself "was ruined by books . . . not by dirty books but by clean books, not by depraved books but by spiritual books. . . . Books ruined her" (64–65). Yet Doris—whom More calls a "priestess of high places," who abandoned her marriage and died in pursuit of her lofty dreams of self-realization—posed little direct danger to the world. Her desires led her away from Tom and into a journey of what she saw as enlightenment. But her lack of religious faith, and her attendant "search" for her own truth, resulted in disaster. The danger in this mode of thinking—exemplified today in popular books like Elizabeth Gilbert's *Eat, Pray, Love*—stems from the way it authorizes a flight from all the restraints of our ordinary life. Such beliefs suggest that if we do not find our authentic selves at home, we must leave, even if this means abandoning our commitments and vows.[21]

Percy's depiction of Doris and Tom reinforces his point that our ideas about the best human life matter in ways modern liberals fear to address: Doris's dreams send Tom spiraling into isolation, and his wife to an accidental death on Cozumel. Much of the danger angelism poses comes in an indirect way: in Doris's case, her abandonment of home and family in favor of some elusive self-discovery poses a grave enough difficulty for More himself; yet for the society at large, the notion that family cannot trump individual desire results in disaster, especially because we need the moral reinforcement a family and community provide to check our disorder.

Percy's concern is the way that any abstract ideal can possess people. He represents this through More's realization that our goodness always remains fragile, and that "what lies beneath, some fault in the soul's terrain so deep that all is well on top, evil grins like good, but something shears and tears deep down and the very ground stirs beneath one's feet" (152). Those who fall into this pattern suffer from a sort of ethical blindness. Having lost their sense of being neither angel nor beast, people possessed by active angelism find it quite easy to commit monstrous deeds in the name of moral ends. Late in the novel, when the crisis induced by misuse of his lapsometer drives a portion of the population into angelism, More encounters a semanticist and his students, who intend to "practice creative nonviolent violence, that is, violence in the service of nonviolence," actions made noble in light of their intention to stand in solidarity with the rebels of South Ecuador (325–26). The influence of heavy sodium ion poisoning on their brains has removed all the sentimental restraints that keep modern humanists from doing violence and has made the victims think and act without moral restraint in pursuit of their philosophical goals.

Understanding the lapsometer metaphorically, we can see how Percy believes that some ideas quite literally rend the psyche. In the book, the lapsometer can cause man to become "totally abstracted from himself, totally alienated from the concrete world, and in such a state of angelism that he would fall prey to the first abstract notion proposed to him and will kill anybody who gets in his way, torture, execute, wipe out entire populations, all with the best possible motives and the best possible intentions, in fact in the name of peace and freedom, etcetera" (328). As a mirror of the twentieth century's ideological wasteland, the description is a chilling one. But Percy moves beyond metaphor in the text. The worst angelism More encounters does not result from the lapsometer but rather from his neighbors' native dispositions and ideologies.

To cite one example, late in the story, More meets a former professor of black studies and pro-football player who adopts the name Uru and leads the novel's "Bantu" guerilla movement against the white Paradise Estates. During a rare moment in the novel where characters acknowledge their real differences, Uru and More discuss the situation frankly. Uru insists he and his people can "build a new society" amid the ruins of old southern culture and displays his willingness to use any amount of violence necessary to accomplish this. He rails against his less ideologically pure comrades who serve in their churches and wish to treat Dr. More with respect. He insists accommodation will get them nowhere, and that their political struggle amounts to civil war (104). Only Victor, a Baptist church deacon and old friend of More's, saves him from Uru's murderous intent (295–302). Throughout these scenes, Percy implies that ideology and abstraction from the ordinary restraints of the self go hand in hand. Both lead to destruction, and apart from community and faith, modern men have all too little defense against these forces—particularly because of the way they subtly warp our understanding away from the truth of our existence.[22]

Although the active version of angelism abets violent, radical politics, Percy suggests it ultimately poses less danger to America than the less obvious passive form.[23] As a force that interprets events and shapes human conduct, passive angelism warps our vision and effaces our ability to recognize the reality of our situation. While some people lose sight of moral restraint and act in monstrous ways pursuing abstract ends, others simply lose their empathy for those who think and feel differently. This appears in various ways. Most characters in the novel continually interpret massacres as the work of madmen (9–10). Instead, More often insists that "there's a reason" for this behavior, that it cannot simply be dismissed as insane and therefore beyond moral judgment. Because these scientists deny the real presence of evil in the world, More's explanation stands outside their modern, secular understanding; people hear what More says but cannot truly acknowledge that he points them back to an absolute morality and the reality of sin (83). At other times, his colleagues see moments of angelism and bestialism inspired by misuse of the lapsometer as nothing more than "mass hysteria" akin to "St. Vitus's dance in the Middle Ages" (241). Beyond acknowledging the strangeness of events around them, none of the characters in the novel comprehend the way their science misleads them.

Passive angelism manifests itself in at least one other way in the novel: the characters' sense of place and time. The novel's events create profound disturbance in men's souls, such that More and his neighbors often seek some refuge from their ordinary lives. More himself creates a new home in an old, abandoned Howard Johnson motel. As the motel is a relic of the "old Auto Age" where no one ventures, More initially sees it as an opportune place to get away with one of his three love interests, an employee in the Love Clinic named Moira Schaffner. The ruin serves as his refuge against the dangerous influence of Immelman's experiment—taking the lapsometers and testing the extent of their capabilities by driving people in the area around Fedville into abstract or animal frenzies.

Later, fearing the impending disaster, More hopes to wait out the lapsometer-triggered heavy sodium ion release by enjoying a "prodigal" woman half his age, living on cartons of canned goods, cases of bourbon and sherry, and "the Great Books stacked alongside." "Think of it," he enjoins his audience: "reading Aeschylus, in the early fall, in old Howard Johnson's, off old I-11, with Moira" (258). The defective nature of this arrangement—its isolation, flight from responsibility for others, and ultimately hedonistic orientation—and its replication of Doris's path away largely escape More's notice. Yet while the abstract idea of life there appeals to More, all his experiences with Moira at the old motel remind him of his old family life. More's dalliances constantly drive him to recollect his pain and sense of loss, giving him no relief from his cares. Despite this, he cannot understand his emotional situation: "Why does desire turn to grief and memory strike at the heart?" (138). More finds no answer; his deceased wife and daughter continue to haunt his memories and stifle his lust for Moira and his other lover, Lola Rhoades.

More knows that aside from a temporary "fix" via the lapsometer, "the only treatment of angelism . . . was recovery of the self through ordeal" or other powerful experience (37). His lost family and ties to the community root him in a specific time and place, but for most of the novel he remains torn between the life of a transient and his longing for a settled existence. Throughout the novel, More's secretary and nurse, Ellen Oglethorpe, retains a quiet role as his conscience and tie to possible future stability. A "strict churchgoer and a moral girl," Ellen nevertheless lacks belief, finding herself embarrassed at the notion of a personal, supernatural God. Instead, she guides herself through the Golden Rule and tries to nudge Tom into doing the same (157).

Like More, Moira and Lola also live an ephemeral and transient existence, lacking the emotional connections of community and physical ties to a home. Twenty-two years old, Moira lives for moments of pure exaltation that draw her out of herself. As More observes, "Ruins make her passionate. Ghosts make her want to be touched." She has traveled constantly; her very lack of rootedness makes her compare the ruined motel to Pompeii, and she "thinks that the great motels of the Auto Age were the haunt of salesmen and flappers of the Roaring Twenties" (133–34). Lola betrays similar tendencies toward historical unconsciousness; however, hers find expression in a nostalgic vision of the Old South. She lives in a "preposterous" re-creation of Tara from *Gone with the Wind*. Also half More's age, Lola plans on staying in her gaudy replica mansion, minding her own business while the heavy sodium disaster proceeds. While Moira remains totally ignorant, Lola knows the world cannot long subsist in its state, but nonetheless gives in to an agrarian fantasy, claiming that she really only believes that "when all is said and done, the only thing we can be sure of is the land. The land never lets you down." As he often does when speaking with a person he opposes, More genially agrees but admits he "never did know what that meant" (279). Percy implies that neither of them really do. Knowing little about history, both women nonetheless place faith in an abstraction rooted in how they *imagine* the past—they flee there from reality. With Moira, this comes from a generic belief in a lost age of mobility and infinite possibilities; Lola's nostalgic imagination places her in an unrealistic pastoral vision. Neither this progressivism nor flight into the idealized past gives them a way to comprehend the political and moral situation in which we find ourselves.

Despite his awareness of the crisis and relative depth of intellectual resources with which to combat it, at different points in the novel More nevertheless betrays all the symptoms of angelism-bestialism. Having initially tested the lapsometer's diagnostic functions on himself, More confesses he discovered "a regular museum of pathology, something like passing a metal detector over the battlefield of Iwo Jima" (32). He finds himself stricken with "attacks of elation and depression, as well as occasional seizures of morning terror" (11). When he avoids ascending into lofty dreams of himself as the Nobel Prize winner who will rescue the world, More's self-awareness saves him: "I, for example, am a Roman Catholic, albeit a bad one. . . . Some years ago, however, I stopped eating Christ in Communion, stopped going to mass, and have since fallen into a disorderly life. I believe in God and the whole business but I love women best, music and science next, whisky next, God fourth, and my fellowman hardly at all. Generally I do as I please" (6). As a result of the contradictions between his beliefs, desires, and actions, More finds himself largely isolated. More's self-awareness is striking: he links his departure from the community of the Church to his descent into disorder. Yet the solitude runs deeper. While married, he never used his wife's living room to entertain, rarely did any of the things ordinary folk did, "never owned a pointer bitch, had no use for friends," and generally lived apart from others (270). While his distance from others abets his tendencies to abstraction, his solitude ironically stems from the grasp he has over the real conditions of his world. It remains an asset—or liability—his colleagues and neighbors largely lack, but undermines his ability to find a home (148).

Where for Nietzsche, the bourgeois last men simply experience life in a flat, uncomplicated lethargy, Percy paints a much richer picture of modern emotional life. Instead of this empty soul, he evokes moody, death-haunted creatures constantly driven to extremes.[24] This becomes even more apparent in the way individual pathologies of angelism-bestialism work together in More's world. Together they foster a peculiar set of political dilemmas and social sensibilities. In the next section, I explore some of the more harrowing dimensions of this imaginary landscape.

The Evacuated Center of American Social Life

Throughout More's misadventures, he observes myriad political, cultural, and theological divisions in his small corner of America. Most of them bear a strong link to his understanding of how the angelic and bestial further derange our fallen nature. While on the basis of More's story, we can infer that Percy's concern with the modern malaise stemmed from a series of deeply existential concerns, we can discern important political consequences that follow from the state of modern souls. For Percy, the relative effectiveness of liberal democracy persuades us into thinking we can live divided lives within a defective self-understanding. The nature of the system encourages this belief: "The center did not hold. However, the Gross National Product continues to rise" (18). This encourages a pragmatic optimism that men can live increasingly disordered lives so long as prosperity endures. He implies that while our society may not require political and theological unity, the absence of even a minimal consensus creates profound distortions in how we live with one another.[25]

In More's America, people view one another not as actual men and women but rather through labels and categories. The most salient abstractions here involve politics, religion, and race: Left versus Knothead, atheist opposed to believer, and black against white. Yet in Feliciana parish, the intellectual and cultural differences that separate these groups also manifest themselves in *literal* geographic and emotional separation. Having broken apart from one another, most people elect to live in separate communities. All the novel's various groups avoid genuine engagement with shared spaces and simply abandon directly contested ones. Whether or not Feliciana parish actually deserves the title of a community, it divides itself quite thoroughly. Rather than fighting to sustain life in common, the people let the public spaces fall into the same disrepair as America's roads.

Percy weaves two exceptions into this overall story and each bears some examination. He presents the first in a vast and disparate collection of "the dropouts from and castoffs of and rebels against" American society who reside in the Honey Island Swamp adjacent to Fedville and the Paradise Estates. These include the African American Bantu guerillas, young whites "who live drowsy sloth-like lives," psychopaths, pederasts, and many others (15–16). The other exists in More's home, Paradise Estates, "an oasis of concord in a troubled land" where both Left and Knothead live in peace (17) but protect their homes with "an electrified ten-foot fence, a guard house at every entrance, and a private patrol" led by a retired colonel who drives an armored car sporting a turreted machine gun (31, 281).

Yet in both places, instead of forming genuine and unified communities where the residents recognize their disagreements and act with charity toward one another in light of them, the residents simply form opposing subgroups. In Paradise, the homeowners pretend they agree and largely ignore one another: "On Wednesday nights one goes to a meeting of Birchers, the other to the ACLU. Sunday one goes to church, the other in search of the lordly ivory-billed woodpecker, but both play golf, ski in the same bayou, and give 'Christmas gifs' to the same waiters at the club" (19). In the swamp, all of the various sects live in splendid isolation from one another, each pursuing its own idealistic or monstrous ends. In Paradise, people talk and act as if everyone around them agrees, and More constantly encounters individuals who assume he concurs with their way of seeing things. Rather than proclaim his differences, More generally keeps silent. Nowhere do people communicate in a way that recognizes the reality of their plight.[26]

Exhaustion and decay rule More's America. While individuals act as if their world proceeds without profound tension or difficulty, in the meantime, they let their physical environment fall into ruin. Roads and sidewalks crack (8–9). Everywhere More looks, weeds and vines sprout uncontrollably (94). In one of his less philosophical moments, More laments: "Don't tell me the U.S.A. went down the drain because of Leftism, Knotheadism, apostasy, pornography, polarization, etcetera etcetera. All these things may have happened, but what finally tore it was that things stopped working and nobody wanted to be a repairman" (62–63). The deteriorating physical environment demonstrates society's failure to care for itself. In More's world, life's prospects seem dim, and the general disappearance of vitality holds other consequences.

Having highlighted the way people divide up their living spaces and find themselves unable to reach any moral compromises, More goes further still. While he claims that "most Americans do well enough," More even identifies peculiar medical complaints that emerge in Left and Knothead. Percy places the Knothead complaints in the body and the Left-leaning ones in the psyche, though neither monopolizes either type of symptom. The conservatives fall into "unseasonable rages, delusions of conspiracies, high blood pressure, and large-bowel complaints." Leftists "contract sexual impotence, morning terror, and a feeling of abstraction of the self from itself." Comically, this mix of symptoms vastly multiplies the number of proctologists and psychiatrists in Paradise (20).

Yet all the residents act and live in similar ways, developing an existential kinship to one another. Despite their divergent maladies, More claims not to "notice a great deal of difference between the two" (15). Both suffer equally from angelism-bestialism: the typical Knothead tends toward biblical literalism; the Lefts generally explain the world via scientific materialism. Both hope to embrace a complete system that orders their universe and eliminates the need to talk to anyone who disagrees. All of them periodically indulge themselves completely in unsatisfying material pursuits. None of them know how to live as whole persons between angel and beast, and their evasion of real community helps them ignore this fact. Throughout, their relationships remain superficial enough to help them evade this and obscure their despair.

Although Percy engages in a bit of imaginative excess in general, the story highlights the ways a purely scientific understanding of the world fails to come to grips with truly human things. To address this, he raises profoundly troubling questions of how we approach issues of human dignity in both sex and death. He does this by describing two interrelated projects More encounters at the Fedville medical complex, the Love Clinic and

Geriatric Rehabilitation. Euphemistically titled departments in the hospital that study sex acts and oversee euthanasia, each represents a case of what Percy sees as scientific materialism run amok. Both projects utilize a behaviorist understanding of human beings as creatures that merely respond to environmental stimuli, and each begins with the presupposition that a utilitarian calculus of pain and pleasure should define the whole of human life. More believes these labs disrespect and deny the essential human experience of self-consciousness, and that in doing so, they rob us of our ability to act as morally significant causes of events in the world.[27]

A tool like More's lapsometer stands at the center of the hospital's many psychiatric projects. Invented by Fedville's director and called the "Skinner box," this device stimulates the brain's pain and pleasure centers to allow doctors to condition their patients' "negative" behavior out of them while encouraging more "positive" varieties. Here, Percy plays on B. F. Skinner's use of testing boxes on animals and hypothesizes what modifying *human* behavior in them might entail, with disturbing effect. Placing all behavior on a scale of sickness and health rather than moral value, Fedville's doctors push their patients into acknowledging only their biological life. The most important difficulty Percy raises here is that science might even partially succeed in eradicating man's natural intuitions regarding a healthy life, and thus cause him to lose his one path back to living well. Percy highlights this through his depiction of the tensions between More's thinking and that of his colleagues.

Precisely because they cannot step outside their materialism, Percy's scientists remain incapable of comprehending More's various moral intuitions. Confronting Tom about his feelings regarding women, his colleague Max fails to understand why More's failure to feel guilt over sleeping with various women bothers him:

> "If you would come back and get in the Skinner box, we could straighten it out."
> "The Skinner box wouldn't help."
> "We could condition away the contradiction. You'd never feel guilt."
> "Then I'd really be up the creek." (118)

Percy seeks to demonstrate the consequences of conditioning away sin as a mere "problem." He reminds us that human dignity inheres in our ability to make morally significant choices in light of a proper understanding of the human condition. By evading the intractability of guilt, depression, and a host of other conditions, Fedville's scientists seek to make people into little more than clever, well-adjusted animals.[28]

In the Love Clinic, doctors observe and record the neurological impulses of individuals and couples engaging in various sexual acts. The entire process removes any emotional or relational component from these performances; the scientists only seek to understand the precise mechanisms of orgasm to maximize the bodily pleasure of those participating. At no point do the doctors or volunteers link their sexual lives to emotion, much less procreation. Percy implies that this way of arranging our relationships is defective in that it effaces love as a generative force that binds people together over a full life. Instead, the doctors in the clinic and many of the characters in the novel embrace ephemeral connections, a way of living that strongly undermines community. Percy uses his story to demonstrate that not only is lasting love necessary for human happiness, but it also reinforces the possibility for genuine human community—the sort Paradise, Fedville, and the swamp lack.[29]

The first and foremost example of this defect is the fact that children hardly appear in *Love in the Ruins*. For a novel largely centering on the life and death of society, this is particularly noteworthy. First, More's long-dead daughter, Samantha, haunts his dreams and he frequently turns to thinking about her at moments when he doubts himself or engages in misbehavior. Her memory tugs at More and reminds him of how his dalliances with younger women merely reinforce his alienation and solitude. With Samantha's memory reminding him of the failings of his present and Ellen nudging him into accepting a new life in community, More eventually finds his way to a stable life.

The second example comes early in the novel when More treats a dehydrated newborn whose parents reside in the swamp. Members of a "love community" there, the parents hope to raise the little boy in "a life of perfect freedom and peace" (50). Of course, no such thing exists among fallen creatures. By stripping away the supposedly social causes of evil, the love community hopes for heaven on earth rather than an actual community realized between flawed human persons. Even at his most confused, More recognizes the unrealistic assumptions that drive people into the swamp: the grateful parents encourage More to join them, but he repeatedly demurs. Through this, Percy conveys the notion that the swamp is not a truly human place. Finally, in the aftermath of the novel's events, More mentions his own two children. But these could come about only after some distinct changes in his life and that of the community as well. The absence of children, and the new life they represent within the novel's events, betrays one of Percy's fundamental concerns about fostering life in a period little inclined to accept its transcendent value. This brings us back to the scientific denial of life More observes in Fedville.

The Love Clinic strips sexual acts of their interpersonal components because no actual communication occurs there. The doctors dictate how and when various acts should be undertaken, measuring and recording the sexual activities without speaking with the subjects, only *at* them. They actively discourage the participants from doing anything but directly engaging in the act. When the couples find performing difficult, the doctors treat the issue as nothing more than a technical problem they must overcome (121–32). Because of its frankly authoritarian character, the entire procedure bears little relation to love. In treating human beings as little more than lab rats, the clinic's doctors break the natural bond sex generally reinforces between couples, instead making sex alone the object of their relationship.[30]

In More's America, old age carries far less pain and decline in bodily functions than today, yet in many ways the senior citizens of his time live profoundly unhappy lives because doctors so frequently separate them from their families and from any organic community. Geriatric Rehabilitation, or "Gerry Rehab," aims at "reconditioning" senior citizens who exhibit "crankiness, misanthropy, malcontent, solitariness, destructiveness, misery" despite the most perfect physical comfort. More tells the reader that this range of behaviors has become known as the St. Petersburg Blues; confronting a life of comfortable exile, perfectly healthy seniors simply lose their will to live. Instead of letting the elderly carry on the way they want, federal policy aims at making them fit in, at forcing them to enjoy their retirement in the way society expects.

When the seniors arrive at Gerry Rehab, doctors implant electrodes in their brains. Following Skinner's model for conditioning rats, they then place the elderly patients in a "recreational environment." They reward those who engage in the suggested leisure activity through a mild electric current that induces "a pleasant sensation, an unlocated euphoria, hypothalamic joy." With all the other patients, the doctors administer "a nasty shock through electrode B inducing a distinct but not overpowering malaise." The government ships those who fail to respond properly to the Skinner box off to the "Happy Isles," a soft euthanasia facility where doctors simply take those who "behave antisocially" and shock them into bliss. Once there, the seniors soon learn "to press the button themselves," inducing a mental state of "dreaming so blissful that they pass up meals"—that is, until they painlessly expire (121–22).

With the Love Clinic and Gerry Rehab, Percy notes how the doctors design procedures to eliminate guilt, painful emotions, and physical suffering. Percy continually draws our attention, however, to the truths that these form necessary aspects of human existence: psychological discomfort can lead us to seek to reintegrate ourselves into our community in a healthy way rather than just treating the outward symptoms of alienation and disorder. Eliminating psychological pain poses a real danger in that we lose our principal signal that something is wrong. Even more profound consequences follow from America's growing failure to reckon with death itself. The practice of sending unhappy seniors to a separate place to die—that is, sparing the healthy and young the burden of knowing what awaits them as well as eliminating one duty of family—places a profound limit on community. Knowing we bear no personal responsibility of care toward our elders may enhance our freedom, but it also allows us to evade the reality of our condition as flawed, mortal creatures.

The novel's central confrontation occurs in a medical theater called "the Pit." A debate between More and a colleague, Dr. Buddy Brown, transpires over the case of Mr. Ives, whose doctors transferred him to Fedville after he engaged in all manner of antisocial behavior at a nursing home. Ives seems immune to the Skinner box, and because he refuses to speak or respond to stimuli for a month, More's opponent Dr. Brown presumes the old man has suffered a stroke and demands that the hospital send him to the Happy Isles center for what he euphemistically terms "separation." Brown and the other behaviorists in the room insist that a man like Ives deserves release from his qualitatively poor existence, and that medical ethics should always lead responsible doctors to recommend a swift end to life.

With the extraordinary power of the lapsometer, however, More is able to "measure the index of life, life in death and death in life" of Ives. He determines that Ives is fully conscious of his activities but is utterly enraged at his situation (190). Dosing him gently, More then coaxes Ives into speaking and he reveals the reasons for previous his silence. The director of the medical center asks:

> "Why have you neither walked a step nor uttered a word during the last month?"
>
> Mr. Ives scratches his head and squints up the slope. "Well sir, I'll tell you. . . . There is only one kind of response to those who would control your responses by throwing you in a Skinner box."
>
> "And what would that be?" asks the Director sourly, knowing the answer.
>
> "To refuse to respond at all." (234)

In the logic of what Percy sees as an inhuman sort of science, an old man who rebels by refusing to act at all denies his right to life.[31]

Through More's eyes, Percy shows us a world where the pursuit of a pleasant, supposedly more fulfilled life overtakes all other priorities. Percy fears that materialism destroys human dignity; the fact his protagonist cannot convey this message to others renders the consequences of this in a very human form. An ambivalent man attached to neither the Knotheads nor the Lefts, More acts as the sole opponent to various "qualitarian" projects aimed at making life more comfortable. Neither Tom nor Ellen supports the geriatric wing's agenda. She simply insists that "it's not right" but, much like many Americans today, she cannot provide reasons for her dissent (158). Like Ellen, More can only bring his Christian moral intuitions to a debate but almost always stops short of explaining them in a direct way. At the same time, however certain his opponents seem in their "reasonable" belief that "it's the quality of life that counts," they all blush at More's use of the word "funeral" in the showdown with Brown (197, 224). In a sense, neither More nor his opponents live in full awareness of their language and beliefs. The behaviorists cannot acknowledge the moral reality of their actions, yet at the same time More remains unable to articulate the depth of his disagreement or ultimately explain the theological basis upon which it rests. Percy implies that a public culture closed to differing beliefs—especially religious ones—makes real communication impossible.

More himself shares some guilt for attempting to manipulate and heal the world through scientific means. In his hubris, he forgets that this is impossible. Nevertheless, he always hopes to use the Ontological Lapsometer in service of an understanding of human beings as more than clever animals or biomechanical machines.[32] Possessed by reductive abstractions, his interlocutors cannot imagine anything beyond their immediate sense perceptions and the scientific theories they use to explain the world. Even the most sympathetic cannot understand More's theological intuitions; instead, most presume their materialism to be something with which no reasoning person could disagree.[33] In many ways, this communicative impasse presents an end to American life. Yet in the end, much of the novel's action occurs under the *threat* rather than the actuality of catastrophe. My final section concerns the political consequences of this conclusion.

A Politics for a Time Near the End of the World

Percy frames *Love in the Ruins* around the possibility that More's lapsometer might cause a chain reaction that would permanently damage enough of the population to cause a national catastrophe.[34] At first, the device *seems* to send the world into a momentary freefall, one profound enough to cause More to view it as perhaps nothing less than the removal of God's blessing from the United States—for as he says, up until this point, America would seem to have enjoyed such good fortune that even atheists almost thanked God (3–4). More's pride causes him to imagine that his lapsometer could either cause such a disaster or, even more absurdly, definitively heal America's damaged psyche. In the same breath as he admits his hubris, More nevertheless hopes that the options remain simple and clear-cut: either the lapsometer "could save the world or destroy it," with no third option (7). More seemingly desires the heavy sodium disaster to herald the end, if only because that would present him a much simpler scenario than the one actual people face: being forced to muddle through life's complexities. This brings the novel's political dilemma to a point because in communities we encounter the subtle variety of human life. There our abstractions fall apart, and our relationships draw us away from mere animal life.

While the "end of the world" Percy heralds in the opening of *Love in the Ruins* certainly does not provide an excess of hope for the future of American politics, it may well have more to do with the failure of modern man's self-understanding than a literal failure of political order.[35] To cite one example, throughout the novel characters repeatedly construe acts of violence and mayhem as nothing more than instances of madness. They never condemn such behavior in a way that implies the culpability of the wrongdoers.[36] This flight from moral praise and blame bears mention because at the end of the novel, More discovers that a "love community" from the swamp committed all the murders throughout the book, a group whose "leader is quoted as saying his family believes in love, the environment, and freedom of the individual" (386–87). Their beliefs in love understood solely as free sex, in the environment as a greater good than human persons, and in the sort of freedom that grants license to murder become something of an ideal type of deranged life—the perfect image of existence oscillating between angelism and bestialism. With those forces walking hand in hand, that "community" embodies all the worst tendencies in More's world.[37]

Despite the love community's violence, More's semi-hallucinated apocalypse never quite materializes. More falls asleep as the entire community appears to stand on the brink of an angelic and bestial civil war. Yet when Ellen wakes him a few short hours later, she assures him that the town has mostly returned to normal while he slept, and that there "was no real trouble" (365–66). Coming from any other character than Ellen, this might seem like yet another example of an individual unable to come to grips with the reality of her situation.[38] Instead of suggesting any one person has "healed" the community, Ellen observes that things returned to normal because "people like it like this," a farcical conclusion in light of Percy's apocalyptic lead-up (366).[39]

By writing *Love in the Ruins*, Percy hopes to avert what he sees as the likely Cartesian End of History. Yet reclaiming the dignity of community cannot eliminate the oscillation between angelic and bestial—after all, fallen human nature persists. However, the restraining influences of faith, community, and family mitigate the worst in human nature. Precisely because the picture Percy paints is *not* that of the utterly vacuous, spiritless nothings Nietzsche evokes, hope may still remain for the world, but only if we find a way to live in the middle ground between the angelic and bestial. Particularly in the novel's conclusion, Percy suggests that only concrete links to a particular community and sacramental faith that works to protect the family will accomplish this. As addled as More often made himself, he never considered genuinely radical changes in human living to be healthy; he never thought he could *change* human nature so much as heal its extraordinary wounds. Even if he did so serially, Tom always envisioned remaining with and marrying only one of his love interests. Here, his utter refusal early in the novel to partake in the life of the swamp bespeaks his rejection of the ethos "love communities" embrace (46–55).

In an epilogue set five years after the novel's events, Tom marries Ellen and makes a new life for himself (396–99). More's lapsometer could not save the world—or even More himself. Instead, Ellen's love helps him recover a more moderate life.[40] He abandons his loftiest aspirations and instead focuses on making a decent life as a small-town doctor and father to his young children. More largely gives up his alcoholic lifestyle and earns a very modest income tending to his neighbors. His life reordered, he even agrees to help his friend Victor—the deacon who saved him from death—manage the local politics of a run for the U.S. Congress (400–401). Most important, the pace of his life changes: "Here's one difference between this age and the last. Now while you work, you also watch and listen and wait. In the last age we planned projects and cast ahead of ourselves. We set out to 'reach goals.' We listened to the minutes of the previous meeting. Between times we took vacations" (381–82). Finally rooted in a community, More recovers a sense of his moral limits. In his new life, he feels guilt and mostly avoids indulging in his old desires. While he changes, he now knows he cannot remake himself or heal the world.

Although Percy sketches elements of a world that might come to pass, he denies any of this might become inevitable. As a "prophecy in reverse," *Love in the Ruins* stands as a warning and as a challenge to reknit community. The crisis More *imagined* in such a disproportionate manner led him into the realization that something had to change. For Percy, moments where civic and political institutions fray along the edges create a similar possibility for society as a whole to recognize its situation. In such moments, the danger opens men up to renewed self-understanding. *Love in the Ruins* conveys the notion that while America's political consensus may be illusory, nevertheless people manage to overcome their differences through life in local communities. Flawed as it is, the American project remains more resilient than its critics would like to admit. This persistent fact may help remind us that our nation began not in real unity but rather in profound disagreement.

More carves out a place for himself in the midst of personal tragedy and disaster, one largely untouched by the manic politics of his age. His pain, suffering, and guilt remain important components of healing and reconciliation. The problem with science, materialism, angelism, and bestialism stems from the way they deaden us to the signs that might drive us to recognize our frailty and seek to reconnect with God and our neighbor. While

Love in the Ruins presents us no clear political prescription, Percy conveys the hope that we might reknit our communities amid the ruins of our old understandings. Leaving the details up to us, he insists that any revival of community must also carry with it a recognition that human fallenness will always push us to extremes, dangers we can resolve only by confronting the real nature of our situation, particularly in the poverty of our current ideas and language concerning how men should live. Only then might love in the fullest sense reign.[41]

Notes

I would like to thank David Alvis, Ralph Hancock, Peter Lawler, Elizabeth Mercurio, Aimee Raile, and Sarah Morgan Smith for their comments on various drafts of this essay.

1. Walker Percy, "Notes for a Novel about the End of the World," in *The Message in the Bottle: How Queer Man Is, How Queer Language Is, and What One Has to Do with the Other* (New York: Picador, 2000), 101.

2. Martin Luschei, *The Sovereign Wayfarer: Walker Percy's Diagnosis of the Malaise* (Baton Rouge: Louisiana State University Press, 1972), 181.

3. Some of the better survey works relevant to this essay include John F. Desmond, *Walker Percy's Search for Community* (Athens: University of Georgia Press, 2004); Mary K. Sweeny, *Walker Percy and the Postmodern World* (Chicago: Loyola University Press, 1987); Patricia Lewis Poteat, *Walker Percy and the Old Modern Age: Reflections on Language, Argument, and the Telling of Stories* (Baton Rouge: Louisiana State University Press, 1985); and Jerome Taylor, *In Search of Self: Life, Death and Walker Percy* (Cambridge, MA: Cowley, 1986). Peter Augustine Lawler is the most prominent analyst of Percy's political import. See his *Postmodernism Rightly Understood: The Return to Realism in American Thought* (Lanham, MD: Rowman and Littlefield, 1999), esp. chs. 3 and 4; and also his *Aliens in America: The Strange Truth about Our Souls* (Wilmington, DE: ISI Books, 2002), esp. ch. 10. For a few other works relevant to this effort, see Daniel Schenker, "Walker Percy and the Problem of Cultural Criticism," *South Atlantic Review* 53, no. 1 (1988): 83–97; Karl-Heinz Westarp, "Message to the Lost Self: Percy's Analysis of the Human Situation," *Renascence* 44, no. 3 (1992): 215–24; and Matthew Sitman and Brian Smith, "The Rift in the Modern Mind: Tocqueville and Percy on the Rise of the Cartesian Self," *Perspectives on Political Science* 36, no. 1 (2007): 15–22.

4. Percy composed *Love in the Ruins* in the late 1960s. While Percy never directly dates the novel, at one point Tom More notes that at age seventy, Perry

Como still regularly performed. This dates the beginning of his "time near the end of the world" to July 1983. *Love in the Ruins* (New York: Picador, 1971), 97. Hereafter, all page references to this book will be given parenthetically in the text.

5. On the complexity of Percy's understanding of the last man, see Lawler, *Postmodernism Rightly Understood*, 10–11, 91–96. In another context, Joshua Mitchell terms this sort of personality that oscillates between extremes of thought and belief the "Augustinian Self." Mitchell's presentation of Augustine and Percy's anthropology overlap considerably. See ch. 2 in his *The Fragility of Freedom: Tocqueville on Religion, Democracy, and the American Future* (Chicago: University of Chicago Press, 1995), esp. 40–42.

6. Friedrich Nietzsche, *Thus Spoke Zarathustra*, trans. Walter Kaufmann (New York: Penguin, 1966), 16–19.

7. Poteat observes that no group eludes Percy's "satiric reach: liberals, conservatives, blacks, whites, Roman Catholics, Protestants—just to name a few—are equally chastised for their complicity in the imminent demise of Western culture" (*Walker Percy and the Old Modern Age*, 70).

8. Compare to Ephesians 6:12: "For we are not contending against flesh and blood, but against the principalities, against the powers, against the world rulers of this present darkness, against the spiritual hosts of wickedness in the heavenly places" (RSV).

9. Percy himself saw the goal of *Love in the Ruins* as "to take a certain point of view of Dr. More's and from it to see the social and political situation in America." See *Conversations with Walker Percy*, ed. Lewis A. Lawson and Victor A. Kramer (Jackson: University Press of Mississippi, 1985), 74.

10. For two accounts of this, see Gary M. Ciuba, *Walker Percy: Books of Revelations* (Athens: University of Georgia Press, 1991), 134–36; and Michael Kobre, *Walker Percy's Voices* (Athens: University of Georgia Press, 2000), 116–18.

11. *More Conversations with Walker Percy*, ed. Lewis A. Lawson and Victor A. Kramer (Jackson: University Press of Mississippi, 1993), 118–19.

12. Alexis de Tocqueville, *Democracy in America*, ed. J. P. Mayer, trans. George Lawrence (New York: Harper, 1969), 507–8.

13. Desmond argues that More cannot act as a doctor and scientist without succumbing on some level to the very scientism he deplores in his opponents. This fundamental paradox undermines everything he attempts in the course of events (*Walker Percy's Search for Community*, 129–30).

14. On this, see ibid., 5–8; and J. Gerald Kennedy, "The Sundered Self and the Riven World: *Love in the Ruins*," in *The Art of Walker Percy: Stratagems for Being*, ed. Panthea Reid Broughton (Baton Rouge: Louisiana State University Press, 1979), 120–21.

15. Kobre, *Walker Percy's Voices*, 133–34.

16. Lewis A. Lawson, "Tom More: Walker Percy's Alienated Genius," *South Central Review* 10, no. 4 (1993): 34, 37–38.

17. For Percy's own account of these issues, see his two nonfiction books, *The Message in the Bottle* and *Signposts in a Strange Land*, ed. Patrick Samway, S.J. (New York: Farrar, Straus, and Giroux, 1991), and his satirical self-help book, *Lost in the Cosmos: The Last Self-Help Book* (New York: Farrar, Straus, and Giroux, 1983).

18. In a 1989 interview, Percy observed that "the only theory of man in the air is what comes from the popular media, which is a kind of pop scientific idea which I saw is fundamentally Cartesian and incoherent. . . . *Love in the Ruins* is really an exercise in Cartesianism" (*More Conversations with Walker Percy*, 232–33). For one account of Percy's assault on modern Cartesianism, see Sitman and Smith, "The Rift in the Modern Mind," 15–17.

19. Aristotle *Politics* 1253a1–20.

20. This distinction may be found in Taylor, *In Search of Self*, 44.

21. Gilbert's best seller (New York: Penguin, 2007) chronicles a similar story to More's Doris: she flees from her marriage, seeking fulfillment in Italian gelato, an Indian ashram, and a divorced Brazilian tourist in Bali. Given the tone of *Love* and Percy's other works, one can only imagine Percy's response to a work like Gilbert's.

22. On this, see Lawler, *Postmodernism Rightly Understood*, 95–96.

23. Taylor, *In Search of Self*, 58.

24. Lawler, *Postmodernism Rightly Understood*, 12.

25. On Percy's desire for authentic community, see the introduction to Desmond, *Walker Percy's Search for Community*, esp. 3–17.

26. For two examples, see *Love in the Ruins*, 47–55 and 126–32.

27. On the sense in which treating human beings via the stimulus-response model precludes real communication, see Desmond, *Walker Percy's Search for Community*, 121–22.

28. Lawler, *Postmodernism Rightly Understood*, 12.

29. In a 1985 interview, Percy remarked that it "seems that the nearest approximation, humanly speaking, of happiness is human love. You would like for your characters to get out of the fix they are in and achieve some kind of happiness. The best way to do it, the easiest way to do it, is to fall in love" (*More Conversations with Walker Percy*, 107). This echoes 1 John 4:7–8, "Beloved, let us love one another; for love is of God, and he who loves is born of God and knows God. He who does not love does not know God; for God is love" (RSV).

30. On the authoritarian nature of the Love Clinic's procedures, see Desmond, *Walker Percy's Search for Community*, 123–24.

31. For two accounts of the scene in the Pit, see Ciuba, *Walker Percy*, 146; and Desmond, *Walker Percy's Search for Community*, 135–36.

32. Poteat, *Walker Percy and the Old Modern Age*, 72–73.

33. On the utter inability of More's interlocutors to discuss or negotiate outside their presuppositions, see Luschei, *The Sovereign Wayfarer*, 203.

34. On what we might call Percy's anti-apocalyptic teaching in *Love*, see Ciuba, *Walker Percy*, 131.

35. Desmond argues that the world Percy sees ending is that of the easy appearance of compromise in the American spirit—a warning to both uncomplicated secular humanism and literalist faith (*Walker Percy's Search for Community*, 119).

36. For one instance, see *Love in the Ruins*, 267.

37. Lawler, *Postmodernism Rightly Understood*, 95–96.

38. On Ellen's role as More's conscience and one of the only characters who truly understands the reality of life in Feliciana parish, see Taylor, *In Search of Self*, 154–55; and Sweeny, *Walker Percy and the Postmodern World*, 22–23.

39. Ciuba, *Walker Percy*, 162–64.

40. On More's reconciliation with sin, see Poteat, *Walker Percy and the Old Modern Age*, 74–76.

41. Desmond, *Walker Percy's Search for Community*, 257.

The Second Coming of Walker Percy

From Segregationist to Integrationist

Brendan P. Purdy and Janice Daurio

This essay looks at three strands of Walker Percy's thoughts through the decade or so before his 1956 *Commonweal* article, "Stoicism and the South."[1] These three strands of thought are semiotics, Catholicism, and Stoicism. Percy's work on semiotics, his reading of Kierkegaard, and his conversion to Catholicism led him to make the change from being a segregationist southern moderate to an integrationist southern moderate. Or, to put it more precisely, Percy realized that being a southern moderate no longer allowed for the segregationist viewpoint. After examining these three strands, we consider "Stoicism in the South" with respect to historical, cultural, philosophical, and theological concerns.

As a frame of reference for this chapter, consider the following story about Percy. During spring break in 1936, Percy and his best friend, Shelby Foote, a novelist and historian (most famously the author of the magisterial three-volume opus *The Civil War: A Narrative*), took a bus trip to New York City. While traveling Foote opined that integration would "probably not be a bad thing." Shocked, Percy replied, "I cannot believe that you, a southerner, would say that."[2] This is the position that Percy began with and the purpose of this essay is to describe the Second Coming that transformed Percy from a segregationist to an integrationist.

Semiotics

Language and Consciousness

As an admirer of Charles Sanders Peirce and a novelist, Percy valued language highly. In fact, the analysis and study of language dominates his nonfictional work. In particular, he was interested in semiotics and the philosophy of language. Percy understood the human person to be a symbol maker by nature, as is clear from his essays on semiotics, for example: "Culture: The Antinomy of the Scientific Method," "Semiotic and a Theory of Knowledge," and "Symbol, Consciousness, and Intersubjectivity."[3] He also understood that changing language changes ideas, and that what language one uses and the manner in which it is used reflect on the unacknowledged body of beliefs of the community. In particular, Percy believed that naming is a social activity. Naming, and the "misnaming" of metaphors, both makes and reflects one's world. Human beings are embodied consciousnesses that are part of the natural world, so it is no radical claim to say that naming objects in the world makes the world. However, there is vigorous debate within contemporary philosophy on proper names, and since this debate can be traced back to Peirce's thought it bears mentioning.

Saul Kripke, in the most important work on the philosophy of language to be published after Wittgenstein's *Philosophical Investigations* (originally published in 1953), argued in *Naming and Necessity* that proper names are "rigid designators," that is, they designate the same object in all possible worlds in which that object exists and never designate anything else.[4] Thus, a rigid designator merely denotes; here Kripke was arguing against the descriptivist theory of naming of Frege and Russell, who argued that all words, including proper names, have both a sense and a reference (*loci classici*).[5] Thus, Kripke was arguing against the Anglo-American analytic tradition.

One important aspect of Kripke's theory is that an object is "baptized" and this fixes the reference of the object. From here the "name denoting that object is then used to refer to that object."[6] From this one can see why Kripke's theory is called a causal theory of reference (as opposed to a descriptivist theory like those of Frege, Russell, Wittgenstein, et al.), since the name is assigned by an initial community of speakers and then from that point on "the name is spread from link to link as if by a chain."[7]

To explain Kripke's thought simply: for example, at a certain point in time, there was a baptism by the New World colonists to call blacks "slaves." One such individual is John Punch.[8] Kripke would argue that while "John Punch" would refer to the same individual in all possible worlds (unless he does not exist in one of those worlds), it is only (tragically) accidental that in this world "John Punch" is the same as "first African slave in the American colonies." From the time of the baptism (1640) until the end of the Civil War and the passing of the Thirteenth Amendment in 1865, the meaning of "black" was generally the same as "slave," at least in the South. However, while the meaning changed (contra Frege, Russell, et al.), the reference remained the same. So at least in respect to looking at the dehumanizing tendencies of speakers, Kripke's theory is existential in a sense that Percy would appreciate: John Punch is a man and it is only accidental that he can be described as a slave, but it is not who he truly is since there are possible worlds where Punch is a freeman. The use of the term "slave" demonstrates the power of language that Percy was so keen on emphasizing.

As is often the case in philosophy, even for such an original mind as Kripke's, there are precursors. Peirce, who so influenced Percy, held a theory of direct reference like Kripke, at least for proper names: "Every language must have proper names; and there is no verb wrapped up in a proper name. Therefore, there would seem to be a direct suggestion there of a true common noun or adjective. But, notwithstanding that suggestion, almost every family of man thinks of general words as parts of verbs."[9]

Through Peirce, part of the landscape of Percy's thoughts on language is a view that shares affinities with Kripke. There is no claim here of any explicit relationship between Percy and Kripke, but elaborating on the affinities between Kripke and Peirce allows for a precise formulation of naming as a communal process. Note that the original title of Percy's "The Mystery of Language" was "The Act of Naming," and unsurprisingly this article is about sense and reference, without all of the logical hand wringing of the analytic tradition.[10] How does this interlude into analytic philosophy relate to Percy becoming an opponent of segregation?

Percy asserts that people don't have an idea and then search for words for it; rather, people become comfortable with certain words and phrases and this ease of use changes our ideas. Words accommodate certain ideas and uses of language and forbid others. The universal dignity of the human person forbids thinking and speaking of any marginalized people as a problem to be solved or a nuisance to be gotten rid of. Returning to the example above, John Punch was clearly treated as a problem to be solved, with horrible consequences for the United States.

An example of the relationship between semiotics and religious belief can be found in the divergent views of the Eucharist within Christianity. The traditional view of Catholicism and Orthodoxy is that the Eucharist is the body and blood of Christ (see John 6:54); however, the Protestant belief is that the Eucharist is merely a symbol. Thus, when the Reformers changed the meaning of the Eucharist, they also changed a number of concomitant theological ideas. For example, "priest" became "minister" and "mass" became "service." Late in his life (1989) Percy quoted Flannery O'Connor on the Eucharist: "If it's only a symbol, then the hell with it," and this gets back to the Eucharist being a rigid designator for the body and blood of Christ.[11]

Percy argues that a common mistake about language (mistaken in being incomplete) is that the purpose of language is to convey information. In addition to conveying information, "words are potent agents," Percy writes in "Metaphor as Mistake."[12] The words *segregation* and *integration* do more than convey information; in fact, conveying information is the least thing they do. A thorough reading of the dictionary entries for these words does not encompass them. Each comes with a long train of history (like Kripke's "links of a chain") and evokes groups of committed persons with complex philosophies; each word has a picture (cf. Wittgenstein's "picture theory").[13] This is undoubtedly true as well about what Percy calls the three mysteries of the Christian faith: the Incarnation, the Trinity, and the real Presence in the Eucharist.[14]

In present thought, there is a wide rift between those who think that the study of consciousness is and only is a "third-person" affair and those who think that first-person, lived consciousness is the primary category. For the former group, psychological consciousness is to be studied objectively and as a matter of science. Once all of the psychological causes of consciousness are stated and neuroscience explains what causes consciousness, then there will be no more left to do.

For the latter group, phenomenal consciousness, individual experience of one's own consciousness, gets the primacy. It is the primacy of lived consciousness, that is, the first-person consciousness of subjective experience. On this view, one cannot give a full and complete account of consciousness with respect to its causes and structure, as studied in cognitive psychology and neuroscience, without remainder. As David Chalmers puts it (using Kripke's notions of possible worlds from *Naming and Necessity*), in creating, once God had fixed all the microphysical facts, he still had more work to do; there was phenomenal consciousness left.[15] In his own way, Percy discusses this in "The Coming Crisis in Psychiatry" (first published in 1957) where he writes that psychiatry must decide if it is a biological science or a humanistic discipline.[16] In other words, is consciousness without or with remainder?

Consider a zombie world: a molecule-for-molecule identical world, but populated with beings without consciousness. Chalmers argues that such a zombie world is conceivable and therefore logically possible. If it is logically possible, then lived consciousness must be something over and above the physical facts. Consciousness supervenes on the microphysical facts in our world, the natural world, but it does not do so in every possible world. Therefore, in the same way that language is more than mere meaning, consciousness is more than mere matter, which is a belief that Percy certainly shared.

In a prescient essay in 1958, Percy suggests a reason for this rift in views of consciousness and a way to close the gap between psychological and phenomenal consciousness. So central does Percy take language to be to human knowledge that he makes this startling claim for its importance: the rift has resulted "from a failure to appreciate the extraordinary role of the symbol, especially the language symbol, in man's orientation to the world."[17] Percy likes the primacy that Husserl gives to first-person consciousness, but regrets Husserl's failure to appreciate the social dimension of that consciousness. Mind and consciousness develop within a social process: that's why the morality of segregation may seem like common sense. Their sensitivities or background commitments are developed within a society with a coherent belief system.

In the article, Percy continues in the Peirce-Kripke vein: he argues that what happens when someone learns the meaning of a word is the grasping of the concept not of a thing but of an event. Further, when we learn a word, "what we wish to know is what happens."[18] The meaning of a (noun) word is as much a reference to what happens between people (speaker, hearer) as it is a reference to a thing. "Denotation is an exercise in intersubjectivity."[19] When two supporters of segregation are talking about segregation, however objective they try to be, this talk is still first and foremost a meeting of two subjects, an "I-Thou" meeting, whose thinking is constrained by their conceptual categories and rigid designators. When they speak of segregation, they are not aware of it (period); they are speaking of what it is for them qua southern Stoics. What seems to be commonsensical and self-evident is always the common sense and self-evidence of the community.

Conversations have a way of reinforcing the beliefs people already have. And this kind of reinforcement is pleasant; it cements the community. The discordant voice of the integrationist, especially when it is the voice of one of the members of the community, is much more jarring. Every act of consciousness is a participation in a community; pace Husserl, there is no isolated ego-consciousness. "The I think is only made possible by a prior mutuality: we name."[20]

Language and the Psalms

The communal language of the Israelites, which became and still is the communal prayer book of the Catholic Church, is the Psalms. It is unsurprising that "Negro spirituals" of the New World were often comprised of the Psalms since these praises of David often have as their subject matter the downtrodden, oppressed, and forgotten, as Jesus Christ during the Crucifixion, as reported by both Matthew (27:46) and Mark (15:34); *"Eli, Eli [Eloi, Eloi] lama sabachthani"* is the first line of Psalm 21 (22): "My God, My God, why have you forsaken me?" Also, as a lay affiliate (oblate) of the Roman Catholic monastic order of St. Benedict, Percy prayed the Office of Lauds. The psalm prayed on Sundays, Feasts, and Solemnities in the Divine Office (Liturgy of the Hours) is as follows:

> O God, you are my God whom I seek; For my flesh pines and my soul thirsts like the earth parched, lifeless and without water. Thus have I gazed toward you in the sanctuary to see your power and glory, For your kindness is a greater good than life; my lips glorify you. . . . But they shall be destroyed who seek my life, they shall go to the depths of the earth; They shall be delivered over to the sword, and shall be the prey of jackals. The King, however, shall rejoice in God; everyone who swears by him shall glory, but the mouths of those who speak falsely shall be stopped. (Psalm 62)

Many of the Psalms take this form: the psalmist praising God while declaring his own unworthiness, followed by stanzas of rejoicing at the destruction of his enemy. The Psalms have spoken to the least among humanity from the times of the Babylonian exile of the Hebrew people (circa 350 BC) until the present day. Why do the Psalms bring so much comfort to the afflicted? And further, what do the Psalms have to do with language and integration?

The theology of the Psalms is the theology of blacks in the South, the less powerful in the land of the powerful, the Africans in the antebellum South held in their own Babylonian captivity.[21] Pity is a distinctly Stoic emotion, and in Walker Percy's uncle and adoptive father Will's *Lanterns on the Levee* (originally published in 1941, republished with Walker's introduction in 1973), he shows himself an exemplar of southern Stoicism. He writes at the beginning of the chapter entitled "A Note on Racial Relations," "A superabundance of sympathy has always been expended on the Negro, neither undeservedly nor helpfully, but no sympathy whatever, so far as I am aware, has ever been expended on the white man living among the Negroes. Yet he, too, is worthy not only of sympathy but of *pity* for many reasons. To live habitually as a superior among inferiors. . . . To live among a people whom, because of their needs, one must in common decency protect and defend."[22] This quotation, in addition to demonstrating the Stoic virtue of pity, also demonstrates the Stoic view of those lower than them socially. This quote is very jarring to modern ears, but one must remember, as Percy pointed out, that his uncle "was regarded as a liberal, a dangerous liberal" by his contemporaries.[23]

But in the Psalms, pity or compassion (*rachamim*) is almost exclusively reserved for God.[24] Therefore, it is inappropriate for the landowner to be compassionate toward his servants. The relationship of humans to each other is as children of the same father. To take a compassionate attitude toward other human beings is to usurp the place that must be held by God alone. It is not pity that is called for, but solidarity and love.

The Psalms contain some the most powerful words in Hebrew Scripture because they demonstrate through poetry and song the closeness of God to his people, particularly the oppressed or forgotten. The Psalms, then, are demonstrative of the potency of language. The theology of the Psalms is in stark contrast to the ethos of the Stoic. In his article "Stoicism and the South," Percy asserts that, with respect to integration, there are just two attitudes available to the southern moderate: either that of the Psalms or that of Epictetus, who ironically was born into slavery himself.[25] Having rejected southern Stoicism, Percy's obvious choice would be the Psalms.

Integration

Through his study of semiotics Percy came to see the power that words have, and how the words of the Psalms or Epictetus are strong enough either to make one firm in one's convictions as a segregationist or to induce one to become an integrationist. Further, since the understanding of a word is, according to Percy's semiotics, experiential, then if one is experiencing the evils of segregation and reflects upon the language of the Psalms and the teachings of the Church, then one must become an integrationist. But before we turn to Percy's awakening, we have to discuss the thought of a Lutheran that led him, in part, to Catholicism.

Catholicism

Kierkegaard

By the end of the 1940s Percy exchanged the southern Stoicism of his early life and of his class for the Christian, specifically Catholic, worldview, shown in his change of heart (and mind) on segregation. How a person comes to change a fundamental worldview remains ultimately mysterious. We can say this of any person, but particularly of a private and scholarly person like Percy. What happens in the internal forum, the place where the self meets and converses with the self—and with God—can only be guessed at, however. Further, when Percy did sit down to explain his conversion in an essay, he left the reason for the conversion unstated, as we will discuss below.

Though Kierkegaard is Protestant and Percy became a Catholic, we can assume Kierkegaard's influence on Percy by his quoting Kierkegaard in the epigraph to *The Moviegoer*. Consider Kierkegaard's signature narratives of the three types of people: the aesthetic, the moral, and the religious. Percy shared Kierkegaard's view of Christianity as a "scandal" to the unbeliever, even the morally upright unbeliever. For Percy to break with his society in general and his family in particular, and that for the sake of the South's minority religion of Catholic Christianity, can rightly be called a scandal.

In Kierkegaard's three stages, one progresses from the aesthetic through the ethical to the religious. The characters in Percy's books often progress through these steps or, as in the case of Binx in *The Moviegoer*, skip the ethical and graduate directly to the religious.[26] The aesthetic man lives for beauty and pleasure, in part as a way to escape boredom and depression. In his college years, Percy pursued beauty and pleasure. As a tuberculosis patient hospitalized for months, Percy, it can safely be assumed, battled boredom. As he was the grandson and son of suicides whose mother died early in a car accident (possibly another suicide), it seems just as safe to assume that Percy battled depression and existentialist despair. As Binx mulls over in his own mind in chapter 3 of *The Moviegoer*, beauty is a strong motivator (though perhaps not as strong as avarice). At this stage, Binx (and, early on, Percy) is Kierkegaard's aesthetic man.

Before his gradual and mostly hidden shift in worldview, Percy personified the ethical man. A good reputation is also a strong motivator: the desire to seem noble in his own eyes and in his community's can carry a person far. Such is the wellspring of action of the moral person, if the person is a southern Stoic in Percy's sense of the term. Such was, apparently, the wellspring of action for William Percy and other southern Stoics. But the highest kind of individual, according to Kierkegaard and certainly affirmed by Percy, is the religious man.

Why isn't morality enough? Why add religion? In the mid-twentieth century, a groundbreaking essay by G. E. M. Anscombe halted the unstinting march of academic ethics toward greater independence from religion by pointing out that rule-based morality, whether consequentialist or deontological, suffered from the incoherence of laws without a lawgiver.[27] But with the Kierkegaardian view, one's religious commitment is rightly restored to its place as the capstone of all other commitments, including ethical ones. Ethics in light of religion looks different and leads to different commitments and positions than ethics on its own, even assuming that there is such a thing.

Those who would consistently develop the virtues over many years require sufficient motivation. Religious commitment provides that motivation. A leap-in-the-dark faith commitment to God, for Kierkegaard, is good in its own right. Returning to the motif of language, one can see a similarity between Kierkegaard and the early Wittgenstein (that is, the Wittgenstein of *Tractatus*): the ineffable begins where language loses its meaning. Percy felt the same way about the ineffability of faith, in particular the Incarnation, the Trinity, and the Eucharist; fiction better suited Percy's purpose than careful philosophical analysis.

When asked in 1971 about the difficulties of being a Catholic writer, Percy responded, "The main difficulty is that of language. Of course the deeper themes of my novels are religious. When you speak of religion it is almost impossible for a novelist because you have to use standard words like 'God' and 'salvation' and 'baptism,' 'faith,' and the words are pretty well used up. They're old words. They are still good words, but the trick of the novelist, as the Psalmist said, is to sing a new song, us new words."[28] So we can see the fundamental problem for Percy when writing about religion: he has to use words, and words are idea formers as much as, or more than, they are idea conveyors. Word choices are also subtle persuaders. The words of the Psalms, the daily bread for Benedictine oblates, must have formed and reflected Percy's intellectual development. Further, Percy's semiotics are reflected in the above quote since the meaning of words are grasped qua experience.

Truth is good in its own right. What Percy takes from Kierkegaard, too, is that truth must be valued, not merely known. It must matter to the individual; it must be true to the individual. Moral values flourish against a horizon of nonmoral values. Rightly understood, the ethical is dependent on the religious. The religious dimension is not an add-on to the ethical, as the example of Binx makes clear. A moral view, that is, a moral view that avoids despair and boredom, can exist only, or can exist best, when there are other things we value more: "Seek first the kingdom of God and all the rest is added." Thus, "What matters is to find my purpose, to see what it really is that God wills that I shall do; the crucial thing is to find a truth that is truth for me, to find the idea for which I am willing to live and die."[29]

For inspiration and motivation for a sustained commitment, morality is not enough. Given the attractiveness of a life of pleasure (the aesthetic life), why be faithful to (moral) laws without a lawgiver? Morality without the religious foundation becomes complacent and accepts the status quo values of the community. Even given its virtues of tolerance and courtesy, the southern Stoic morality is little more than the life of pleasure, the life of the aesthetic, or at best like Uncle Will, the ethical man. It seems as if morality without the inspiration of being a Catholic, at least for Percy, left him unable to see the wrongness of segregation. It took the jolt to his imagination that came with his conversion and religious commitment to break through to integration.

In *The Moviegoer*, Kate Cutrer says that she knows herself and wants to be a religious person: someone who, with her last rational act, surrenders her rationality to one who will guide her. It does not take a novel-as-autobiography view to see that Percy was thinking out his own decision in a piece of fiction; novelists write about what they know. Kate will make the leap of faith; so had Percy.

A religious commitment, at least of the kind that Percy made when he became a Catholic, helps in a system of morality in a number of ways. It provides motivation and inspiration; it serves as a reminder that the moral life is never finished, that perfect justice is a hope and not a premortem reality. It provides a way of seeing. One's religious commitment is always in tension with one's political commitment. Percy's becoming a Catholic endangered his membership in the southern Stoic community.

There is a bumper sticker that reads: "You cannot be both Catholic and pro-abortion." Is this true? Walker Percy's bumper sticker might read: "You can't be both Catholic and pro-segregation." Can one? As a matter of empirical fact, one can, since some Catholic groups favored segregation. But of course the point of our hypothetical bumper sticker is to proclaim that segregation, and the set of principles in which it is nested, is inconsistent with Catholic principles.

Percy's segregationists are nice people; above all, they are polite. Percy's southern white segregationist contemporaries graciously accepted their position of superiority in the community, but treated their black inferiors well. It took a jolt in the form of a religious conversion to move Percy from silent advocate of segregation to active spokesperson for integration. Not only had he moved from the ethical to the religious; the religious had transformed the ethical.

Conversion

Walker Percy traded the metaphors and myth of the American South's version of Stoicism for the more demanding and more complex metaphors and myth of the Catholic vision of reality. Walker Percy is first and foremost a literary man, not a philosopher. His argot is myth and metaphor. In "Metaphor as Mistake" he expresses his approval of "what [Owen] Barfield called 'that old authentic thrill which binds a man to his library for life: the metaphorical.'" He notes: "The theorist is insensitive to the beauty of metaphor." Welcoming myth and metaphor, the fiction writer, like "the primitive," "comes face to face with something . . . so distinctive that it might be said to have a presence." Myth and metaphor are associated in Percy's mind with the thing apprehended and validated for you and me by naming.[30]

The Catholic myth's answer to the old philosophical problem of appearance and reality is this: the way things appear to be is not the way things are. The new myth for Percy was the Catholic vision of the way things really are: despite appearances, all human persons have infinite worth and are deserving of unqualified and undifferentiated respect. The worth of persons is not dependent on how they look, on what they do, or on their contributions to society. This myth grabbed Percy's intelligent and active imagination.

The myth Percy embraced is the inspirational one captured in *Corpus Christi*, a daring idea that takes the preposterously high view of human beings implied by a high Christology. The commingling of human beings with the divine in the person of Christ is not to be understood primarily as the lowering of the divine to the human but as the uplifting of the human into the divine. In the words of the Catholic liturgy when the wine is mixed with the water: "May we come to share in the divinity of Christ, who humbled himself to share in our humanity."[31]

Percy explained the other part of the appeal of Catholicism in the essay "Why Are You Catholic?" Percy wrote, "The reason I am a Catholic is that I believe that what the Catholic Church proposes is true."[32] This answer is evasive, a kind of nonanswer. In fact, although the article is purportedly written to answer the question, Percy spends the first half of the essay saying he won't and then the second half going no further than stating that he accepts the Judeo-Christian viewpoint but explicitly refusing to state why he picked the "Catholic brand." So the reader is left at the end of the essay where he was at the beginning: Percy is a Catholic because he believes that the Catholic Church is the guardian of *depositum fidei*, the deposit of faith.

Percy accepted what the Catholic Church teaches on moral, social, and political issues (Kierkegaard's ethical man) because he first accepted the Catholic vision of the way things should be. His imagination guided his reason; as befits a disciple of Kierkegaard, his being as a religious man guided his being as an ethical man. In fact, Percy gives Kierkegaard's *The Difference between a Genius and an Apostle* partial credit for his conversion.[33] The relationship between religion on the one hand and politics and morality on the other is asymmetrical. The former shapes and evaluates the latter but not vice versa.

That one's religious commitment is first and foremost an act of the imagination might help explain why many an intelligent person stays Catholic even in the face of the current scandals over the abuse of children and adolescents by Catholic priests and the concomitant cover-up by bishops. It makes all the more sense to think that imagination is the organ of commitment, especially for Walker Percy, since he was a religious man and not just a literary man, just as Kierkegaard regarded the religious man as higher (in fact, two steps higher) than the aesthetic man.

A person committed to a certain religious tradition does not and should not tolerate everything in moral matters; his religious commitment alters and shapes his imagination to see beyond conventional morality. He returns to the vision of that tradition through imagination, and works out the moral system from that insight of his imagination. It is tempting to reduce Catholicism to moral theory or a political theory, but it is neither.[34] It is being committed to a comprehensive, sacramental view that is a kind of seeing-as. Being a Christian is not a matter of becoming one more political party;[35] it is being formed as a person of a certain sort who brings the vision of who he is to his decision about what he does.

Kierkegaard's Individual View vs. Catholic Community View

Part of the Catholic version of the Christian view is the priority of the communal over the individual. Percy rejects what could be called the Lockean "punctuated self" and what Charles Taylor calls "the buffered self."[36] In his otherwise superb biography of Percy, Jay Tolson misrepresents Percy's position as solitary and isolated.[37] It is true that his position was solitary and isolated in the sense that he was very nearly the lone dissenting voice in the southern Stoic community, but as a Catholic he understood himself not as an isolated individual but as a member of a worldwide community, "the Church militant." He was very much alone in that he broke with his family's—and especially his influential uncle's—southern Stoicism, but what Tolson calls his "solitude" is better described as his leaving one community to join another, effected by his conversion. Like many early Christians, he left his biological family to join his adopted church family, which is what Christ called his followers to do: "If anyone comes to me without hating his father and mother, wife and children, brothers and sisters, and even his own life, he cannot be my disciple. Whoever does not carry his own cross and come after me cannot be my disciple" (Luke 14:26–27).

But once Percy got to that new community, the Catholic community, he was unfortunately alone, there, too. Many of his white Catholic contemporaries were segregationists. A white person living in the South at Percy's time who failed to be a Stoic might be one who rejected his superior status, as perhaps Thomas Merton did, as a contemporaneous southerner (via France, England, Rome, and New York) at Gethsemani monastery. Flannery O'Connor, or at least many of the characters in her short stories, did, too. For example, in "A Good Man Is Hard to Find," the grandmother sees the murderer as her son: a relationship of family. Also, in O'Connor's "The Displaced Person," the old priest, representing the Catholic world order, sitting on the porch with the white landowner for whom the Polish refugee worked, sees all before him as God's created order.

Embracing a Catholic Identity

It is rare to find people who say that they reject morality. Some people espouse a view of morality that we would rightly call faulty or have their own code of ethics: it is disordered, distorted, or incomplete; they are like members of the Mafia, who hold themselves to elaborate rules of conduct founded on a sharp distinction between their own and those who are not their own. Their code is similar to the personal code of Count Vronsky in *Anna Karenina*. "These principles were laid down as invariable rules: that one must pay a cardsharper, but need not pay a tailor; that one must never tell a lie to a man, but one may to a woman; that one must never cheat any one, but one may a husband; that one must never pardon an insult, but one may give one."[38]

The moral rules of the southern Stoic, like the Mafia's and Count Vronsky's, are based on the dichotomy of self and the other. The southern Stoic must welcome other southern Stoics to his club but must not let in blacks; he addresses whites with titles and by their last name and his black servants by their first names. He is polite to all, because politeness self-valorizes.

A change in a moral code comes with the widening of the scope of those included as one's own. To return to the previous example, an improved Count Vronsky would see that he must repay all his legitimate debtors, not just those to the right people; that women as well as men have intrinsic moral worth and deserve honesty; that no one should be cheated, and so on. Such changes are much more likely to result from a burst of imagination than an improvement in reasoning. Thus, the grandmother in Flannery O'Connor's short story "A Good Man Is Hard to Find" speaks from a sudden burst of insight, seeing the serial murderer as one of her own, not the other. And Thomas Merton, walking down a familiar street, sees passersby no longer as not-monks, as "other," but as his own. He sees that his status as a monk does not privilege him over others. In fact, it is this very status as a monk that requires him to give up seeing himself as privileged. The preconverted

Percy, so strongly influenced by his Uncle Will, thought it was ethical to treat blacks differently from whites in a way that confirmed the former's status as occupying a lower place in society. The postconverted Walker could not; he sided with Archbishop Joseph Rummel of New Orleans, of whom more is said below.

Kant and other modern deontological moral philosophers think that the properly exalted view of a human being is attributable to his status as an individual, acting alone, with the aid of the categorical imperative. Even Kant's "community of ends" is best thought of as a cohesive set of independent agents. But for Percy, that exalted status, including and exceeding a proper morality, follows from the whole human community's relationship as community to the divine. It is his acceptance of the Christian exalted view of the human person—or, more accurately, the Catholic Christian view of the human community—that marks the turning point for Percy. The modern scientific view, definitionally separated from the religious view, is, like the purely ethical nonreligious view, "radically incoherent when it seeks to understand man qua man."[39] In his acceptance of the Catholic communal view, Percy truly is isolated in the sense that he is part of the diminishing minority of Americans who reject the radical individualism of the self characteristic of the twentieth-century United States.

Even those blacks who accepted their stable but inferior position in the mid-twentieth century South still tried to limit the boundaries of their inferiority. The black servant in the Cutrer family, in *The Moviegoer*, shows by his posture that although he is a chauffeur he is not a servant.

> Mercer lets me in . . . Today he does not say "Mister Jack" and I know that the omission is deliberate, the consequence of a careful weighing of pros and cons. Tomorrow the scales might tip the other way (today's omission will go into the balance) and it will be "Mister Jack."
>
> For some reason, it is possible to see Mercer more clearly today than usual. Ordinarily it is hard to see him because of the devotion. . . . He is thought to be devoted to us and we to him. But the truth is that Mercer and I are not at all devoted to each other. My main emotion around Mercer is unease that in threading his way between servility and presumption, his foot might slip. I wait on Mercer, not he on me.[40]

This passage is rich with insights into Percy's incipient move toward an antisegregationist view. Mercer's superficial politeness layers over and belies his rebellion against inequality, especially insofar as that inequality follows not so much, or not fully, from his having willingly accepted the position of servant but from white society's expectation of blacks as "naturally" occupying that position. Finally, note that "devotion" is a virtue of the southern Stoic; so is politeness. Alas, the part of the southern Stoic code prescribing politeness might not only hide but exacerbate the enmity between classes; it is this Stoicism that is discussed next.

Stoicism

Historical Considerations

George Washington, commander in chief of the Continental army and first president of the United States, was the quintessential Southern Gentleman in the cavalier tradition. The cavaliers came from the south of England to Virginia predominantly between 1642 and 1675, the second wave of permanent English immigration to North America.[41]

The society of the cavaliers was founded on a "moral of manners" much stronger than a mere sense of appropriate behavior. These morals became part of the fabric of culture for the young gentry through formal education (for example, memorization and writings) as well as informally by experiencing colonial Virginian culture. For example, among the earliest writings of Washington is a list of 110 rules of manners. The young cavaliers like Washington were given "freedom of will" not as end in itself, but in the Greek manner as a means of achieving virtue. As David Hackett Fisher writes in his seminal *Albion's Seed* about the colonial cavaliers, "It was a stoic ideal which cultivated a calm acceptance of life. It taught that one must fear nothing and accept whatever fate might bring with courage, honesty, dignity, and grace. The mastery of this stoic creed was one of the central goals of socialization in Virginia."[42]

While Washington was not a bibliophile, he is known to have read and owned a copy of an English summary of Seneca's *Dialogues* and Addison's *Cato*. Further, as has oft been told of Valley Forge, Washington ordered and attended a production of *Cato* for his officers during the bleak, bitter winter of 1777–78. If one peruses his corpus, one sees that Washington returned again and again to *Cato*.

The difficulty that all Americans must face is the irreconcilable tension between two facts: two of their greatest Founding Fathers, Washington and

Jefferson (of whom more will be said later), created a nation founded on the inalienable rights of "justice and liberty for all" yet owned slaves. In the case of Washington, he directed that his slaves were to be freed upon his wife Martha's death (in fact, she freed them in 1800, two years before her death). So in some sense, Washington must have known that slavery was wrong, yet he was bound by an evil current in his time and place.[43]

This cavalier tradition was epitomized in the gentry of the American South and with it came the tensions between the highest Stoic ideals and slavery, and later segregation. This contradiction between slave owner and Founding Father can be properly understood only in light of the Stoic influence on the cavalier. This tension did not go away with the abolition of slavery—the evil festered with Jim Crow laws. A Stoic, as Seneca taught, must treat both those below him and those above him in status with respect and kindness. This is why the southern Stoics crusaded against both the Ku Klux Klan (KKK) and the integrators. They were opposed to the former since the KKK used fear and violence (two non-Stoic attributes) against those "beneath them in dignity," and they were opposed to the latter since they were upsetting the social order of master and servant.

Philosophical Considerations

Why didn't good people in the mid-1800s figure out, all on their own, that slavery is wrong? Why didn't good people in the mid-1900s in the South figure out, all on their own, that segregation is wrong? For one thing, as mentioned above, change happens with community. Also, it must be said, no coherent worldview is wholly devoid of praiseworthy elements. The American myth of slave owners and slaves living in peace, although false, must have been in some instances at least somewhat true. And the word "separate" in a phrase with "but equal" has an undeniably intuitive appeal.

The appeal of both myths, the peaceful slave/master relationship and peaceful segregation, is founded on that quintessential American value: individual freedom, at least for the slave owner and the white segregationist. The myth is threatened by the same value: blacks did not freely choose either arrangement. Arguably, however, even whites in the South did not fully agree to segregation, even when they thought that they did. Consider these three elements in the acceptance of a moral theory.

First, moral theories, like all theories, including scientific ones, require imagination as much as rationality. It takes a significant infusion to the imagination by a powerful counter-myth to awaken change. White southern landowners might have agreed to segregation because they lacked the imagination to picture anything else. Their own paradigm of morality—Stoicism—worked well for them. Furthermore, blacks themselves, for a long time, did not protest; they might not have been able to imagine another way, given the violence they faced in retribution if they did imagine freedom and equality.

Second, the general moral theory of Stoicism, or more precisely the specific theory of southern Stoicism, succeeded well enough. And at first it succeeded very well. The southern Stoicism of upper-class whites in the South succeeded well enough to scare off the "scalawags" and "carpetbaggers." But, like the characters in *Alice in Wonderland* who had to run just to stay in place, southern Stoics would have to change their concept of morality in order to keep moral.

Third, an individual's views of morality depend strongly on the views of his community. It has to be this way for most people, who are not visionaries. Percy was a visionary and even he, after his conversion, never entirely repudiated his southern Stoicism.[44] Like the prisoner in Plato's cave who escaped into the full light outside the cave and then returned to report his vision, he had to lead his fellow southern Stoics from Stoicism to a new vision of morality: a view he described as the true Christian one.

A way to bring these three elements of the acceptance of a moral belief together is with evolutionary game theory. Evolutionary game theory is the analysis of dynamic strategic interactions using such notions from biological evolution as replication and mutation. The theory is widely used in all of the biological, social, and behavioral sciences. A germane application of evolutionary game theory is to the evolution of norms, which is of particular interest to philosophers.[45] What evolutionary dynamics elucidates about a culture is that if a large proportion of the population has a certain belief, in this case "Segregation is correct," then it is difficult for mutants to invade (a "mutant" in this sense being an individual who has beliefs that differ from the norm). Thus, evolutionary game theory tells us that Percy's decision to become a mutant (that is, an integrationist) in a population of segregationists was a very difficult one to make. Note we are using game theory not to explain why Percy became an integrationist but rather, again, to demonstrate the difficulty of a minority belief becoming a majority belief.

Last, returning to the questions posed at the beginning of this section, it is difficult for an otherwise intelligent and moral individual to pull back the veil of his prejudice. While this difficulty may help explain why good people believe in an evil societal structure, it by no means justifies such a belief.

Southern Stoicism

There are many kinds of Stoicism, including the ancient Greek one (Epictetus) and the ancient Roman one. The latter is obviously important to Percy. *The Moviegoer*'s aunt leaves a quotation from Marcus Aurelius at Binx's door after the two have a particularly important conversation.[46] But the main Stoicism here is what Percy calls Southern Stoicism. In general, Stoics—Greek, Roman, cavalier, and southern—believe that while all should be treated with respect; those beneath in dignity, such as slaves, are to be treated with a kindly paternalism. This kindly paternalism, of course, masks an inherent belief in the inequality of men and thus violates the modern notion of egalitarianism. An important example of this egalitarianism is the 1954 Supreme Court case *Brown v. Board of Education,* which ruled that separate is not equal.

To get a grasp of the thought of Stoicism, consider Roman Stoicism's most eloquent proponent, Marcus Aurelius: "If it turns out that there is no life beyond the grave, then be assured that this is for the best. The gods would not have arranged it that way if it were not for the best."[47] Tranquility is Stoicism's emblem, as can be found in Epictetus as well as Marcus Aurelius: "Begin therefore from little things. Is a little oil spilt? A little wine stolen? Say to yourself, 'This is the price paid for apathy, for tranquility, and nothing is to be had for nothing.'"[48] One can say that the South's social arrangements between classes are also, presumably, for the best; otherwise, whatever god or gods there are would not have so arranged things or allowed such things. And regardless, the Stoic bears suffering with tranquility, making it an eminently traditional philosophy that doesn't really lend itself much to change.

This emphasis on tranquility leads to the more political notion that the status quo should be kept because that is what the gods intended. Marcus Aurelius continues, "When thou art troubled about anything, thou hast forgotten this, that all things happen according to the universal nature."[49] Noble submission to what is constitutes the hallmark of Stoicism. Therefore, accepting the status quo is morally right, and trying to change it is not only morally wrong but impious. Trying to change things is a rebuke to the gods.

In the case of the southern Stoics, they were trying to keep the status quo from attacks by the Ku Klux Klan on one side and by the integrationists on the other. While their opposition to the Klan is admirable, it is hard to parse: Was this done for true moral reasons or merely to defend the status quo—that is, to keep society tranquil?

However, defense of the status quo is not automatically the morally wrong choice; it depends on the status being defended. For example, the current status quo in the United States is integration, and this should be maintained. A moral individual has to be able to look beyond the norms of the culture and consider whether certain behaviors are right or wrong. This is where the southern Stoic clearly failed. For example, the early Christians in the decadent and bloody pagan Roman society stood out from their contemporaries because they were opposed to abortion, infanticide, adultery, and a whole litany of behaviors acceptable in Roman society.[50] Thus, defense of an indefensible status quo is a negative outgrowth of the Stoic emphasis on tranquility.

It is easy to judge the sinners in the past when one has the benefit of enlightened views, which is why taking contemporary historical and philosophical considerations into account is so important.[51] In particular, it is easy to say to Percy, "Why did you not realize that segregation is evil earlier?" Given that the southern Stoicism of the cavalier tradition permeated Percy's life, one can see that his rejection of the status quo was difficult for him and thus all the more admirable. In the context of evolutionary game theory, it was difficult for Percy to become a mutant. Percy's rejection of segregation means that not only did he come to the morally correct conclusion about integration, he went one step further by publicly proclaiming his moral dissatisfaction with segregation. Both of these acts oppose the heart of Stoicism; the second act must have been more difficult than the first, since in performing it Percy publicly rejected southern society.

Perhaps one of the reasons that Stoicism was so prevalent in the American South, in addition to the cavalier tradition, is that it shares some affinities with the "Protestant" (broadly conceived) view that most southern Christians held. That view makes a distinction between the saved and the damned, where no action of the individual can change things. In fact, thinking that one's actions can effect the most important change, salvation, is sinful. So while it cannot be said that a Protestant view supported southern segregation, it might be said that destabilizing the current order needed an additional push from a non-Stoical ideal—in this case, Catholicism.

It is easy to see that a society permeated with both the cavalier tradition and Calvinist predestination would find it difficult to break free from the status quo. Of course, there were various events that broke the unholy edifice of treating blacks as second-class citizens, and we highlight a handful of the more notable ones here. First, there was the integration of the U.S. Armed Forces by Harry Truman in 1948 by executive order, first proposed by the Gillem Board in 1946. Second, *Brown v. Board* in 1954 (referred to by Percy as "the Decision") was a momentous decision by the U.S. Supreme Court. The economist Thomas Sowell eloquently expresses how important this Supreme Court decision was:

> May 17, 1954, was a momentous day in the history of the United States, and perhaps the world. Something happened that afternoon that was all too rare in human history. A great nation voluntarily acknowledged and repudiated its own oppression of part of its own people. . . . *Brown v. Board of Education* was clearly much more than another legal case to go into the long dusty rows of volumes of court decisions. It represented a vision of man and of the world that touched many hearts across the land and around the world. The anger and rancor it immediately provoked also testified to its importance. In a larger historical context, that such an issue should reach the highest court in the land was itself remarkable. In how many places and in how many eras could an ordinary person from a despised race challenge the duly constituted authorities, force them to publicly defend their decisions, retreat, and finally capitulate?[52]

President Dwight Eisenhower used the National Guard to enforce *Brown* and to compel integration of Central High School in Little Rock, Arkansas, in 1957. This was a watershed moment in the struggle for civil rights since the federal government was finally formally acting to end American apartheid. In addition to these federal actions, the organic growth of the civil rights movement, led by (the Protestant) Martin Luther King (most publicly from 1955), contributed to the demise of the status quo.

Percy's conversion to Catholicism influenced his transition to the integrationist viewpoint. Percy never alluded to Protestant/Catholic difference, but Tolson suggests it in his biography of Percy. He says that Percy "might even have been attracted to the idea of Catholicism as the foundation for a renewed human community, though Percy's concern for the social dimensions of his faith seems to have come somewhat later" than his conversion.[53] The Stoic view is a moral view, but it is a moral view in which some set the standards for all. Whether it's whites setting standards for blacks or the reverse, southern Stoicism seems to betray the ancient classical Stoicism, which moves toward equality based on shared rationality. But because classical Stoicism's inclusivity is founded on shared rationality, it is very different from any kind of inclusivity in the Judeo-Christian order upheld by Percy. On the Christian view, inclusion comes from shared membership in the kingdom of God: very different from the Stoic or the Enlightenment ideal.

As Percy began to publicly enter into the debate over integration, he realized that his conversion to Catholicism a decade or so earlier put him in a unique position as a southern moderate. Uncle Will, William A. Percy, Percy's larger-than-life hero and adoptive father, was also a southern moderate, as were almost all of those in the upper-class cavalier tradition. But Uncle Will instantiated the model southern cavalier in the Stoic tradition. Will considered himself a moderate: he battled against one extreme, the violence and fear of the KKK, and against another, those blacks who no longer would accept apartheid.[54] Will could not countenance the civil rights movement because he could not support the overturn of the established social order of the grand southern tradition. In this sense, one can see why Uncle Will considered himself a moderate: a moderate was for tranquility and tradition.

Percy wanted to both honor his uncle and support desegregation; he tried to serve these two masters but could not (cf. Matthew 6:24).[55] What Percy received from the Catholic Church and what he learned from Kierkegaard was confirmation of his repudiation of Uncle Will's admiration for Stoicism. While the Stoic-Christian southerner thought that he was living as a Christian, Percy pointed out in the 1956 *Commonweal* article that he was not. He was living the life of the Stoic, and while being a southern Stoic and a Christian are not mutually exclusive, a true Christian Stoic is a Christian first and a Stoic second.

It is easy to understand why Thomas Jefferson who, like Washington, was a Virginian of the cavalier tradition, famously modified the New Testament as the *Life and Morals of Jesus of Nazareth*, wherein he excluded the Trinity, divinity, miracles, angels, and the rest but kept the "moral" teachings of Jesus. For the cavalier Jefferson, Jesus is no longer Christ, but in fact merely another Stoic thinker. One may wonder what Jefferson's response was to the *Acts of the Apostles,* chapter 17, when St. Paul directly confronts the Stoics at the Areopagus with the Gospel of Christ.[56] The Athenians would not have been upset if Paul had merely proclaimed the morals of Jesus, but claiming a man as God was more than they could countenance.

It is too simple to say merely that Will was a segregationist and Walker was not. It is too simple because for a long time Walker did accept Uncle Will's romanticized view of the South, with everyone in a segregated status quo enjoying bucolic peace with politeness and deference, as Tolson notes: "The romance of the Old South had never been more slickly packaged, but Walker fell for [Margaret Mitchell's] *Gone with the Wind* at least as hard as Uncle Will did. . . . Apart from its anecdotal interest, Percy's enthusiasm for *Gone with the Wind* sheds some light on what he then [summer 1936] thought about southern society and history. It suggests that for all his wariness about the southern romance—the idealized picture of the southern gentry, the happy submissiveness of blacks, the codes of honor and chivalric heroism—he was still [then] very much under its sway."[57]

"Stoicism and the South"

In his important contribution to *Commonweal* in 1956, Percy judges between Epictetus and the Psalms in favor of the latter. Percy begins the article by discussing the current state of the "upper-class white Southerner," who is no longer the "champion of the Negro" but rather has "unshouldered his burden for someone else to pick up"; "he is either silent or he is leading the Citizens Councils." The reason the cavalier has laid down Kipling's white man's burden is that he is "now fighting the same good fight as his fathers, who kicked out the scalawags and carpetbaggers and rescued the South."[58] But, Percy argues, while the southern Stoic believes himself to be unchanged and thereby fighting the same fight as his forefathers, he is not. He has changed, and further, the societal structure has changed. The edifice of the southern stoa is collapsing, since the cavalier ethos can no longer support it.

These white southerners fought the fight and won the race against past villains (scalawags, carpetbaggers); are they not entitled to rest from their labors and enjoy the respectability those victories bring them in society? The simple answer, according to Percy, the self-described moralist, is no, and that for two reasons.

First, if one's society changes around one, then one is required to adapt. (The general principles of morality, at the most abstract level, do not change, but the immediate rules of everyday existence have to change, precisely in order to be faithful to the unchanging general principles!) If for no other reason, because blacks themselves no longer found the peaceful imbalance acceptable, white southerners must change their mores. While morality and culture are intrinsically related in societies, the former must supersede the latter; otherwise, the culture dissolves into anarchy and violence. A recent example of this is the August 2011 riots in Britain that were initially a protest against the Metropolitan police but became destructive and bloody. And while governments can support morality, they cannot properly create it, and if their policies help to destroy the family unit (the foundation of all morality), as slavery did to black families and social welfare policies have done in the West, then we are left amoral narcissists with a sense of entitlement that is matched only by our refusal to accept responsibility for our own actions. Such a society cannot survive since there will be no one left who cares enough to save it, and in the end it will die in indifferent despair.

Second, social change can reveal that an apparently just societal arrangement in the past not only does not work now but did not even work that well in the past. That societal arrangement never was what it claimed to be. The protective (because respectable) label "Christian" does not and did not ever apply to the imbalance of respectability between whites and blacks in the South.

While there are various reasons for the societal change (*Brown v. Board*, most prominently), none sufficiently explains why Stoicism is a failed ethical theory. Percy elaborates on how the "greatness of the South, like the greatness of the English squirearchy [that is, the cavaliers], has always had a stronger Greek flavor than it ever had a Christian."[59] Percy describes in poetic terms how the southern Stoic differs from the Christian, and while the upper-class white southerner lives in a Christian edifice, it is but an illusionary edifice that masks the stoa.

The segregationist arrangement was Roman Stoical, not Christian. In the *Commonweal* essay, Percy quotes the very passage from Marcus Aurelius that Binx's aunt puts in her note to him in *The Moviegoer:* "Every moment think steadily, as Roman and a man, to do what thou hast in hand with perfect and simple dignity, and a feeling of affection, and freedom, and justice."[60] This moral system, according to Percy, is inconsistent with the call to bravery in "the Decalogue, the Beatitudes, the doctrine of the Mystical Body," and shows that the southern Stoics' allegiance is to Epictetus, not the Psalms.[61] In their condescending attitude to blacks, whites displayed an arrogance that showed that they considered themselves to be superior. Note what Binx's aunt says at the end *The Moviegoer*:

> I'll make you a little confession. I am not ashamed to use the word class. I will also plead guilty to another charge. The charge is that people belonging to my class think they're better than other people. You're damn right we're better. We're better because we do not shirk our obligations either to ourselves or to others. We do not whine. We do not organize a minority group and blackmail the government. We do not prize mediocrity for mediocrity's sake. Oh I am aware that we hear a great many flattering things nowadays about your great common man—you know, it has already been revealing to me that he is perfectly content so to be called, because that is exactly what he is: the common man and when I say common I mean common as hell.[62]

Most important, as a result of the old (unjust) societal structure in the South, "the white man has lost his *oblige*, the black man has lost his manners, and insolence prevails." And then echoing Washington, Jefferson, and all the other cavaliers: "Southern society was above all a society of manners." But the Stoics have a further problem—while Christians consider hope to be a virtue, the Stoics do not have real hope; rather, their "finest hour is to sit tight-lipped and ironic while the world comes crashing down around" them.[63] But irony does not support a crumbling empire nor lead to salvation.

Christianity has a way to build a New Jerusalem from the ruins of the Stoic South. The southern Stoic sees insolence in his former charge, "and this is what he can't tolerate, the Negro's demanding his rights instead of being thankful for the squire's generosity." For the Stoic this "insolent" attitude is particularly troublesome since the individual is not intrinsically precious; rather, it is one's attitude toward him that matters. Thus, the insolence of the Negro reflects poorly on the southern Stoic.[64] Thus, the decay of good manners and respect between black and white meant that the whites were failing as good Stoics. One can see the helplessness of the southern Stoics and understand why they remained silent among the debris of a shattering apartheid. But for the Christian, the human person is not, to paraphrase Percy, lost among the ruins; all humans have intrinsic, sacred worth. The way to rebuild the structure of southern society is through Christ.

Toward the end of his article, Percy talks about Archbishop Rummel. As archbishop of New Orleans from 1935 to 1964, though largely lacking support from his own flock, Joseph Francis Rummel desegregated the archdiocese and, more slowly, the Catholic schools: "Ever mindful, therefore, of the basic truth that our Colored Catholic brethren share with us the same spiritual life and destiny, the same membership in the Mystical Body of Christ, the same dependence upon the Word of God, the participation in the Sacraments, especially the Most Holy Eucharist, the same need of moral and social encouragement. Let there be no further discrimination or segregation in the pews, at the Communion rail, at the confessional and in parish meetings, just as there will be no segregation in the kingdom of heaven."[65] Percy writes that unfortunately, "again the upper-class white Catholic has not distinguished himself. . . . They can no longer afford the luxury of Creole Catholicism." Percy points out that the "Stoic-Christian Southern is offended" when Rummel calls segregation sinful since he "cannot help feeling that religion is overstepping its allowed area of morality"—sexuality, alcohol abuse, and gambling. The southern Stoic "is therefore confused and outraged when Christian teaching is applied to social questions."[66] In recent times, American life has not become any less complicated for the Christian in the public square. When Christian leaders speak out for life (from the moment of conception to natural death) or marriage, they are often met with a misunderstanding of the First Amendment. Whether attacked by the cavaliers of the 1950s South or the moral relativists of today, the Christian faces scorn and hatred for living and proclaiming the Gospel of Christ.

Percy concludes his article by stating that the South must answer Rummel's question, but as of yet it has not been answered. "And the good pagan's answer is no longer good enough for the South."[67]

In this essay we have argued that there are at least three strands that led to Walker Percy's Second Coming from segregationist to integrationist. To purposefully use a religiously loaded term, Percy had to be converted from his belief in an immoral social system to a moral one. These three stands of Percy's thought detailed here are semiotics, Catholicism, and Stoicism. While for the purposes of exposition, these strands were pulled apart, they are actually intertwined and form a cord. Since this cord is, in the end, held together by truth—that is, the Gospel of Christ—it is unbreakable.

Notes

1. The article is reprinted in Walker Percy, *Signposts in a Strange Land,* ed. Patrick Samway, S.J. (New York: Picador, 1991), 83–88.

2. Jay Tolson, *Pilgrim in the Ruins: A Life of Walker Percy* (New York: Simon and Schuster, 1992), 129.

3. "Culture: The Antinomy of the Scientific Method" was originally published in *New Scholasticism* 32 (October 1958): 443–75; "Semiotic and a Theory of Knowledge" in *Modern Schoolman* 34 (May 1957): 225–46; and "Symbol, Consciousness, and Intersubjectivity" in *Journal of Philosophy,* June 17, 1958, 631–41. All three essays are included in Walker Percy, *The Message in the Bottle: How Queer Man Is, How Queer Language Is, and What One Has to Do with the Other* (New York: Picador, 1975), at 215–42, 243–64, and 265–76 respectively. There is also an entire section on semiotics in Percy's *Lost in the Cosmos: The Last Self-Help Book* (New York: Picador, 1983), 85–136.

4. L. Wittgenstein, *Philosophical Investigations,* trans. G. E. M. Anscombe (New York: Blackwell, 2001); Saul A. Kripke, *Naming and Necessity* (Cambridge, MA: Harvard University Press, 1980), 48.

5. G. Frege, "On Sense and Nominatum" (1892), and B. Russell, "On Denoting" (1905), in *Contemporary Readings in Logical Theory,* ed. I. M. Copi and J. A. Gould (New York: Macmillan, 1967), 75–92, 93–105.

6. Kripke, *Naming and Necessity,* 106–7.

7. Ibid., 91.

8. Punch was in fact the first African slave in the English colonies. He was one of three indentured servants (the other two being James Gregory and a man known only as Victor) who ran away from their master, Hugh Gwyn, in Virginia in 1640. The trio was caught after only three days and later brought to trial. The judge, in addition to sentencing all three to whippings, added four more years to Gregory's and Victor's terms of indentured servitude and condemned Punch to lifelong servitude—slavery. The tragedy, of course, is that Punch was black while the other two were white, and this set in motion the idea of racial slavery in the Americas. This is in contrast to the Romans who were, at the least, egalitarian with respect to the evil of slavery.

9. C. S. Peirce, *The Essential Peirce,* vol. 2, ed. Pierce Edition Project (Bloomington: Indiana University Press, 1998), 285. See J. R. Di Leo, "C. S. Peirce's Theory of Proper Names," in *Studies in the Logic of Charles S. Peirce,* ed. N. Houser, D. Roberts, and J. Van Evra (Bloomington: Indiana University Press, 1997). For an interpretation of Peirce that is non-Kripkian, see D. Boersema, "Peirce on Names and Reference," *Transactions of the Charles S. Peirce Society* 38, no. 3 (2002): 351–62.

10. Percy, *Message in the Bottle*, 150–58.

11. *More Conversations with Walker Percy*, ed. Lewis A. Lawson and Victor A. Kramer (Jackson: University Press of Mississippi, 1993), 235.

12. Percy, *Message in the Bottle*, 64–82.

13. Ludwig Wittgenstein, *Tractatus Logico-Philosophicus,* trans. D. F. Pears and B. F. McGuinness (New York: Routledge, 2001), 29–39.

14. *More Conversations with Walker Percy*, 106.

15. D. Chalmers, "Consciousness and Its Place in Nature" (2003), 6, http://consc.net/papers/nature.pdf (accessed November 14, 2010).

16. Percy, *Signposts.*

17. Percy, *Message in the Bottle*, 265–76. For completeness, it should be mentioned that when Percy speaks of symbol, he is using it in the sense of Susanne K. Langer. In particular see Langer's *Philosophy in a New Key*, which was originally published in 1941. *Philosophy in a New Key: A Study in the Symbolism of Reason, Rite, and Art,* 3rd ed. (Cambridge, MA: Harvard University Press, 1957).

18. Percy, *Message in the Bottle*, 268.

19. Ibid., 271.

20. Ibid., 270.

21. Jean-Pierre Prevost, *A Short Dictionary of the Psalms* (Collegeville, MN: Liturgical, 1997), 33.

22. William Alexander Percy, *Lanterns on the Levee: Recollections of a Planter's Son* (Baton Rouge: Louisiana State University Press, 1973), 298; emphasis added.

23. *Conversations with Walker Percy*, ed. Lewis A. Lawson and Victor A. Kramer (Jackson: University Press of Mississippi, 1985), 262.

24. Prevost, *Dictionary of the Psalms*, 50.

25. Percy, *Signposts*, 343.

26. See *Conversations with Walker Percy*, 66. Since Binx has been gradually transitioning from the southern Stoic worldview but his aunt has not, she cannot understand him, and continues to judge him by its standards.

27. G. E. M. Anscombe, "Modern Moral Philosophy," *Philosophy* 33, no. 124 (1958), http://www.philosophy.uncc.edu/mleldrid/cmt/mmp.html (accessed November 14, 2010).

28. *Conversations with Walker Percy*, 41.

29. S. Kierkegaard, *Either/Or,* ed. and trans. V. H. Hong and E. H. Hong (Princeton, NJ: Princeton University Press, 1988), 361.

30. "Metaphor as Mistake," *Sewanee Review* 66, no. 1 (1958): 82, 85.

31. The phrase before the comma comes from Romans 5:2 and 2 Peter 1:4 and the phrase after the comma is from Philippines 2:8. This collect is present in the Roman Catholic liturgy of both the Extraordinary ("Tridentine") and Ordinary ("*Novus Ordo*") forms, albeit the version in the Ordinary form is abbreviated.

32. Percy, *Signposts*, 304.

33. *More Conversations with Walker Percy*, 137.

34. This is in spite of the contentious debates over moral theories by the Dominicans, Franciscans, and later the Jesuits in the Middle Ages and the Renaissance.

35. Jonathan Malesic, "Is There a Light under That Bushel? Hidden Christian Identity in *Wise Blood* and *The Moviegoer*," *Annual Publication of the College Theological Society* 54 (Maryknoll, NY: Orbis, 2008), 117.

36. Charles Taylor, *A Secular Age* (Cambridge. MA: Belknap Press of Harvard University Press, 2007), 37–42, 134–42, 300–307.

37. Tolson, *Pilgrim in the Ruins*, 167–68.

38. Leo Tolstoy, *Anna Karenina*, trans. Richard Pevear and Larissa Volokhonsky (New York: Penguin, 2000), pt. 3, ch. 20, 304–5.

39. Walker Percy, *The Fateful Rift: The San Andreas Fault in the Modern Mind*, National Endowment for the Humanities, May 3, 1989, C-Span Video Library, http://www.c-spanvideo.org/program/id/159052 (accessed November 14, 2010).

40. Walker Percy, *The Moviegoer* (New York: Knopf, 1966), 21–22.

41. The first wave, of course, was the Puritans to Massachusetts.

42. David Hackett Fisher, *Albion's Seed: Four British Folkways in America* (Oxford: Oxford University Press, 1989), 316.

43. Washington's will specified not to break up the families and to have the freed slaves educated. However, the dowry slaves, those who were part of Martha's dowry to George, were not freed.

44. In a 1985 interview, when Percy was asked if one has to reject Stoicism to be a good Catholic, he answered emphatically in the negative (*More Conversations with Walker Percy*, 106). In fact, Percy stated, "I don't see Christianity and Stoicism as antithetical."

45. For the best introduction to the subject, see Brian Skyrms's trilogy on using evolutionary game theory in philosophy: *Evolution of the Social Contract* (Cambridge: Cambridge University Press, 1996); *The Stag Hunt and the Evolution of Social Structure* (Cambridge: Cambridge University Press, 2004); and *Signals: Evolution, Learning, and Information* (Oxford: Oxford University Press, 2010).

46. Percy said in an interview that in *The Moviegoer* "Southern Stoicism [is] represented by Aunt Emily" (*Conversations with Walker Percy*, 125).

47. Marcus Aurelius, *The Meditations*, trans. George Long, book 12, http://classics.mit.edu/Antoninus/meditations.html (accessed November 14, 2010).

48. Epictetus, *The Enchiridion*, trans. Elizabeth Carter, http://classics.mit.edu/Epictetus/epicench.html (accessed November 14, 2010).

49. Marcus Aurelius, *The Meditations*, book 12.

50. See Apostolic Fathers, *The Didache*, in *Early Christian Writings*, trans. Maxwell Staniforth and Andrew Louth (New York: Penguin, 1987), 2, 2. While

we are not aware of any influence of the early Christian tract *The Didache* (c. AD 50–120) on Percy, it is a very Catholic (meaning Roman Catholic, Eastern Catholic, and Orthodox) text since it combines strict moral imperatives with a discussion of the liturgy of the Eucharist (187–99). In other words, one should be able to recognize a member of the "one holy, catholic and apostolic church" by his deeds, both morally and liturgically.

51. By no means is the claim being made that morality is relative to culture, but rather that, when criticizing the errors of the past, one should take into account the given culture to try to understand why people held morally wrong beliefs. Again, evolutionary game theory shows how difficult it is for mutants to arise and challenge the status quo.

52. Thomas Sowell, *Civil Rights: Rhetoric or Reality?* (New York: William Morrow, 1985), 13.

53. Tolson, *Pilgrim in the Ruins*, 198.

54. Will Percy describes the Percy family battle with the Klan in *Lanterns on the Levee*, ch. 18. This battle is further described in Bertram Wyatt-Brown, *The House of Percy: Honor, Melancholy, and Imagination in a Southern Family* (Oxford: Oxford University Press, 1994), where he emphasizes that without the Percy family, this reincarnation of the Klan would have taken over Greenville (227).

55. From a letter to his cousin Phinizy Spalding, "I might even say that everything I am interested in writing about is a result of the impact of Uncle Will's world-view upon me and what has germinated as a result of the ferment which followed" (Tolson, *Pilgrim in the Ruins*, 267). Whether he was in sync with Uncle Will or opposing him, he was guided by Uncle Will's vision.

56. At least to our knowledge, Jefferson never directly wrote about this.

57. Tolson, *Pilgrim in the Ruins*, 129.

58. Percy, *Signposts*, 342–43.

59. Ibid., 343.

60. Percy, *The Moviegoer*, 78.

61. Ibid., 343, 344.

62. Ibid., 222–23.

63. Percy, *Signposts*, 343, 344.

64. Ibid., 344.

65. Joseph Francis Rummel, *Blessed Are the Peacemakers*, Pastoral Letter 15 (Archdiocese of New Orleans, 1953).

66. Percy, *Signposts*, 344.

67. Ibid.

Walker Percy, Alexis de Tocqueville, and the Stoic and Christian Foundations of American Thomism

Peter Augustine Lawler

According to John Courtney Murray in *We Hold These Truths,* the task of American Catholics is to supply a theory adequate to the greatness of our Founders' practical accomplishment.[1] The dominant theory of our nation is Lockeanism, the theory of a middle-class country. We Americans, so the thinking goes, are basically beings with "interests" and so beings with "rights." We are free beings who work and demand that everyone work for him- or herself. We are middle class insofar as we're free, like aristocrats, to work like slaves, and we're enlightened enough to know we risk being suckered if we rely on the love or the trust of others instead of ourselves. So we pride ourselves in methodically resisting social instinct with selfish calculation. Each of us is compelled to sustain his or her being in freedom, and so we work hard to push back our dependence on nature—including our dependence on the instincts we're given as social animals. That understanding of the "abstract" individual, everyone knows, doesn't do justice to the experience of free persons who love and die. It doesn't do justice to us as either relational or properly proud beings, as beings personally privileged by the longings and capacities that distinguish each human soul.

For the American Catholic novelist/philosopher Walker Percy in *Lost in the Cosmos* (1983) and elsewhere, there are two indigenously American ways of criticizing or elevating the middle-class way of life.[2] The first is the experience of the southern aristocrat—more specifically, the Stoic or philosophic consciousness of the best of those aristocrats. The other is Christianity. Percy was raised by perhaps the most remarkable and penetrating of those Stoics. From his "Uncle Will" (the poet William Alexander Percy), he learned to appreciate the place of the aristocratic virtues of generosity and magnanimity in the formation of the character of a properly proud human being. And he learned what's true about the aristocratic criticism of the petty, calculating materialism of the American middle class. This criticism is of people without "class," without a social, rooted orientation in habit and thought that would tell them who they are and what they're supposed to do as ladies and gentlemen in the world—and as beings open to the genuine, moral responsibilities they've been given by their natures and by their place in the world.

By turning to Christianity, Percy also learned the limits of such Stoicism: its denial of human equality, of justice, of rights, of what we owe in love to our fellow creatures. For Percy, American Thomism is what comes from an honest, Christian correction to what's true about the Stoic criticism of middle-class life. That correction results in a very tentative, but very real, appreciation of the gains achieved by ordinary people—such as African Americans—under the influence of the middle-class conception of justice. Rights can be understood as not merely or even mainly the possession of self-interested individuals in competition with each other for scarce resources, the possession of producers and consumers. They can also be understood as what's given to free, loving, truthful, lying, wondering, wandering, irreducibly mysterious, unique, and irreplaceable beings under God. They can be understood to be rooted in the full, natural truth about the ontological difference that privileges members of our species.[3]

Because the South is now both the most aristocratic and the most Christian part of our country, Percy makes it clear that American Thomism could originate nowhere else. But American Christianity hardly originated in the South, and the southern, Stoic aristocracy was not really Christian at all. And we can turn to our friendly French observer, Alexis de Tocqueville, for evidence that Percy's Thomistic insight about America is hardly new. For Tocqueville, too, reconciling human greatness or the full truth about human individuality with the egalitarian justice that has its source in our Creator depends upon both Christian and aristocratic corrections to the middle-class American's self-understanding about what human liberty is. Tocqueville, like Percy, occupied a kind a privileged position as a person with a genuinely aristocratic social and intellectual inheritance living in a democracy, and both men saw, finally, that Catholic Christianity, purged of aristocratic prejudices (but not aristocratic wisdom), is both the religion and the philosophy or metaphysics (Thomism) most suited to defend the truth about human liberty.

My purpose here is to show the similarity between Tocqueville's and Percy's analysis of American disorientation, of a people confused by not knowing the whole truth about who they are and what they're supposed to do. So my purpose is to show that the seeds of American Thomism, at least, are already in Tocqueville's two-volume *Democracy in America* (1835, 1840).[4] American Thomism, of course, might describe the project of Walker Percy—the attempt to put together what is true about southern Stoicism, Christianity, modern science, and even middle-class egalitarianism in a comprehensive understanding of who we are.[5]

The Pop Cartesian Americans

Percy remarks that he especially admires Tocqueville's remarkable insight that the Americans are Cartesians without having read a word of Descartes.[6] The Cartesian method is also the democratic method, and it's that democratic method that keeps Americans from reading the words of philosophers—Descartes or anyone else. Democratic intellectual freedom means thinking for—and finding what one most needs in—oneself. Modern democracy—based as it is on individual rights—depends upon skepticism or Cartesian doubt when it comes to being ruled by the words of others. I see no reason to privilege any opinion over my own, over my own view of my own interests, of what's best for me. The "I" or the self is disconnected from other "I's" in order to be autonomous or self-determining. And so the "I" denies that self-consciousness is essentially knowing with or for others. The "I"—in truth, an abstraction from the whole social being—confuses the experience of "selfish" disconnection with the whole truth about who he is. He does so to maximize his freedom, but in such a way as to make the real exercise of freedom, of conscious, responsible choice, impossible.

For Tocqueville, some shared dogma or shared certainty about who we are is a "salutary bondage" that makes free thought and action possible. Having to invent oneself out of nothing is an impossible task, one not even shared by God himself (2.1.2). The result of experiencing oneself as being stuck with that task is anxious, paralyzing disorientation, what Percy describes as the hell of unguided or pure possibility.[7] I know I'm not nothing, but I might be anything. So I find it impossible to choose to be anything in particular. I can't simply choose to be who I am. To live well, I must somehow know who I am and what I'm supposed to do, and I can't do that all by myself.[8]

So Percy and Tocqueville agree that the pop Cartesian "I" lacks the resources to separate himself from what Percy (following Heidegger) calls the "they" and what Tocqueville calls anonymous public opinion—opinion determined by no one in particular.[9] The Cartesian self, untethered from others, turns out to have no content beyond the ineradicable experience of its "leftover" existence. I refuse to be ruled by other persons—to be suckered out of love. But public opinion, being an anonymous, unerotic force that envelopes us all equally, doesn't involve the same sort of undemocratic submission. The "I," by rejecting all personal authority—the authority of beings with names—ends up submitting to anonymous self-surrender. My particular being becomes filled up with opinions that come from no one in particular. The individual, by regarding the social passions of love and hate as dangerous threats to his own self-sufficiency, becomes unerotically locked up in his petty self, unable to be moved to thought or action on his own.

The isolated or abstracted "I" has no intellectual or emotional point of view—no spirit of resistance—to display the unique and irreplaceable individuality characteristic of real or whole human persons. Doubt that animates resistance to personal rule by others is turned on oneself and eradicates the possibility of proud self-rule. The good modern, egalitarian news, Tocqueville observes, is that I can say nobody is better than I. The corresponding bad news is that I have no reason to say I'm better than anyone else (even if I deeply desire to do so). And so I—in particular—can't say why I shouldn't submit to public opinion, just like everyone else. Public opinion provides ready-made answers to the questions anyone needs answered in order to live well, answers I'm in no position to discover for myself (2.1.2.)

That's why, Percy and Tocqueville agree, the modern tendency is to replace the egalitarian and personal religion of Christianity with the egalitarian and impersonal religion of pantheism (2.1.7).[10] There's no better relief for the anxiety of being an isolated "I," it would seem, than the thought that we're all alike—everything is alike—and we're all God—or lacking in nothing. Percy and Tocqueville both show that pantheism—in forms such as Western Buddhism—should be attacked as an enemy of human freedom or real individuality. Pantheism is a diversion from what we really know fueled by the isolated "I's" impulse toward self-surrender. It's a seductive lullaby that pushes individuals away from truthful thought and effective action.

The individual aims to lose himself in a whole in which he is a perfectly indistinct part by drawing upon the mind's desire for a unified vision that admits of no irrational or accidental exceptions. So the movement from personal to impersonal religion today is the surrender of any attempt to understand or defend one's own particular existence. Percy makes it clear that pantheistic self-surrender is finally impossible, but that's not to say we aren't personally diminished by the effort.

Percy does worry a good deal about the possibility of the chemical suppression of the anxiety that accompanies self-consciousness. Drug-based psychiatry promises quick relief without any need for self-understanding. But even here, Percy is more worried about what such efforts will do to us than any real chance of their ultimate success.[11]

Tocqueville agrees that the reason poetry will never fade away, even in the seemingly most unidealistic or unadorned of democratic times, is that our most truthful or least deluded experience is of the particular, contingent individual existing for a moment between two abysses, stuck, as it were, mysteriously between ignorance and knowledge when it comes to himself (2.1.17). Tocqueville sometimes echoes the Christian Pascal in describing the greatness and misery characteristic of particular members of our species alone, which will always be fit subjects for the poetic imagination.

Tocqueville and Percy agree that Christianity, as Pascal says, knows man, or sees each of us as the "who"—not just the "what"—each of us really is. And that is why they defend personal religion—religion that distinguishes between Creator and creature and sees each and every particular creature in his or her uniqueness—against every alternative, ancient or modern, superstitious or seemingly scientific (2.1.3–7). That's not to say that for either Tocqueville or Percy Pascal's unadorned Christianity expresses the whole truth, maybe even about Christianity. Pascal is too much about anxious misery—about the absence of God and the experience of personal contingency—to account for the joy that we're given as beings who can know something, if not everything, about ourselves, each other, and the world we share in common.[12] The truth is that we necessarily wander, as the beings who are self-conscious and wonder in the cosmos, and that the being who knows is necessarily somewhat of a mystery to himself. So our anxiety and joy are inseparable, and we're much more than miserable accidents.[13]

Tocqueville and Percy also agree that the Cartesian self too readily defers to the impersonal or materialistic authority of modern science. To say you should do what I think is my attempt to rule you. So you—the Cartesian "I"—won't defer to allegedly reasonable words of intrusively personal philosophers like Socrates, especially if I display my personal wisdom by recommending them to you. But if I recommend that you do what "studies show," we both defer to the impersonal, objective authority of science.

Science becomes objective by abstracting from the "I," by displaying material or "objective" or impersonal reality as the whole of reality. The scientist can't help but detach himself as scientist from the reality his study displays, but the status of the scientist is not the topic of his study. He doesn't hesitate to explain that the "I" that I think I am is an illusion, that he can explain what I am and what I do. The self-help he offers me is explaining that my experience of being a leftover can be alleviated by embracing scientific truth and living according to the insight that my desires can be satisfied in the way those of the other social animals can. Tocqueville follows Pascal and Percy follows Kierkegaard in observing that science has nothing to say about the situation and destiny of a particular individual, and it is powerless, of course, to theorize the irreducible fact of individual particularity out of existence (2.1.17, 2.2.15).[14]

Tocqueville says that what offends him about materialistic theoreticians is that they proudly turn themselves into gods by reducing those they study to brutes. Percy says that they understand themselves as pure minds orbiting a cosmos of pure bodies. They describe people as organisms-in-an-environment and then exempt the experience of themselves as minds—meaning their intellectual, social experience of the joy of shared discovery—from that description. The experience of being pure mind isn't that of the Cartesian "I." For the scientist, consciousness is consciousness with other scientists, and truthful discovery that's not self-discovery is a social experience not shared with other social animals. But when the ordinary pop Cartesian turns to the scientific expert for help, he finds only what the scientific studies show without the experience of the scientist.[15]

The scientists are surely right to show that there's no place in the cosmos for an isolated, pointless "I," just as they're surely wrong in implicitly understanding themselves as a community of pure minds wholly detached from ordinary human concerns. The scientists, as more or less than minds, are stuck with reentering the social world of parents, children, friends, and so forth, and this they can't do so as scientists. They can't help but find ordinary lives dreary, and so it's not so surprising that nothing they say can make us nonscientists as happy as they think we should be with the way they think we live. The scientist—by thinking in terms of minds and bodies—offers no insight into the connection between mind and body, and he thinks of both himself and nonscientists too simply.[16]

That's why Tocqueville says that "aristocratic science"—which is all about the pleasures of the mind—is too proud and "democratic science"—which is all about satisfying the pleasures of the body (that is, technology)—is too humble (2.1.10). And that's why Percy is so clear that people are neither minds nor bodies nor even some mixture of the two. To be human, to be self-conscious as we are, is to be born to trouble in many senses, but one is to be full of longings that can't be attributed to either minds or bodies, which elude theoretical articulation, simple satisfaction, and scientific measurement.[17] The aristocrat Leo Strauss rightly said that the world is the home of the human mind, but Strauss himself was more or less than simply mind. The world described by the physicist, as Percy adds, has no place for the physicist.[18] And Tocqueville experienced a kind of dizzying disorientation when thinking too purely or apolitically, because the reality he experienced had no room for Tocqueville or any great defender of human liberty as something more than mere philosophy.[19] For Tocqueville and Percy, human reality is irreducibly personal or particular, and the universal truth can only be known by particular persons. The Christian and genuinely scientific teaching is that logos can only be found in persons, in the only relational, the only alienated, and the only creative beings in the cosmos.

What the allegedly pure minds offer the isolated, displaced "I" is the relief from anxious, dislocated human misery that accompanies experiencing oneself as other than a body or an organism in an environment. That program of self-help through self-denial, Percy and Tocqueville agree, mainly makes at least lots of people more anxious and restless than ever. They try, as Tocqueville emphasizes and Percy observes, to lose themselves in materialistic or consumerist diversions, sometimes, as Tocqueville says, with an insane ardor (2.2.13). The seemingly decent American materialists, Percy and Tocqueville observe, are actually loony; they don't know why they're doing what they're doing. Their material calculation only diverts them quite imperfectly from what they think they really know. As the great anti-Communist dissident Aleksandr Solzhenitsyn put it, it's easy to find just under the surface of their methodical pragmatism the howl of existentialism.[20] Percy writes to replace that howl with the possibility of delight in sharing what we really know by putting back together what's true about modern science with what's true about European existentialism.[21]

Tocqueville says only the Americans' religion keeps their self-destructiveness from literally becoming suicidal. When they lose their religion or some other limiting explanation for their experiences of displacement, Percy agrees, the more thoughtful or insistently self-conscious or undiverted among them do become suicidal. Despite our best efforts, we're unable to find in public opinion or scientific expertise the guidance we need in knowing who we are or what we're supposed to do. Not knowing how to live, we either lose ourselves with uneven success in diversions, or decide not to live at all.

Both Tocqueville and Percy seem to class Americans as either shallow and easily diverted—those Tocqueville calls decent materialists (2.2.11)—or deep and self-destructive, at least when their individualism isn't countered by religion or the pleasures of political life. For Percy and Tocqueville, the struggle of our time is to come to terms with the possibility of suicide and reject it (2.2.13).[22] That struggle, in other words, is to rediscover the goodness and gratuitousness of created being, including one's own being.[23] For Tocqueville, much of the goodness of being human can be discovered through the proud pleasures of political responsibility. Percy, of course, was aware of that possibility through the southern Stoics, and he understood the proud rational man ruling himself and others, with Tocqueville, as a form of natural human perfection. But it was not, he thought, given to him or as a real possibility for most prosperous Americans today.

For Percy, the remedy of faith in a personal Creator whose infinite and loving being corresponds to our deepest longings is the only one available, in most cases, these days. Percy, of course, thought that remedy was not only effective but true, the one that corresponds best to what we really know through science about who we are. Tocqueville, meanwhile, while open to faith and especially the Pascalian thought that Christianity knows man, thought himself unfortunate because he couldn't quite believe. He was, to some extent, stuck with his anxiety insofar as he couldn't quite accept—while denying that he had any privileged right not to accept—the Christian account of the creation of particular persons by a personal, relational Creator.

Tocqueville seemed to worry that unerotic individualism would make American materialists so decent or herdlike that they would surrender any thought about their futures (including, of course, about their mortality) to a providential soft despotism of meddlesome, schoolmarmish bureaucrats (2.4.6). But he also said that religious madness was the inevitable result of the attempt to divert oneself from the needs of the soul (2.2.13). And Percy seems to agree that both the religious madness and the secular ideologies of the twentieth century—especially ideological wars or, in a way, huge wars over nothing—were natural reactions to the emptiness of pop Cartesianism. Some Brave New World or therapeutic despotism might come, Percy was able to see, but probably not. He, as a believing Christian, may have had a bit more faith in the resilience of the human soul or distinctively human nature than did Tocqueville. He seemed pretty certain, at least, that we would remain ensouled creatures until the end of time. As he shows, for example, at the end of *Lost in the Cosmos*, our efforts to drug ourselves into serenity or blow ourselves out of existence will likely fail, and love, faith, and politics will emerge from again from the ruins.[24]

That the pop Cartesian experts offer us no guidance concerning who we are and what we're supposed to do is the point of Percy's hilarious "Last Donahue Show" in *Lost in the Cosmos*.[25] Appearing on that show out of nowhere are two figures from America's allegedly discredited but genuinely countercultural past—Colonel John Pelham, Jeb Stuart's legendary artillerist, and John Calvin. Both the southern Stoic warrior Pelham and Calvin, of course, are certain about who they are and how to act. They are equally—if differently—repulsed by the sexual and personal irresponsibility displayed on the *Donahue Show*, by the ignorant indifference to our duties as self-consciously relational beings.

Calvin can't grasp what "sexual preference" could possibly mean; it doesn't occur to him that acting or being sexual is just a personal whim. For him we're creatures, made to obey God's toughly judgmental law. Pelham, a gentleman who knows who he is, a rational man and a member of a noble class, has no trouble knowing how to treat a lady. His knowledge owes nothing to religion; he respects such belief, he says, but he adds he doesn't give it a second thought. Pelham defines himself by having fought for his way of life. He doesn't regret fighting, although he knows he lost. So he accepts what, to him, is the obvious result—the rule of "white trash."

We can also turn to Tocqueville to flesh out Percy's insight that the American "countercultures" are Calvinist, Protestant Christianity and southern Stoicism (1.1.2, 1.2.8, 1.2.10). Americans aren't Cartesian to the extent that they're either Christian or aristocratic. The first Americans, he reminds us, showed up in New England and Virginia. The New Englanders were the pilgrims; they left their homeland in the service of an idea that's both religious and political. They were enlightened family men and women, out to found an egalitarian city in accord with Christian, biblical principles. And so they did. New England was the most democratic place in the world since ancient Athens. It was, more precisely, the most democratic place ever. The Puritan "idea" wasn't like the Platonic "city in speech." It was intended to and did become real, and it was based on an "idea" that extended equally to all human beings. The Puritans' idea of justice was far more universal or nonexclusionary than the one found either in Athenian practice or Socratic theory, but it still remained political or embodied in a real place in this world (1.1.2). The ancient democracy, of course, was composed only of citizens and depended on slaves; equality was merely political or conventional and didn't extend beyond the gates of the city or to all people living within those gates.

So even ancient democracies, Tocqueville observes, were really aristocracies, and even their best thought was distorted by aristocratic prejudices (2.1.5). But the Puritan city included, in principle, all human beings, and it was based on the biblical principle that all human beings are equally ensouled creatures under God. On that faith-based idea the Puritans built, in this world, in the direction of universal civic participation and universal education. No creature rules another by right, and every such creature, to avoid being seduced by vain or satanic frauds, has to read the world of God for himself. On that egalitarian insight, the Puritans' political theory, Tocqueville observes, was amazingly free from prejudice (1.1.2).

In middle-class America, universal literacy was caused by the requirements of earning a living for oneself. For the Cartesian, individualistic, egalitarian American, nobody is above—and nobody is below—having interests (1.1.3). The Puritan agrees that everyone has a duty to work for himself and in service to others, and so education, contrary to what aristocrats believe, isn't all about the cultivation of some leisure class. But, not sharing the Cartesian skepticism about the spiritual dimension of our existences, the Puritan adds that each of us is more than a being with interests—and so universal education is about much more than techno-utility. The Puritan finds content and so social duties and an eternal destiny in the irreducible, irreplaceable "I" each of us knows ourselves to be. So for the Puritan, egalitarian education is also liberal education or "higher" education.

Tocqueville, it's true, didn't call the Puritans Calvinists, but he described them as much like the idealistic citizens of Calvin's Geneva, about whom Tocqueville knew much, at least through his reading of Rousseau. The downside of the Puritans, in his eyes, was their ridiculous and tyrannical legislation, their attempt to draw their law from the Old Testament books of Exodus, Leviticus, and Deuteronomy, their attempt to criminalize every sin. Tocqueville himself didn't regard such legislation as properly Christian, but peculiarly Puritanical or Calvinist.

Tocqueville explains that the Gospels themselves don't contain any specific political teaching and so are compatible with a variety of political orders, including easygoing liberal modern democracy. Tocqueville emphatically distinguishes Christianity from Islam insofar as Christianity isn't about the "law" in the sense of political legislation (2.1.5). It's Christianity, by teaching the equal freedom of all human beings from enslavement by any particular political "cave" and its degrading civil theology, that freed every particular individual from political domination. That's what Tocqueville means when he says that Jesus Christ had to come to earth to show us the ways in which all human beings are equal (2.1.3). What Jesus shows us, he believes, is true—even if what Jesus claims about being God isn't. (There's no evidence at all that Tocqueville thought Jesus was God, that the Resurrection actually occurred, that the Trinity is credible, and so on.) The aristocratic philosophers, Tocqueville does say, were blinded by their class insofar as they accepted slavery as inevitable, just as Percy said (and the example of Uncle Will confirms) that the southern Stoics were blinded by their class to their racist paternalism. The Christian teaching concerning equality differs from Cartesian skepticism in not being focused on the isolated individual. It is, as Tocqueville explains, the main antidote to American self-obsession (2.1.3). Christianity, like every religion, teaches creatures that they have duties they share in common. They have such common duties because their souls have some shared content, a foundation in their Creator through which they can know and love one another. Christianity teaches Americans that they are more than empty or self-contained "I's"—psychologically self-sufficient yet dependent for their very beings on their contingent and ephemeral bodies. American preachers, Tocqueville explains, speak about humility, and so officially are against pride. But by telling people each of their lives has a unique and irreplaceable immortal destiny, and that there are pleasures far higher than the pleasures of the body, just as there are duties that go far beyond mere material utility or deference to the rights of others, Christian preaching actually inspires the pride connected with any form of irreducible individuality or moral responsibility or experience of soul (2.2.15).

Tocqueville does find what can be called secular justifications for some residually Puritanical American legislation—which has to be taken as evidence that he sees Christianity's personal "anthropology" as true even in the absence of revelation (2.2.15). He praises how seriously the Americans take the virtues of chastity and marital fidelity, as well as the ways in which they exempt women from the rigors of middle-class productivity (2.3.8–12). American women calculate that religion serves their true interests as beings born to be wives and mothers, and they, in a seemingly Christian way, surrender many of their claims for justice to sustain personal love. Tocqueville displays the alliance of American priests and American wives and moms against the ridiculous claims for the unerotic self-sufficiency of American men.

Christianity, Aristocracy, and the Greatness of Human Individuality

Tocqueville's final discussion (2.2.15) of religion in America moves away from any concern about political utility toward sustaining the sublime qualities that distinguish human individuality from all else that exists, from being absorbed into some homogeneous, materialistic account of the world. There, he calls Americans' religion their most precious inheritance from aristocratic times, and the way they have known the aristocratic truth, found in the philosophic doctrine of Socrates and Plato, that we are beings capable of transcending our biological limitations in the direction of immortality. Tocqueville praises the rest commanded by American law and belief on what might be called the Puritans' Sunday. That leisure is for beings who know their longings to be more than mere bodies can be satisfied, for reflection on who they are in light of their true destiny. Without Sunday, the Americans could easily lose themselves in the frenzy of restless diversion. They could easily, by thinking of themselves as less than they really are, become less than they are meant to be.

Christians believe, against the pretensions of the materialistic experts, that they are more than material beings, and so they're inspired to have thoughts and perform deeds that stand the test of time. Christianity also curbs their restless materialism by giving them a view of humanly worthy leisure (which they enjoy on Sunday), by keeping them from believing that they need to be constantly diverted from the ephemeral insignificance of the isolated "I." Tocqueville, in evaluating Christianity's effect on the individual, divides the philosophers into pre-Socratic and Epicurean materialists and the Platonists serious about the soul's immortality. Christianity originally emerged, he explained, as part of the soul's rebellion against the Epicurean excesses of the Romans (2.2.12). The pre-Socratic claim about the transience of everything human was a kind of self-fulfilling prophecy. None of the pre-Socratics' writings were preserved intact over time. Meanwhile, the works of Plato, attuned as they are to the true longings of souls, remain with us as wholes.

Tocqueville pointedly says that Christianity expresses, for Americans, what's always true about the aristocrat's proud view of the high purposes of particular individuals. According to Tocqueville, Christianity functions for the Americans as a kind of Platonism for the people, a kind of aristocracy that includes everyone—the egalitarian aristocracy of the Puritans. For Nietzsche, Platonism for the people suggests that Christianity is a religion for slaves being diverted from living well now by illusions about their true home in some other world. Christianity is a diversion or opiate for the weak.

The southern Stoics, Will Percy reminds us in *Lanterns on the Levee*, actually agree with Nietzsche (310–21). He explains with elegant directness that the Christian hope for personal salvation is what "the Negroes," given their natural and social incapability for truthful self-rule, can't help but believe. Christianity frees people from any sense of responsibility for what they do in this world, and it exalts emotional enthusiasm at the expense of reason. It's true that Will Percy's aristocratic criticism here is clearly of southern fundamentalism—the religion shared, in his view, by Negroes and white trash. It's not of the kind of Christianity that Tocqueville praises, the source of the Americans' common moral code that limits their self-obsession. Will himself was a Catholic as a young man, and he understood his belief as an admirable—almost fanatical—code of personal perfection. But he took it as a sign of Stoic or rational maturity that, one day, he just couldn't believe. He was stuck with living without hope, stuck with himself as he experienced himself through reason alone (95–96).

For Will Percy, the road traveled reached the serenity that comes through the accepting of undeniable facts (176). Knowing the truth becomes heartening or invigorating only with patience, and eventually it becomes compatible with some personal happiness. Will knew that he was, in many respects, from his rational unbelief to his homosexuality, the exception to the rule, and so he knew that he was to some extent a tourist—a wanderer—wherever he was (156). He was, to a remarkable extent, at home with his homelessness, and his deep loneliness didn't lead him to either suicidal despair or political fanaticism (158, 223, 348). He did his duty to his children and his community as a member of his class. Will Percy was not as lonely as a man can be; he was not nearly as displaced as the American Cartesian. No Cartesian could write: "I have seen the goodness of men and the beauty of things. I have no regrets. I am not contrite. I am grateful" (348).

The only way to think truthfully about death, for Will, is to surrender any vain or anguished claims for personal significance. It is to rise above Christian and aristocratic nobility in the usual senses. Being a Stoic in the full sense is learning how to die, to free oneself from fear and anguish through truthful self-surrender. In this respect, his advice was to listen to the thought of Buddha. Our anguish is called by our apartness or experiences of personal contingency. Why would we want this miserable experience, Percy asks, to continue after death? Death is the surrender of apartness through becoming nothing more than an indiscriminate part of the whole that is Creation. We know, Percy claims, that we are most ourselves when we're most not ourselves, when we lose ourselves in another or in beauty. So death is a kind of coming home, the definitive cure for our homelessness (310–21).

For Walker Percy, Will's personal loneliness was based on a misunderstanding. Will also wrote he was most himself through his poetic sharing of what he knew through words that gave voice to experiences that many people held in common (172, 313). His deepest longings were personal, and, although death surely cured his deep loneliness, it didn't do so, in his own eyes, in a way that corresponded to his longing not to be alone, to be personally transparent before another who loved him the way he was. Will loved the good things and the good persons of life too much to be a Buddhist, and he accepted death rather than embraced it. He was the least suicidal of the Percys, and he seems to have contemplated self-destruction far less than the Stoics in Percy's novels, the real-life other Percys, and even Walker Percy himself.

For Walker, Buddhism, like science, expresses well who human beings are in general, but not the particular longings that are the sources of both our irreducible joys and our irreducible anxiety.[26] For Walker, Will's denial of the possible truth of Christianity was a kind of self-denial. Will—the wonderer and wanderer—didn't reflect sufficiently on the cause of his homelessness, and so his life might have been more joyful and less merely serenely lonely. And Will, despite his protestations, never surrendered his concern for his personal significance as a rational being and a dutiful member of a noble class. His Socratic Buddhism, Walker also noticed, contradicted his Stoic pride. Will, in fact, knew well enough that his "democratic" account of the equal personal dissolution of us all couldn't quite be satisfying to the aristocrat who overcomes his fear of death through his courage, even if both ways of overcoming fear or materialistic determination are marks of the true Stoic, of the philosopher-emperor.

Tocqueville would have denied that the serenity of Will Percy was inconceivable. Like Walker Percy, he would have appreciated him, as he did Pascal, as one of a kind. But even in Tocqueville's own case, disbelief filled him with dizzying disorientation, the intellectual and emotional loneliness he discerns in the American Cartesian. His remedy was less serene and accepting than throwing himself into a passionate defense of political liberty. He embraced a cause that transcended material determination and would produce accomplishments that would stand the test of time.[27]

Tocqueville's own experience, together with his observations concerning the materialism generated by democratic, Cartesian skepticism, suggests that only if people believe that they're more than the biological beings scientists describe or the empty leftovers the Cartesians describe can they live well—or achieve their true greatness—in this world (2.2.15). As Percy puts it, only if we have some credible explanation for our experiences of homelessness can we be at home as well as can be with the good things of this world.[28] Christianity is the antidote to materialism, which is what Tocqueville calls the probably untrue and certainly pernicious theoretical diversion that makes the weak—the displaced "I"—weaker (2.2.15). Materialism can't extinguish but it can intensify the experience of the "I" as pointless leftover in a world otherwise perfectly comprehensible by impersonal theory. Materialism can have the effect of turning the sublimity of human longings—and the great thoughts and accomplishments—into nothing but dizzying, paralyzing disorientation. Christianity, we learn from the Stoic Will, may not be the only antidote to materialism, but it is the one that's most credible and effective in democratic times, and it's certainly the one most compatible with the egalitarian understanding of justice. So it is the antidote to materialism that corresponds mostly fully with what we really know about ourselves.

No materialist can explain the hopes and longings of the being capable of experiencing himself as existing for a moment between two abysses. And Tocqueville agrees with the Socratic Christian Percy that there's nothing more mysterious and wonderful than the particular human being, the being who knows but who can't be fully known to himself (2.1.17). Tocqueville, by connecting magnanimity and humility or pride and the anxious experience of personal insignificance, comes close, in his own way, to Thomism—meaning a way of showing that aristocratic Christianity or classical Christianity or philosophic Christianity aren't oxymorons. His Platonic or aristocratic affirmation of the truth about the soul or the sublimity of the highest forms of human thought and action isn't meant to negate the distinctive contribution of Christianity to the whole truth about who we are.

We can say that Tocqueville offers a Platonic criticism of Pascal on behalf of the thought that our true greatness includes some justifiable pride in who we are, but he also offers a Pascalian criticism of the absolutely self-sufficient pretensions of classical magnanimity and Socratic philosophy. We can see, in fact, that Tocqueville's talking up of both the aristocratic and the egalitarian Christianity corresponds to the measured approach he takes to more pure or complete displays of aristocracy in America. That's why he and Percy described for our qualified admiration what aristocracy they could find in America, and it's why they made it clear that the aristocratic or Stoic criticism of the middle-class reduction of the human being to a being with interests—a consumer and producer—has great weight. The aristocrats are undeniably strong where the clueless, merely "leftover" democrats are weak.

Tocqueville and American Aristocrats

Tocqueville, in the last chapter of *Democracy*'s volume 1 (1.2.10), reports that he found aristocrats in America among both the Indians and the southern slaveholders. In each case, men prided themselves on not working, and they regarded their leisure as noble. They ranked their own beautiful and useless activity over the productive lives of most men. They regarded themselves as more free than those whose lives were dominated by work, material desires, and slavish fear. Both the Indians and the southerners regarded the tasks worthy of men as hunting, fighting, and giving speeches about hunting and fighting (political life). Tocqueville rightly regarded the Indian way of life as defeated by its own vanity and the greedy techno-power of the American middle class.

The southern aristocracy—although based on the monstrous institution of race-based slavery—was still in some ways a worthy alternative to the middle-class, democratic way of life of most Americans. Each alternative, Tocqueville makes clear, has its distinctive virtues and vices, and the southerners basically had the virtues and vices of any aristocracy. They were both more spontaneous and more spiritual than the northerners, and so they had a better sense of how to enjoy life. They found joy in leisurely self-contemplation, and they didn't work themselves to death in a futile attempt to transform themselves or their world. They were distinguished by their proud sense of who they are and what they're supposed to do in ruling themselves and others as members of a particular class in a particular time and place. They were, as Percy writes, distinguished by the classical virtues of magnanimity and generosity, and they displayed the flourishing of a kind of natural human excellence in our hemisphere.[29] But they were also lazy, selfish in the sense of privileging their class over humanity in general, and so unjust.

In some ways, Tocqueville presents the southern aristocracy as the result of an impulse opposite to that which animated the Puritans. New England was founded on selfless, egalitarian idealism. Its Puritanical vice was taking the idealistic formation of every human soul through political legislation far too seriously—or at the expense of individual liberty. Virginia Tocqueville presents as founded in pure selfishness. The first Virginians were "classless" in the precise sense: they lacked the manners and morals—the decency—that come from being formed according to a moral code.

They were solitary adventurers—coming to America without family or friends—in search of easy money. They lacked the self-discipline that came either from being Christians or being productive members of the middle class. They unjustly wanted to have plenty of everything with very little work. They were pretty much pirates. It's hardly surprising that slavery so readily took root in Virginia and the rest of the South (1.1.2).

That founding selfishness was transformed into an aristocracy through generations of experience with slavery. The Virginians began to take pride in their noble leisure, and they began to take on the habits and opinions of cultivated gentlemen. They began to think of themselves as members of an aristocratic class, and they developed both the virtues and vices of any such class. They were both better and worse than the Puritans. They were better insofar as they displayed a kind of intellectual and political greatness not characteristic of either Puritanical or later middle-class America. But that really meant that their selfishness was sublimated or elevated, and it continued to depend on the monstrous, increasingly spiritualized despotism of race-based slavery. They attempted to degrade a whole class of human beings to subhuman servitude, to reduced beings without the longings that flow from their freedom (1.2.10). The Puritans idealistically devoted themselves to displaying the qualities of soul of everyone through political and religious life, and they thought that no creature was above working both for himself and for the service of others. The Virginians, in the name of a certain vanity about their own souls, worked harder and harder to deprive other men of their souls, to turn them into beings fit for nothing more than working for others.

The Virginians' criticism of the Puritans was their repressive moralism. They regarded "abolitionism" as one example of many of the fanatical tendency to both criminalize every sin and to judge the diverse choices of others as sins. Aristocratic manners and morals, there are—there's class! But it can't be required by law. The Virginians weren't about outlawing sin, and they had a sophisticated tolerance when it came to diverse displays of individuality. So it was a Virginian who wrote the unforgettable words about the inalienable rights of individuals and established in our country the principle of pure religious liberty. When the classical or Epicurean (or basically Greek and Roman) Jefferson thought about a free display of one's individuality, he wasn't thinking at all about the decent "bourgeois" materialism of members of the middle class. For him, religious liberty was primarily about protecting the cultivated gentleman and his refined skepticism from those who would use popular piety as a political tool. Tocqueville rightly never describes the leading men—the aristocratic class—of the South as fundamentally Christian. When he says that it was a lucky accident that our Framers—the men who came up with the Constitution—were basically aristocrats, he was thinking in some large part about southerners (1.1.7).

Education for Civilization

The Puritan and the American aristocrat are, when it comes to justice and moral legislation, opposite extremes. But they unite in opposing the materialism of the solitary "I" or self-obsessed individual that is the purely middle-class American. They were clear on who they are and what they're supposed to do as members of a class or community. And they agreed that education is, most of all, about the soul—for the cultivation of a being not determined by the impersonal forces that surround him or defined merely by the requirements of earning a living. The Puritans and the southerners were about, in different ways, civilization. Restlessly opposed to civilizing influences, Tocqueville shows, were middle-class Americans who thought of education as merely indispensable for acquiring technical skills, and who identified philosophy and science with technology or the transformation of nature with bodily need in mind. The American individualist is constantly running from civilization to some solitary place on the frontier (2.2.13). The individualistic or emotionally self-absorbed American, on his own, resists having his heart and soul enlarged by a particular "city" or political and religious society.

The aristocrat, in Tocqueville's eyes, is about reading the Greek and Roman authors to learn how to govern himself and others, and to learn the proud truth about what it means to be a rational man born to use his leisure to take pleasure in discovering the truth for its own sake (2.1.4-10, 15, 20).

Aristocratic science, Tocqueville observes, is about pleasures of the soul, democratic science about pleasures of the body. The truth, the aristocrat believes, is pleasurable because it enhances his self-conscious pride in his soulful human greatness; the democrat is too skeptical about the soul or immaterial being to believe that he can know anything more than what he can use to sustain his biological being. About himself, the democratic "I" only knows that he's not nothing, and he's stuck with sustaining his characterless and so anxiously displaced being on his own. But the aristocrat, as they say, knows that he's somebody, a being with the significance of both individuality and a secure location in a particular place or class. So he has confidence in his personal capabilities, that he, as a moral and political being, can have a real effect on the world.

Percy adds what Tocqueville couldn't have known: the American southern masters—before, during, and after the Civil War—were only superficially Christian. They understood themselves, in a way Tocqueville would have appreciated had he known, as Roman patricians reading Greek philosophers. Their models were the Stoic philosopher Epictetus and especially the philosopher-emperor Marcus Aurelius. They thought of themselves as a class of men generously and magnanimously responsible for others, men who would never think or do anything that was beneath them. The Stoic does right by you not out of love of you or out of respect for your rights. He does what's right in all circumstances because he won't compromise the "inner fortress" that is himself as a rational, moral being—a self-understanding that finds its social embodiment in the honor code of his class. He displays his greatness of soul by benefiting his inferiors, while not forgetting who he is and why they are inferior.[30]

The southern Stoic, the true aristocrat, is both radically solitary and quite social. He doesn't depend on anything outside of himself, which is why, as both Tom Wolfe and Admiral James Stockdale have shown us, the writings of the Stoic philosopher-slave Epictetus are best suited to guide a man in securing his freedom and dignity in a maximum security prison or as a North Vietnamese POW. He's a member of a class that's both natural and conventional.[31] As both Colonel Pelham and Will Percy explain, they recognize their kind whenever they've appeared in history (61). So Stoicism in the South was a kind of conventional aristocracy displaying, at its best, a natural perfection—a perfection, as Marcus Aurelius said, available to all beings equipped with speech and so reason but achieved only by a few. It's a perfection that is both theoretical and practical, linking together truth and courage by taking responsibility for what we can't help but know. Tocqueville, and of course Percy, didn't think America could or should have aristocratic rulers. So Tocqueville recommends that, in democracy, those following literary careers should read the Greek and Roman authors in their original languages. We can easily say, after reading Percy, that Tocqueville recommends for democratic writers a kind of Stoic education, the education

Walker Percy received from Uncle Will. That way our writers will acquire aristocratic habits of mind, and they'll learn how to read books written with care for a small audience that has the leisure to read closely.

The danger is that metaphysics and theology will lose ground in democratic language, and words will become more exclusively technical, commercial, and administrative (2.1.16). A corresponding danger is that people will lose confidence in being able to rule themselves and others, and so the very words they use will suggest their passive, fatalistic dependency (2.1.20). One antidote to this abstract and shallow impoverishment of democratic language is the best aristocratic books. They can be expected to infuse democratic language with words that express the distinctions and longings democracy can't help but neglect. Democratic prejudices or partial truths will be countered by aristocratic prejudices or partial truths. The truth is, Tocqueville says, that aristocrats unrealistically exaggerate, for example, the effect of great men on historical change, just as democrats—with their impersonal theories all about "forces"—unrealistically or dogmatically deny that effect (2.1.20).

Tocqueville doesn't recommend close study of the Greek and Roman authors for most Americans. It will arouse in them longings that can't be satisfied in the routine of middle-class life, making them more restless and more dangerous than they need be (2.1.15). In most cases, it appears, Tocqueville is, in democratic times, for technical education supplemented by religion and some involvement in local politics. He's with the Puritans insofar as he notices that everyone has the needs of the soul, which get distorted and disoriented when they're ignored (2.2.12). That doesn't mean that, on education, he was as idealistically egalitarian as a Puritan. Because the Puritan idea was radically Christian, it couldn't distinguish between a class suited for what we call liberal education and a class suited for work in the ordinary or technical sense of the term. Both liberal education and work—truth and justice or leisure in the aristocratic sense and productivity in the middle-class sense—are for everyone. From Tocqueville's view, the Puritans expected too much of ordinary people.

Tocqueville, insofar as he criticizes Americans for their lack of great literature and free thought, is for the development of some higher education in America. He seems to be close to the suggestion that American higher education, outside of the sciences, should be some combination of aristocratic and Christian books. What's best about the greatness of proud, aristocratic individuality should be tempered by Puritanical devotion to egalitarian justice, and vice versa. Surely American education, in his eyes, wouldn't be merely some combination of aristocratic prejudices and democratic technology. The Christian element, surely, would have to be somehow more than mere dogma; otherwise the educated American would embrace Christianity only for its political utility, with no sense of why he or she should be devoted to the proposition that all men are created equal. Surely he makes it abundantly clear that the Lockean/Cartesian defense of that proposition is inadequate. One way, of course, is by tellingly not talking about Mr. Jefferson's *Declaration of Independence*.

So Tocqueville seems, from this view, most attracted to a kind of Catholicism purged of any connection with the prejudices of aristocratic injustice, which wouldn't be so different from the Puritanism he described purged of a kind of un-Christian political fanaticism, a Puritanism transformed by a criticism based on both the purely Christian and aristocratic views of freedom. Tocqueville would be most for a religion that corrected classical magnanimity—with its devaluing of the lives or freedom of most human beings—without obliterating it. He's for preserving the real truth it teaches about human greatness and the real—if quite imperfect and finally ambivalent—pleasures of political life.

The dialectic between pride and anxiety or magnanimity and something like humility—between overvaluing one's personal significance and experiences of utter personal contingency or insignificant emptiness—is what animated Tocqueville's own life. It's the one that expresses what's true about both the aristocratic and too radically Christian (in his eyes, Pascalian) experiences of the human soul. In Tocqueville's most truthful reflections about himself, he found his pride in personal, political significance and virtue to be genuine, but his anxiety about his real significance equally so. He presents the most characteristic human experiences as the pride or greatness of statesmanship (purely aristocratic truth) and the anxiety in the face of the truth about the personal contingency of us all (purely democratic truth). For anyone who really tells the truth to himself about himself, as Tocqueville says he does in his *Souvenirs*, self-confidence never exists without self-doubt, and no confident display of human greatness is completely free from diversion.[32] That's why Percy says we have a right to our anxiety as an indispensable clue to the truth about our being, which is not to say that the truth revealed by anxiety—our homelessness or displacement—is the last word about who we are. Self-doubt or self-irony may have overwhelmed the confidence of the Stoics in Percy's novels, but that's only because they couldn't either properly understand their anxiety or see that it's properly alleviated not only by pride but by personal love—by what displaced persons can share in common even in the midst of civilization's decline and fall.[33]

The Delayed Contribution of the South

We have to remember Tocqueville doesn't highlight the ways the southern aristocracy could contribute to a more general American understanding of who we are. He doesn't describe the southerners as particularly attached to Greek and Roman literature (although they were) or as elevating the general quality of American language. He says there's no American literature worth talking about, and he doesn't, as anyone would today, talk about the distinctiveness of southern literature. That's probably because, as Percy observes, the southerners expended all their literary energy in the decades immediately prior to the Civil War defending race-based slavery, a singularly indefensible cause for any decent man. Tocqueville saw the South as doomed—and rightly so—and as making no contribution to our country's or the world's increasingly modern future. He really can't explain why the study of the Greek and Roman authors won't just wither away in America or why American education became more purely technical or utilitarian. From Percy's perspective, Tocqueville's American seems to need a more literary version of the aristocratic South than he could actually find.

The thought that the South might make an enduring contribution to curbing American pop Cartesianism, it seems, couldn't be taken seriously until after the Civil War. The South, we might say, is liberated to make that contribution by being freed of the monstrous task of defending slavery in thought and deed. Orestes Brownson, in the unjustly neglected *The American Republic* (1865), said, immediately after the war, that the true interpretation of the American Constitution, the one that does justice to the whole truth about the material, political, and spiritual dimensions of being human, combines southern particularity with northern universality. The South is all about the assertion of the particular individual—by itself a tyrannical assertion—but an assertion that displays emphatically part of the greatness of who each of us is. The South is, in this sense, too personal.

The North—both in its materialism and in the fanaticism of Puritanical abolitionism—is too universal or general or destructive of human distinctiveness. The particular individual is dissolved into a kind of abstract humanitarianism—a seductive doctrine that preys upon the weakness of the displaced "I" in an anonymous world. Northern abolitionism, in Brownson's expansive understanding, culminates in the homogeneity of both materialism and pantheism. But the North, of course, is also strong on the universal principles of justice, on not exempting proud individuals from the social and political responsibilities we are all share.

So Brownson suggests, thinking along lines remarkably similar to Tocqueville, that the proper combination of southern particularity—or its concern for particular persons and places—with northern universality—especially at its highest levels of coming to terms with our shared embodiment and equality under God—is pretty much the real truth about who we are as whole human beings. So it turns out, Brownson concludes, that America is the most Catholic of nations.[34] I say this only in passing because his admirably subtle philosophic and poetic attempt to convince Americans of that fact didn't catch on anywhere. I do say it in passing to show that a strongly antislavery, Yankee, very deep, and fairly astute thinker could say that the aristocratic South was partly right in its criticism of the emptiness of American Cartesianism. Surely Tocqueville writing later would have done the same.

We know, of course, that the southern aristocrats returned to power for a while after the Civil War. They lost the war, but through what amounted to a successful terrorist movement forced the Union troops out of their states and restored "white rule." The southern Stoics viewed themselves as ruling the blacks and ordinary whites paternalistically, as gentlemen who by nature and education deserved to rule. Their class was displaced in the early twentieth century by more "populist" or angrily racist and vulgarly democratic political leaders, and the Stoic self-consciousness morphed into being members of an honorable class that had ruled responsibly, fought nobly against overwhelming force in a great war, and had been involved in a futile effort to resist its inevitable decline and fall in a democratized world where there would be no place for them. Freed from having to defend slavery, their literary efforts turned to the articulation of the experience of sustaining oneself in a world where one had been morally and politically dispossessed. It became a criticism of a world in which those in charge were incapable of recognizing who they are. It's these dispossessed Stoics—such as Will Percy—who achieved the greatest self-consciousness about who they are, writing, as did Tocqueville, at a privileged moment after the incomplete fall of aristocracy and just before the full rise of democracy.[35]

Tocqueville and Walker in Relation to Will: The Friendly Criticism of Both Aristocracy and Democracy

The southern Stoic, as presented by the Percys, is not so different from Tocqueville himself. They're both open to the possibility that being human is some kind of cosmic accident, and they identify the loneliness of being lost in the cosmos as a truthful insight. Will Percy aside, most southern Stoics, like Percy's characters in his novels, divert themselves through the pride that comes from knowing their place and doing their duties. He, like Tocqueville, experiences the political pleasure that comes from ruling himself and others; his high opinion of himself is confirmed by what he actually does. True individuality—true greatness—comes through the development of character, through the acquisition of the virtues that make easygoing, confident self-respect possible.

Walker Percy, we can say, didn't write on behalf of political liberty, but to examine the predicament of the heir of the dispossessed Stoic, the being who, as "the last gentleman," experiences life as pure possibility.[36] He thinks he can't be a Stoic, but he knows enough from the Stoics to be aware that the pop Cartesian expert doesn't offer him even a clue about what a being like himself is supposed to do. Still, many of the differences that separate Tocqueville from the aristocrats he describes apply to Walker Percy too. They are both touched by the Christian, egalitarian claim for justice, and so they don't join the Stoics in viewing progress toward democracy as nothing but decline. Democratic progress, in truth, makes the world better in some ways and worse in others. There's more promise and more greatness in ordinary lives than the Stoic aristocrats suggest. And so southern Stoicism failed, most of all, in mistaking the clamor for equal rights of the civil rights movement as ungrateful insolence.

Walker Percy comes close to Tocqueville in his balanced and quite political account of the strengths and weaknesses of the political dimension of his uncle's singular version of southern Stoicism.[37] He begins by noting, as Tocqueville does, that aristocrats are typically willfully naïve about the injustice or exploitation that accompanies any form of paternalism. Uncle

Will wrote, as Tocqueville would have also noticed, as if he was too noble to think about his self-interest, but it was in his interest, after all, to regard his sharecroppers as beings unfit to care for their own interests. The aristocratic doctrine of noble self-forgetfulness had its use as an ideology, which doesn't mean it was completely untrue.

It's true, after all, that words like *noblesse oblige* refer not to privilege but to magnanimous and generous duty. It certainly couldn't have been wrong for the southern Stoic—such as Will Percy or Atticus Finch—to believe that his position in society entails a responsibility to others—to the poor, vulnerable, and the otherwise needy. Walker compares Will's real-life courageous confrontation with the Klan on behalf of endangered Negroes (see also, of course, *To Kill a Mockingbird*) with a fearful and otherwise emotionally stunted individual in a democratic city closing his blinds rather than getting himself involved with a neighbor being murdered. It's true enough that Uncle Will or Atticus Finch were wrong not to believe black people or white trash could rule themselves, and their relationship with their inferiors had nothing to do with love or rights. But justice understood simply as the protection of rights wouldn't have inspired their undeniably noble and indispensable deeds.

Noblesse oblige, for Percy, is a criticism of what Tocqueville calls individualism, meaning apathetic indifference to the virtue or welfare of others (2.2.2). From Percy and Tocqueville's view, democratic relationships are more egalitarian and so more just, but also more utilitarian, less caring, and less personal. Individualism is the emotional result of the intellectual self-absorption of pop Cartesian skepticism. Because individualism is the cause of the passive detachment that makes us all easy prey for despots, Tocqueville actually claims it's more dangerous for human liberty than the passionate selfishness of the aristocrat's devotion to members of his class to the exclusion of others.

Percy, in that spirit, provocatively suggests that paternalism "might even beat welfare." Welfare seems better because the individual is not treated as a child by being degraded by a particular person. But it's really worse precisely because it's so impersonal or unresponsive to the person's real needs. Worse than the aristocratic form of aristocratic injustice (except racially based slavery), in Tocqueville's eyes, is the schoolmarmishness of the bureaucratic control of every feature of our lives that would be the logical culmination of our creeping individualism (2.4.6). Equality would be preserved insofar as people wouldn't think of themselves as dominated by anyone in particular, but the result might be that we'd all be reduced to less than we're really meant to be as free and relational persons. Better than paternalism, Percy suggests, would be a world that's both egalitarian and personal, a world governed by charity. But his search for that Christian solution began with the southern, Stoic criticism of the impersonality that comes from a world full of equally contentless democratic "I's." That northerners have a loving concern for humanity and southerners for particular people is a criticism that is equally aristocratic and Christian.

Tocqueville was, compared to Percy, a little weak on Christian charity and personal love, just as he was a bit too much about the anxiety of the wonderer and wanderer and not enough about the corresponding joy. He didn't really seem to believe, with Pascal, that the true explanation of our homelessness—our wandering—is that our true home is somewhere else. Still, he did what he could to reconcile aristocratic greatness with democratic justice by trying to see with the eyes of the Creator. Aristocrats, he says, see things too particularly, and so they miss what's true and good about what all of us share in general. Democrats think too generally, and so they miss what distinguishes one human being from another; they miss the particular content that is the source of irreducible personal significance. God himself, Tocqueville sees, doesn't need general ideas or "theories." He sees each of us as we really are in our unique particularity, in how we are alike and how we are distinguished. Democracy that does justice to human particularity, it seems to me, can only be grounded in a Christianity that preserves what's true about aristocracy.

The first form of that mending—but not ending—of the aristocratic account of personal significance can be found in Thomas Aquinas's realistic correction of Aristotle's description of the classical virtue of magnanimity.[38] Tocqueville and Percy continue that great tradition of Christian realism which, in our time, mends democratic tendencies toward personal emptiness and disorientation through elevation in the direction of our true greatness.

Notes

1. John Courtney Murray, *We Hold These Truths* (Lanham, MD: Sheed and Ward, 1960). For this interpretation of Murray, see my *Modern and American*

Dignity: Who We Are as Persons, and What That Means for Our Future (Wilmington, DE: ISI Books, 2010), ch. 8.

2. Walker Percy, *Lost in the Cosmos: The Last Self-Help Book* (New York: Farrar, Straus, and Giroux, 1983).

3. Will Percy's stunningly coherent and rather deeply philosophical southern Stoicism is found in his *Lanterns on the Levee* (Baton Rouge: Louisiana State University Press, 1973); originally published in 1942. My main source for how Walker Percy's thought relates to what he learned from his Uncle Will is the novelist's introduction to the 1973 edition. Subsequent page references to Will Percy's work will be given parenthetically in the text.

4. Alexis de Tocqueville, *Democracy in America*, trans. H. Mansfield and D. Winthrop (Chicago: University of Chicago Press, 2000). Subsequent references to Tocqueville, given parenthetically in the text, will be by volume, part, and chapter number, in that order.

5. On Walker Percy, this essay is an overview of his thought based mainly on *Lost in the Cosmos* and his essays collected in *Signposts in a Strange Land*, ed. Patrick Samway, S.J. (New York: Farrar, Straus, and Giroux, 1991) and *The Message in a Bottle: How Queer Man Is, How Queer Language Is, and What One Has to Do with the Other* (New York: Farrar, Straus, and Giroux, 1975). Most of what I say about Walker Percy and Stoicism depends on "Stoicism in the South," found in *Signposts*.

6. Walker Percy, *More Conversations with Walker Percy*, ed. Lewis A. Lawson and Victor A. Kramer (Jackson: University Press of Mississippi, 1993), 232–33.

7. Walker Percy, *The Last Gentleman* (New York: Picador US/Farrar, 1999), 3: "Lucky is the man who observes and not necessarily believes that every possibility is open to him." The book was originally published in 1966.

8. See Percy, *The Last Gentleman*.

9. Percy, *Lost in the Cosmos*, 127–40.

10. Ibid., 252.

11. See Walker Percy, *The Thanatos Syndrome* (New York: Farrar, Straus, and Giroux, 1987).

12. See my *The Restless Mind: Alexis de Tocqueville on the Origin and Perpetuation of Human Liberty* (Lanham, MD: Rowman and Littlefield, 1993).

13. Percy, "A Space Odyssey (II)," in *Lost in the Cosmos*, 225.

14. Percy, "The Coming Crisis in Psychiatry," in *Signposts in a Strange Land*, 251.

15. Percy, *Lost in the Cosmos*, 172.

16. Ibid.

17. Ibid.

18. Ibid.

19. See my *The Restless Mind*.

20. Aleksandr Solzhenitsyn, "We Have Ceased to See the Purpose," 1993 Address to the International Academy of Philosophy in Lichtenstein, in *The Solzhenitsyn Reader: New and Essential Writings, 1947–2005*, ed. Edward E. Ericson and Daniel J. Mahoney (Wilmington, DE: ISI Books, 2009).

21. See my *Postmodernism Rightly Understood: The Return to Realism in American Thought* (Lanham, MD: Rowman and Littlefield, 1999), ch. 3.

22. See Percy, *Lost in the Cosmos*, 78.

23. Percy, *Signposts in a Strange Land*, 221.

24. Percy, "A Space Odyssey (II), " 225.

25. Percy, *Lost in the Cosmos*, 45.

26. See ibid., 11.

27. See my *The Restless Mind*.

28. Percy, *Lost in the Cosmos*, 132.

29. Percy, "Stoicism in the South," in *Signposts in a Strange Land*, 83.

30. Ibid.

31. Tom Wolfe, *A Man in Full* (New York: Bantam Books, 1998).

32. On Tocqueville's self-understanding in his *Souvenirs*, see my *Modern and American Dignity* (Wilmington, DE: ISI Books, 2010), ch. 7.

33. This is the theme of Percy's novel *The Last Gentleman* most of all. See my *Aliens in America* (Wilmington, DE: ISI Books, 2002), ch. 10.

34. Orestes Brownson, *The American Republic* (Wilmington, DE: ISI Books, 2002). The observations on Brownson here are explored in much greater detail in my introduction to this ISI edition.

35. This paragraph is based on William Alexander Percy's *Lanterns on the Levee*, as illuminated by Walker Percy's "Stoicism in the South."

36. Percy's critical appraisal of the decline and fall of southern Stoicism in his novel *The Last Gentleman* is explored in greater detail in my *Aliens in America*, ch. 10.

37. What follows is drawn from Walker Percy's "Introduction" to the Louisiana Sate University Press edition of *Lanterns*.

38. On the Thomistic correction to Aristotle, see Mary M. Keys, *Aquinas, Aristotle, and the Promise of the Common Good* (New York: Cambridge University Press, 2006); and my *Modern and American Dignity*, ch. 7.

Selected Bibliography

Primary Sources

Conversations with Walker Percy. Edited by Lewis A. Lawson and Victor A. Kramer. Jackson: University Press of Mississippi, 1985.
The Correspondence of Shelby Foote and Walker Percy. Edited by Jay Tolson. New York: Norton, 1998.
Lancelot. New York: Farrar, Straus, and Giroux, 1977. Reprint, New York: Picador, 1999.
The Last Gentleman. New York: Farrar, Straus, and Giroux, 1966. Reprints, New York: Avon, 1978; New York: Picador, 1999.
Lost in the Cosmos: The Last Self-Help Book. New York: Farrar, Straus, and Giroux, 1983.
Love in the Ruins. New York: Farrar, Straus, and Giroux, 1971. Reprints, New York: Avon, 1978; New York: Picador, 1999.
The Message in the Bottle: How Queer Man Is, How Queer Language Is, and What One Has to Do with the Other. New York: Farrar, Straus, and Giroux, 1975.
More Conversations with Walker Percy. Edited by Lewis A. Lawson and Victor A. Kramer. Jackson: University Press of Mississippi, 1993.
The Moviegoer. New York: Knopf, 1961. Reprints, New York: Avon, 1980; New York: Vintage, 1998.
The Second Coming. New York: Farrar, Straus, and Giroux, 1980.
Signposts in a Strange Land. Edited by Patrick Samway, S.J. New York: Farrar, Straus, and Giroux, 1991.
The Thanatos Syndrome. New York: Farrar, Straus, and Giroux, 1987.
A Thief of Peirce: The Letters of Kenneth Laine Ketner and Walker Percy. Edited by Kenneth Laine Ketner. Jackson: University Press of Mississippi, 1995.

Selected Biographical and Historical Works

Coles, Robert. *Walker Percy: An American Search.* New York: Little, Brown, 1979.
Harwell, David Horace. *Walker Percy Remembered: A Portrait in the Words of Those Who Knew Him.* Durham: University of North Carolina Press, 2006.
Percy, William Alexander. *Lanterns on the Levee.* Baton Rouge: Louisiana State University Press, 2006.

Samway, Patrick. *Walker Percy: A Life.* Chicago: Loyola, 1999.
Simpson, Lewis P. "Walker Percy, 1916–1990." *Southern Review* 26, no. 4 (1990): 924–29.
Tolson, Jay. *Pilgrim in the Ruins: A Life of Walker Percy.* New York: Simon and Schuster, 1992.
Wyatt-Brown, Bertram. *The House of Percy: Honor, Melancholy and Imagination in a Southern Family.* Oxford: Oxford University Press, 1994.
———. *The Literary Percys: Family History, Gender and the Southern Imagination.* Athens: University of Georgia Press, 1994.

Selected Interpretive Works

Akins, Adrienne V. "Failure of Love: Racism and Original Sin in Walker Percy's *Love in the Ruins.*" *Southern Quarterly* 47, no. 1 (2009): 65–73.
Broughton, Panthea Reid, ed. *The Art of Walker Percy: Stratagems for Being.* Baton Rouge: Louisiana State University Press, 1979.
Ciuba, Gary M. *Desire, Violence and Divinity in Modern Southern Fiction: Katherine Anne Porter, Flannery O'Connor, Cormac McCarthy, Walker Percy.* Baton Rouge: Louisiana State University Press, 2007.
———. *Walker Percy: Books of Revelations.* Athens: University of Georgia Press, 1991.
Crowley, J. Donald, and Sue Mitchell Crowley, eds. *Critical Essays on Walker Percy.* Boston: G. K. Hall, 1989.
Desmond, John M. *At the Crossroads: Ethical and Religious Themes in the Writings of Walker Percy.* Troy, NY: Whitson, 1997.
———. "Fyodor Dostoevsky, Walker Percy, and the Demonic Self." *Southern Literary Journal* 44, no. 2 (2012): 88–107.
———. *Walker Percy's Search for Community.* Athens: University of Georgia Press, 2010.
Dupuy, Edward J. *Autobiography in Walker Percy: Repetition, Recovery and Redemption.* Baton Rouge: Louisiana State University Press, 1996.
Elie, Paul. *The Life You Save May Be Your Own.* New York: Farrar, Straus, and Giroux, 2003.
Elliot, Carl, and John Lantos, eds. *The Last Physician: Walker Percy and the Moral Life of Medicine.* Durham, NC: Duke University Press, 1999.
Gray, Rich. "Walker Percy's Appeal to Searchers: *The Last Gentleman* and *The Second Coming.*" *Christian Scholar's Review* 41, no. 1 (2011): 15–34.
Gretlund, Jan Nordby, and Karl-Heinz Westarp, eds. *Walker Percy: Novelist and Philosopher.* Jackson: University Press of Mississippi, 1991.
Hardy, John Edward. *The Fiction of Walker Percy.* Urbana: University of Illinois Press, 1987.

Ketner, Kenneth Laine. "Rescuing Science from Scientism: The Achievement of Walker Percy." *Intercollegiate Review* 35, no. 1 (1999): 22–27.
Kobre, Michael. *Walker Percy's Voices*. Athens: University of Georgia Press, 2000.
Lawler, Peter Augustine. *Aliens in America: The Strange Truth about Our Souls*. Wilmington, DE: ISI Books, 2002.
———. *Postmodernism Rightly Understood: The Return to Realism in American Thought*. Lanham, MD: Rowman and Littlefield, 1999.
Lawson, Lewis A. *Still Following Percy*. Jackson: University Press of Mississippi, 1995.
Marc'hadour, Germain. "Walker Percy in the Wake of Thomas More." *Moreana* 32, nos. 123–24 (1995): 127–36.
Montgomery, Marion. "Walker Percy and the Christian Scandal." *First Things*, April 1993, 38–44.
———. *With Walker Percy at the Tupperware Party: In Company with Flannery O'Connor, T. S. Eliot, and Others*. South Bend, IN: St. Augustine's, 2009.
O'Gorman, Farrell. *Peculiar Crossroads: Flannery O'Connor, Walker Percy, and Catholic Vision in Postwar Southern Fiction*. Baton Rouge: Louisiana State University Press, 2007.
Poteat, Patricia Lewis. *Walker Percy and the Old Modern Age: Reflections on Language, Argument and the Telling of Stories*. Baton Rouge: Louisiana State University Press, 1985.
Prigden, Allan. *Walker Percy's Sacramental Landscapes: The Search in the Desert*. Selinsgrove, PA: Susquehanna University Press, 2009.
Quinlan, Kieran. *Walker Percy: The Last Catholic Novelist*. Baton Rouge: Louisiana State University Press, 1996.
Sitman, Matthew, and Brian A. Smith. "The Rift in the Modern Mind: Tocqueville and Percy on the Rise of the Cartesian Self." *Perspectives on Political Science* 36, no. 1 (2007): 15–22.
Smith, Brian A. "Losing Sight of Man: Percy and Tocqueville on the Fate of the Human Sciences." *Perspectives on Political Science* 40, no. 3 (2011): 140–46.
Sweeny, Mary K. *Walker Percy and the Postmodern World*. Chicago: Loyola University Press, 1987.
Sykes, John D. *Flannery O'Connor, Walker Percy, and the Aesthetic of Revelation*. Columbia: University of Missouri Press, 2007.
Tharpe, Jac, ed. *Walker Percy, Art and Ethics*. Jackson: University Press of Mississippi, 1980.

Contributors

Elizabeth Amato recently received her doctorate in political science at Baylor University, where she is currently an adjunct professor. Her interests in politics and literature and in the relationship between happiness and modernity served as the focus for her dissertation, "Happiness and Modernity: The Pursuit of Happiness and the American Regime."

Nathan P. Carson is visiting assistant professor of humanities and philosophy in Christ College (the Honors College) at Valparaiso University. He recently defended his dissertation at Baylor University in virtue ethics, on the concept of appreciation as a form of moral understanding, wisdom, and attention. His primary research is in Aristotelian and contemporary virtue ethics and nineteenth-century philosophy (especially Kierkegaard), with secondary interests in twentieth-century Catholic literature, including Walker Percy and Flannery O'Connor. He has a forthcoming article on Cormac McCarthy appearing in *Film and Philosophy* and a forthcoming article on Kierkegaard's epistemology appearing in *Journal of Chinese Philosophy.*

Janice Daurio is professor of philosophy at Moorpark College, where she teaches introductory courses in philosophy, ethics, Western religions, and critical thinking. She was educated at Hunter College, CUNY, St. Mary's University, and Claremont Graduate University.

Peter Augustine Lawler is Dana Professor of Government at Berry College. He is the author of numerous books, including, most recently, *Modern and American Dignity: Who We Are as Persons, and What That Means for Our Future.* He is also the editor of the journal *Perspectives in Political Science* and the codirector of the Stuck with Virtue conference series. He served on the President's Council on Bioethics from 2004 to 2009.

Micah Mattix is assistant professor in literature at Houston Baptist University. His essays and reviews have appeared in *New Literary History, Applied Semiotics, First Things, Books & Culture, Pleiades,* and numerous other publications. He recently published a book on Frank O'Hara.

Woods Nash is a lecturer in philosophy at the University of Tennessee. His research focuses on representations of medicine, health, and illness in southern fiction and contemporary film. His essays have appeared in various journals, including *Cormac McCarthy Journal*, *Catalyst: A Social Justice Forum*, and *Perspectives on Political Science*.

Farrell O'Gorman is professor of English at Belmont Abbey College. He is the author of *Peculiar Crossroads: Flannery O'Connor, Walker Percy, and Catholic Vision in Postwar Southern Fiction*. His articles have appeared in such publications as Blackwell's *Companion to the Regional Literatures of America*, *Southern Literary Journal*, *Mississippi Quarterly*, and *Critique: Studies in Contemporary Fiction*.

Brendan P. Purdy teaches mathematics at Moorpark College and directs the campus math learning center. He was educated in philosophy and mathematics at UCLA, California State Polytechnic University, Pomona, and the University of California, Irvine. Purdy does research in the fields of mathematical psychology and game theory as well as in the intersection of literature, philosophy, and theology in Catholic thought.

Richard M. Reinsch II is a fellow of Liberty Fund, Inc., where he is also the founder and editor of the Online Library of Law and Liberty. He is the author of *Whittaker Chambers: The Spirit of a Counterrevolutionary*. In addition, his writings have appeared in *Perspectives on Political Science*, *Religion & Liberty*, *The City*, *Modern Age*, *Intercollegiate Review*, *Society*, *Touchstone*, *American Conservative*, the Heritage Foundation's *First Principles*, and *University Bookman*, among other publications. He received his JD from the University of North Carolina School of Law in 2004.

James V. Schall, S.J., is professor of government at Georgetown University, where he has taught political philosophy since 1977. He is the author of numerous books, most recently *The Classical Moment*.

Brian A. Smith is assistant professor of political science at Montclair State University, where he teaches courses in political thought and international affairs. His work has appeared in *Polity*, *Interpretation*, *Perspectives on Political Science*, *Anamnesis*, the *Journal of Libertarian Studies*, and the *Journal of Markets and Morality*. He is working on a book about Walker Percy's political and social thought.

Ralph C. Wood is University Professor of Theology and Literature at Baylor University, where he teaches in both the Great Texts program and the Department of Religion. His most recent book is *Chesterton: The Nightmare Goodness of God*.

Index

abolitionism, 260
abortion, 27, 62, 82
abstraction, 170, 191, 192, 194, 199;
    of "angelism," 102; from the
    body, 135; ideology and, 189;
    individualism as abstraction from
    social being, 239
academia, 74–75
African Americans. *See* blacks
Agrarians, 2, 132, 136
AIDS, 58, 61, 63
Alanen, Lilli, 43n3
alienation, 25, 42, 84, 167, 170, 196;
    imposed by the Fall, 184; "theorist-
    consumerism" and, 174; treated as
    outward symptom, 198
Amato, Elizabeth, 7
American Jeremiad (Bercovitch), 150
American Republic, The (Brownson),
    259
"Angelic Imagination, The" (Tate), 132
"angelism," 186–87, 188, 201, 202;
    Aristotelian tradition and, 84;
    passive, 189–90; scientific self-
    abstraction of, 102
Anna Karenina (Tolstoy), 220
Anscombe, G. E. M., 215
anthropology, 87, 110, 111n4;
    anthropological incoherence,
    88–90; Christian, 7, 125; religiously
    grounded, 166
anxiety, 58, 101, 110, 114n26, 165;
    as clue to truth about being,
    258; disappearance of, 145;
    Enlightenment and, 65; inability to
name oneself and, 150; of isolated
    individual, 240; joy inseparable
    from, 242; objectless, 94–95;
    scientism and, 169; transcendence
    and, 94, 96; unsignifiability and,
    95–96, 114n25
apes, language/thought and, 69, 73, 77,
    112n10, 145
Apology (Socrates), 71
Aristotle, 3, 69, 70, 71, 116n41, 263;
    on animality, 116n38; friendless
    divinity of, 72; on man as beast
    or deity, 186; theory of virtue,
    83–84, 106; on true and false
    views, 73
Arrowsmith (Lewis), 16
art, 70, 76, 88, 115n30
Arthurian legends, 120, 134, 136
atheism, 1, 3, 16, 182, 200
atomic family, 174
Augustine, St., 19, 72, 177–78n27;
    Confessions, 1, 124, 150;
    Manicheanism of, 83
autonomy, individual, 8, 50, 60, 61, 64,
    101–4. *See also* individualism

Bakhtin, Mikhail, 123
Barrett, Will (fictional character),
    40, 96–97, 100, 104–5, 108, 167;
    marital difficulties of, 174; search
    for God, 170–73
becoming, 93, 94
behaviorism, 88, 185, 195, 199
being, 79, 103, 106, 147, 166, 168
Benedict XVI, Pope, 82

Benson, Robert Hugh, 79
Bercovitch, Sacvan, 150
Berrigan, Daniel and Philip, 24
"bestialism," 186, 189, 201, 202
Bible, 4, 80, 204n8, 205n29, 212–13, 219; Jefferson's modification of, 228–29; Old Testament, 247
Birmingham, Alabama, 11–12
"Black Cat, The" (Poe), 127
blacks (African Americans, Negroes), 12, 14, 63, 83, 182, 238; "Bantu" guerrilla movement, 188–89, 193; baptized as "slaves," 209; civil rights of, 23–24; fundamentalist religion and, 249; "Negro spirituals," 212; Psalms as theology of blacks in South, 213; Stoic moral theory and, 223–24, 231
Bolling, Binx (fictional character), 7, 31, 48–50, 106; Cartesian self of, 30, 34, 39; conversion of, 26, 38, 40–41; life situations mediated by movie screen, 35–38; "Little Way" of, 48, 66n3; on nonliteral sense of moviegoing, 31–32; as representative of social condition, 41–43; "vertical" search of, 33–34; as "victim" of Descartes, 29. *See also Moviegoer, The*
Book of Common Prayer, 15
Boone, Daniel, 136
Boyle, Nicholas, 142n22
brain, human, 68, 90, 180
Brave New World (Huxley), 54
Brioche, Janet, 17–18
Brothers Karamazov, The (Dostoyevsky), 121
Brownson, Orestes, 2, 6, 259–60
Brown v. Board of Education, 225, 227, 230
Buckley, William, 11
Buddhism, 81, 241, 251
Bunting, Charles, 72

Calvin, John, 245–46, 247
Calvinism, 127, 227, 246, 247
Camus, Albert, 14, 25
capitalism, 160
captivity narratives, 134
Carnap, Rudolf, 25
Carr, John, 69, 78
Carson, Nathan P., 8
Cartesian theory, 4, 5, 7, 10, 43n3; Americans as pop Cartesians, 239–48, 259, 262; *cogito*, 98, 99; screen of ideas, 37; split between things and thought, 76; theory of knowledge, 83. *See also* Descartes, René
"Cask of Amontillado, The" (Poe), 125, 133
Cassirer, Ernst, 25, 90
Castle of Otranto, The (Walpole), 127
Catholicism, 15, 22, 132, 212; in American South, 175; British Gothic and, 126–27; Catholic identity, 220–22; community view of, 219–20; dogma of Catholic Church, 85; Eucharist in traditional view of, 210; Kierkegaard's influence on Percy and, 214–17; in *Lancelot*, 137–40, 143n41; in Louisiana, 134; in *Love in the Ruins*, 183; Percy's conversion to, 207, 217–19, 227–28; Protestant rivalry with, 9; race and, 232; theological system of, 23. *See also* Thomism
Cato (Addison), 222
Cavell, Stanley, 128, 129
Chalmers, David, 210–11
Chandler, Raymond, 135
Chappell, Vere, 43n3
Charterhouse of Parma, The (Stendhal), 32
Cheney, Brainard, 121, 141n8
Chernyshevsky, Nikolai, 123

Chesterton, G. K., 2
children, 196
"chivalry," in American South, 135
Chomsky, Noam, 90
Christianity, 120, 136, 137, 140, 175–76; aristocratic, 10; Christian anthropology, 7, 125; democracy grounded in, 263; early Church, 176, 226; evangelical, 162; human as pilgrim or wanderer, 3, 242; humans as fallen beings, 53; as personal religion, 240, 241, 245; religious conversion, 26, 38, 40–41; in romantic novels, 134; science and, 1–2; Stoicism and, 224, 235n44; "theory of man" as apologetics, 5; three mysteries of, 210; Tocqueville's views on, 241, 247–52
Christology, 218
Churchill, Winston, 154
civilization, 71, 115n36, 136, 175; education in America and, 255–59; Judeo-Christian teachings and, 89; plantation aristocracy and, 126; recovery and flourishing of, 174; utopia and, 54
civil rights, 160, 228
civil society, 175
Civil War, 209, 256, 259
Civil War, The (Foote), 207
Collier, Elijah ("Lije"), 12
"Coming Christ, The" (Percy), 114n25
"Coming Crisis in Psychiatry, The" (Percy), 95, 114n25, 211
community, 10, 45n27, 110, 185, 189; care of elders and, 198; Catholic, 191, 219–20; disorder held in check by, 180, 188, 189; Eucharist and, 133, 143–44n44; individualism against, 128; institutionalized, 5; I-Thou relation and, 105; love and, 196; "love community," 201;

reinforcement of beliefs and, 212; revival of, 203; scientific knowledge and, 112n6; unhappiness and, 58; utopian, 52–54, 57; virtues and, 106; of writers, 120, 140
Concept of Anxiety, The (Kierkegaard), 94–95
Confederacy, romanticization of, 132–33
Confederacy of Dunces, A (Toole), 27
confessional narrators, 131–32
Confessions (St. Augustine), 1, 124, 150
Conrad, Joseph, 13
conscience, 5
consciousness, 91, 92, 110, 113n17, 115n30; expansion of, 149; human distinction from animals and, 184–85; intersubjective constitution of, 99, 104; language and, 98, 208–12; self-consciousness, 101, 105; socially constructed, 98, 115n28; unfallen or "preternatural," 101, 115n36
consent, informed, 62
"controverted feminine," 142n22
conversion, religious, 26, 38, 40–41, 207, 217–19
Covington, Louisiana, 23, 78, 85
Crime and Punishment (Dostoyevsky), 121
Crockett, Davy, 136
Cromwell, Oliver, 134
"culture of death," 27, 80
"Culture: The Antinomy of the Scientific Method" (Percy), 208

Dante Alighieri, 130, 131, 132, 150, 152
Darwin, Charles, 162, 166
Darwinism, 1, 3, 87, 111n5
Daurio, Janice, 9
Day, Dorothy, 23

death (mortality), 71, 131, 167, 173, 232; "culture of death," 27, 80; failure to reckon with, 198; human dignity and, 194–95; individualism and, 245; Nazi cult of death, 154; personified in Poe stories, 127; self divided at death, 130; as surrender of apartness, 250
Declaration of Independence, 2, 5, 6, 258
democracy, 126, 159, 192, 239, 247, 256; Christianity and, 263; fall of southern aristocracy and, 261
Democracy in America (Tocqueville), 239, 253
Democratic Party, 181–82
Derrida, Jacques, 148
Descartes, René, 3, 7, 29–30, 43, 98; American individualism and, 128; antebellum South and, 132; Archimedean leverage point and, 34; Cartesian theater replaced by cinema, 33; *Meditations*, 35, 43n4, 129; mind-body split of, 130, 144n44; Percy's antipathy toward, 40, 41, 76, 186; theory of knowledge, 83; on two senses of idea, 30–31. *See also* Cartesian theory
Didache, The (early Christian tract), 235n50
Difference between a Genius and an Apostle, The (Kierkegaard), 218
"Displaced Person, The" (O'Connor), 220
Divine Comedy (Dante), 131
doctors, 69–71, 135, 180, 197–98
Donahue, Phil, 73
Dostoyevsky, Fyodor, 16, 120–21, 126, 136, 140; Christian anthropology and, 125; egoism as target of, 122; Orthodox Christian faith reclaimed by, 121, 123, 125, 133; as Percy's model in writing *Lancelot*, 133

Dracula (Stoker), 125
Dream of Descartes, The (Maritain), 32–33, 35
drugs, 4, 53, 58, 65
dualism, 4, 89, 111n4, 148
dyadic signification, 90–91, 112n10, 145–46, 153

Eat, Pray, Love (Gilbert), 187, 205n21
Eden, Garden of, 128
ego, 58, 68n14, 98, 99
egoism, 107, 122, 123, 132
Eisenhower, Dwight, 227
Eliot, T. S., 119
Ellison, Ralph, 143n39
Emerson, Ralph Waldo, 128, 161
empiricism, 99
Enlightenment, European, 88, 122, 127, 130; in antebellum South, 132; Christian view contrasted with, 228; rationality prized by, 126, 165; as source of anxiety and unhappiness, 65
Epictetus, 213, 225, 229, 231, 256
Epicurus, 3
Episcopalianism (Anglicanism), 134, 156, 164
ethics, 70, 116n38, 123, 166, 215
Eucharist, 143–44n44, 215, 232; divergent Christian views of, 210; in *Lancelot*, 133, 139, 140; liturgy of, 236n50; in *Love in the Ruins*, 168, 170; in *The Thanatos Syndrome*, 153
"Eudora Welty in Jackson" (Percy), 84
eugenics, 59, 68n13
euthanasia, 61, 67–68n13, 154–55, 182, 195, 198
evolution, 5, 58, 88, 138
evolutionary game theory, 224, 236n51
existentialism, 99, 114n26, 244; on anxiety and freedom, 96;

Christianity and, 25; novelists, 4; science and, 1, 3
extraterrestrial intelligence, 4

Fall, the, 128, 180
"Fall of the House of Usher, The" (Poe), 120, 130–31, 133
family relationships, 162, 174–75, 178n27
Faulkner, William, 14, 15, 25, 104, 126, 161
female body, 128–29
feminists, 54
Fisher, David Hackett, 222
Foote, Shelby, 15, 20, 26, 76; agnosticism of, 27 integration supported by, 207
Fortugno, Art, 22–23
Foucault, Michel, 148
Founders: of United States, 2, 6, 222–23, 237
Fourier, Charles, 121
Frankenstein (Shelley), 125
freedom, 4, 83, 237; anxiety and, 94–95, 96; Cartesianism and, 239; as wandering, 5
Frege, Gottlob, 208
Freud, Sigmund, 162, 166
Fromm, Erich, 95, 114n24

Gilbert, Elizabeth, 187, 205n21
Gnosticism, 163–64
Gone with the Wind (Mitchell), 191, 229
"Good Man Is Hard to Find, A" (O'Connor), 220
Gordon, Caroline, 25, 132
Gothic fiction, Anglo-American, 120, 125–31, 132
"Gramercy Winner, The" (Percy), 18
Greeks, classical, 1, 2–3, 10, 254
Grey, J. D., 20–21
Growths of Civilizations, The (Toynbee), 33
Gulledge, Jo, 74–75

Hamlet (Shakespeare), 120, 140n2, 150
happiness, pursuit of, 5–6, 47–48; contrarian view of, 7; in *Lost in the Cosmos*, 48, 51–57; in *The Moviegoer*, 48–50; quest for health compared to, 69–70; rejection of, 48; in *The Thanatos Syndrome*, 48, 57–66
Hardart, Frank, 22
Hawthorne, Nathaniel, 161
Hegel, G. W. F., 21–22
Heidegger, Martin, 1, 25, 79, 240
Henry IV (Shakespeare), 53, 55
heterosexuality, 75
Hinduism, 81
hippies, 54
Hispanics, 54, 83
history, end of, 180, 201
Hoeveler, Diane Long, 126, 128
homosexuality: in *Lost in the Cosmos*, 73–74, 75; in *The Thanatos Syndrome*, 63; of "Uncle Will" Percy, 15, 17, 250
Howland, Mary Deems, 34, 37, 44n6, 60, 67n12
humanism, 19, 21
human nature, 81, 87, 102, 109; American Adam and, 128; fallen, 60; flaw in Percy's theory of, 8; healing wounds of, 201
Husserl, Edmund, 25, 211, 212
Huxley, Julian A., 16

identity, 1, 171, 220–22
ideology, 163, 166, 189
Idiot, The (Dostoyevsky), 121
immanence, 21, 49
Incarnation, of Christ, 153, 210, 215
Independent Presbyterian Church, 12

individualism, 7, 8, 98, 125, 177n26; American, 128, 136, 183; Cartesian, 132, 137, 262; Catholic communal view at odds with, 221; Christian, 140n4; Gothic literature and, 126; inattention to mortality and, 245; modernity and, 120; pervasive influence in Western culture, 119. *See also* autonomy, individual
Inferno (Dante), 150, 152
integration, 210, 213–14, 227
intelligence, 80, 101
intersubjectivity, 99, 104, 106, 107; denotation and, 211; virtue predication and, 108, 110
Invisible Man (Ellison), 143n39
"Is a Theory of Man Possible?" (Percy), 113n17, 146
Islam, 247
I-Thou relation, 99–100, 104, 105, 107, 109, 211
Ivanhoe (Scott), 134

Jaspers, Karl, 25
Jefferson, Thomas, 131, 132, 136; Declaration of Independence and, 6, 258; religious liberty and, 254–55; Stoic tradition and, 228–29
Jews, 12, 54, 83, 153
John Paul II, Pope, 27, 80
John XXIV, Pope, 173
Joyce, James, 25
Judeo-Christian order, 81, 82, 89, 111nn4–5, 218, 228

Kafka, Franz, 19, 99
Kant, Immanuel, 221
Katallagete (radical Protestant journal), 24
Keller, Helen, 25, 91
Kennedy, John F., 26
Kierkegaard, Søren, 9, 10, 25, 38, 84, 218; on anxiety, 94–95, 96; on genius, 21; on Hegel, 21–22; individualism of, 140–41n4; on possibility as temptation and threat, 19; on religious versus aesthetic man, 219; self-as-relation, 100; on self-becoming, 72
King, Martin Luther, Jr., 227
Kipling, Rudyard, 229
knowledge, 31, 148–49; Cartesian theory and, 36, 39, 83; as intellectual virtue, 102; language and, 211; perfection of, 73; self-knowledge, 51; symbolic communion and, 93
Korean War, 36, 48
Kripke, Saul, 208–9
Ku Klux Klan (KKK), 13, 14, 23, 225; Percy family battle against, 228, 236n54, 262; violence of, 223
Kurth, James, 175

Lamar, Lance (fictional character), 8, 122–23, 133; Catholic Church and, 137–40; as detective and scientist, 135–36; as Gothic villain, 134; romanticism of, 134–36; scientifically detached violence of, 129; violent frontiersman figure and, 136, 137
Lancelot (Percy), 8, 26, 119–21, 150; detecting reality beyond individualism in, 131–40; *Hamlet* compared with, 120, 140n2; movie cameras in, 40; *Notes from Underground* compared with, 120, 121–25, 138, 139, 140; Poe's legacy and, 125–31
Langer, Suzanne, 25, 90, 234n17
language, 4, 25, 78; apes taught to talk, 69, 73, 112n10; consciousness and, 98, 208–12; knowledge mediated through, 104; mystery of,

79, 146–47; Psalms and, 212–13; quest to grasp reality through, 171, 177n20
Lanterns on the Levee (Wm. A. Percy), 15, 213, 236n54, 249, 264n3
Last Gentleman, The (Percy), 13, 20, 26, 40
Lawler, Peter, 6, 10
Lawrence, D. H., 25
Lawson, Lewis A., 34, 42, 45n28, 141n8
Lee, Robert E., 134, 136
Lévi-Strauss, Claude, 148
Lewis, Matthew, 127
Lewis, R. W. B., 128
Lewis, Sinclair, 16
liberalism, 2, 9, 48, 63, 121, 187
Life and Morals of Jesus of Nazareth (Jefferson), 228–29
linguistics, 148
Locke, John, 5, 6, 32, 132
logos, 3, 171
Lord of the World, The (Benson), 79
Lost in the Cosmos (Percy), 26, 69, 148, 150, 237; academic reception of, 74–75; on consciousness, 101, 115n36; hostility toward Descartes in, 40; "The Last Donahue Show" in, 73–74, 245; pursuit of happiness critiqued in, 48, 51–57, 65; on scientific theories, 72–73; on transcendence of signs, 151; on unsignifiability, 93–94, 113n18
Love in the Ruins (Percy), 9, 11, 26, 40, 119, 179–80; American decline in, 181–84; apocalyptic politics in, 200–203; Cartesian self in, 184–92, 205n18; children largely absent from, 196–97; difficulties of married love in, 163–70, 173; love of domestic family in, 162; Presbyterianism in, 12; as "prophecy in reverse," 179, 202; return to paradise as theme, 112n5; scientific materialism run amok in, 192–200

MacIntyre, Alasdair, 103, 116n38, 116n41
Magic Mountain, The (Mann), 18
Manicheanism, 84, 138
Mann, Thomas, 18, 19
"Man on the Train, The" (Percy), 25
Marcel, Gabriel, 25
Marcus Aurelius, 225, 230, 256
Maritain, Jacques, 25, 32–33, 35, 83
marriage, 162, 174; in *Love in the Ruins*, 163–70; in *The Second Coming*, 170–74
Marx, Karl, 162, 166
masculinity/masculine rationality, 127
"Masque of the Red Death, The" (Poe), 127
materialism, 7, 19, 124, 183, 202; of American middle class, 238; anxiety and, 243–44; Christianity as antidote to, 249, 252; liberals ("Lefts") and, 194; in Northern states, 160–61, 259–60; physical understanding of human existence, 16, 156; of science, 4, 195; trashiness of, 10
Mattix, Micah, 8
Mead, George H., 98, 99, 115n28
medicine, 122, 124
Meditations (Descartes), 35, 43n4, 129
Melville, Herman, 161
Merton, Thomas, 219, 220
Message in the Bottle, The (Percy), 25, 72, 111n1
"Metaphor as Mistake" (Percy), 147, 149, 210, 217
metaphors, 208
metaphysics, 6, 33, 70, 79, 123, 239
Methodism, 52
middle class, 237–38, 239, 252, 253, 257

mind, as inner theater, 7, 32–33
Mirrilees, Doris, 25
Mitchell, Margaret, 229
modernity, 110, 120, 126, 171, 179, 180
Monk, The (Lewis), 127
More, Thomas, 22
More, Tom (fictional character), 58–59, 145–46, 152, 153, 156, 195; Cartesian self and, 184–92; Catholicism of, 180, 183; failed marriage of, 163–64, 174; as first-person narrator, 119
Moviegoer, The (Percy), 2, 26, 29–30, 51, 119; Christian conversion in, 38, 40–41; critique of film world in, 16; ghostly Cartesian mind in, 33–35; Kierkegaard's influence and, 214–16; lack of community in movie theater, 40, 45n27; moviegoing as nonliteral activity, 31–32; movie screen as mediator of life situations, 35–38; as National Book Award winner, 38; *Notes from Underground* as influence on, 121, 141n8; pursuit of happiness critiqued in, 48–50, 65; race relations in, 221–22; screen culture and Cartesian society, 41–43; Stoicism in, 225, 230–31; theory of man and, 87; virtue ethics in, 104. *See also* Bolling, Binx
Murdoch, Iris, 105–6
Murray, John Courtney, 2, 6, 237
"Mystery of Language, The" (Percy), 146–47, 209

naming, 103, 147
"Naming and Being" (Percy), 79, 147
Naming and Necessity (Kripke), 208, 210
"Narcissus as Narcissus" (Tate), 133
National Book Award (NBA), 26, 38
Native Americans (Indians), 134, 253

nature, 3, 6, 136, 255
Nazism, 4, 16–17, 82, 154–55
Negroes. *See* blacks
neuroscience, 3
Newkirk, Terrye, 66n3
New Orleans, 15, 21, 26
Newton, Isaac, 166
Nietzsche, Friedrich, 116n41, 192, 201, 249; "last man" of, 9, 180–81; Übermensch of, 104
North (U.S. region), 2, 259–60
"Notes for a Novel about the End of the World" (Percy), 79, 151
Notes from Underground (Dostoyevsky), 120, 121–25, 131, 138, 139; Percy awakened to calling as writer by, 19; self-reflection at conclusion of, 140
novelists, 4, 76, 151, 179
"Novel-Writing in an Apocalyptic Time" (Percy), 151

O'Connor, Flannery, 2, 80, 138, 144n45; Catholic community and, 219–20; on the Eucharist as symbol, 210
"Ode to the Confederate Dead" (Tate), 133
O'Gorman, Farrell, 8
O'Neill, Eugene, 19
"On the Difference between a Genius and an Apostle" (Kierkegaard), 21
original sin, 124
Origin of the Species (Darwin), 166
Orthodox Christianity, 121, 123, 133, 210, 236n50

pantheism, 240, 241, 260
Pascal, Blaise, 25, 241, 251, 252, 263
Paul, St., 176, 178n27, 229
Pavlov, Ivan, 146
Peirce, Charles Sanders, 77, 90, 100, 146, 208, 209

Index

Pelham, Col. John, 245–46, 256
Pentecostalism, 156
Percy, Ann (daughter of W. P.), 25
Percy, Charles (family ancestor), 13
Percy, Leroy Pratt (father of W. P.), 11, 13
Percy, Mary Pratt (adopted daughter of W. P.), 25
Percy, Walker (W. P.): antipathy toward Descartes, 40, 41, 76; as apocalyptic writer, 79–80; biography and family history of, 7, 11–27; Catholicism of, 22, 23, 207, 217–19, 227; as moviegoer, 33, 41; on science, 69, 76–77, 112n6; Stoicism and, 10, 15–16; theory of man, 5, 78, 87, 102, 110, 111n1; Thomism of, 2, 4, 238; transformation from segregationist to integrationist, 23–24, 207, 214, 217, 221–22, 232
Percy, William Alexander ("Uncle Will"), 14–16, 22, 23, 215, 236n55, 261–62; confrontation with Ku Klux Klan, 14, 262; death of, 18, 19; homosexuality of, 15, 17, 250; *Lanterns on the Levee*, 15, 213, 236n54, 264n3; segregation and, 221, 229; Stoicism of, 15–16, 216, 228, 238, 247, 250–51, 256–57
Petrarch, 131
"Philosophy of Composition, The" (Poe), 131
Philosophical Investigations (Wittgenstein), 208
philosophy, 21–22, 208, 209, 255
Phinizy, Martha Susan [Mattie Sue] (mother of W. P.), 11, 12, 14
pilgrimage, 26, 81
Pilgrim in the Ruins (Tolson), 11
"Pit and the Pendulum, The" (Poe), 127
Plato, 3, 15, 52, 248; allegory of the cave, 33, 224; on duality of doctors, 70; on improvement of the soul, 83
Poe, Edgar Allan, 120, 123, 127–35, 139, 140
poetry, 149, 213, 241
politics, 70, 79, 81, 181, 183; abstraction and, 192; for the end of the world, 200–203; radical and violent, 189; religion in relation to, 218
Poor Folk (Dostoyevsky), 121
pornography, 145, 194
Possessed, The (Dostoyevsky), 121
postmodernism, 6
Poteat, Patricia Lewis, 39, 204n7
Presbyterianism, 12, 134
Protestantism, 9, 126, 134, 210, 226
psychiatry, 211
psychoanalysis, Freudian, 17–18
psychotherapy, 73
public opinion, 240
Punch, John, 209, 210, 233n8
Purdy, Brendan P., 9
Puritans, 246–47, 249, 254, 257
"Purloined Letter, The" (Poe), 132, 135, 141n6

"Questions They Never Asked Me" (Percy), 69, 79, 85

racism, 24, 126, 247, 260
Rand, Ayn, 163
Randolph, John, 131
rationalism, 122
"Raven, The" (Poe), 131
Reformation, 142n22
Reinsch, Richard M., II, 8–9
Republican Party, 181
Roe v. Wade, 81–82
romanticism, 122, 123, 132–33
Rome, ancient, 10, 174, 175, 254; early Christianity in, 226; slavery in, 233n8; Stoicism in, 225, 230

Rousseau, Jean-Jacques, 124
Rummel, Archbishop Joseph, 24, 221, 232
Russell, Bertrand, 25, 208
Ryle, Gilbert, 35

Sagan, Carl, 3, 4–5
Samway, Patrick, 79
Sane Society, The (Fromm), 114n24
Sartre, Jean-Paul, 1, 25, 95, 100
Saussure, Ferdinand de, 148
Schall, Father James V., 7–8
Schopenhauer, Arthur, 16
Schuyler, Capt. Marcus Aurelius (fictional character), 51–57, 66n8
science, 5, 16, 41, 149, 202, 239; anxiety and, 95; "aristocratic" and "democratic," 243; birthplace of, 53; Cartesian self and, 39, 135; evolutionary science, 4; impersonality of, 1–2, 242, 251; literary culture and, 76; materialism and, 4, 195; monopoly on explaining reality, 130; postmodernism and, 6; self-consciousness and, 4; soulcraft blended with, 185; technology identified with, 255; theory as common sense, 72–73; understanding of human condition and, 69, 76, 77; utopian societies and, 54, 55; worldview of, 165, 170; worship of, 122
Science of Life, The (Huxley and Wells), 16
scientism, 23, 122, 145–56, 165–66, 169–70
Scott, Sir Walter, 134
Searle, John, 148
Secada, Jorge, 33
Second Coming, The (Percy), 26, 80, 96–97, 100, 167; difficulties of married love in, 170–74; love of domestic family in, 162; Sartrean stare in, 108; suicide as possibility in, 20
segregation, racial, 160, 209, 211, 216, 223–24
self-placement, in symbolic world, 94, 97–102
"Self-Reliance" (Emerson), 128
"Semiotic and a Theory of Knowledge" (Percy), 148–49, 208
semiotics, 25, 52, 74, 90, 113n17, 207; integration and, 213–14, 232; language and consciousness, 208–12; language and the Psalms, 212–13
Seneca, 222, 223
sex, 40, 53, 55, 128, 139; anxiety and, 97; "bestialism" and, 186; human dignity and, 194–95; in *Lancelot*, 125; "love communities" and, 201; in *Love in the Ruins*, 196, 197; obsessive genital sexuality, 84; separated from personality and responsibility, 75; sex education, 74; sexual energy and genius, 59; sexual revolution, 135; in *The Thanatos Syndrome*, 58
Shakespeare, William, 11, 15, 21; *Hamlet*, 120, 140n2, 150; *Henry IV*, 53, 55
sign language, 25
Signposts in a Strange Land (Percy), 26, 81
signs, 25, 92, 94, 97, 102, 153; linguistic symbols and, 147; transcendence and, 151; triadic theory of, 146, 152. *See also* dyadic signification; triadic signification; unsignifiability
Skinner, B. F., 53, 88, 91, 112n10, 146, 197
slavery, 160, 223, 230, 262; defense of, 259; first slave in English colonies,

209, 233n8; Southern aristocracy and, 253–54; Stoic acceptance of, 247
Smith, Brian A., 9
Smith, Father (fictional character), 23, 59–60, 63, 67n10, 150, 152–56
Smith, Norman Kemp, 34, 43n4
social Darwinism, 147
socialism, 1, 121
Socrates, 71, 242, 248
solipsism, 123
Solzhenitsyn, Aleksandr, 244
"Sonnet—to Science" (Poe), 130
Sound and the Fury, The (Faulkner), 16, 104, 126
South (U.S. region), 8–9, 176; aristocrats of, 253–55; as bastion of Christian faith, 9, 162; cavalier tradition, 222–23, 228, 229; "Christ-haunted," 2; delayed contribution of, 259–61; merging with rest of America, 160; nostalgic vision of Old South, 191; Percy's quest to save the Union and, 159, 162, 175; popular culture of, 161; racial integration in, 10; restoration of "white rule" in, 260; slavery in, 209, 253–54; Stoic code of honor in, 104, 220, 225–29, 237–38
Southern Gothic literature, 8, 126
Souvenirs (Tocqueville), 258
Sowell, Thomas, 227
Spe Salvi (encyclical of Benedict XVI), 82
Stalinism, 4
"State of the Novel, The" (Percy), 149
Stockdale, Adm. James, 256
Stoicism, 2, 10, 107, 211, 246; in ancient world, 15, 225, 228, 256; in aristocratic ideals of South, 104, 220, 225–29, 237–38; Catholicism at odds with, 217; democracy and, 261; education and, 256–57; Founding Fathers and, 222–23; in

Lost in the Cosmos, 52, 56; in Percy family, 15–16, 19, 213, 215, 216; philosophical considerations, 223–25; Walker Percy and legacy of, 7
"Stoicism and the South" (Percy), 207, 229–32
Stoval, Harry, 22
Strauss, Leo, 3, 243
Streetcar Named Desire, A (Williams), 126
structuralism, 148
suicide, 58, 89, 151, 170, 171; awareness in death-in-life and, 173; in Percy family, 13, 14, 17, 20, 214; rejection of, 244
Sullivan, Annie, 25, 91
superego (Freudian concept), 58, 68n14
"Symbol, Consciousness, and Intersubjectivity" (Percy), 208
"Symbolic Imagination, The" (Tate), 132
symbols, 25, 90–91, 112–13n14, 113n16; communion through naming, 91–97; Eucharist as symbol, 210; identity and, 148–49; self-placement in symbolic world, 94, 97–102; signs distinguished from, 147; virtues of symbol-mongering self, 102–6

Tate, Allen, 131, 132–33, 134, 151
Taylor, Charles, 219
technology, 45n28, 128, 185, 255
television, 40, 64, 135
"Tell-Tale Heart, The" (Poe), 129–30, 133
Thales, 3
Thanatos Syndrome, The (Percy), 8, 26, 79, 119; "culture of death" in, 80; pursuit of happiness critiqued in, 48, 57–66; scientism critiqued in, 145–56

theology, 22, 70, 185, 213
"theorist-consumerism," 163, 164–65, 167, 168, 174
theory of man, 5, 102, 110, 111n1, 205n18
Third Reich, 59
Thomas Aquinas, 19, 23, 25, 83, 263
Thomism, 2, 10, 77, 252; as correction of Stoicism, 238; Declaration of Independence and, 6; on wondering/wandering being, 4. *See also* Catholicism
Thoreau, Henry David, 161
Thus Spoke Zarathustra (Nietzsche), 181
Tocqueville, Alexis de, 5, 10, 128, 183, 238–39; American aristocrats and, 253–55; on Americans as Cartesians, 239–48; aristocracy and democracy criticized by, 261–63; on education in America, 255–58; on religion and individuality, 248–52; southern particularity and, 259, 260
To Kill a Mockingbird (Lee), 262
Tolson, Jay, 11, 13, 17, 26, 219, 229
Toole, John Kennedy, 27
Townsend, Mary Bernice ["Bunt"] (wife of W. P.), 20–21, 27
Toynbee, Arnold, 33
Tractatus (Wittgenstein), 215
"Tradition and the Individual Talent" (Eliot), 119
transcendence, 21, 96, 114nn25–26, 151, 165, 168
triadic signification, 90–91, 92, 98, 106; humans distinguished from animals by, 145; Peirce's theory of, 146; social origin of, 115n30; in *The Thanatos Syndrome*, 152
trinitarian revelation, 72
Trinity, 210, 215, 247
Truman, Harry, 227

trustee family, 175
Twomey, Father Louis, 23

United States, 11, 42; American Adam mythology, 136; Americans as pop Cartesians, 239–48; Cartesianism in early republic, 128; literature of, 121; potential of South to save, 8–9, 159; removal of God's blessing from, 200; sexual revolution in, 135; social decay of, 163, 179, 181–84
unsignifiability, 88, 93–94, 95, 96, 113n18, 114n25; anxiety as despair, 96; of autonomous self, 101–4; intersubjective communion and, 108; I-Thou relation and, 100; other-regarding virtues and, 105, 106
utopianism, 53–57, 122, 123

Vietnam War, 24, 183
violence, 58, 151, 154, 189, 200; of American frontiersman, 134, 136; bestial, 128; of Ku Klux Klan, 223; in *Lancelot*, 125, 129, 136; in *Love in the Ruins*, 182; morality and, 230; pursuit of happiness and, 50
Violent Bear It Away, The (O'Connor), 80
virtues, 87, 116n44, 165; of acknowledge dependence, 103–5; intellectual, 102–3; other-regarding and communal, 105–6; practical and theoretical, 71; predication of, 106–10, 117n52
Voegelin, Eric, 81

Walden II (Skinner's utopian society), 53
Walpole, Horace, 127
war, 40, 51, 52, 53, 89
Washington, George, 222, 228, 235n43

We Hold These Truths (Murray), 237
Weimar Germany, 17, 82, 154
Wells, H. G., 16
Welty, Eudora, 84, 161
West, American, 20
White Citizens' Councils, 23, 229
Whitehead, Alfred North, 25
whites, Southern, 53–54, 223, 230, 231, 234, 260
"Why Are You Catholic?" (Percy), 218
Williams, Tennessee, 126
Wittgenstein, Ludwig, 98, 208, 210, 215

Wolfe, Tom, 256
women: death of beautiful woman in poetry, 131; female body, 128–29; in *Lancelot*, 133–34, 135, 138–39, 143n39; in *Lost in the Cosmos*, 52, 55
Wood, Ralph C., 7, 156
World War, First, 14
World War, Second, 18

Zimmerman, Carl, 174–75, 177nn26–27

POLITICAL COMPANIONS TO GREAT AMERICAN AUTHORS

SERIES EDITOR
Patrick J. Deneen, University of Notre Dame

BOOKS IN THE SERIES

A Political Companion to Saul Bellow
Edited by Gloria L. Cronin and Lee Trepanier

A Political Companion to Walker Percy
Edited by Peter Augustine Lawler and Brian A. Smith

A Political Companion to Ralph Waldo Emerson
Edited by Alan M. Levine and Daniel S. Malachuk

A Political Companion to Walt Whitman
Edited by John E. Seery

A Political Companion to Henry Adams
Edited by Natalie Fuehrer Taylor

A Political Companion to Henry David Thoreau
Edited by Jack Turner

A Political Companion to John Steinbeck
Edited by Cyrus Ernesto Zirakzadeh and Simon Stow

www.ingramcontent.com/pod-product-compliance
Lightning Source LLC
Chambersburg PA
CBHW020640230426
43665CB00008B/249